Turn Neither to the Right nor to the Left

A Thinking Christian's Guide to Politics and Public Policy

D. Eric Schansberg

Alertness Books
Greenville, SC

Author Contact Information:
Professor of Economics
Indiana University (New Albany)
New Albany, IN 47150
dschansb@ius.edu
http://homepages.ius.edu/dschansb

Published by:
Alertness Ltd.
P.O. Box 25856
Greenville, SC 29616
Phone: 1-864-444-3728
Fax: 1-413-622-9441
Email: alertness@policyofliberty.net

Library of Congress Control Number: 2003106916
Publisher's Cataloguing-in-Publication Data
Schansberg, D. Eric, 1965-
Turn Neither to the Right nor to the Left: A Thinking Christian's
Guide to Politics and Public Policy / by D. Eric Schansberg
Includes Endnotes and index.
ISBN 0-9729754-5-4 (paperback)
ISBN 0-9729754-4-6 (electronic book)
1. Bible—Civil Government. 2. Public Policy. 3. Economics Policy.
4. Civil Government—History. I. Title II. Schansberg, D. Eric

83,280 words

Table of Contents

Preface and Acknowledgments

Why Christians Shouldn't Legislate Morality

Why and How Christians Should Legislate Justice

Preface and Acknowledgments

This book has many roots. In general, it is a synthesis of my theology, political views, and training in economics. Although my worldview has evolved over time and, by God's grace, will continue to improve, this is my confident representation of what the Bible says about Christians and government.

More specifically, the impetus for the "legislating justice" portion of the book—to combine economic policy and Biblical Christianity—was Ron Sider's popular book, *Rich Christians in an Age of Hunger*. In the spring of 1992, my brother, who was a student at a Southern Baptist seminary, read Sider's book for a Christian Ethics course and recommended it to me. After reading it, I was deeply troubled by the impractical and unbiblical methods prescribed to reach sometimes dubious goals, and promptly wrote a 20-page rebuttal.

The catalyst for the "legislating morality" portion of the book—to combine social policy and Biblical Christianity—occurred in September 1992 when I attended a large conservative, evangelical church. The church reacted very strongly to a decision that week by the state's Supreme Court to abolish the state's sodomy law. Prompted by the tone of the rhetoric and a surprisingly heavy reliance on political means, I wrote a letter to the pastor which amounted to "the top ten reasons not to legislate (social) morality."

Although the project had been percolating in my mind for three years, the final motivation came from the gauntlet-throwing of two Evangelical scholars. Os Guinness' *Fit Bodies, Fat Minds* and Mark Noll's *The Scandal of the Evangelical Mind* convinced me of the need for a comprehensive Christian "political philosophy." When, why, and how should Christians advocate government activism? Both authors argue that there has not been a substantive effort in this arena for at least 100 years. As such, this book seeks to answer their challenge to provide an evangelical public philosophy—to establish a cogent framework for Christian political practice in 21st century America.

A word about the title: It is a politically-applied pun on a relatively famous Biblical injunction. Taken one way, it could be understood as a call to moderation or even political indifference. But neither is necessarily intended here. Biblically, the phrase meant that Israel should not turn from the path of following God to pursue sin—from adding idols to their worship of God, to ignoring God altogether; from legalism and ritualism to libertinism and carnality. That said, the call was not to spiritual moderation or indifference, but to live a full life—in passionate communion with God and in passionate service toward others.

Taken from another angle, the title is simply meant to underline one prominent theme of the book: that the Political Left and Political Right—and their cousins, the "Religious Left" and "Religious Right"—do not offer a coherent political philosophy and are deeply flawed in their approach to political activism. In addition to the negative goal of refuting popular political views, I have the positive goal of developing a consistent Christian philosophy of government—motivating an ethical and practical framework for Christian political involvement— and providing some examples of constructive and Biblical approaches to issues of social and economic concern for contemporary Christians.

Much of my case will be inferences drawn from the Bible. For non-Christians and Christians who take Scripture as less authoritative, my argument may be somewhat less persuasive. That said, the Bible is still a good starting point which provides at least some common ground; many Biblical principles are a mix of common sense, logic, and universally-held beliefs (e.g., "Do not steal."). And many of my arguments will be more practical than Biblical. Finally, those who disagree with my mode of argument, or even my conclusions, will at least be afforded insights into how "the other side" thinks.

In a sense, this book is a supremely academic effort—deriving a consistent Christian philosophy of government from an authoritative text. In fact, a distillation of the book's argument was published in the Fall 2002 issue of an academic journal, *Markets and Morality*. This is an attempt to look at all relevant Scripture and present a comprehensive and orderly approach to public policy advocacy for Christians. As such, the challenge in writing this is to prevent it from being too, well, academic. To pursue these ends, I have made liberal use of endnotes. The more casual reader won't miss anything of substance by skipping them; the more serious reader will find everything from supporting quotations to clarifying and provocative tangents. (They may be read alongside or after each chapter.)

Moreover, making my case is made considerably more difficult because my conclusions are so rare (although far from unique). It helps that we'll be relying on a common text. And I can tell you ahead of time that the arguments offered here always engender respect and thought—if not immediate and complete agreement. That said, when one writes a book that is, in essence, a thumb in the eye to both the Religious Left and the Religious Right, the "burden of proof" *should* be on the writer. I don't mind the challenge—and I merely ask for your patience and open-mindedness as you consider whether I am a true or false prophet on these matters.

As such, I seek an audience with academics—both secular and Christian. But I also hope to reach interested laypeople—from homeschoolers in high school to Sunday School teachers and seminarians. Of course, this book ultimately provides "answers"—prescriptions for activism in terms of both social morality and economic justice—and should be of interest to those who are interested in the use of political means to reach godly goals.

Finally, I owe a debt of gratitude to the many friends and colleagues who helped me in editing the manuscript. Many of them were chosen specifically because I suspected that they would fervently disagree with many of my conclusions. Some of them still do, and as such, one should not infer that they necessarily endorse every argument in this book. In large part, they have helped me write a book which is coherent in its substance and readable in its style. As a result, I hope you find this book thought-provoking and enjoyable to read.

In particular, Rev. Ross Brodfuehrer, Martha Dennis, Rev. Chuck Lee, Edward Lopez, and Jessica (Phipps) Ingram were helpful with the "legislating morality" portion of the book; Dr. Rick Axtell, Rev. Lon Cullen, and Steve Rickner provided useful comments on "legislating justice"; Martha Dennis, Rev. Greg Huguley, Th.M., and my brother, Rev. Chris Schansberg, offered valuable counsel on the abortion chapter. Thanks as well to David W. Hall for his comments on the entire manuscript. My dear friend, Dave Borden, read all of the above; as with my first book, *Poor Policy: How Government Harms the Poor* (Westview Press, 1996), his comments were remarkably insightful, especially for someone whose worldview is so similar to mine.

And this has been very much a family affair. In addition to my brother Chris providing useful input on part of the manuscript, my sister Cathy produced the book cover, my Dad's print shop provided technical support, and I'm sure I can count on my Mom to buy a few copies! Last but certainly not least: my wonderful wife Tonia provided comments and encouragement throughout the preparation of the book. (She never finished reading my first book, but she gobbled this one up!) I deeply appreciate her love in our marriage and her patient support for my various endeavors.

Thanks as well to *Market and Morality* and *Indiana Policy Review* for publishing parts of what later became this manuscript. *M&M* is published by the Acton Institute in Grand Rapids, MI—an institution devoted to educating seminarians and the general public about the intersection between religious and economic liberty. The *IPR* is published by the Indiana Policy Review Foundation, one of the many state think tanks around the nation seeking to encourage research on "the primacy of the individual in addressing public concerns at the community level." Finally, I want to give as much thanks and glory to God as possible—for graciously giving me the providence to enter this project, the passion to pursue it, and especially, the patience and perseverance to bring it to completion.

D. Eric Schansberg, August 2003

Chapter 1:
Introduction

When should Christians advocate government solutions? The Bible does not provide a clear answer to this question. The traditions of the church as well as the winds of economic, cultural, and political change have served to muddy the waters further. However, one thing is crystal clear: Christians have not spent enough time thinking about the proper role of government in a Christian worldview.[1]

As Lynn Buzzard notes, "Christians need to think more carefully about politics and government... Evangelicals haven't given an iota of thought to what government ought to do. Evangelicals want the government to interfere in issues of pornography and not interfere with private Christian schools. Why? Because evangelicals think a lot about what governments should and should not do? No, because they like the one interference and don't like the other."[2] Rather than a consistent application of Biblical principles, evangelicals often reach conclusions in a piecemeal manner, based on limited information, personal preferences, cultural influences, and political biases.[3]

In particular, perhaps due to their reticence (relatively speaking) to depend on government solutions, politically conservative Christians have been especially lax in reasoning through a political philosophy.[4] And although politically liberal Christians have devoted some energy to devise rationales for a more intrusive State, I will argue that their solutions are too often inconsistent with God's character and Christ's ministry. In sum, we must do better in answering this question: What is the proper intersection between Christians and government?[5]

The Economic Way of Thinking

As a Christian who sees the Bible as authoritative, my first priority will be to properly interpret what the Bible says about Christians and government, justice and righteousness, means and ends. That said, Scripture gives few direct answers to contemporary policy issues. Instead, we are left to draw inferences from revealed principles. Four times in Acts, we're told that Paul "reasoned" from the Scriptures[6]; we need to use both Scripture and reason to reach valid conclusions. To this end, we will cover everything from the character of God to the New Testament's specific instructions to believers concerning the State. Along the way, we will discuss a number of related Biblical topics: idolatry, Old Testament judges accepting bribes, the use of force, legalism, evangelism, and so on.

I am also a Christian economist—or more accurately, a Christian who is trained in, and makes his living through, economics. Many economists are fond of talking about "the economic way of thinking"—a capacity to rigorously identify the costs and benefits of personal decisions and public policies. Although this skill may seem elementary, there are innumerable bad decisions in both realms which stem from our failure to weigh costs and benefits appropriately. Most notably, we fail to weigh costs and benefits accurately whenever we engage in sin. Assuming that God wants the best for us, our failures to "keep in step with the Spirit" must be because we underestimate the costs or exaggerate the benefits of sin.[7]

Likewise, we can fail to implement good policies when we don't see all of their benefits. And we can easily implement poor policies, particularly when we don't see all of the costs of government activism. In this latter sense, economists are often considered "pourers of cold water" on proposals for government activism since we insist on analyzing relatively subtle costs.[8]

In the context of public policy, thinking clearly is made more difficult by at least three factors. First, players in the political arena typically describe only "half the picture"—proponents of a policy advertise the benefits of a policy; opponents are vocal about the costs. Second, both sides are rarely at the height of objectivity. Third and most important, the benefits of good policies and the costs of bad policies are often, by their nature, relatively subtle. For example, funding a new government program with deficit financing (future taxes) is more politically attractive than increasing taxes now since the costs would be pushed into the future. In any case, the political arena features information which is rarely balanced or complete.[9]

In this book, I will focus on applying this way of thinking to the intersection between Christian activism and public policy. In general, I will argue that the benefits of pursuing government activism are rather obvious while the costs are relatively subtle. Thus, my job is typically to make those costs more visible. In addition to the Biblical problems with many types of government activism, after recognizing many of its practical costs, readers will often find government solutions less attractive, and in many cases, prohibitively so. And beyond becoming newly troubled by a number of current policies, I hope to make readers aware of more just and effective policy proposals and non-government means of reaching the same goals.

Because the costs of government activism are relatively subtle—and because I will focus on these costs—most readers will leave this book less excited about the use of public policy as a means to godly ends. This is not, however, to throw the baby out with the proverbial bath water. "We know that the law is good if one uses it properly."[10] To apply Paul's words in another context: the question then becomes how to use it properly.

The Christian Way of Thinking...or Not Thinking
Mark Noll's *The Scandal of the Evangelical Mind* and Os Guinness' *Fit Bodies and Fat Minds: Why Evangelicals Don't Think and What to Do About It* trace the historical roots of what they call "evangelical anti-intellectualism."[11] Although this broader topic is important, for our purposes, one should note that religious conservatives have not formulated a consistent Christian philosophy of government, particularly with respect to social policy. Likewise, many Catholic and mainline Protestant leaders have been notoriously soft-headed about economic prescriptions—what has amounted to "wishful thinking" about the nature of man and the practice of government. In contrast, Blaise Pascal argued that "working hard to think clearly is the beginning of moral conduct." To honor God and serve people well in the political arena, we must do this in the realm of public policy analysis.[12]

As Bertrand Russell cynically noted, "Most Christians would rather die than think—in fact they do."[13] Although too caustic and not nearly universal, his criticism is too often true. The costs of our failure in this realm are tremendous. We fail to glorify God sufficiently with what distinguishes us from the rest of Creation—our ability to reason. As such, Guinness repeatedly exhorts his readers with the Biblical command to love the Lord their God with all of their minds.

The costs of well-intentioned but misguided policies are difficult to underestimate—both in their capacity to harm others and to harm God's reputation. To be sure, advocacy of government mandates is not often an attractive position, especially when accompanied by some combination of ignorance about economics and politics, strident rhetoric, personal hypocrisy, and philosophical inconsistency. As Guinness firmly criticizes the modern church: "anti-intellectualism is both a scandal and a sin. It is a scandal in the sense of being an offense and a stumbling block that needlessly hinders serious people from considering the Christian faith and coming to Christ. It is a sin because it is a refusal...to love the Lord our God with our minds."[14] Or as C. S. Lewis put it: "God is no fonder of intellectual slackers than of any other slackers."[15] When non-believers stumble, it should be because of their difficulty with accepting the Gospel, not our poor reasoning skills, legalisms, obnoxiousness, and so on.

Ideally, as Dorothy Sayers once remarked, "the Christian mind is a combination of intellectual light and spiritual ardor that is simply a mind in love with God."[16] How often do we relish the opportunity to learn, to stretch our belief systems, or to engage in active debate with people who can challenge our thinking? As Guinness argues, "it is as integral to think Christianly as it is to live Christianly...[it is] a form of active obedience. Like every other part of the Christian life, thinking Christianly is active and demanding."[17] Too often, we fail to focus on the intellectual aspects of our faith and our world. The apostle Paul would have been deeply troubled by such laxity. One can easily imagine the overflowing zeal in his remarks about intellectual rigor to the Corinthians: "We demolish arguments and every pretension that sets itself up against the knowledge of God, and we take captive every thought to make it obedient to Christ."[18] Is this true for us?

That said, "thinking Christianly" is not simply thinking about Christian topics. We are called to be "salt and light" in an often rotten and dark world. This is impossible without reasoning through some of the world's favorite topics, including politics. In addition, thinking Christianly does not mean adopting a Christian answer for every issue. The church—whether the "Religious Left" or "Religious Right"—already has too much of this kind of thinking already. Joel Belz pokes at Christians "whose whole political experience has been unblemished with a single compromise of any kind. In fact, they've probably never even been tempted to political compromise for the simple reason that they've never carried on a serious political conversation with someone they disagree with."[19]

There is an interesting tradeoff in this regard. Those who are relatively open-minded are more prone to wrestle with incorrect ideas, but more likely to encounter and accept new insights into truth; those who are relatively close-minded are more likely to reject heresy, but more likely to adhere to tradition when they should not. Our primary concern should be on "right thinking"; "right beliefs" will follow. Some of us are too ideological and partisan; some of us are too reluctant to consider arguments that we claim are "one-sided." What matters is whether one's thought process glorifies God; what matters is whether one is "one-sided" on the side of truth and God.

Going Against Tradition and the Status Quo when Appropriate

For those who tend to rely heavily on tradition, this book is likely to make you uncomfortable at times. My prayer is that you would wrestle with these issues earnestly and honestly, seeking to sift through any chaff to reach valuable wheat. We are not to follow tradition, but God. We are not to follow a particular political party, but truth. We are not to blindly believe what we are told by pastors, teachers, our parents—or authors for that matter! We are not to have our theology unduly influenced by culture and political ideology. We are to search the Scriptures like Bereans, to reason as passionately as Paul, to wrestle with God like Jacob, and to love those in the world as deeply as Christ.

Traditions certainly have a place within the Christian experience. But they can also be misleading and misused. Adhering to tradition implies that what we have thought in the past was correct then, and continues to be correct today. But as Leo Tolstoy noted, it is sometimes exceedingly difficult to walk away from incorrect traditions: "I know that most men—not only those considered clever, but those who are clever and capable of understanding the most difficult scientific, mathematical or philosophical problems—can seldom discern even the simplest and most obvious truth if it obliges him to admit the falsity of conclusions they have formed, perhaps with great difficulty—conclusions of which they are proud, have taught to others, and on which they have built their lives." Forsaking an incorrect tradition requires keen insight, humility, and often, the courage to run counter to one's peers. Despite the challenges of shedding inappropriate traditions, Christians need to be careful that tradition does not become an idol in any area of their lives.

It has been said that in some sense, the role of a Christian is "to comfort the afflicted and to afflict the comfortable." As such, I hope that this book is read as an exhortation to minister more passionately and effectively within the church and particularly, to the world. And given that many of us have become comfortable in our beliefs about the role of government, I hope to afflict some of those articles of faith as well. As Flannery O'Connor noted, "The novelist with Christian concerns will find in modern life, distortions which are repugnant to him, and his problem will be to make these appear as distortions to an audience which is used to seeing them as natural." This book will address many such "distortions."[20]

As one who writes much against the political status quo, I am comforted by the thought that at least I am in good company. Of course, our Savior was anti-establishment with respect to both traditional religious and political powers. And I am willing to risk being called "crazy" for my policy stances and what I see as the proper role for Christians and government. Some of their contemporaries thought Christ was possessed and believed Paul to be "out of his mind"[21]. The question is not whether my ideas are wild or unconventional, but whether they are true. Are my critiques of traditional thought and my prescriptions both Biblical and practical?[22]

In Sum...

I will address three broad questions in this book. First, how should Christians respond when acted upon by government? And how should this response differ if the government is legally prohibiting a righteous behavior, if it taxes a rightcous behavior, if it subsidizes sinful behavior, or if it legally mandates sinful behavior? Second, when should Christians seek government policy as a means to an end? In particular, when should we use the government to prohibit or tax sinful behavior, or to subsidize or mandate righteous behavior? Third, to what extent do the above answers depend on the type of sinful behavior (e.g., murder, gluttony, practicing a false religion) or the type of righteous behavior (e.g., charity, being a good steward of the environment]?

In trying to answer these questions, the structure of the book is as follows. I will set the table with three more chapters—two on Christians and government in general, and another one on the importance of pursuing godly goals with godly methods. From there, the first major section will begin with the Biblical evidence concerning the Christian pursuit of government to reach "social morality" goals. I will then add other practical reasons why this is a costly strategy and conclude with some Biblical and practical propositions for dealing with some social issues. The second major section deals with the Biblical case for using government to promote "economic justice"—in certain settings, and with "justice" properly defined in terms of both means and ends—in particular, to identify ethical and practical ways to help the poor and oppressed. The book finishes with two chapters on abortion and a chapter with concluding remarks. In a word, I find a role for Christians to pursue the use of government as an appropriate means to just ends, but my diagnoses and prescriptions for activism will differ considerably from those that are commonly proposed.[23]

It is my belief that wrestling with the ideas in this book will allow us to have a greater impact in the political realm—bringing more glory to God and more souls into His kingdom. II Timothy 2:15 says to "Do your best to present yourself to God as one approved, a workman who does not need to be ashamed and who correctly handles the word of truth."[24] I am not ashamed of the way I have handled this fascinating, complicated, and controversial topic. My hope and prayer is that I have correctly handled both the "word of truth" and truth in general, and that the truthful seeds will find fertile soil in your heart and mind.

Chapter 2:
The Bible on the Role of Government

Most Biblical episodes involving human government are rather ugly. Foremost, sin can be viewed as our failed attempts at self-governance—outside of God's will. As such, the Bible records the opening of our history—Adam and Eve's disastrous failure to self-govern properly. In Genesis 4, we are told that the family tradition of poor self-governance continued when Cain killed Abel. Interestingly, Cain then left the presence of the Lord and built a city—a center of human government.[1]

Government in the Old Testament
Government and the Israelites

From there, Biblical encounters with formal government are relatively non-descript until the book of Exodus tells us that the Israelites were brutally oppressed by Pharaoh before being delivered from Egypt through Moses by God's hand.[2] After God rules through Joshua to establish the Israelites in Canaan, God chooses to work through judges to govern His people. The book of Judges highlights the Israelites' repeated failures to follow God and recounts how judges were empowered by God to deliver His people from the bondage and oppression that had resulted from their disobedience.

After a time, the Israelites began to grow dissatisfied with this form of divine government, and under Samuel, they clamored for a human king. They wanted a king "like other nations...to govern us and go out before us and fight our battles."[3] They wanted to be ruled—by someone other than God, and they wanted someone to fight their battles for them. God identified their desire as a rejection of Him and His way and then told Samuel to "solemnly warn them and show them the ways of the king who shall reign over them."[4] His subsequent speech to the Israelites in I Samuel 8:11b-18 remains one of the great descriptions of the abuse of power, and too often, the standard for human government:

> He will take your sons and appoint them to his chariots and to be his horsemen, and to run before his chariots; and he will appoint himself commanders of thousands and commanders of fifties, and some to plow his ground and to reap his harvest, and to make his implements of war and the equipment of his chariots....He will take the best of your fields and your vineyards and olive orchards and give them to his courtiers....the best of your cattle and donkeys, and put them to his work. He will take one-tenth of your flocks and you shall be his slaves. And in that day you will cry out because of your king, whom you have chosen for yourselves; but the Lord will not answer you in that day.

Samuel warned the people that the king would use their sons for his military. And in a perverse twist on "putting others first," their sons would run ahead of his chariots! The people would be subject to heavy taxation and slavery. The king would take 10% (if only it were so little today!), but more importantly, he would take their best—what should have been set apart for God.[5]

The people were not persuaded by Samuel's reasoning; their response was a determined refusal to follow Samuel and God. Saul, the new king, had a promising start, but after he was disobedient twice, God withdrew His support. The rest of Saul's rule—a waiting period to establish the credentials and develop the character of David—was marked by inconsistency, fits of jealousy, and a penchant for using force on his opponents. His successor, King David ruled well in general—as "a man after God's own heart," but the quality of the subsequent kings mostly degenerated from Solomon through the kings of Israel and Judah.[6] Only a few of the later kings ruled well, most notably Josiah. But by then, the country had degenerated so far that the priests and the people had completely forgotten about God's Law.[7]

Israelite "Adultery" with Government

A believer's relationship with God is frequently described in the Bible as a marriage.[8] The unfaithfulness of the Israelites in their relationship with God—by worshipping other gods—is graphically portrayed as committing a variety of sexual sins.[9] Likewise, various alliances with the governments of foreign powers were condemned by the prophets as "adultery"—seeking solutions, sustenance, and security from an entity other than God, depending on man instead of God. As Isaiah preached, "Stop trusting in man, who has but a breath in his nostrils. Of what account is he?"[10]

Isaiah 20:5-6 condemns Israel who "trusted in Cush and boasted in Egypt." Isaiah 30:1-3 announces a "woe to (God's) obstinate children" for "forming an alliance...looking for help to Pharaoh's protection, in Egypt's shade for refuge." Isaiah 31:1 pronounces another warning: "Woe to those who go down to Egypt for help, who rely on horses, who trust in the multitude of their chariots and in the great strength of their horsemen, but do not look to the Holy One of Israel." And in the most sexually graphic language in the Bible, for the same sins,

Ezekiel 23 condemns their prostitution, lust, nakedness, promiscuity and lewdness, and predicts their resulting "defilement."[11]

Samuel closed his sermon about the dangers of having a king with an ominous warning: God would not respond to them when (not if) they cried out to Him about their choice of government. In Judges 10:10-14, God initially refused to help the oppressed Israelites. Instead, He said "go and cry out to the gods you have chosen; let them deliver you in your time of distress." In II Chronicles 12:8, God said His people would become subject to an enemy king "so that they may learn the difference between serving me and serving the kings of other lands."

As G. Campbell Morgan notes: God gave them a king so that "they might learn the folly of their choice. In this is revealed a constant method of the Divine government. When men fail to rise to the height of the purpose of God, and clamor for something lower, He gives them what they ask, and then watches over them and guards them as they work out their low choice to its ultimate conclusion, and thus are eventually brought back to His purpose with a full understanding of its perfection."[12] Similarly, in Romans 1:24-28, concerning godless and wicked men, we are told that God "gave them up" to the desires of their hearts. Given the desires of many Christians throughout the 20th century to use government—to provide security and sustenance, to enforce moral standards, and so on—and Christian disappointment with contemporary government policy, perhaps God has "given us up" to our gods as well.[13]

Government in the New Testament
Christ and the Temptation of Government

Christ's earthly opponents tempted him to say things that would get him in trouble with the Roman government. Christ's response to one such question—that one should "give to Caesar what is Caesar's, and to God, what is God's" is probably the most famous Biblical remark concerning Christians and government.[14] Notably, Christ was answering a question intended to trap him "so that they might hand him over to the power and authority of the governor"—they were hoping to use the power of the State to stop his ministry[15]

In Matthew 4, we are told about the three temptations that Christ faced before beginning his ministry in earnest.[16] Satan tempted Christ to "tell these stones to become bread." But Christ rejected that suggestion, citing the larger issue: "Man does not live on bread alone but on every word...of God." In addition to his personal hunger, by extension, Christ also faced an ongoing "social" temptation—to end all hunger by turning stones into bread or to seize popularity or political power with a food give-away. Christ could have diminished income inequality through miracles or bought the allegiance of people with hand-outs, but he didn't. Although dealing with "felt needs" is important, Christ showed us that it must be kept in a proper perspective with God's agenda and a focus on the Gospel. Likewise, our "quick fix" solutions often are outside of God's will— because there are unintended consequences or because the means to the end are not appropriate.

Satan also tried to tempt Christ with inappropriate religious means, suggesting that Christ throw himself off the top of the Temple so that angels would rescue him.

Christ refused this method of sensationalism and "church growth." Satan also proposed a political temptation, but Christ refused to rule through traditional government institutions, replying that we are to worship God and serve Him alone.[17] Here, the broader implication of this question for us is whether we worship, serve, and depend on government—or God alone.

Christ was often tempted to push the timing of God's plan and especially to substitute another, less divine agenda—to establish an earthly kingdom. At the end of his life, the temptations were the same—to avoid the cross, to call down angels to help him, and so on. Notably, at Gethsamene, Peter inappropriately uses force by engaging in sword play, cutting off a servant's ear. Christ's rebuke of Peter probably has broader application to Christian proposals for the use of force and government: "all who draw the sword will die by the sword."

It is also noteworthy that the recorded temptations of Christ all relate in some way to pursuing seemingly reasonable yet inappropriate means and ends. Further, we are not told about any of the other temptations that we know Christ must have faced. As John Yoder notes: "Being human, Jesus must have been subject somehow or other to the testings of pride, envy, anger, sloth, avarice, gluttony, and lust; but it does not enter into the concerns of the Gospel writers to give us any information about any struggles he may have had with their attraction."[18] It is probably true that Satan thought the social, religious, and political temptations were pivotal. It is definitely true that God and the divinely-inspired Gospel writers viewed these as the most important and dangerous of the temptations Christ faced. It seems likely that God meant to convey their gravity for us as well.

In addition to eschewing the temptation to use earthly government, Christ was critical of the methods of earthly rulers and told his disciples not to follow in their footsteps. In Matthew 20:25-26, Christ said "you know that the rulers of the Gentiles lord it over them, and their high officials exercise authority over them. Not so with you." Luke 22:25-26 adds that the officials called themselves "Benefactors." Notably, government's use of force is frequently accompanied by the claim that it is helping those who are forced to do something they wouldn't have done otherwise.

The Israelites and the disciples had expected the Messiah to be a political leader, but Christ had an entirely different agenda.[19] Somehow, today's Christians fall into an eerily similar position, at least implicitly believing that Christ's words and actions do not at all discourage the use of government. Their chief argument is that this tool was unavailable to him in the contemporary Roman political structure. However, the "cultural" argument is at worst, disingenuous or dangerous—or at best, unsatisfying. First, Christ was offered political power and refused it. Second, Christ could have taken actions to ensure a substantial degree of economic and political power, but didn't. Third, if the use of government was supposed to be an important tool in the Christian arsenal, a God who is sovereign over history could have sent Christ at a different, more democratic, time. And finally, any "cultural" argument is potentially dangerous since it opens the door for its use on a wider variety of issues.

Christ told Pilate, "My kingdom is not of this world. Otherwise my followers would fight."[20]

Apparently, this statement and the rest of Christ's ministry reflect God's will—in order to protect and extend the integrity of the gospel. Is it the same today? Are we arrogant for claiming that we can use government effectively and appropriately? Up to this point, I have not at all proven that Christians should avoid using government as a tool in any given context. But at the least, theological and Biblical integrity require that we reflect long and hard on whether the principles that governed Christ's ministry are true today. Certainly, some burden of proof should be on those who wish to use government to try to accomplish godly goals.

In Scripture, Christ only mentions the most powerful man in the world (Caesar) once. But when looking at Christ's life, we cannot say that we should ignore politics or politicians. Christ warned the disciples about the Herodians and the politically-astute Sadducees. And he did not avoid personal contact with individuals from the ruling social, religious, or political classes. Christ was anti-Religion, yet befriended Nicodemus; he was anti-Politics, yet befriended tax collectors and the Roman centurion. They were identified with oppressive institutions, yet Christ dignified and respected them independent of their career choices.

Perhaps most important, Christians should soberly recognize that it was the State along with religious leaders that put Christ to death. That Christ was killed by a combination of the religious and state authorities is no accident. Thankfully, John 19:10-11 records that Pilate did not have the ultimate authority to forcefully take his life; Christ willingly gave it for our salvation.[21]

The Writings of the Apostles on Government

The rest of the New Testament also displays a surprising lack of interest in political issues. There were no political protests or calls for the government to prohibit abortion and slavery, gambling and drinking, or to expand government programs to feed the poor and increase the minimum wage. The complete absence of Biblical text devoted to these topics is astounding given the level of rhetoric and the number of proposals for activist government from both ends of the contemporary Christian political spectrum today.

That said, the apostles did write a good deal about our relationship to political authorities. Romans 13:1-7 instructs all believers to "submit to the governing authorities." Moreover, Paul said that these authorities are established by God, and thus, that rebellion against authority is equivalent to rebellion against God. In I Peter 2:13-17, Peter instructs us to submit ourselves to every authority "for God's sake." These are provocative passages, especially in light of their recommended submission to Nero—a pagan ruler who inflicted substantial persecution on the early church. Apparently, submission to God-established authority shows faith in God's sovereignty over rulers—that God is working through, or in spite of, our leaders.

In I Timothy 2:1-3, Paul's first instructions to Timothy about worship are for believers to pray, intercede, and give thanks for "all those in authority." Paul then points to the reason for this: "that we may live peaceful and quiet lives in all godliness and holiness."[22] Although Paul was quite willing to rankle his religious foes, he recommended the pursuit of tranquility in political matters. Paul concludes by saying this approach is "good, and pleases God."

The Romans 13 passage concludes by telling us to pay our taxes and to give honor and respect where it is due.[23] The I Peter 2 passage closes with a command to "fear God [and] honor the king." In Luke 12:4-5, Christ tells his followers to fear God but "not [to] be afraid of those who kill the body but can do no more." Thus, we are supposed to honor and respect both God and our rulers, but God's authority takes precedence. Both intuitively and from Scripture, the line is drawn where submission to the State interferes with our submission to God.[24] The early church battled this often. Two examples are chronicled in Acts, the most famous of which is the retort by Peter and the other apostles: "We must obey God rather than men."[25] When there is no conflict, we are to submit to the State; when the two conflict, our primary allegiance is to God.[26]

Finally, the first Beast and Babylon—spoken of so harshly in Revelation—are most likely representations of human power and government. Revelation 13:8,14 probably speaks to (false) religion encouraging the worship of the State. Revelation 2:10, 13:7, and 16:14 speak to the State warring against God and His people. Revelation 17 prophesies the destruction of Babylon. And Revelation 19:20 speaks to the end of State power. As the two beasts in Revelation 13 underline, the combination of Satan, false religion, and the State can be dragon-like (emphasizing power) or more serpent-like (emphasizing deception and idolatry).[27] And perhaps most sobering, the only warning in Revelation to Christians—outside of the letters to the seven churches in chapters 2-3—is the call to leave Babylon and its enticements in chapter 18.

Scripture speaks at great length about the problems with human government—from the agenda at Babel in Genesis 11, to the staggering warning about kings in I Samuel 8, to the repeated idolatry of the Israelites toward government, to the anticipation of a political messiah throughout the Old Testament, to the temptations of Christ in Matthew 4, to the meaning of the first beast of Revelation 13. In a word, the sum of the Biblical evidence indicates that we should be leery about attempting to harness the power of government.[28] And before we criticize political leaders or even think about using government for whatever purpose, a prerequisite is that we do first what the Bible has explicitly prescribed concerning government—in particular, giving thanks and praying for our leaders.[29]

Chapter 3:
The Theory vs. the Practice of Government

Another key introductory point is to distinguish between government activism as it might work—in contrast to how it is likely to work in reality. As such, it is important to distinguish between utopian theory and practical application—and discuss the extent to which there is a divorce between the two in certain contexts. The history of Christianity, the history of the world, and the disciplines of political science and economics have much to contribute about the difficulties in going beyond good intentions to good policy.

Past and Present Christian Pursuits of Government
In practice, the intersection between Christianity and government has had a checkered past. Constantine established Christianity as the officially sanctioned State religion of the Roman Empire early in the 4th century, but mandating praise and worship is far from Biblical. Persecution of pagans was a regular practice—once Christians were in positions of power.[1] And arguably, the "Crusades" are the most infamous "religious" episodes in history outside of the crucifixion of Christ. One can question whether the combatants were misguided believers using an improper method or warmongers who usurped the banner of a Holy War for their own purposes. Either way, God's name has been dragged through the mud as a result.

The origins of colonial American history have their roots in concerns about religious freedom from the State.[2] Although far from consistent and totally free, the nation was founded on an inherent, God-given right to religious, political, and economic freedoms.[3] Arguments persist to this day about the religious beliefs of the Founding Fathers, but whether they were deists, theists, or Christians, it is curious that some politically conservative evangelicals have spent so much energy on defending mere men.[4] Moreover, many of the Religious Right's legislative efforts to restrict freedom probably cause many of the Founders to spin in their proverbial graves.[5]

In the middle of the 19th century, Christians transferred their activist zeal from abortion and infanticide to slavery, and were at the forefront of efforts to end the practice. In the late 19th century, Protestants encouraged the movement from private to public schools to use the State to indoctrinate the children of primarily-Catholic immigrants.[6] The turn of the century also saw the Christian-led transition from private and largely Christian-based welfare efforts to government-run programs—believing that the government could help the poor in a more effective and comprehensive manner. Into the 20th century, Christian faith in, and use of, government grew more rapidly—with its Social Gospel and calls for protective legislation and income redistribution, its impact on the Progressive Era's reforms, its insistent calls for prohibition against alcohol, and its battle against teaching macro-evolution in the government schools.[7]

After World War II, conservative Christians were prominent in the battle against communism. One manifestation of this passion was the inclusion of "In God We Trust" on our money and "one nation under God" in the Pledge of Allegiance during the Eisenhower administration.[8] The timing reminds one of King Saul building his first altar to God—after he had begun to fall away from God.[9] By the time we added four words to our money and our national creed, this country was well on its way to falling away from its belief in God. The children of the 1950's then became the adults of the 1960's, and members of the Religious Left became active in promoting civil rights and the rapid expansion of welfare programs for the poor.

Today, the Religious Left focuses on using government to protect the environment and especially, to try to help the poor—to "legislate (economic) justice."[10] Concerning the latter, they invoke government force to regulate labor and product markets and to take money away from taxpayers to fund income redistribution to the poor. Meanwhile, the Religious Right is not excited about that agenda, but instead promotes the use of government to "legislate (social) morality"—typically to use the power of government to regulate the behavior of consenting adults engaging in "sin." These battles include the realms of prostitution, gambling, "gay rights," and so on.[11] Thus, many Christians are actively involved in pursuing government solutions—but their goals differ considerably. In a word, the problem is that "We criticized big government, but what we were really criticizing was the other guys who had control of it when we wanted control. So it wasn't big government per se that was evil. Our primary objection was that we weren't running it."[12]

As James Haltemann notes, "This curious contrast begs for an integration where either a non-interventionist position is taken on both [kinds of] issues or an interventionist position on both..."[13] This "curious contrast" is one of the catalysts for this book—an attempt to find a consistent Christian philosophy of government from Scripture. While not having a well-formed political worldview, most Christians look to government to solve many or even most social and economic problems. Reminiscent of the Israelites in I Samuel 8, we often look to government to fight our battles for us—from the War on Poverty to the War on Drugs.

Unfortunately for past and present Christian advocates of government activism, there is no clear mandate from Scripture endorsing many of their uses of government. For example, concerning the U.S. Catholic bishops and their desire to "legislate justice," Paul Heyne comments that they "want to transform institutions; they are therefore wise to focus on gaining control of governmental policies. However, honesty requires they give up the authority of the New Testament as support for what they are doing."[14]

With God's preferred method of voluntary behaviors, one typically finds slow progress. But because government is powerful, it can enforce great change—at least externally. It can certainly "get things done"; the questions are whether those are "the right things" and whether government is an appropriate means to the chosen end.[15] Heyne argues further that "the determination to have as little to do with [government] as possible is far closer to the spirit of the Gospel than are the persistent efforts of church officials since Constantine to gain control of government for their own ends."[16]

The Theory vs. the Practice of Government

Government is capable of promoting, if not mandating, certain outcomes. Government is also responsible for establishing the "rules of the game" for individuals in a country—everything from the integrity of the monetary and judicial systems to penalizing or subsidizing certain behaviors. But as the purveyor of the "legitimate" use of force, in the hands of sinful man, this ability is subject to degrees of abuse. The irony is that we wouldn't need government if men were angels, but since they are not, we must rely on non-angels to govern.[17] In other words, when government is in charge—and particularly when it has a large degree of political power—there is a significant danger that the subsequent outcomes will be rather unpleasant.

To note, human government is responsible for the most gruesome events in history. Taking the 20th century as a prime example, the world has endured the likes of Hitler, Stalin, and Pol Pot, as well as the brutality of the Chinese Communists, a number of oppressive African regimes, and the persecution of innumerable Christians.[18] And although less deadly, our government has engaged in other appalling uses of force: slavery, Jim Crow laws, Japanese internment camps, discriminatory laws against the Chinese, and so on. Scripture describes the grisly use of power as well: from Nebuchadnezzar killing the sons of King Zedekiah just before putting out his eyes to the persecution of believers in Revelation.[19]

If it so chooses, government is in a position to impose tremendous costs on groups and individuals. In recent years, there have been complaints about racist police officers, racial discrimination in criminal sentencing, and gender bias in government schools. Although the widespread existence of each is debatable, the point remains that government is certainly capable of imposing such costs. George Washington noted that "government is a dangerous servant and a fearsome master." Christians should avoid giving control to this "master" whenever possible. As Thomas Paine wrote, "government, even in its best state, is but a necessary evil;

in its worst state, an intolerable one." It follows that one should be wary of giving government more power and control.

Even without malevolence of this extent leveled at individuals or groups, in a fallen world, it seems unlikely that the many arms of the State will operate under anything close to pure motives, complete knowledge, and the ability to enforce order without improperly restricting freedoms.[20] (An interesting counter-example is Joseph and Pharaoh imposing taxes to store up food in anticipation of the seven-year famine. Note, however, that success required a benevolent dictator and omniscience in that area—a rare combination!) In a word, there is a potentially vast divide between the theory and practice of government.[21] (And this still leaves unanswered the question of whether advocating a government solution in any particular instance is Biblical.) In practice, government policy can range from the good to the bad to the ugly. The job of the politically-active Christian is to find the instances when policy can be good and to fight against those policies which are bad or ugly.

Ten Principles on the Theory vs. the Practice of Religion and Government

Aside from the general practice of government, there are further concerns specifically related to the prospect of politically-active believers. First, in practice, which Christians would likely become involved? Aside from those led by the Spirit, there will be a bias toward those led by a relatively power-hungry spirit.[22] Others will be attracted to politics who lack perspective and objectivity in the pursuit of their political goals. As Blaise Pascal remarked, "Men never do evil so completely and cheerfully as when they do it from religious conviction."[23] Or from Richard John Neuhaus: "When it is the Lord's battle you are fighting, politics takes on an aura of deadly earnestness."[24] These are likely to be among the worst potential representatives of the church and a source of innumerable black marks on God's reputation.

Second, those in politics are likely to be further enticed by the trappings of power.[25] Richard Reeves argues that "Politicians are different from you and me. The business of reaching for power does something to a man—it closes him off from other men until, day by day, he reaches the point where he instinctively calculates each new situation and each other man with the simplest question: 'What can this do for me?'"[26] Ultimately, as Henry Kissinger wryly notes: "Ninety percent of the politicians give the other ten percent a bad reputation." While not inevitable that one will join the 90%, it is a difficult temptation to avoid.[27]

Moreover, politics virtually requires salesmanship and the art of compromise. Neither is inherently wrong, but both are fraught with potential dangers.[28] Where is the line between aggressively promoting a bill and tilting the debate by leaving out relevant benefits and costs? Where is the line between appropriate cooperation and inappropriate compromise? It is difficult to maintain objectivity and integrity while practicing politics.[29]

Third, to the extent that we seek to use government as a tool, we must take great care to "do it right." Whenever laypeople or leaders in the church speak on social and political issues, they implicitly play the part of "mouthpiece for God."[30] This is a role we should not take lightly. Of greatest seriousness, we risk a violation of the 3rd Commandment—misusing God's name.[31] With ill-advised policy prescriptions, we do a great disservice to others, our faith, and our Lord.

Fourth, political activity in the church promotes division within the church and with the world around relatively unimportant issues. Philip Yancey explains that "a political movement by nature draws lines, makes distinctions, pronounces judgment; in contrast, Jesus' love cut across lines, transcends distinctions, and dispenses grace. If [my] activism drives out such love, I betray his kingdom."[32] Former Senator Bill Armstrong put it this way: "I am a conservative, and yet, if I were a pastor, I would want to be very careful not to do something that would make it hard for a liberal to know Jesus and worship in my church."[33] Notably, when Paul used the word "preach" to describe his speaking, he always talked about preaching Christ, grace, or the gospel—never about preaching morality or justice. Before we eagerly pursue any political agenda, we need to ask ourselves whether the action will be a stepping stone or a stumbling block for others' reception of the Gospel. As John MacArthur notes, "By making activism our priority, we fashion a reputation as rabble-rousing malcontents and foster hostility toward unbelievers that alienates us from them, and them from us."[34]

Fifth, political activity in the church promotes unity around improper and distracting issues. As C.S. Lewis reasoned for two hypothetical demons working on a believer: "Let him begin by treating patriotism...as part of his religion. Then let him, under the influence of partisan spirit, come to regard it as the most important part. Then quietly and gradually nurse him on to the stage at which the religion becomes merely a part of the 'cause' in which Christianity is valued chiefly because of the excellent arguments it can produce."[35] The use of political means and the pursuit of political ends is not nearly as important as the Gospel itself.

Sixth, assuming that political means have some validity, we still run the risk of putting too much emphasis on "good things" at the expense of "best things." Ironically, a focus on politics may be sub-optimal, futile, or even counter-productive. David Gushee argues that "Jesus chose to establish evangelism and disciple-making as the fundamental task of the church—even as its fundamental political (or, if you will, pre-political) task— because he knew how human character and human societies operate. Changed people bring changed values into public life...[It] will, perhaps paradoxically, prove impossible for Christians to have a significant impact on politics through a disproportionate focus on politics itself. Political change will emerge primarily from the bottom up rather than the top down."[36] Are you more worried about the White House or your house? Are you more focused on your family and ministry or on politics and the sins of others?[37]

Seventh, the practice of politics in a democracy promotes a "rights" mentality. In the United States, we are trained by our culture and society to believe that we have rights—and as citizens we do. But one would be hard-pressed to find the concept of "Christian rights" in the Bible. And even if one developed such a case, they would have to quickly admit that those rights should be sacrificed in ministering to others.[38] For example, even when Paul used his citizenship to appeal to Rome, it was not to benefit himself, but to strengthen the Philippian church and to gain an audience with Caesar for the Gospel.

Eighth, the church has to be careful that it does not become just another special interest group or group of "concerned citizens"—especially one that has become "the servant of class, material interest, or national spirit."[39] Or as Neuhaus observes: "It is degrading for religion to divide its influence by providing little more than moralizing appendages to the right wing of the Republican party and the left wing of the Democratic."[40] For instance, when we lobby for favorable tax treatment for churches or for environmental protection laws, we are often indistinguishable from those in the world. Whether reality or merely perception, it is unfortunate to signal to the world that our primary goals on earth are temporal and political. One sad indication of our failure here was the certainty with which the world believed that Promise Keepers was—or would become—a political movement. At its worst, political activity by Christians is viewed by the world as merely a means to earthly (and questionable) ends.[41]

Ninth, Christians should have concerns about using worldly things to promote godly ends. Of course, the things of this world can be redeemed at the foot of our Savior's cross. The world is content to be active in using the force of government to fulfill its agendas. However, the work of God starts with grace and free will. Thus, the church is called to *persuade* others to follow God. As Paul writes, "For though we live in the world, we do not wage war as the world does. The weapons we fight with are not the weapons of the world. On the contrary, they have divine power to demolish strongholds." And although the words are forceful, the context is not at all political. Paul is pointing to the use of Truth to "demolish arguments," in aggressively trying to evangelize and minister.[42]

Finally, Christians should give great pause and reflection to attempts to bridle the powers of the State. Besides the Biblical and practical concerns, government is not only powerful, but imminently reversible. "Everyone who preaches the right of the stronger considers himself as the stronger."[43] In other words, we risk "dying" by the same sword we attempt to use on others. Likewise, if one believes that end-times prophecy involve a one-world government, then giving more power to the State is a remarkably short-sighted strategy. Moreover, across the world, there is a negative correlation between the size of government and basic freedoms, including religious practice. In a word, we advocate additional government intervention at substantial risk to our future freedoms.

Chaos vs. Order; Democratic Governance and Political Force

It is clear that effective government must be between the two extremes of full-blown anarchy (which given sin nature, would result in [too much] chaos) and complete totalitarianism (which would result in stasis and would achieve order but without freedom). The question then becomes where the most effective government would be on that spectrum. The potential range of answers can be narrowed considerably by recognizing the importance of both order and, especially, freedom. As A. W. Tozer expressed it: "Ideally the object of government is to achieve order with a minimum of restraint while permitting a maximum of freedom to the individual."[44]

One should also recognize that government is ultimately about the use of force. As Daniel Webster said, "There are men in all ages who mean to govern well, but they mean to govern. They promise to be good masters, but they mean to be masters." Moreover, politics and government are about the exercise of power. Neuhaus again: "Politics is the business of governing. It has to do with power—getting, keeping, and exercising it...Power, in turn, is the ability to get other people to do what you want, and not to do what you do not want...Every system of government, no matter what it is called, is a system by which some people rule over other people...I am aware that this is not a very elevated view of politics. Politics can involve nobler works and even visions. But they are not essentially what politics is about."[45]

Of course, this is a troubling view of the exercise of power, especially in light of sin nature—and points to the efficacy of limited government and democracy.[46] But as C. S. Lewis argues, "There are two opposite reasons for being a democrat. You may think all men so good that they deserve a share in the government of the commonwealth, and so wise that the commonwealth needs their advice. That is, in my opinion, the false romantic doctrine of democracy. On the other hand, you may believe fallen men to be so wicked that not one of them can be trusted with any irresponsible power over his fellows. That I believe to be the true ground of democracy."[47] It follows that democracy is a far-from-perfect form of government that may nonetheless be the best, realistic alternative in a fallen world.

And all this is troubling from the view of the one over whom power is prospectively going to be exercised. As G. K. Chesterton notes, "[Governance] is...a thing analogous to writing one's own love letters or blowing one's own nose. These things we want a man to do for himself, even if he does them badly...In short, the democratic faith is this: that the most terribly important things must be left to ordinary men themselves."[48] It will be important for us to wrestle with this vital question later: in what matters should the governors exercise force over those the governed? More to the point: when should Christians advocate the use of coercion over others?

Finally, there are number of inherent ethical tensions in decisions based on coercion: When the interests of human beings are antagonistic, these interests are either left unresolved, one party voluntarily submits to the other, or their interests will be resolved using coercion. But coercion presents a number of difficulties. "Among the infinite variety of plans that employ coercion to organize society, which is best? Furthermore, even if the 'best' plan could be identified, why would we expect people to submit to it...And if you consider individual self-interest as antagonistic to the general interest, where do you propose to establish the acting principle of coercion?"[49]

The Advocacy of Force and the Atrophy of Virtue

Doug Bandow has argued that "statism has become the basic theology for those committed to using government to coercively create their preferred version of the virtuous society."[50] From the Religious Left, the preferred view of society involves community virtues—for instance, taking care of the poor and the environment. From the Religious Right, the preferred view involves individual virtues—forcing people to adhere to a moral code of conduct. But as Bandow notes, "government is not a particularly good teacher of virtue. The state tends to be effective at simple, blunt tasks, like killing and jailing people. It has been far less successful at shaping human consciences."[51] Again, in theory, government can change externals and can perhaps influence internals, but this "shaping" is fraught with ethical and practical difficulties.

Mark Skousen argues further that "every time we pass another law or regulation...we are admitting the failure of individuals to govern themselves. When we persuade citizens to do the right thing, we can claim victory. But when we force people to do the responsible thing, we have failed."[52] Or as Bandow notes, "A country full of people lusting in their hearts who don't consummate their lust out of fear of arrest is scarcely better than one full of people acting on their sinful whims. It is, in short, one thing to improve appearances, but quite another to improve society's moral core. And God, Jeremiah tells us, looks at the heart."[53]

Christian advocates of government solutions implicitly view freedom and virtue as antagonists. Instead, freedom is a prerequisite for virtue. "Coerced acts of conformity with some moral norm, however good, do not represent virtue; rather, the compliance with that norm must be voluntary."[54] By preventing, punishing, subsidizing, or mandating behaviors, government necessarily reduces or eliminates the virtue and morality behind those decisions. In addition, government activism reduces the vitality of other institutions that are typically responsible for promoting virtue, most notably the church—whether in helping the poor or ministering to "sinners." Moreover, the availability of government solutions is a temptation to abuse power and to improperly seek power. Finally, Augustine argued that any exercise of power tends to feed violence—which in turn, threatens to undermine loving one's neighbor.[55] In sum, restricting freedom is not typically consistent with promoting virtue.[56]

Government as an Idol or as a Tool?

Tim LaHaye once remarked that "the only way to have a genuine spiritual revival is to have legislative reform."[57] In contrast, many prominent, politically-conservative Christians have become increasingly disenchanted with the pursuit of government activism. For example, syndicated columnist Cal Thomas speaks critically of the modern church's pursuit of government: "too many members of the church are seeking a shortcut to righteousness, preferring the ways of government to the way of its savior." In particular, Thomas is critical of the agenda of the Religious Right, concluding that the danger for "the Religious Right is that they are making the same mistakes the Religious Left made. To solve the moral problems of the nation, they are looking to government rather than the author of their faith and His strategies."[58] Charles Colson argues that this fallacy stems from "too low a view of the power of a sovereign God and too high a view of the ability of man."[59] Likewise, Bill Bennett claims that "we place too much hope in politics...[It] has too often become the graven image of our time."[60]

Although the contemporary level of government worship is troubling, it was especially prevalent among Christian leaders at the turn of the 20th century. For example, Marvin Olasky quotes the Canon of Canterbury, William Fremantle, concerning the State: "It calls forth a worship more complete than any other..." and only government "can embrace all the wants of its members and afford them the universal instruction and elevation which they need." Olasky argues that "the worship of power had rarely been stated so explicitly by a church leader" before quoting Fremantle a final time: "when we think of the Nation as becoming, as it must do more and more, the object of mental regard, of admiration, of love, even of worship (for in it God preeminently dwells), we shall recognize to the fullest extent its religious character and functions."[61]

Of course, explicit worship of an entity other than God is an atrocity. But oftentimes our faith is more implicit, relying on government for sustenance, security, and the solutions to many of our problems. Part of this is a failure to understand the limitations of government. For instance, Pope Paul VI once said of government: it "always intervenes with careful justice and with devotion to the common good for which it holds final responsibility."[62] Fortunately, contemporary and more realistic observers would be far more reticent to use such terms as "always," "careful justice," "devotion to the common good," and "holds final responsibility" in their assessment of government's role and abilities.

Our faith in government (or not) is also crucial because our policy recommendations will follow closely. Given his faith in government, the Pope's subsequent conclusions should not be surprising: "It pertains to the public authorities to choose, even to lay down, the ends to be achieved, and the means of attaining them, and it is for them to stimulate all the forces engaged in this common activity."[63] Whether our worship of government is explicit or more subtle, we need to be careful that we do not view government as an idol.

As Robert Sirico has said, "the United States is a remarkably religious nation. Our god is not the God of traditional faiths, however. It is the modern state."[64] Until this faith fades, we will continue to grasp for government solutions and prevent God from moving through us in other ways. Like the Israelites in Samuel's time, we too often look to human government to "fight our battles for us." Or as David Chilton exclaims: "Already, it is common to find people (even Christians!) who simply cannot conceive of certain tasks being performed without state aid. It is a marvel to them that people have ever had housing, education, health care, jobs, transportation, postal service, food, and money apart from [the] state."[65]

For advocates of government activism, there is a fine line between pursuing government as an appropriate means to an end and idolatry of government as provider, protector, and even, as savior.[66] For some avid opponents of government activism, idolatry takes a different form— believing that what government does and doesn't do is essential to God's kingdom. As Jonathan Rauch notes, "Liberals scheme day and night to expand government; conservatives, to shrink it. All of them are governmentalists, in the sense that they define their ideologies and social passions in relation to government." Neither form of "governmentalism" is an appropriate option for a Christian.

I realize that idolatry is a serious charge, but the potential consequences are severe. There is perhaps no greater sin than turning away from God to follow other gods. The sin of idolatry is so serious that the Israelites were commanded to stone to death a wife, family member, or best friend who tried to lead someone to serve other gods; in fact, the one tempted was to throw the first stone.[67] If the inhabitants of a city tried to lead Israelites away from God, they and their city were to be completely destroyed.[68] Because God seeks an intimate relationship with us, to trust in other gods, including government, is a reprehensible sin. Although we laugh at the Old Testament worshippers of stone and wood, we must take care not to fall into dependence on a variety of more subtle idols—money, prestige, power, and government.[69]

Keeping Government in Perspective

In terms of justification, human efforts to self-govern result in eternal separation from God (outside of our acceptance of His grace). In terms of sanctification, self-government comes at the expense of the Spirit's impact on our lives and our ability to glorify God. And human government, often dominated by people who do not have a heart to love God or others, too frequently results in displays of power far outside the will of God.

Peter Wehner argues that Christ was "intentionally ambiguous" with his "Caesar vs. God" response and notes that Christ didn't provide a checklist for believers on this question.[70] But because the issue was not completely resolved, Christians have since engaged in a lively debate over their appropriate relation to, and use of, government. It is that debate to which I hope to provide some useful input.

Regardless of one's conclusions about matters of government, it should be clear that the power of God working independent of the power of the State presents the greatest opportunities to glorify God. After quoting a Roman official's observations about early Christians caring for others, Cal Thomas concludes: "There is power in that, real power. Why would anyone want to settle for less? The church has the power to transform our nation into what most of us would like it to be. But it will not do so if it joins another religious crowd that said 2,000 years ago: 'We have no king but Caesar'."[71]

The Bible teaches that Christians should depend very little on government—either personally or for solving social problems. And to the extent that Christians want to use government as a means of glorifying God, they should take great care in attempts to manipulate its power. Are the goals Biblical—righteousness, justice and so on? Are the methods Biblical, appropriate, and practical? Are there significant or even prohibitive costs to those methods? It is to these questions that we now turn.

Chapter 4:
Pursuing Godly Goals with Godly Methods

At least implicitly, one of the most prominent themes in the Bible is the pursuit of godly goals using godly methods. This begins with the most important issue—seeking justification before God and obtaining eternal life. In so doing, a person can make one of two mistakes: to be unconcerned with obtaining the goal or to seek it earnestly but incorrectly. The latter is probably the more frequent error as people seek to justify themselves before a perfect and Holy God by their works—rather than accepting God's grace, best represented by trusting solely in the atoning death and blood of Jesus Christ. As Ephesians 2:8-9 says "For it is by grace you have been saved, through faith—and this not from yourselves, it is the gift of God—not *by* works, so that no one can boast."

After a (positive) relationship with God is established, the second goal is sanctification—how to grow in our faith, how to obey God and bring Him glory, and how to love others. The very next verse in Ephesians tells us that Christians are "God's workmanship, created in Christ Jesus *to do* good works." Likewise, we are to be His "instruments of righteousness" and we are to be remembered for "our work produced by faith, our labor prompted by love, and our endurance inspired by hope."[1] Unfortunately, many Christians have little passion for pursuing God's goals for their lives. They have a flawed understanding of the character of God, are side-tracked by sin and other worldly pursuits, are unwilling to risk going God's way, and so on. Many other Christians have an earnest desire to fulfill God's design for their lives, but use improper means in trying to reach those goals.

In general terms, the prescribed means for living the Christian life are following the word of God and submitting to the Holy Spirit who dwells in the heart of every believer. The former is well understood as an authority (although some of the details are misunderstood or at least debated fervently); the latter is more subjective and tougher to define. Nonetheless, "keeping in step with the Spirit" is crucial. As Paul says, "I have been crucified with Christ, and I no longer live, but Christ lives in me."[2] Christians are to bring forth the "fruit of the Spirit" and we are to avoid "grieving" and "quenching" the Spirit.[3] We are to avoid giving up our freedom in Christ for bondage—whether to the law, to "basic principles of this world," to carnality, or to anything else.[4] We are to walk in faith, because "everything that does not come from faith is sin."[5] All this is for the purpose of loving God and other people more effectively.

In contrast to what we have the opportunity to do, the Bible is filled with stories of people who pursued the wrong goals or no goals in particular, and those who pursued the right goals but used inappropriate methods. We should take this as a general warning against each type of mistake. In a sense, this book is concerned with the question of whether our agendas for government activism represent the pursuit of appropriate goals and the use of appropriate methods. In this chapter, we will describe the three types of mistakes, discuss the importance of avoiding each, and provide a number of Biblical examples.

A Lack of Passion for the Things of God

Some of the Bible's strongest words are reserved for the "lukewarm"—those who don't care enough about things that matter. Christ warned the church at Laodicea: "I know your works, that you are neither cold nor hot. I wish you were either one or the other! So, because you are lukewarm—neither hot nor cold—I am about to spit you out of my mouth."[6] Perhaps surprisingly, God prefers us to be cold rather than tepid, and ironically, His response to lukewarm is a polar opposite—a remarkably intense disgust.

Intuitively, it should be clear to us why God would prefer cold to lukewarm. Room-temperature food is rarely enjoyable to eat; mediocrity in personality and character are not attractive; we tend to appreciate firm handshakes and resolute voices. We know where we stand with people who are hot or cold. We know what to expect from strong-willed people; we respect their convictions independent of whether we agree with them. Likewise, God can more effectively deal with those of us who are on fire, even if we're going the wrong direction. As Simone Weil noted, "if the [Prodigal] son had lived economically, he would never have thought of returning."[7] And to note, some of Christianity's most fervent and effective defenders have been people who initially set out to prove Christianity wrong.

Why do believers fail to treat the things of God more seriously? One reason is that we tend to "hedge our bets." In I Kings 18:21, Elijah asks the Israelites, "How long will you waver between two opinions? If the Lord is God, follow him; if Baal is God, follow him." Polytheism and idolatry are similar—banking on God *and* something else in pursuit of abundant life. James 1:6-8 describes the "double-minded man" who asks, but doubts as he is asking. He is "unstable" and "should not think that he will receive anything from the Lord." For instance, we do this when we ask for "input" from God rather than agreeing beforehand to surrender to His revealed will. Why would we be so arrogant as to ask for God's advice while reserving the right to refuse it?

Hedging one's bets may be prudent financial advice, but is patently unwise in spiritual matters. As Christians, we are called to put all of our eggs in one basket, to bank on the one sure investment—the blood and cross of our Lord and Savior, Jesus Christ. As Jim Elliot once said, "He is no fool who gives up what he cannot keep to gain what he cannot lose." Investing fully in the things of eternity is the smartest way to use our time, talent, and treasure.

Sometimes we're lukewarm because we trifle with things that God cares deeply about—we don't go far enough with obedience or we condone what should be condemned. On one hand, in I Corinthians 5:1-2, Paul chastises the church of Corinth for tolerating tremendous sexual immorality in the church—"and of a kind that does not occur even among the pagans...and you are proud! Shouldn't you have rather been filled with grief and have put out of your fellowship the man who did this?"[8] On the other hand, in Galatians 1:8-9, Paul rips into the purveyors of a legalistic heresy as "anathema," preaching that they should be eternally condemned. Tremendous immorality among believers or a "grace plus" theology taught in the church were to be fervently rebuked—in order to maintain the reputation of God's church and to more effectively communicate the infinite value of Christ's atoning blood.

Sometimes we're distracted from the things of God by overtly sinful things. Hebrews 12:1 encourages us to "run with perseverance the race marked out for us"— which includes "throwing off everything that hinders and the sin that so easily entangles." Galatians 1:10 describes a common but regrettable phenomenon—being distracted by peer pressures, wanting to please men instead of God.

Sometimes we're distracted by "good things" (as opposed to the "best things"), succumbing to the busyness of life. The Gospels record many who chose not to follow Christ, deciding instead to pursue lesser goals—the rich young ruler who wouldn't give up all he owned, the man who wanted to bury his father before he followed Christ, and so on. Others are distracted from their walk with Christ—like the seed cast among thorns which "does not mature."[9] In addition, the Gospels implicitly ignore countless others who couldn't be bothered to sacrifice their favored activities for the opportunity to sit at Christ's feet.

Sometimes we are unwilling to take risks by stepping out in faith—either in our requests to God or in our actions. In either case, our cowardice is unfortunate since we miss out on the great opportunities that God would afford us. Again, Scripture records numerous examples: Pilate deferring to the hostile crowd, the cowardly conclusion of the ten Israelite spies in the wilderness (vs. the courage and faith of Joshua and Caleb), Barak requiring Deborah to go along for the battle against the Canaanites, and so on.[10]

Sometimes we care about the things of God—but not enough. Jim Wallis distinguishes between whether one is *for* righteousness and justice and whether one is hungry and thirsty for righteousness and justice.[11] Or as the famous basketball philosopher Bobby Knight has said, "It is not the will to win that is important; everyone has that. It is the will to prepare to win that is important." Are we willing to "prepare"—to sacrifice for the greater things of God?

Worst of all, sometimes we fail to care at all.[12] It is a tremendous error to be apathetic—in particular, to have no concern for the things of God. As such, Esau is described as "godless" in Hebrews 12:16 since he "sold his inheritance rights as the oldest son" for a bowl of soup and some bread. To treat the promises of God so lightly is an unspeakable insult to God.

Are we passionate about anything? Are we lukewarm, or are we cold or hot? An unwillingness to be passionate stems from a failure to understand God's character, to have an eternal and divine perspective, and ultimately, to trust God.

Passion for the Wrong Things

Often, the problem is not the absence of zeal, but rather, having a zeal that is misplaced or misdirected. "It is fine to be zealous, provided the purpose is good."[13] For instance, one wouldn't criticize Jonah for lacking passion or resolve. When asked to preach to the Ninevites, Jonah "ran away from the Lord" and headed in the exact opposite direction of God's will. From the belly of the fish, Jonah turns to God in repentance: "in my distress I called to the Lord...I will look again toward your holy temple." When Jonah finally preaches the word of the Lord, the Ninevites respond favorably. But instead of rejoicing at their repentance, Jonah "was greatly displeased and became angry." Jonah's strange but heartfelt opinions—not wanting the "evil" Ninevites to have access to a relationship with God—continue as he twice asks God "to take away my life, for it is better for me to die, than to live." A passion for God's agenda would have been preferable to his merciless and discriminatory rants, but in each case, God was still able to use Jonah's far-from-tepid responses.

The Bible also frequently portrays what one could describe as a passion for sin. Two of the more stunning instances are in the strikingly similar accounts of Genesis 19 and Judges 19.[14] The former's prologue to the destruction of Sodom and Gomorrah is well-known, but the latter is equally sinful—if not more so, given who the sinners were. The passion and the parallels between the pagans and the Israelites to commit carnal and violent sins are staggering.

In Genesis 31 and Judges 18, the Bible again provides two similar stories—when a pagan and an Israelite are distraught about losing their household gods. In the latter, a militarily over-matched Micah nonetheless sets out to retrieve his defenseless idols. His statement of faith in Judges 18:24 is poignant, but sorely misplaced: "You took the gods I made, and my priest, and went away. What else do I have? How can you ask, 'what's the matter with you?'"

The pagans of the Old Testament are also memorable for the passion with which they worshipped their many gods. Often, their dedication was truly impressive. They were willing to spend their money, slash their bodies, and even sacrifice their children to these gods. And all this for gods who were "like a scarecrow in a melon patch; [they] cannot speak; they must be carried because they cannot walk."[15] Even today, many non-believers are extremely passionate in their worship of false religions and an assortment of false gods. We should be shamed by the efforts they put into worshiping false gods when we fail to put the same energy into worshipping the one true God.

As noted earlier, the Israelites exhibited great passion for avoiding the government of God. They clamored loudly for a human king in I Samuel 8. Ezekiel graphically describes Israel fervently chasing after its "lovers" (other nations and other gods). Jeremiah also paints a vivid picture of their passion: "Long ago you broke off your yoke and tore off your bonds; you said, 'I will not serve you!' Indeed, on every high hill and under every spreading tree you lay down as a prostitute...You are a wild donkey sniffing the wind in her craving—in her heat who can restrain her? Any males that pursue her need not tire themselves; at mating time they will find her...You said, 'It's no use! I love foreign gods, and I must go after them.'"[16]

Often, Christians are passionate about sin as well. On one hand, we misuse our freedom in Christ as a license "to indulge the sinful nature"—our addictions to, or indulgences in, carnality.[17] On the other hand, we fail to stand firm in our freedom in Christ, becoming "burdened again by a yoke of slavery"—by earnestly trying to win God's approval, by actively imposing rigid legalisms on ourselves, and judgmentally forcing those man-made standards on others.[18]

We may not worship gods of stone and wood, but we have other passionate idolatries: looking to government for solutions, sustenance, and security; over-indulgences in sports, shopping, or soap operas; addictions to work or leisure; "co-dependencies" in our relationships with others. And sometimes the idols are more subtle—elevating family to too high of a level (vs. Christ's call to "hate" one's parents), believing every word of a particular preacher or teacher (vs. the Bereans in Acts 17:11), being completely immersed in the church and its activities (vs. I Peter 2:12's "Live such good lives *among* the pagans..."), and so on. Such subtle idols are arguably more dangerous. As C.S. Lewis noted, "Brass is more easily mistaken for gold than clay is."[19]

Passion is a prerequisite for following Christ, but that passion should be applied to the right issues. Moreover, the appropriate goals should be pursued with methods endorsed or approved by God.

Godly Goals, Ungodly Methods

As Christians, we are called to have tremendous passion for many things: the unsaved and the Gospel, God's name and reputation, justice, righteousness, and so on. But pursuing godly goals is no assurance that it will be done in a way that honors God. We can err by being unable to discern the proper approach to a given situation, choosing the wrong timing, using the wrong strength, or having improper motives.[20] After all, zeal without knowledge or charity are not praiseworthy in God's kingdom.[21]

The Bible is replete with examples of people pursuing honorable or at least reasonable goals, but with flawed methods. For Christians, the most important general example is a reliance on the flesh as opposed to the Spirit.[22] As Ian Thomas notes, "the devil does not mind whether you...succeed or whether you fail in the energy of the flesh, whether you are filled with self-pity or self-praise, for he knows that in both cases you will be preoccupied with yourself, and not with Christ."[23]

Less complicated examples of the same principle are a prominent theme in the Old Testament—particularly when we pursue our preferred timing and agendas. Earlier, we noted Esau's apathy toward God's promises and the inheritance through Abraham. In contrast, his younger brother Jacob exhibited great interest in what Esau had forsaken. However, Jacob's methods for pursuing the inheritance were far from ideal. In Genesis 27, younger son Jacob deceived Isaac into giving him the blessing of the firstborn; in Genesis 25, Jacob had already bought the firstborn's birthright from Esau for a bowl of soup and some bread.[24] God had promised that "the older will serve the younger" earlier in Genesis 25, but instead of relying on God's timing and methods, Jacob took matters into his own hands and improperly pursued the things of God.

Throughout I and II Kings, Israel's rulers were frequently accused of "committing the sins of Jeroboam." What was his sin? In I Kings 11:29-39, God had promised Jeroboam kingship over ten of the tribes of Israel. In I Kings 12:20, the Israelites rebelled against King Rehoboam and the prophecy was fulfilled. But Jeroboam failed to trust God's promise to him. In I Kings 12:26, Jeroboam reasoned that the people would revert back to Rehoboam if they continued to return for worship in Jerusalem, so he built two golden calves to hold their religious and political allegiance. In a nutshell, Jeroboam's sin was to take what God had already promised him—but in his own strength, chasing his own agenda in his own timing, and failing to trust in God.

Abraham and Sarah's failure to wait on God's timing for a child is probably the most famous example of this principle.[25] In Genesis 15:1-4, Abraham asked God if his servant Eliezer was to be his heir. But God promised Abraham that instead, he would father a son—the one to whom God's blessings and Abraham's inheritance would go. Although Sarah was not directly mentioned by God, they surely assumed initially that she was to be the mother. But some time later, her faith faded: "The Lord has kept me from having children." She suggested that Abraham sleep with her maidservant so that they would have a child. Abraham consented and within the year, Hagar bore Ishmael. Clearly, the goal was reasonable—to have the child that God had promised, but the chosen means to the end were a failure to trust in God's timing and methods. Perhaps the most sobering detail of this story is that Abraham believed that Ishmael was "the child of the promise" until God told him 13 years later that Sarah would bear Isaac. He had used ungodly methods, but for many years, had been convinced that he had acted appropriately.

Other Israelites also convinced themselves that seemingly reasonable methods were appropriate to use. In Genesis 34, Shechem pursued his "love" for Dinah in a strange way—by raping her and then "speaking tenderly to her." In response, Jacob's sons consented to intermarry with the Shechemites, conditional on them becoming circumcised. While recovering from "surgery," Levi and Simeon put them to the sword. Although their passion for revenge is understandable, the chosen method was equally sinful—deception, murder, and trivializing one of God's holy ordinances. In Exodus 2, Moses killed an Egyptian who was beating a fellow Israelite. His emotions are understandable, but as a result of his poorly chosen method, Moses spent 40 years as a shepherd in the wilderness.[26] In II Samuel 6, Uzzah reached out to steady the Ark despite strict instructions not to touch it. His actions were understandable and his intentions were honorable, but the result was instant death. And in I Kings 15, King Asa purchased a treaty with the Arameans by handing over all of the temple's gold and silver—instead of pushing for spiritual renewal and trusting God to deliver Israel.

The same theme is prevalent in the New Testament. The disciples and many of Christ's other followers had anticipated a political Messiah. Although an understandable scenario to anticipate and even desire, it was not at all within God's will. When Peter insisted strongly that Christ should avoid the cross, he responded by telling Peter, "Get away from me, Satan!" In Matthew 20:20-22, James and John asked to sit on each side of Christ in his kingdom. Their desire was legitimate; they wanted to be great in Christ's kingdom. Note that Christ did not rebuke their goal per se, but merely said that they didn't understand what they were asking. Likewise, Peter's swordplay before the crucifixion and the disciples' desire to call down fire from heaven were understandable but improper responses.[27]

Many of the Pharisees were passionate in pursuing what they thought to be God's goals; the result was Christ's harshest criticisms.[28] Remember that before becoming a Christian, Paul believed that persecuting the Christians was the godliest thing he could do. To illustrate the extent of his Pharisaic zeal, he notes that he intensely persecuted the church.[29] And concerning the Jews, Paul testified that they were "zealous for God, but their zeal is not based on knowledge."[30] Because they sought to "establish their own righteousness," their passion was for naught in God's economy.

One cannot pigeon-hole how Christ responded in each situation—except that in each instance, he obeyed

God and loved others perfectly, and that he had perfect motives in the perfect timing with the perfect strength and the perfect method. To focus on outcomes without analyzing methods is dangerous. Implicitly, it is an argument that the means justify the ends. As such, the crux of this book will be to argue that in using government, we typically fall far short of following God's standards and emulating Christ's ministry. We often have the right goals, but are using inappropriate methods.[31]

Godly Goals, Godly Methods

Clearly, we want to pursue the right goals with the right methods. In I Samuel 17, the Israelite soldiers were understandably but inappropriately paralyzed by their fear of Goliath. A young man, David, emerged from the crowd with a passion for defending God's name and a confident faith in, and dependence on, God in the battle. He eschewed the armor and weapons of King Saul—improper for him to use—for his beloved slingshot. The outcome: the severed head of the dreaded Goliath, faith in David as a (future) leader, and glory to God. In contrast to the soldiers' insufficient passion for the things of God, David had passion for the right things and used an appropriate method.

In I Samuel 14, a similar adventure for Jonathan is sandwiched between three instances when Saul chose sinful methods in his battles against the Philistines. In I Samuel 13, Saul acted in his own timing, failing to patiently wait for Samuel until the appointed time. I Samuel 14 opens with Saul's legalism that no soldier should eat until the Philistines were vanquished. And in I Samuel 15, Saul ignored Samuel's instructions, disobeyed God, and followed his own agenda. Instead of totally destroying the Amalekites and their possessions, he saved the best of what God had condemned—in order to sacrifice it to God! Jonathan's faith and dependence on God stand in stark contrast to Saul's "reasonable" but sinful choices to depend on his own methods as opposed to God's.

The Biblical stories of passion for godly goals and methods are endless—Gideon's decision to follow God by cutting down his father's idols, building an altar to God, and using his father's best bull as a sacrifice to God; people who went to great lengths to receive healing from Christ (through a roof, by touching his cloak, etc.); the extent of the Israelites donating time and money to building the Tabernacle and their precision in building it "just as the Lord had commanded Moses"; Caleb who passionately wanted what God had promised to him earlier; and so on. But the moral of each story is the same. We are to be passionate people, having a zeal for obeying God and loving others. And we are to use methods that are approved by God or consistent with Christ's ministry.

Too often, we settle for so much less in our Christian walk. In contrast, the Bible's most frequent description of God's relationship to us is that of a passionate lover. The "agape" love described in the Bible is unconditional, risk-taking, enemy-loving, and totally unreasonable. The Old Testament repeatedly instructs the Israelites to love God with all of their mind, soul, heart, and strength. When describing the Christian life, Paul uses phrases like "press on toward the goal to win the prize," "whatever you do, work at it with all your heart," and "fight the good fight." Christianity is not about the rigidities of legalism or the ability to avoid sin; it is about freedom from bondage to sin and freedom to love God and others effectively. It is not a religion of politely attending church a few times a week; it is a life-changing splash into an otherwise stagnant world that needs to hear and see the Gospel.

We are to be as passionate in our giving as Mark 12:41-44's widow giving her two mites. We are to be as passionate about others in ministry and discipleship as Luke 15 portrays the rejoicing angels and the loving father. We are to be as passionate in our petitionary prayers as Luke 18's persistent widow. We are to be as passionate in our questions to God as Habakkuk, Job, and the Psalm-writers. We are to be as passionate about God's name and reputation as Christ was in clearing the temple. *And* we are to pursue those goals using methods that will bring glory to God.

In terms of public policy activism, four criteria emerge from these principles.[32] First we must determine whether the prospective goal is godly. Second, a given public policy must be an *ethical* means to godly ends. Pursuing reasonable goals or even godly goals does not ensure that any particular method will be appropriate. Although homosexuality is a sin, carrying a sign that says "God hates fags" is hateful and violates the 3rd Commandment. Likewise, using a gun to take money from people to pay a poor man's hospital bills is not a Biblical approach to charity. Third, a given public policy must be an *appropriate* means to godly ends. For example, if one does nothing to support the needy, is it appropriate to vote to spend other people's money for that task? If there are gambling-like activities that occur in the Church, should Christians deal with gambling in the world before it deals with gambling within? Fourth, a given public policy must be a *practical* means to godly ends.

For example, assuming for the moment that advocacy of government redistribution to the poor is ethical and appropriate, we're not assured that the redistribution will actually promote the spoken end of helping the poor. Without meeting all four of these criteria, Christians will have no Biblical ground on which to stand in their public policy activism.[33]

There is a bumper sticker that says "If you're not outraged, you're not paying attention." There are plenty of candidates for our attention, but are we passionate about godly goals? And in the pursuit of those goals, are we using godly means? In particular, is the use of government troubling? Are all uses of government equally valid? We turn now to the agendas of the "Religious Right"—to "legislate (social) morality," and then, the "Religious Left"—to "legislate (economic) justice."

A Note on Defining
Legislating Morality and Justice

In any discussion, it is important that all parties understand the terms being used. Unfortunately, as noted earlier, Christians have had a shotgun approach to what they consider to be appropriate roles for government intervention. In the attempt to form a coherent and consistent philosophy, we will have to be more precise. As such, this is an important mini-chapter. I encourage you to read this section carefully and to think through alternative ways to define the key terms. This will enable you to better understand my arguments and to test them properly.

In defining "morality" and "justice" in the context of government activism, I am using the terms as they are commonly (although not exclusively) used in the political arena. I will refer to "legislating morality" (LM) as efforts to regulate and restrict consensual but sinful acts between two adults in which no significant, direct costs are imposed on others. Although both parties enter the agreement willingly and expect to benefit, Christians believe that, as sin, the activity is, on net, harmful. But the key point is that the behavior is voluntary for both parties and both parties expect to benefit—what economists call "mutually beneficial trade." Examples of this include sex outside of marriage and drug use. (A second category of LM is using government to force or legitimize "good behaviors" such as prayer in schools.)

In contrast, "justice" issues will be those in which someone's rights are directly and significantly violated. Obvious examples of this include murder, rape, and theft. In other words, one party uses force of some type to directly harm another party; someone benefits directly at the expense of another. It follows that "legislating justice" (LJ) is the use of government to try to improve justice and to reduce or eliminate unjust outcomes. There is a long and involved debate about whether the focus of justice should be on opportunities or outcomes. Christians should be interested in both. As such, I will focus on the use of just methods to reach just outcomes.

Thus, the key distinctions in my two definitions are the extent of the earthly consequence of the sin and whether those costs are imposed directly on others or not. Pope John Paul II draws the same line: "each individual's sin in some way affects others. Some sins, by their very matter, constitute a direct attack on one's neighbor."[1] Lysander Spooner distinguished between vices ("those acts by which a man harms himself or his property") and crimes ("those acts by which one man harms the person or property of another").[2] Ralph Reed makes a similar distinction when he concludes that "the best standard for government is still John Stuart Mill's principle of allowing the greatest liberty possible until someone else's life or liberty is jeopardized."[3]

Of course, such a distinction between "morality" and "justice" issues is a simplification. First, the two terms are intertwined—to act justly is a matter of morality and the morality of one's actions often determines the justice of the subsequent outcome.[4] That said, the distinctions between mechanisms (voluntary or coercive) and anticipated outcomes (mutually beneficial or not) will still serve as a useful model.

Second, both justice and morality issues involve costs imposed on others. (In fact, everything we do or don't do affects other people.[5]) Proponents of LM often argue that other parties are indirectly harmed by gambling, prostitution, etc., and thus, that government activism is warranted.[6] However, their view becomes untenable if extended very far.[7] For example, consider a new college graduate who enters a profession. Although he enters into a mutually beneficial trade with his employer, he indirectly harms other workers in his field by competing with them and lowering the market wage. Moreover, when you buy something from X, you decide not to buy it from Y, making Y worse off. In a word, if we were to use the government to prohibit all (consensual) economic activity that has some negative impact on others, we would never be able to engage in trade—except *that* decision would harm X and Y as well![8]

At the least, this framework is helpful in distinguishing between more and less significant and direct costs—from murder to second-hand cigarette smoke. Clearly, there are important distinctions between the size of the costs imposed on others from a variety of sins—for example, by not being charitable to the needy, driving too fast, believing in the central tenets of a false religion, being a serial rapist, and eating an extra piece of pie. Should the government legislate against all of these sins? When do the costs become significant enough to allow Christians to righteously invoke government solutions? To the extent that these costs can be mapped on a spectrum, one could argue that as the costs become larger and more direct, there is a greater potential role for government activism.[9] Likewise, on a practical level, it will be much easier to advocate the reduction of clear and direct costs than subtle and indirect costs (or whose definition as a significant cost requires Biblical revelation.)

In sum, I recognize that morality and justice are connected in practice, but given the need for some sort of framework, for the sake of convenient labels, and recognizing their popular usage, these terms would seem to be a reasonable basis for our discussion.

A Few Other Points...

First, we must distinguish between instances when the government allows people to sin and when the government forces people to sin (through omission or commission). And we must distinguish between what the Bible calls for in terms of the behavior of believers and what God expects from non-believers. In discussions about God's standards and our response to the authority of government, believers are often unclear, or at least sloppy, about the Biblical differences between these concepts.

Second, abortion is too complicated to cover in the LM/LJ framework without further development, and thus requires a separate treatment. Further, the discussion of abortion and subsequent prescriptions is rather voluminous, and thus requires a separate section with two chapters. I will cover this topic after developing the LM and LJ sections of the book.

Third, proponents of LJ typically focus on equality of outcomes as opposed to equality of opportunity. There is a good reason for this: it is difficult if not impossible to directly observe "opportunity." Unfortunately, outcomes are only a proxy for opportunity. Moreover, a preoccupation with outcomes is equivalent to a focus on the ends rather than the means to those ends. Do any means justify godly ends? Instead, Christians are called to think through the question of whether the prescribed means are godly and practical, as well as whether the ends are godly. As Jim Wallis notes, "We need a...commitment to justice...but to shape a new future we must find the moral foundations and resources for a new social vision."[10] Unfortunately, many Christian prescriptions for government activism fail to have those foundations.

Fourth, the frequent comparison of LM sins to LJ sins is inappropriate and amounts to sensationalism. The former sins involve consent and voluntary behavior where both agents believe that they benefit; the latter sins involve the use of force and coercion where one party is clearly and directly made worse off by the actions of the other. Of course, all sins are equal in that they require the blood of Christ for atonement. But if one insists on treating all sins the same politically, they are stuck in the untenable position that all sin should be punished (equally) by government.

Fifth, proponents of LM are fond of noting that "all laws legislate morality by definition"—thus defining LM as all-encompassing. But there are a number of problems with such a broad definition. Although the statement is true, it does not prove that Christians should engage in any particular legislative agenda. Again, we must study the means to the ends. Moreover, the fact that government policy can affect behavior is also not a proof that Christians should pursue such restrictions. For example, the government could "crack down" on Buddhism and co-dependent relationships, but that doesn't make it an ethical or practical method. Note that despite their immorality, many sins are not the subject of any Christian legislative efforts. In a word, such a broad definition of LM gets us no closer to studying this important question. Hopefully my definitions will allow us to reason through what God wants us to do—and not to do—with the tool of government.

Sixth, failing to invoke government solutions—as in the above examples—is not equivalent to the government endorsing the behaviors. Thomas Aquinas said that "Human law cannot, therefore, prohibit whatever is contrary to virtue; it is enough for it to prohibit whatever destroys social intercourse, allowing everything else to be permissible, not in the sense of approving it, but of not attaching a penalty to it."[11]

If you're not satisfied with my definitions of LM and LJ, find your own. But distinctions must be made; as noted above, an all-encompassing definition for LM is of no use in forming a consistent Christian philosophy of government.[12] Without a viable alternative framework, a rejection of the LM/LJ model—a spectrum of the costs that a variety of sins impose on others—implicitly equates rape and murder with smoking marijuana, eating too much junk food, and going to the horse track too often. After all, each of these impose costs on other people.[13] Likewise, people often throw around the terms "justice" and "social justice" without defining them or wrestling with whether they have found appropriate means to these vague ends.

It is crucial that we believe the right things for the right reasons. As Greg Jesson notes, "When people abandon truth, all they are left with are personal feelings expressed in indignant and self-justifying language...We are left with phrases such as, 'I just personally believe it' or 'That's the way I feel, so that's the end of it.'"[14] If you find yourself saying those phrases in the face of legitimate questions about your beliefs on political activism, I encourage you to wrestle earnestly with the issues that follow. Paraphrasing Plato: "An unexamined faith is not worth having."

Chapter 5:
Why Christians Shouldn't Legislate Morality (Part 1)
What Does the Bible Say?
What Would Jesus Do?

When one presents an argument against "legislating morality," a frequent concern is that it is a ploy to excuse sinful behavior. This is not my purpose. Rejecting or downplaying the sinfulness of immoral behavior is sinful. But dealing inappropriately in other ways with "sinners" is also sinful. Christians are called to deal with sinners using conviction and compassion, in truth and love. This is not a rationalization of immoral behavior or its sinfulness, but rather a question of identifying godly responses to it.[1]

As we developed earlier, good intentions are not sufficient for godliness. Zeal and proper motives are not enough; we must use godly methods as well. This presents an important question: Is legislating morality an appropriate tool for Christians to embrace? For instance, should Christians be active in fighting for legislation that prohibits homosexual conduct and gambling? Should Christians lobby for prayer in public schools? How should we address these issues from the pulpit and in more public forums? This section of the book will focus primarily on appropriate responses to non-Christian adults engaging in consensual activities—when no one's rights are directly and significantly violated.[2] We will deal with the topic of "legislating justice"—when someone's rights have been directly violated—in the next section of the book.

When trying to choose the correct response in any given situation, Christians often use two standards: "What does the Bible have to say?" and "What would Jesus do?" The same questions are useful here as well.

What Does the Bible Say About Legislating Morality[3]?

The Bible is clear about God's view on many "social morality issues"—sex outside of marriage, the abuse of alcohol, and so on. But that is not the issue at hand. The question is: When God's moral standards are clear, should Christians actively pursue a legislative agenda to promote or enforce those standards?

Although the Bible is often clear about what God wants for individuals, it says nothing about believers using human government to legislate morality for non-believers. Most notably, the teachings of Christ and the writings of the apostles fail to mention using the State to enforce morality or to pursue spiritual goals. One should note that the Old Testament is replete with references to God directing people to use human government to impact other people. But this intervention was limited to impacting *His* people—the Israelite community. Moreover, the Israelites were to enforce the dictates of the Law—but only within their community.[4]

An important exception was God's desire for His people to settle in the Promised Land, which included instructions for the Israelites to destroy the pagan nations who until then had controlled Canaan. However, this exception cannot serve as a model for contemporary efforts to legislate morality. These efforts were undertaken 1.) by a nation set apart by God; 2.) with God's explicit direction and command; 3.) for a specific purpose—to prepare Canaan for Israelite occupation and dominion; and 4.) to simultaneously render God's judgment—death and destruction—to a prohibitively sinful people[5] through a mixture of natural and supernatural means. None of those conditions is relevant today.

Worshiping a God of Freedom

We worship a God who is concerned with freedom over virtually everything else. To note, He gave us a free will. Why? Voluntary praise is far better than coerced praise.[6] And free will allows us to develop character and other attributes God wants His children to have. In addition, free will and the subsequent cause and effect of our "reaping and sowing" can serve as an incentive to continue positive behaviors or change negative behaviors.

Notably, the Bible opens with the theme of freedom as Adam and Eve choose to disobey God. He had given them one restriction. They were tempted by it and fell. It was not God's will that they should sin, but it was God's will that they should have the choice—the opportunity to glorify God or to separate themselves from God.[7] It is also striking that the theme of the entire New Testament is freedom—freedom from sin, from death, from bondage, freedom to enjoy the abundant life, to better love God and others. "It is for freedom that Christ has set us free....But do not use your freedom to indulge the sinful nature; rather, serve one another in love."[8]

Further, the Bible does not portray God forcefully intervening in the course of human events—unless it is to affect judgment or to help believers. There are no apparent instances when He steps in to prevent people from committing sins beforehand. Sometimes He sent warnings through prophets, but He did not interfere with their choices to engage in the behavior. In fact, God frequently allows people to "hang themselves" with the desires of their heart—to bring them to their knees.[9] By legislating, and thus, limiting certain behaviors, we may be standing in the way of His redemptive plan for some individuals.

In the context of freedom, intuition from life's experiences presents us with an interesting dichotomy: there are times when parents should prevent children from making mistakes, but there are other times when it is best to let children make mistakes so they can learn from them. The same tension is evident in the debate about legislating morality. One side believes that God wants people to have the freedom to make their own mistakes; the other side believes that God wants us to restrict others from making those mistakes. Certainly, the case can be made for parents restricting their children at times. However, the Bible provides no support for Christians restricting the behavior of other adults, particularly non-believers.

If there had been religious conservatives around in the Garden of Eden, one wonders if they would have built a fence around the "tree of the knowledge of good and evil," or perhaps, even chopped it down—for themselves or others.[10] In a creative twist, Rob Bass asks us to consider

the most famous story of substance abuse in the Bible. The substance was mind-altering. There was a pusher. The people involved were warned of its dangers. There were disastrous consequences for others as well. Their situation was under the direct control of God. If there was a case for prohibition, this was it. Infinite Wisdom could determine what to prohibit; Infinite Power could provide enforcement. Yet, God refrained. It is the story of Adam and Eve in the Garden of Eden. Every argument from within the Judeo-Christian tradition for legal prohibition runs up against this rock: that it is an attempt to second-guess Infinite Wisdom. It is not just an attempt to substitute our judgment for our neighbor's, but an attempt to substitute our judgment for God's.[11]

In sum, there can be no moral choices without the freedom to choose. As Dallas Willard notes, we are given "a life in which we alone among living beings can stand in opposition to God—in order that we may also choose to stand with God."[12]

Arguing from "Silence"

When the Bible is clear about a topic, debate among Christians is rendered moot or confined to the fringes of orthodox belief. If the Bible is unclear or silent—as in the case of the details of Christian political involvement—any such debate becomes more interesting. In the case of silence, there are two general approaches to interpreting the Bible as a guide to behavior.

A conservative way to deal with silence is to avoid the behavior if it is not recorded. For instance, some people argue that since the New Testament does not mention the use of musical instruments in the worship of the early church, contemporary worship should omit them as well. This principle is difficult to apply consistently and rigorously.[13] More to the point here, proponents of this mode of applying the Bible cannot advocate legislating morality (or political involvement at all) because the early church did not engage in such activities.

Most Christians at least implicitly believe that "silence equals inactivity" is too rigid, not allowing for "the spirit of the Law." As such, they make decisions with the assistance of the Holy Spirit, prayer, wise counsel, and reason. While more flexible, this approach is more dangerous since it elevates reason—or more accurately, poor reasoning—to a potentially harmful level. As such, one can argue to be active from silence, but should be careful when doing so.

Since Scripture is silent on the matter, the next step is to consider whether legislating morality is "Christ-like" behavior. Would Christ have lobbied the government to pass certain laws? When would Christ have advocated putting his neighbor in jail? If Christ were here today, in what contexts would he pursue human government as a means to divine ends?

"In His Steps"? "What Would Jesus Do?" (or What Would Jesus Have Us Do?)

Let's start with a thought experiment. Imagine Christ in the middle of a busy day of teaching, healing, working with his disciples, and rebuking the Pharisees. He takes a break to call a few legislators who are pivotal to the passage of a state sodomy law. Then, he appears on a local radio talk show to argue against a referendum to allow legalized gambling. Finally, from the pulpit, he devotes half of his sermon to harping on the pagans for their sexual immorality and exhorting his followers to make their voice known on the important social morality issues of the day. If it is difficult to imagine these activities in Christ's agenda, we should reconsider whether such methods are appropriate for us.[14]

Next, let's consider what the Bible says about the way Christ interacted with people. Although he never "legislated morality," perhaps his methods were consistent with using that tool. Or maybe his behavior will provide clues about why this tool is inappropriate. What did he say? How did he say it? How did he treat people? What actions did he take? To what extent was his response conditional on their background? Did he have varying expectations for disparate groups of people? Was there a significant difference between his teaching "from the pulpit" and his discipling one-on-one? Usually, when we think about how Christ interacted with people, we are better able to determine proper courses of action for ourselves.

Christ's Encounters with Individual Unbelievers

To those who approached him asking to become a disciple or to receive eternal life, he provided case-specific instructions about what was necessary to follow him. Luke 9:57-62 records three such instances. In each case, Christ recognized each individual's top priority— fame/prestige, love for a father, love of family—and prescribed putting it aside to pursue the Kingdom of God. A more famous story is that of "the rich young ruler."[15] After the young man claimed that he had kept all of the commandments since the time he had been a boy, Christ responded with "one thing you lack. Go, sell everything you have and give it to the poor...then, come follow me." Some have incorrectly interpreted these passages as universal injunctions for Christians—for instance, that all believers should pursue poverty.[16] Instead, the point of the stories is that for unbelievers, there is often "one thing" they idolize above God, "one thing they lack" in their ability to follow Christ. But this "one thing" varies between individuals. Thus, optimal solutions must differ as well.

Likewise, with those who approached Christ wanting to be healed, he used a variety of methods. He healed by touching, being touched, and without any contact at all; he cured blindness by word and by touch, with spit and with mud; he raised people from the dead by word and by touch; he required faith at times and other times, not; he rebuked demons and sent them into a herd of pigs. Christ chose to heal people in a variety of ways.

In contrast to Christ's individual-specific approach, legislating morality is much less flexible in dealing with widely different situations.[17] Moreover, just before Jesus delivered the critical line to the rich young ruler, Mark 10:21 records that "Jesus looked at him and loved him." In contrast, legislating morality cannot confer a tone of love or be communicated in the one-on-one approach Christ used so often. And legislating morality moves us from persuasion to coercion.

Finally, we know that Christ was known for consorting with the "heathen." His reputation implies that he did this often and in a way that those people found appealing. As such, it seems unlikely that his conversations contained any of the rhetoric often laced into the diatribes of religious conservatives. Did he pull any punches with his pagan companions? No, but we can be assured that he approached each situation with perfect wisdom and tact, in truth and love.

Christ's Preaching to the General Public

As one characterizes the style and substance of Christ's sermons to the general public, one realizes how much his approach deviates from verbally lambasting the "heathens" and attempts to legislate morality. First, his preaching was more alluring and persuasive than heavy-handed and condemning. While his words pierced hearts, they were never the equivalent of a sledgehammer over

the head—except with the Pharisees. He encouraged—and
allowed rather than forced—people to change. And when
he preached on sin, it was often with the use of parables—
in a creative, less direct fashion. In contrast, legislating
morality is negative and direct, rarely appealing to non-
Christians, and at least perceived to be a condemnation of
the sinner.

Second, his preaching placed an emphasis on
"being" rather than "doing." He spoke about the "heart"
and focused on internal sins of the spirit more than
external sins of the flesh. Why? He recognized that
immoral actions spring from the heart; he talked about the
disease rather than merely the symptoms. In contrast,
legislating morality focuses on externals and perhaps
squelches any subsequent discussion of the condition of
the heart. With legislation, guilt and resentment may be
more likely, but salvation may be more elusive. In
response to the enslaving power of sin, human law has
some power to change behavior, but simultaneously, it
may also hinder the power of Christ to transform lives.

Third, he was able to challenge more of his
audience given the breadth of his messages. He placed
more emphasis on the spirit rather than the letter of the
law. Thus, instead of merely harping on the "sinners," he
took a poke at those who had "sinned in their hearts." For
example, Christ used all but one of his mentions of
adultery for purposes other than directly criticizing sexual
immorality.[18] With such preaching, the self-righteous
could not escape so easily or so smugly. In contrast, a
focus on legislating morality—or preaching about
immorality outside the norm for most Christians—
encourages pride and is largely irrelevant to helping
believers walk more closely with God.

Fourth, his style was creative and constantly surprising; his responses to questions were unorthodox and unexpected. He used examples and language his listeners could understand, showing empathy and an obvious desire to reach his audience. In contrast, legislating morality is wooden, pedestrian, and shows no empathy or desire for a relationship with the sinner. "When the only tool you own is a hammer, every problem begins to resemble a nail."

Finally, what Christ did *not* preach is perhaps of greatest importance. "The Roman pagan of Jesus' day was committing the same sins as the American pagan of today. Nowhere does the Bible quote Jesus condemning the Romans or their sins. There is no biblical or historical evidence that Jesus engaged in any anti-Roman political activity."[19] In short, it is difficult to imagine Christ harping on the behavior of non-Christians or being an advocate of legislating morality.

Christ with his Followers

The above categories are noteworthy because they were largely one-time or impersonal encounters. When Christ built relationships—most notably with the disciples—his behavior was markedly different. In short, he was much tougher on them, holding them to a higher standard and saying the stronger things that are more acceptable within more intimate relationships. As opposed to the less direct approach he used with those who did not know him well, at times he was painfully direct with his followers. For example, Christ chastised the disciples twice for having little faith; he asked them "Are you still so dull?" when they failed to understand a particular point; he rebuked them for wanting to call down fire from heaven to punish a group of disinterested Samaritans; and instead of remaining silent, Christ chose to tell Peter he would deny him three times.[20]

But Christ was also patient in the development of his followers' faith. One is reminded of the stories of "doubting Thomas" and Mary and Martha.[21] When James and John asked for positions of prestige within his kingdom, Christ didn't chastise them for such a crass request, but merely asked if they had counted the costs.[22] Christ was also encouraging. One imagines that his response to Peter's attempt to walk on water was delivered with a smile, expressing his pleasure with Peter's growing faith.[23] And Christ's actions to restore his relationship with Peter after the resurrection remain a model for all to emulate.[24]

In contrast, we often fail to confront, challenge, or encourage our fellow believers enough.[25] Instead of developing these skills through interaction with non-believers, legislating morality takes us out of the mode of dealing with people directly and intimately, by using government as the agent of behavioral change. Likewise, when we focus on the behavior of strangers, we simultaneously ignore relevant issues in our own lives and in the lives of our Christian friends.

Christ's Encounters with the Pharisees

It was only with his disciples and the Pharisees—the "religious people"—that he harshly reprimanded certain behaviors. And while he was demanding of the disciples (for their own good and the glory of God), he was most stringent in his dealings with the Pharisees and their hypocrisy. The Pharisees combined Christ's concern for the effect of "religious" people on God's reputation with the strong approach that hardened hearts require.

Christ's ministry was marked by a number of encounters with the Pharisees—long discussions, short debates, their foiled schemes, and his memorable rebukes. Matthew 23 is the most potent example—an entire chapter devoted to Christ pinning back their ears. He described them as hypocrites, blind guides, blind fools, snakes, and a brood of vipers, and then backed up the labels with specific charges. First, he addressed the crowd about the Pharisees: "...do everything thcy tell you. But do not do as they do, for they do not practice what they preach... everything they do is done for men..." Then, he spoke directly to the Pharisees: "you travel over land and sea to win a single convert, and when he becomes one, you make him twice as much a son of hell as you are...you have neglected the more important matters of the law— justice, mercy and faithfulness...you appear to people as righteous, but on the inside you are full of hypocrisy and wickedness..."[26]

Of course, Christ responded positively when the Pharisees were inquisitive, seeking truth rather than pursuing power. Nicodemus visited Christ at night and their discussion about becoming "born again" highlights the memorable third chapter of John's Gospel. Apparently Nicodemus was convinced by the Light because he later rose to Christ's defense in the midst of a verbal attack by other Pharisees; later, he helped to bury Christ.[27] The goal of Christ's interaction with the Pharisees—whether teaching or rebuking—was always repentance and relationship.

Christ had much to fear from the Pharisees—in earthly terms. In fact, they were the ones who eventually arranged his death. But he did not shy away from speaking the truth about them or to them. It is then even more noteworthy that he never said anything derogatory about the (secular) State or Caesar, but saved such a fiery tongue exclusively for the (religious) Pharisees.[28]

Why Christ Demanded More from "Religious People"

With respect to salvation, God is not particularly interested in the behavior of those who are outside of a relationship with Him; "the wages of sin is death" for all who have not accepted the gracious gift of God. With respect to the church, more is at stake when His representatives fall; God's reputation is on the line when His supposed followers misbehave.[29] In addition, the 3rd Commandment and the history of God's responses to Israel make it clear that God is extremely concerned about what happens to His name.[30]

As such, Paul instructs believers to "keep away from...those who cause divisions and put obstacles in your way that are contrary to the teaching you have learned" and to "keep away from every brother who is idle and does not live according to the teaching you received from us."[31] Christ also taught that believers were to disassociate with those who failed to repent on the word of witnesses and the church.[32]

Paul is most explicit about this theme in I Corinthians 5—when he rebukes the church at Corinth for being proud about harboring a man who was sleeping with his father's wife. After chastising the church, he then makes an interesting comparison to how we are to treat *un*believers:

I have written you in my letter not to associate with sexually immoral people—*not at all meaning the people of this world who are immoral*...In that case, you would have to leave this world. But now I am writing you that you must not associate with anyone who calls himself a *brother* but is sexually immoral or greedy, an idolater or slanderer, a drunkard or a swindler. With such a man do not even eat. *What business is it of mine to judge those outside the church?* Are you not to judge those inside? God will judge those outside..." (italics added)[33]

In other words, we are to have very high standards for people within the church and few expectations of those outside.[34] We are to deal strictly with sinful people in the church; and in large part, we are to leave outsiders to a God who is perfect at judging behavior and motives, as well as taking vengeance.[35] In contrast, we often focus too much on the actions of non-believers. And we typically get the order backwards—spending the least energy on ourselves, more on others in the church, and most on those outside the church.[36]

Conviction and Compassion

One of Christ's encounters bears further mention: John 8's story of "the woman caught in adultery." The teachers of the Law and the Pharisees used force to bring the accused woman to Jesus and humiliate her. They incorrectly paraphrased the Law's punishment for her sexual immorality and then asked what should be done. The motivation for the episode was an attempt by the religious authorities to trap Jesus into going against Old Testament Law or the Roman law that Jews could not carry out executions. But as with the cross, Christ grasped victory out of the jaws of defeat—this time with a brilliant answer: "If any of you is without sin, let him be the first to throw a stone at her." Once the accusers left, Christ sent her away, saying "Go now and leave your life of sin." Christ had freed her and tried to persuade her to obey and follow God.

There are a number of relevant points here. The Pharisees were not equitable in their rendering of justice since they only apprehended the woman. They failed to note that the Law specifies that both adulterous parties should die and they supplemented the Law by specifying the means of execution.[37] But note that Christ did not choose to ask them any clarifying questions, point out their error in recalling the Law, or focus on their lack of equity. Instead, he chose to make a different and crucial point—one that must have been best since he chose it. Appealing to technicalities might have allowed him to avoid this situation, but it wouldn't have answered the larger question: what should one do when dealing with "sinners"?

While giving the perfect answer to a seemingly impossible question, Christ provided us with the framework for how to deal with acts of immorality. He neither condemned the woman nor condoned the woman's sin. He neither validated her lifestyle nor allowed the Pharisees to use her for their own gain. Instead, he convicted the prideful Pharisees, restored the dignity of the woman, and challenged her to do what was in her best interests—to leave her life of sin. In sum, he perfectly balanced conviction with compassion, truth with love.

Thus, we too need to approach "social morality issues" with 100% conviction and 100% compassion. Although each of us tends to err on one side or the other, a truly loving response can have no compromise with either.[38] I John 3:18 instructs us not to "love with words or tongue but with actions and in truth." Lacking conviction, we are "too soft," too lenient, too unwilling to confront people with the loving truth that their choices are harmful to themselves and others. Lacking compassion, we are "too hard," too unsympathetic, too eager to confront people who are broken and hurting inside. While liberal churches often ignore or downplay the conviction, evangelicals too frequently leave out the compassion. Both are wrong.

The answer cannot be avoiding the sinners either; evangelism and ministry don't work well from a closet—especially the closet of legislating morality. Unlike today's stereotypical religious conservatives, instead of attacking the heathen, Christ was famous for being with them—the Samaritan, the tax collector, the prostitute. Unlike today's stereotypical religious liberals, he didn't stop at merely interacting with them, he said what needed to be said. In sum, he was remarkably accepting of them, but not their behavior.

When we fail to use both conviction and compassion, we fail to be truly loving. In contrast, Christ's encounters with individuals always sought the best for them. When the one man who could have rightfully thrown some rocks protected "the woman caught in adultery" from stoning, his primary concerns were battling religious hypocrisy and restoring relationship with the woman. His closing remark to the woman was an injunction to "go and sin no more"—don't harm yourself any longer, establish relationship with me instead. Why did Christ want her to change? Not for community standards of morality. Not because he was offended by her actions. But because ultimately, he loved his neighbor, he wanted the best for her, and he knew his prescription was in her best interests.[39]

Christ's Creative Style

Christ used many different approaches, but in general, his methods were extremely unorthodox. Reading the Gospels, one is struck by the creativity of his parables and how his responses surprised the recipients, his followers, and today, us. He led his life in vigorous opposition to the religious and political status quo. In fact, Christ's entire ministry can be viewed as a break with conventional wisdom and religious formulas.

In contrast, legislating morality is wooden and as a popular instrument of force, remarkably unoriginal. It amounts to the threat of unyielding, human, negative reinforcement—hardly the epitome of a Spirit-led change in individuals' lives. In addition to other concerns about the effectiveness of legislating morality, such a blunt, brute-force, universal approach is unlikely to yield optimal solutions.[40] As Ralph Reed explains, "After my faith experience, I became more skeptical of government's ability to legislate morality or reform people's souls."

While Christ was often indirect in method, he was always direct in purpose. In contrast, believers do not often act with the same convictions. If so, we would confront people individually when we had the opportunity (and we would look for more opportunities).[41] Are we too busy, too scared, or too callous to follow his example? Are we too afraid of what people will say if we confront them directly? If so, we fear men more than God and legislating morality is merely a cop-out.

Further, the Bible records only a few instances when Christ became angry. But there is an interesting pattern to his wrath: it occurred only when God's name was being abused (the Pharisees in general, and in clearing the temple) and when someone wanted to directly interfere with another's rights (Christ wanted to help someone and was encountering interference—"Let the children come to me," healings on the Sabbath, and so on). To frequently preach angry denunciations of the heathen from the pulpit is not consistent with Christ's approach. Likewise, preachers should save most of their vitriol for religious hypocrisy (protecting God's reputation) and those who directly harm others (in other words, what I have defined as "justice" issues).

Christ's style was always measured and rarely inflammatory. He saved his denunciations for the disciples and religious leaders. Christ always treated people with dignity—except perhaps the people who might have had "too much" dignity: the Pharisees and the disciples when they struggled with pride. His interactions were less accusatory than promoting introspection. His words and parables were chosen so well that they often spoke to more than one group. In contrast, denunciations of "sinners" or sinful behaviors from the pulpit or from "concerned Christians" are often single-minded, indignant, and filled with fiery rhetoric.

In sum, legislating morality is neither explicitly condemned nor encouraged in the Bible. But notably, politics and concern for "social morality issues" (outside of the church) are absent from the teachings of Christ and the apostles.[42] And most important, legislating morality is inconsistent with the style of Christ's preaching and the substance of his message. If one of our goals is to become more Christ-like, we need to determine what Christ would do. As such, it is difficult to imagine him advocating the use of legislating morality.

Chapter 6:
Why Christians Shouldn't Legislate Morality (Part 2) Practically Speaking—What Are the Costs?

Outside of our knowledge about God's character and our inferences about what Jesus would do, there are often practical reasons for participating in or abstaining from certain activities. Christ instructed his disciples to "count the costs"—presumably, not just the cost of following him.[1] These rationales should not supersede the Bible, but may be useful to consider in supplementing Biblical truths and our worldview. If God does not want us to use human government to legislate morality, can we determine the practical reasons for why this is not within His will? In a word: what are the practical costs of legislating morality?

Judgmentalism
Legislating morality increases the world's perception that Christians are judgmental. By focusing on immoral behavior, we often give the impression that we dislike the person engaged in that activity. We claim to adhere to the dictum "hate the sin and love the sinner," but this line is harder to walk than to talk. And even if one maintains a good balance internally, perceptions may still lead outsiders to form a different conclusion. We often speak about not engaging in certain behaviors to avoid making our brothers stumble. But in this case, we can easily become a stumbling block for unbelievers.

Moreover, it probably does encourage judgmentalism in the Christian community. If we take an honest look at the church, we see a significant amount of judgmental behavior toward the sinners within the church and the heathens outside. How well does the church balance compassion and conviction in dealing with homosexuals and divorcees? It's easier to point fingers at someone else and still easier to point them at people we don't even know.

Ironically, this is analogous to the Pharisees. As John Ortberg notes, "In the culture wars of the first century, there was a group of activists who came down on the right side of all the values questions...But it is interesting that the people who held the 'right' values were the ones least responsive to Jesus' message and most likely to receive his reprimands...The ironic result of their 'rightness' in belief and practice was that they became unable to love."[2] Given Christ's fiery response to this type of error, we should be especially leery of stumbling in this regard.

Christ came "to seek and to save what was lost."[3] To do likewise, we should read John 3:17 more often after we quote 3:16: "Indeed, God did not send His Son into the world to condemn the world, but in order that the world might be saved through him." Before we embraced the blood and cross of Christ, we too were completely unworthy; "there is no difference—all have sinned and fallen short of the glory of God."[4] We need to remember that we were once "objects of wrath," now brought into relationship by our acceptance of God's grace through Christ's atoning death on the cross.[5] Even the most outrageous sinner is that same one short step away from a relationship with God.[6]

Finally, by definition, a focus on behavior promotes comparisons to others and instills the pride that comes from saying "I don't do that!". Of course, discerning and identifying immorality can be done appropriately. But if it isn't, it is also sinful. In addition, such rhetoric fosters an atmosphere that makes vulnerability and accountability more unlikely within the church, especially on difficult issues like marital turmoil and personal finances. "If someone knew what I've been doing or what I did in my past, they wouldn't accept me." It is exceedingly difficult to toe the line between harping on the sinners outside the church and exhorting the sinners inside the church. Outside of pride, is there any greater enemy to dealing with sin than secrecy and a lack of accountability?

Works-Based Religion?

Christianity features grace—a salvation that yields works instead of being caused by works. Unfortunately, efforts to legislate morality tend to change the world's perspective from grace to works. When Christians focus on morality issues, an unfortunate but inescapable consequence is that we perpetuate the deadly myth that Christianity is just another salvation-by-works religion. Will focusing on or even changing these behaviors help or hinder people from entering into a relationship with Christ? Are we working to turn them into white-washed tombs or cups that are clean outside but dirty inside, having a "form of godliness but denying its power."[7] As John MacArthur expresses it: "Forcing people to adopt our Biblical standards of morality only brings superficial change and hides the real issue—sin and their need for rebirth in Jesus Christ."[8]

In addition, we paint a picture of a God who requires something before He establishes relationship with a prospective believer. While there remain many sins to repent from and many behaviors to change after salvation, repeated attempts to legislate morality may result in the misperception that Christ's message about the "one thing they lack" to follow him is, instead, many issues. This encourages the unfortunate mindset that one needs to "get their life together" before coming to God. Paul labels these additions to the Gospel of Christ "anathema."[9]

Works preceding salvation is heresy; preaching morality over the Gospel is ascriptural and largely ineffective. Notably, when Paul uses the word "preach," it is always followed by "the Gospel," "grace," or "Christ"—never "morality." Too often, our preaching is not centered on what's great about Christ, but incorrectly, on what's wrong with the world. In fact, preaching morality to someone before they have accepted the Gospel is exactly backwards. David Brainerd, an early American missionary to the American Indians, once said, "I never got away from Jesus and him crucified. When my people were gripped by this great evangelical doctrine, I had no need to give them instructions about morality. I found that one followed as sure an inevitable fruit of the other. I find my Indians begin to put on the garments of holiness and their common life begins to be sanctified, even in small matters, when they are possessed by the doctrine of Christ and him crucified."

A focus on morality also reinforces a works-righteousness attitude among believers. With such a heavy emphasis on specific behaviors—a checklist of acts of commission—we feel guilt if we're not doing well and pride if we're meeting "the standard." Consequently, we often fail to look any deeper—to spiritual sins and our motives, becoming complacent and arrogant in our walk with God.

Legalism

With "gray" issues—where morality is dependent on context; e.g., gambling and alcohol consumption—adamant attempts to prohibit certain behaviors are merely legalisms.[10] Again, self-righteousness and making Christianity unnecessarily less attractive are some of the "fruits" of these efforts. With respect to those who taught legalism within the Galatian church, Paul said "the one who is throwing you into confusion will pay the penalty."[11]

Christ hammered the Pharisees for their legalism: "Woe to you experts in the Law, because you have taken away the key to knowledge. You yourselves have not entered, and you have hindered those who were entering."[12] Christ spent much more time criticizing the Pharisees for their arrogance, hypocrisy, and legalism, than on the "sinners" who are so frequently the target of religious conservatives. Legalisms are a stumbling block to those who are misled in their walk with God and to those who might otherwise choose to follow Christ.

As such, Paul exhorted the church at Colosse to refuse the arguments of the legalists among them:

Since you died with Christ to the basic principles of this world, why, as though you still belonged to it, do you not submit to its rules: 'Do not handle! Do not taste! Do not touch!'? These are all destined to perish with use, because they are based on *human* commands and teachings. Such regulations indeed have *an appearance of wisdom*, with their *self-imposed worship*, their false humility and their harsh treatment of the body, but they *lack any value* in restraining sensual indulgence. (Colossians 2:20-23; italics added)

If an activity is not forbidden by the Bible, then we should not judge others, especially non-Christians, for doing it—and should certainly not pursue laws to prohibit it. And all of the talk among conservative evangelicals about the exercise of liberty as a potential stumbling block should be accompanied by discussions about legalism and political activity as potential stumbling blocks.

How About a Little Consistency?

Consistency is not the highest of virtues, but it is usually a worthy pursuit. In this context, if one tries to motivate an argument for legislating morality, where should we draw the line? Adultery, misusing alcohol, and believing the doctrines of false religions are all wrong—and arguably more damaging than the subject of contemporary evangelical efforts in the legislative arena—yet we don't see any attempts to make those things illegal.[13] If legislating morality is appropriate, we should be even more active in restricting these evils.

Moreover, we are not particularly consistent in pursuing laws within general areas. We want to keep certain drugs illegal. But what about alcohol and tobacco which cause much more harm? We want laws against prostitution to be vigorously enforced. But how is that different than "one-night stands" or repeated fornication? And are we even consistent within the Christian community? Some evangelicals campaign against gambling without rooting out all of its manifestations within the church body. Some rip homosexuality while leaving other extra-marital sex and divorce virtually untouched. Some actively advocate using others' money to help the poor but do little to help the poor personally. When Christians fail to "clean house" first—personally or within the church—they are subject to Christ's critique of judgmentalism.[14] We need to be discerning, but the way in which we confront evil is as important as the evil itself. We need to remove the plank out of our own eye before we begin to think about pointing out the plank in the world's eye.

Further, religious conservatives are fond of illustrating that liberals are unrealistic about how the government's economic policies work—in reality as opposed to in theory. Ironically, the same critique is relevant in this realm of government activism as well. How legislating morality works in practice is the key question—not how we'd like it to work.

Finally, note that allowing something to be legal is not equivalent to approving or even condoning the behavior. Should we admonish our elected officials because pre-marital sex is still legal? If we do not pursue laws against Moslems, does that mean we approve of their theology? Remember that there is a sizable difference between a law forcing you to do something immoral (or keeping you from doing something moral) and allowing others to do something immoral.[15]

Dimming the Light?

In Matthew 5:14, Christians are identified as the "light of the world"—and are called to be a light in contrast to the world's darkness. We can be a light, because we have the Light and this light presumably affects our behavior for the better. Our light is to be a beacon to those outside the Light, making them aware of the abundant life available in Christ.

If effective, legislating morality causes people to improve their behavior to avoid punishment under the law. For proponents of legislating morality, this is an explicit goal. However, it is not a goal that particularly interests God. Outside of a relationship with Him established by belief in the gracious, redeeming power of His Son's blood, works are largely irrelevant. And to the extent that non-believers improve their behavior, the Christian's light in contrast to the world's darkness is muted. Well-behaved pagans make the witness of Christians more difficult to perceive. As C.S. Lewis said, "Brass is more easily mistaken for gold than is clay."[16] Unfortunately, as a result, we are not as set apart since many behave more outwardly moral—looking more like Christians, but only because the laws of the State constrain them.[17]

For example, one way for Christians to provide a good witness is to provide meals for neighbors who are enduring an illness, recovering from a death in the family, etc. Imagine that a group of "concerned Christians" recognizes this and lobbies Congress for a bill that makes it a crime not to take dinner to a neighbor in distress. The result would be greater morality but how many more Christians? While it could be argued that the group's efforts would bring some glory to God, the instrument of choice would be force and most of the glory would probably go to the State.

This has application to a number of arenas. For instance, should Christians lobby for "tougher marriage laws"? The goal is to reduce the number of divorces—aside from the method of legislating morality, certainly a laudable goal. But outside of protecting children (a "justice" issue), is it a godly goal? At the least, we should recognize that if more non-Christian marriages stay together, the light of good Christian marriages is diminished.[18]

Other Practical Issues...

First, given the tradeoffs we must make with our time and other resources, by definition, this pursuit takes our energies from other things.[19] Is this appropriate? Should a pastor spend much time criticizing the heathen instead of convicting his congregation of relevant sins? Should laypeople devote time and money to lobbying their state legislatures to pass legislation on social morality issues instead of building relationships with neighbors and helping the needy? At any point in time, we make a decision to devote our time, talent, and treasure to one activity over all others. Our choices in this realm do not reflect God's will often enough.[20]

And when it comes to dealing with sin, it would seem that we have plenty to do within the Church and within our own souls. As Lysander Spooner said: "If those persons, who fancy themselves gifted with both the power and the right to define and punish other men's vices, would but turn their thoughts inwardly, they would probably find that they have a great work to do at home."[21]

Second, even if legislating morality is an appropriate tool, such efforts are bound to be largely ineffective in curbing behavior.[22] This is because the parties directly involved in the sin perceive that they benefit. By definition, consensual behaviors are more difficult if not impossible to stop, because nobody has an incentive to report the activity. And perversely, in the case of an illegal market—e.g., illegal drugs, gambling, and prostitution—more stringent enforcement of the law makes those items more valuable, further increasing the financial incentive to enter the market and supply the good or service. In these cases, only tremendous punishment is likely to have a significant impact. Further, increased punishment can actually serve as an allurement for consumers—who reason that the prohibited activity must be awesome if people are willing to risk so much to do it. And others, most notably teenagers, may be attracted by the "forbidden fruit" aspect of rebelling against legal standards.

Even trying to form laws against "vices" is, by definition, far more difficult. Spooner notes that "Crimes are few, and easily distinguished from all other acts; and mankind are generally agreed as to what acts are crimes. Whereas vices are innumerable; and no two persons are agreed, except in comparatively few cases, as to what are vices. Furthermore, everybody wishes to be protected, in his person and property, against the aggression of other men. But nobody wishes to be protected, either in his person or property, against himself..."[23]

Third, a related problem is that it can be very difficult for us to sit on the sidelines while society or people who we care about are chasing false gods on a collision course with disaster. But we need to remember that false gods always fail and that the subsequent crises are often how God reaches people.[24] Moreover, taking the false gods from people by force may, in fact, be counterproductive. As Walter Wangerin argues, "What we *don't* want to do in this culture is to reach out and snatch people's false gods away from them. That is not effectual because the people will hold onto their false gods all the more, and they will hate us besides."[25]

Likewise, note that Paul's chief concern was his obedience and perseverance in running the race, not the response of the audience, his faithfulness to his ministry rather than his success in the ministry. Isaiah was commissioned into a ministry of "hardening hearts" (6:11-13), knowing ahead of time that most people would be deaf and blind to his exhortations. And the "watchman" in Ezekiel 33 is held to the same principle: his sole responsibility was to tell the people. If he failed to deliver the message, their blood was on his hands; if they failed to accept the message, their blood was on their own hands.

Spooner concludes about "legislating social morality" that "so long as [people] are sane, they must be permitted to control themselves and their property, and to be their own judges as to where their vices will finally lead them. It may be hoped by lookers-on...that the person will see the end to which he is tending, and be induced to turn back." [26] But if not—"if he chooses to go on to what other men call destruction, he must be permitted to do so. And all that can be said of him...is that he made a great mistake in his search after happiness, and that others will do well to take warning by his fate." [27] We need to instruct people about the fruit of disobedience, but then allow them the freedom to go their own way.

Fourth, on popular issues, some Christians have appealed to satisfying the "wishes of the majority." [28] This is remarkably inconsistent and tremendously short-sighted. While majority rule and democracy are good institutions in general, they are not universally desirable. Should slavery have been treated in an equivalent manner? Is the morality of abortion dependent on what a majority believes? What about a day in the future when the majority thinks Christianity is dangerous or a folly? [29]

Matthew 26:52 warns us against the use of force: "all who draw the sword will die by the sword." In fact, if anything, we should err on the side of defending the freedom of others to do what they please (assuming it doesn't harm others directly), even if we disagree with their choices.[30]

Finally, Christians should realize that when we focus on the world's immorality—whether in casual conversation, from the pulpit, or in the public square—we are asking if not begging for attacks on our behavior and any hypocrisy in the church.

"But Our Morals Are Declining..."

Scripture records numerous assessments of community morality. For example, at different times, Christ called the people of his time wicked, unbelieving, adulterous, and perverse.[31] And we know that the people of Israel weren't exactly saints—the prophets actively condemned the seemingly incessant immorality and idolatry of the Israelites. In fact, Ezekiel compared Sodom favorably to the Jerusalem of his time.[32] Thus, God allows Himself the freedom to assess community morality. For better or worse, Christians often take the same liberty, typically arguing that morals today are "bad and getting worse." Most trace this decline to the 1960's, harkening back to the "glory days" of the 1950's. But is this wholly accurate?[33]

First, one should note that making a comparison of moral standards across time is probably a futile exercise. It is impossible to see inside hearts where an optimal "measurement" would be taken; actions are only a proxy for what concerns God. Further, it is difficult to even measure behavior—especially sins of omission. For example, people often forget that the parents of the 1950's raised the children of the 1960's. (Where did Ward and June Cleaver go wrong and why don't they get more of the blame?!) But even accepting such an imperfect measure, we should also note that there are a number of factors which might cause us to bias our "estimate."

Second, we know that people tend to inappropriately exaggerate the "good ol' days." We tend to believe "our times" are far better or worse than the past—probably overestimating the differences.[34] For example, while abortion increased after *Roe v. Wade*, Marvin Olasky illustrates that the abortion rate in the 1860's was approximately equal to the rate today.[35] Concerning the 1950's, Tom Sine argues that "conservative Christians were as alarmist then as they are today."[36] Frederica Mathewes-Green notes that movies in the 1930's glorified adultery and drunkenness.[37] And David Neff cites survey research indicating that those under 40 years old have more orthodox Christian views that those over 40.[38]

Third, people often focus on certain trees rather than the entire forest. In this context, we focus on particular evils while ignoring improvements in other areas. For example, when people roundly assert that the "good ol' days" were better, I ask whether that would include how society treated blacks and the disabled. As Lynn Buzzard notes, "People read American history and conveniently forget an awful lot of evil."[39] Frame and Tharpe argue that "by wanting to return to the 'Golden Age' of the 1950's, conservatives needlessly offend many of those in our society for whom life, in some important ways, was not so great in the 1950's."[40] Moreover, Christian scholarship has blossomed in recent decades.

"Back in the 1940's, not even Sherlock Holmes could have found evangelical fingerprints on any field of academic endeavor."[41]

Fourth, it is easy to confuse the level of discussion about a particular sin with the amount of that sin. For example, the physical, sexual, and mental abuse of children receives considerably more attention today than in the past. However, those sins may not be more frequent, but merely more openly discussed.

Fifth, we are subject to more temptations over time, as we grow wealthier and have more opportunities to sin (or to glorify God). For example, Olasky notes that prostitution increased dramatically in the 18th century as men traveled more, and had greater incomes and more leisure time. Were 17th century men more wholesome or merely less able to fulfill those lusts of the flesh?[42] Moreover, community standards may increase or reduce the "cost" of engaging in certain behaviors. Perhaps the permissiveness of the 1960's allowed many people to do what had been in people's hearts throughout the 1950's. For example, to what extent is our country's higher divorce rate today a function of longer lifespans, greater capacity for economic independence, and cultural influences—allowing people to leave poor marriages far more easily than in the past? Moral and immoral behaviors are influenced by both character *and* circumstance. To the extent that past moral behavior was determined by mere circumstance, one's excitement about that era should fade.

Finally, why do people behave themselves? Sometimes, they are motivated by love for people. Other times they are motivated by selfish reasons—"If I treat this person well, they will treat me well also." Therefore we tend to see civil behavior—even among those who aren't Christian—when people "need" to please others. In a market economy, people usually satisfy others to earn a larger income. In contrast, when someone has power over others, we are less likely to see friendly behavior, since they don't need to please others nearly as much.[43] With the increase in the size and power of government over the last 40 years, the realm in which people exert power over each other has grown tremendously. This factor may explain an increase in sinful behavior and our continued confusion between external actions and internal motives.

All of these points are interesting and relevant, but probably not wholly convincing to an avid fan of the "good ol' days." But even if one accepts the supposition that morality has declined, it is possible if not probable that we had a lot of nice, moral people in the 1950's, but fewer and/or less passionate Christians.[44] The goal is not greater morals per se, but more people in the kingdom of Heaven and greater discipleship on Earth. And focusing on morality may cause one to miss the far more important topic of grace.

Politically active groups of religious conservatives often fall into this trap—by equating "pro-family-values,"[45] patriotism[46], and in general, a conservative social agenda with Christianity. In his political manifesto, Ralph Reed described his wish: "In short, we desire a good society, a decent society based on shared values of work, family, neighborhood and faith."[47] While I understand the desire of a political group to exert influence and appeal to conservatives of all religious stripes, it would be difficult to describe that effort as Christian or godly. Moreover, it may perpetuate the confusion between works and salvation.

Ultimately, the debate over whether the United States is, was, or can again be "a Christian nation" may be interesting, but it is not fully resolvable or particularly useful.[48] Whether we are more or less moral than 50 years ago is a provocative question, but the answer is irrelevant to living our lives in a God-honoring manner today. We should take the current level of morality as a given and concentrate on glorifying God in the circumstances we face.[49] Christ said that "because of the increase of wickedness, the love of many will grow cold."[50] Christians are called to stand firm on issues of private and social morality—not only in conviction, but in compassion; not only in truth, but in love.

Law as Teacher, Student or Both?

All things equal, those who advocate using the law to impact behavior at least implicitly believe that the law is more teacher than student. John Calvin argued that the law served three purposes from a Christian perspective: to demonstrate unrighteousness to non-Christians so that they would embrace God's grace (justification); to instruct Christians on how properly to walk with God (sanctification); and to restrain the evil acts of individuals for the good of society (order vs. chaos).[51] But there are a number of problems with this view: When law is inconsistent with Christian morality, it fails to accomplish these purposes; civil law is not necessary for instructing non-Christians or Christians; and it leaves unasked and unanswered which evil acts should be restrained by law.

Paul seemed to recognize the tension in this debate.[52] In Galatians 3:24, he says the law "was put in charge," using the Greek to term to describe a child's relationship to a nanny and implying some degree of teaching. But in Romans 2:14-15, Paul argues that the law is written on our hearts, implying little or no need for an external law as teacher. Is law an effective teacher? When one looks at current events and the world, it seems that law is at least as often led by cultural norms as the law shapes those norms. Could law be a more effective teacher? Probably at the margin. But all of this still ignores the key question: Is coercion appropriate and practical for Christians to use on non-Christians to enforce social morality goals? Again, in what contexts should we seek to put our neighbors in jail?

A Note on *Blinded by Might*

In their book, Cal Thomas and Ed Dobson criticize the "Religious Right" and have stirred quite a debate in conservative evangelical circles.[53] It has been the subject of numerous book reviews[54], colloquies in *World* and *Christianity Today* to discuss the merits and weaknesses of their critique[55], a book-length response from Tom Minnery[56], and general angst in Christian public policy circles.[57] In a word, Thomas and Dobson call for a reformulation of the Religious Right's political involvement, a reconsideration of the limits of politics, and a renewed commitment to engage the world and spread the Gospel. As John Bolt says, "There is much in this book that is wise counsel for Christian political activists and for concerned Christian citizens."[58]

That said, their prescriptions have led to a certain amount of confusion. In particular, some have interpreted this as a call to isolationism and withdrawal from politics. For example, James Dobson says they are "suggesting that conservatives quit trying to influence local and national governments."[59] More objectively, James Hitchcock writes that "despite occasional disclaimers, it can only be read as calling on Christians to abandon politics completely."[60] Or from Bolt again: "They oppose retreat and withdrawal from politics by Christians yet describe it in terms so polarizing...that the subliminal message decidedly encourages distance rather than involvement."[61]

The problem is that their advice looks like withdrawal to those so avidly involved in politics, and in any case, resembles withdrawal because it doesn't provide a substantive, alternative political agenda. Don Eberly sums it up best: They are not "calling for a complete retreat...[They] have done the Christian world a service in pointing out...the limits of politics in confronting deep moral and spiritual conditions...Neither retreat nor the status quo is acceptable. The debate should not focus on methods of retreat, but on new models for engagement and new strategies that focus more on culture than on politics..."[62]

Thankfully, Thomas and Dobson have been able to kick open the door on an important topic. But their effort falls short of the task at hand—to formulate a comprehensive and consistent Christian philosophy of government and to determine potential plans of action in the realms of social morality and economic justice. As such, I have further developed the case against the political activities and rhetoric of the Religious Right. And I will soon be addressing economic justice issues and discussing positive options for engaging our world in terms of both social morality and economic justice issues.

Conclusion

I used to be more tolerant of the belief that Christians should legislate morality. I remain tolerant in the sense that many evangelicals have been deluded into worshipping the State as an agent of social change—by surface logic and the prodding of politically active religious conservatives. And as a teacher, I can empathize with how easy it is to avoid saying tough things from the "pulpit" and instead, to appeal to the audience's "itching ears."[63] But to believe in this idol after the last two chapters requires that one downplay important practical considerations and make some curious assumptions about the Bible, Christ's life, and their application to our lives. It is the pursuit of a forced morality for others, using a method that is difficult, if not impossible, to defend biblically.

Os Guinness notes that "outsiders tend to view evangelicals' public involvement as constitutionally legitimate but intrusive and unwelcome." He assesses this flawed strategy as trying to change society through politics with a reliance "on a rhetoric of protest, pronouncement and picketing, rather than persuasion."[64] Of course, there are times to eschew peace and rankle our foes. But if our behavior is not godly, the subsequent persecution is deserved, not a badge of martyrdom.

What do we gain by "beating the drums"? Are people in our congregations persuaded, convicted, or challenged by our sermons? Do we promote pride and comparisons to others instead of to God's standards? Are we encouraging people to be judgmental? While the costs are significant, it is difficult to find any substantial benefits.

Christ told us to love our enemies and pray for those who persecute us. We need to put this into practice much more often; sinners are not our enemies, they're our mission. Is the appropriate response condemnation or pity? I Corinthians 13 tells us that if we do anything, but have not love, we are nothing; truth without love is worthless in God's economy. Merely speaking the truth in a random fashion does not constitute the sum of our responsibility. Speaking truth without love about immorality is also immoral.

And how is legislation useful for ministering to those who need Christ? With the force of law, there can only be an identification of the sin and a rigidly prescribed punishment. It is impossible to communicate love along with truth using that tool. Legislating morality will thus always be interpreted as too much conviction. With little or no interaction between a "sinner" and someone who can share the Good News, the enforcement of laws will result in too little compassion. Likewise, legislating morality might point out the disease, but it does not provide the only true cure. It encourages the pride of the self-righteous. It begs for counterattacks on instances of Christian hypocrisy.

If believers rely on the Law, they stay in the closet. And to the extent that the laws are effective, they chase law-breakers into a different closet. Efforts to legislate morality at the expense of forming relationships with struggling sinners outside of God's love cannot be a part of God's will. Moreover, pursuing legislation is the easy way out. Maybe this is its attraction for us. "What makes the temptation of power so seemingly irresistible? Maybe it is that power offers an easy substitute for the hard task of love. It seems easier to be God than to love God [and] easier to control people than to love people..."[65] Instead, we should be in the trenches with the heathen, not driving sinful behavior underground and having the State imprison people for these types of sin.[66]

In closing, there are three particularly bitter ironies here. Politically active conservative evangelicals consider themselves patriotic with a focus on the intents of the Constitution and the Founding Fathers. Yet they support a method that was roundly criticized and feared by our country's early leaders—the abridgement of freedom by government. Moreover, they end up supporting the method for which they criticize liberals so fervently—the embrace of government as a means to an end. They also consider themselves to be among those who take the Bible most seriously. However, in legislating morality, they ignore Scripture to continue their idolatry of the State.

Chapter 7:
Why Christians Shouldn't Legislate Morality (Part 3) What Should We Do Instead?

In the previous two chapters, I have developed a substantial case against Christians legislating social morality. It is not endorsed in the Bible and it goes counter to the style and substance of Christ's ministry. Moreover, in practice, it is fraught with unfortunate side-effects that make it an unattractive option.

Zeal and Understanding: We Need Both

I respect the passion and zeal of those who have chosen this method. Unfortunately, at least in this area of their lives, they have been running fast in the wrong direction. As such, they have missed opportunities and caused damage to the kingdom of God with these pursuits. The "good news" here is that if they run or even walk in the right direction, these same people can bring tremendous glory to God.

Peter is an excellent example of this principle. He was a man known for his great triumphs and ugly mistakes. He was the antithesis of "lukewarm" and thus, was someone who could be used in mighty ways by God. Matthew 16 provides a capsule of Peter's desire to run passionately *and* his battle to run in the right direction. In response to Christ's "But who do you say I am?", Peter had the courage to answer "You are the Messiah, the Son of the Living God"—the first time any of the disciples labeled Him as divine. Christ then blessed Peter and promised to build His church on him. But in the next vignette, Christ told the disciples He would be killed.

Peter "took him aside and began to rebuke Him." Then Christ followed with His own rebuke: "Get behind me, Satan!"[1]

Once Peter better understood the character of Christ and the will of God—and once he was empowered by the Spirit—he was able to channel his zeal to obey God and love others more effectively. The same is true for us. We cannot glorify God using methods He does not endorse. While zeal is a prerequisite for effective ministry, it is not sufficient.

Walking in the correct direction is preferable to running in the wrong direction. This walking can most directly be accomplished by one-on-one ministry and by speaking and living the Good News—the method practiced by Christ and the early Church. With respect to changing sinful behavior, this approach is seemingly less practical than legislation, but more godly. It is slower in human terms, but more effective in God's economy; it places its faith in a God who can change hearts rather than a State that can merely change behavior. Why have we pursued this idol? As Christ opened his remarks to the Pharisees in Matthew 22:29, "you are in error because you don't know the Scriptures or the power of God."

I want to conclude this section of the book with a discussion of our shortcomings in evangelism and discipleship, followed by some important considerations for three important issues within "legislating morality" (LM): homosexuality, gambling, and reforming the public schools. In these and other areas, are there more appropriate ways to reach the same goals? Are there other methods that will bring more glory to God?

I. Discipleship and Evangelism: Getting Our Hands Dirty

The idea that we should avoid legislating morality because it is not Christ-like should cause us to consider what Christ did instead. First, He built up his disciples with the equivalent of "small groups" and "accountability partners." He challenged them, rebuked them, and encouraged them when appropriate. How deep are our relationships with other Christians? Are we mentoring anybody and are we being mentored? Does your church promote discipleship as well as evangelism?[2] Do you have a plan to follow Christ in the path of discipleship?[3] Do we have truly intimate friendships where we make ourselves vulnerable with other Christians—or do we just participate in activities with them? In social occasions, do we spend most of our time criticizing others, gossiping, and talking about sports or the weather—or do we spend much of our time building significant relationships with our siblings in Christ? We need to stretch ourselves within our Christian relationships. After all, Paul calls us to meat, not just milk; the Great Commission calls us to make disciples, not just converts.

Second, Christ rebuked "religious people" who were out of line. Are we harsher on those inside or outside the church? Do we downplay carnal sins or ignore spiritual sins within the church? Are we too slow to deflate a fellow Christian's pride, question their legalisms, point out their judgmentalism, and rebuke their hypocrisies? Do we have the courage to stand up for truth within the church, despite the costs? It is often easier to take pokes at those outside the church, but unfortunately it is not Christ-like.

Third, Christ came "to seek and save the lost." He encouraged them to follow him, to walk away from their sins, to turn away from their idols. He dealt with their physical, psychological, and spiritual needs. He "loved them where they were." In a word, he got his hands dirty in the business of ministry and evangelism. What about our relationships with non-Christians? Do we have any contact with them beyond brief encounters at work, school, or the grocery? Do we know them; do they know us? If not, evangelism will be difficult. Too often, we stay isolated from the world around us. (Of course, being immersed in the world is another issue.) Arc we "too involved" in the church? John Stott has called this version of our religion "rabbit-hole Christianity," where our only contacts with the world are our mad, brave dashes to and from Christian activities.

Instead, we are to behave as Christ did—to help the poor, to befriend the promiscuous, to be there for the grieving. And not just to provide a few dollars to buy a meal or a shoulder to cry on, but to say the tough things that need to be said, the truly compassionate words of someone who wants the best for that individual.

Finally, Christ preached the good news to those who voluntarily came to hear him speak. Are we so bold? Do we miss many opportunities to share the Gospel with those who want to hear? Are we quick to give an account of our peace and joy in Christ? Too often, we preach to those who have not asked to hear and we fail to grasp our opportunities to reach those who are seeking Christ. And too often, we preach about morality instead of sharing the Good News.

As Tony Evans argues throughout his book, *Are Christians Destroying America?*, "the spiritual decline of American culture" is the result of two factors: "the failure of non-Christians to take the Person and Word of God seriously" and "the Christian community's seeming inability to impact our culture for Christ at the deepest levels." As Evans concludes, "while we have done an admirable job of cursing the darkness, we have done a poor job of spreading the light."[4] George Sweeting makes the same point: "The biggest obstacle to the salvation of Nineveh was found in the heart of a pious, prejudiced man named Jonah. There was no deceitfulness in all of Nineveh like the deceitfulness in Jonah's heart." Or as Larry Crabb notes, "Social crusading is so much easier than finding God...The great need of our day will not be met by...leaders calling us to join the fight against moral pollution in our society. The greatest need in our world today is simply this: godly men and women who possess and display a quality of life that reflects the character of God, and that provokes curiosity in others about how they too can know God well."[5]

People often quote II Chronicles 7:13-14 but misunderstand its context and misapply its message: "When I...send a plague among *my people*, if *my people*, who are called by name, will *humble themselves* and pray and seek my face and *turn from their wicked ways*, then I will hear from heaven and will forgive *their sin* and heal *their land*." (italics added) The sin spoken of here is among God's people, not out in the world somewhere. Likewise, in Psalms 139:23-24, David implores, "Search me O God and know my heart; test me and know my anxious thoughts. See if there is any offensive way in me, and lead me in the way everlasting." We are called to be introspective instead of throwing rocks at non-Christians.

The story is told about a man who had pain all over his body. When the doctor asked him where it hurt, the man touched his arm, his leg, his stomach, and his head, and said that they all hurt. After X-rays, the doctor came back with the man's problem: "You have a broken finger." Before we begin to consider pointing (broken) fingers at others, we need to get our spiritual houses in some semblance of order.

II. Homosexuality: Conviction and Compassion Revisited

There are few Christians who handle this topic well.[6] "Liberal" Christians often focus on compassion, while ignoring or downplaying conviction. Many condone the behavior, twisting or dismissing Scripture to reach their conclusions.[7] Because homosexual conduct is a sin (and thus, not in our best interests), failure to recognize it as such leads to prescriptions that are not in the best interests of homosexuals. Thus, while appearing to be loving, such "tolerant" responses are either ignorant or callous.[8] "Conservative" Christians often focus on conviction, while ignoring or downplaying compassion. They are quick to cite Bible verses to prove their stance on this issue, but slow to recognize the verses which describe how Christ treated the sexually immoral. They frequently cross the line from hating the sin to (at least being perceived as) hating the sinner.[9] And they fail to recognize that they are implicitly aligning themselves with people whose response to homosexuals is horrific. As Joe Dallas argues, "We have plenty of evidence that we hate the sin, but I think we're a little short on evidence that we love the sinner."[10]

Although we should not ignore homosexuality as a topic, sermons, casual conversations, and public policy pronouncements in conservative circles often spend too much time on this one issue. As David Gushee notes, "the homosexuality issue does not exhaust the content of

Christian social ethics, and sexual ethics do not exhaust the content of the Christian moral vision."[11] And besides, what proportion of the congregations in conservative evangelical churches struggle with homosexuality? Among sexual morality issues, the church needs to address adultery, divorce, pornography, and premarital sex far more than homosexuality.[12] And we need more on how to minister to homosexuals instead of yet another reminder that homosexual acts are sinful. Finally, as argued earlier, it is unbiblical and impractical for Christians to seek anti-sodomy laws[13] and so on—to legislate morality and restrict the freedom of unbelievers involved in consensual activities.[14]

"The Sin of Sodom"

Aside from the Biblical references that directly condemn homosexual acts, the root of the standard Christian position against homosexuality is the destruction of Sodom in Genesis 19. Unfortunately, most people hold the incorrect belief that Sodom was destroyed strictly because of homosexual acts. This stems from a careless inference about Genesis 19 and a failure to know or understand what other Bible verses say about Sodom.

The Bible records that God had decided to destroy Sodom in Genesis 18:17—before the infamous incident in chapter 19. Further, there are no specific reasons given then—only 18:20-21's hint: "the outcry against Sodom and Gomorrah is so great and their sin so grievous." After Abraham pleads for the righteous people of Sodom, two angels visit the city. They are hosted by Lot and then threatened with violence and the height of inhospitality by the mob that appears outside Lot's door. Although the threat of homosexual *rape* triggers the fateful events later in the chapter, we are not told that homosexual acts are the sole reason that Sodom was to be destroyed.

Moreover, we have good reasons to believe that homosexual acts were not even a primary reason for Sodom's destruction. First, the Genesis 18 passage speaks of God responding to an "outcry." We don't know who "cried out" or why.[15] But we do know that people cry out when they believe they have been wronged; people are unlikely to cry out if they engage in a behavior voluntarily. Thus, the "cries" heard by God were probably due to some (involuntary) injustice—some violence against people such as murder, rape, or oppression, not homosexual acts between consenting adults.

Second, Ezekiel 16:49-50 provides us with a direct answer—a description of "the sin of Sodom": they were "arrogant, overfed and unconcerned; they did not help the poor and needy. They were haughty and did detestable things before me. *Therefore* I did away with them..." (italics added) Pride, apathy and not helping the poor? That sounds like elements of the church today! This is especially sobering when we consider that Ezekiel was comparing Sodom *favorably* with the Jerusalem of his time![16]

In fact, the use of Sodom as a point of comparison seems to be its primary Biblical purpose. In the other 18 references to Sodom, only Jude 7 mentions sexual improprieties: they "indulged in sexual immorality and pursued unnatural lust." In six cases, Sodom is used for a direct comparison to the Israelites;[17] in four cases (including two by Christ), Israel is described as *worse* than Sodom.[18] And if the Israelites did not engage heavily in homosexuality, but were judged more harshly than

Sodom, homosexual acts could not have been the primary sin of either.

Two passages explicitly refer to Sodom's purpose as a point of comparison. Jude 7 says Sodom "serves as an example by undergoing a punishment of eternal fire." II Peter 2:6 notes that God "made them an example of what is going to happen to the ungodly." Why was Sodom destroyed? Obviously not because its sins were the greatest, but rather, to make it an example—the first judgment against a city. Sodom was the first city to receive judgment, not the worst. (Note also that this closely follows Genesis 6-8's *worldwide* judgment example—the flood.)

Christians don't need Genesis 19 for a Biblical case against homosexual behavior. Besides, for all the energy some evangelicals spend on the destruction of Sodom and that destruction's tenuous connection to homosexuality, they virtually ignore other sexual sins. And we're told repeatedly in Scripture that in God's economy, Sodom's sins were mild compared to the immorality of His people. Yes, homosexual acts are sinful, but not the "mother of all sins." Therefore, we should spend less time criticizing homosexuals outside the church and more time dealing with serious sins within the church.

Finally, it is ironic that the church today is often guilty of what the Bible defines as the "sin of Sodom"— pride, apathy, and failing to help the poor. Tony Evans makes a similar point when he casts most of the blame for Sodom's destruction on Lot's failure to impact his community for God. "Sodom wasn't destroyed only because the sinners were sinning. It was destroyed because the saints were nowhere to be found."[19] Lot was righteous, but his influence was so inconsequential that there weren't ten believers in the whole city and his son-in-laws ignored his warning and even thought he was joking.[20] Moreover, his wife and daughters weren't exactly God-fearing women. In fact, if Lot had been salt to his family, perhaps his wife wouldn't have turned to salt! Rather than pointing fingers at the homosexual community, we should be engaged in active lifestyle evangelism, as salt and light in a rotting and dark world.

The Red Herring of Orientation vs. Choice

The current popular and scientific debate on homosexuality centers on the extent to which a homosexual's orientation is determined by genetics or environment, by nature or nurture. Although this is an interesting question, it is largely irrelevant to a Biblical perspective.

The question of whether or not many homosexuals are "oriented" toward homosexuality is innocuous. We recognize that alcoholism and many other proclivities are determined to some extent by genetics. Further, we know that environment plays an important role in the raising of a child. But the crucial point is that one's orientation and background do not determine behavior, merely one's preferences and "tendencies." We are still fully responsible for the choices we make. (The fact that I am attracted to women would not excuse unfaithfulness to my wife!) To argue otherwise is a tremendous insult to those making the decisions—a claim that they cannot control their own bodies!

Frederica Mathewes-Green notes that the origins of many of our other "preferences" are equally mysterious—why we're attracted to certain hair colors, body types, senses of humor, worship styles, etc. Again, while interesting, it's irrelevant to the morality of our choices. The important issue is the decisions we make—who we choose to follow and what we choose to do and say.[21] Concerning homosexuals who turn to God, she concludes that "for some, persistence and prayer will lead to reorientation, while for others there will be the difficult lifelong discipline of celibacy. They'll find on that path a crowd of heterosexuals two thousand years long: never-married Christians, those widowed or divorced, those caring for critically-ill spouses."[22]

Thus, for sex outside of marriage, the call for people with a homosexual orientation is perhaps longer and lonelier, but in type, no different than for those with a heterosexual orientation: abstinence.[23] The battle is the same—a war against powers and principalities, a war between spirit and flesh. The necessary faith is the same as well: to believe in a God that wants the best for all of us—so much so that He would send His only Son to die for sinners like us. With that belief, the proper choice becomes obvious: do what is in our best interests and obey the word of God by abstaining from all types of sexual immorality.

Conclusion

Legislating against homosexual behavior is arguably an effective way to reduce its incidence.[24] In addition, it is perhaps useful for "sending a signal" that these behaviors are undesirable or wrong. Unfortunately, as I have described in the last two chapters, such a legislative agenda is not consistent with God's will.

We need to reach out to practicing homosexuals as Christ ministered to the "woman caught in adultery."

Practically, this does not mean condoning their immorality, but instead, treating them with dignity and encouraging them to do what is in their best interests—forming or deepening a relationship with God and turning their back on all forms of sin.[25] Moreover, Christians should be amenable to meeting the physical and emotional needs of those struggling with AIDS. As Thomas Schmidt notes, "the body of Christ is not just a mouth. Christians should be known for the kind of hands-on help that characterized the ministry of our Lord."[26] Biblically, we need to re-read the Parable of the Good Samaritan and substitute a homosexual for the hero of the story.[27] Practically, we need to ask whether anyone has ever been humiliated, vilified, or ridiculed into the kingdom of God. Theologically, we need to recognize that outside of God's grace to us, He would not view us any differently than the most promiscuous homosexual with respect to salvation. God has hope for the homosexual—does the church?[28]

III. Gambling: What is the Proper Response?

Webster's Dictionary defines gambling as "to play games of chance for money or other stakes."[29] It is typified by lotteries, casinos, horse tracks, sports betting, and so on. Ironically, gambling was at the very heart of the American Colonial experience—since the first settlement in Jamestown was underwritten by a lottery in England and the Revolutionary War troops were supported to some extent by lotteries.[30] In general, most colonialists strongly opposed gambling until the early-18th century when a pressing need for capital—for infrastructure, colleges, and even churches—and a dislike for taxation led to more than 150 lotteries.[31]

Christians were instrumental in restricting its practice early in the 20th century, and in recent years, after its renaissance in the 1960's, some on the Religious Right have actively sought its restriction or prohibition. But is gambling inherently wrong? If not, are there principles which can illustrate why some gambling is wrong? And if so, in what other contexts are these principles an issue? Beyond all that, is there any Biblical case to be made for Christians seeking to prohibit its practice? Is such a legislative agenda consistent with God's emphasis on freedom and the characteristics of Christ's ministry? Would prohibition be effective? Is it worth our time and energy?

The Case Against Gambling?

Typically, the arguments against gambling from Christians are pragmatic and socially conservative more than Biblically-based.[32] And practically, proponents of legal restrictions on gambling have a tough road to hoe—with support mostly from some segments within the church and those who don't want gambling in their back yards.[33] In fact, many people apparently enjoy gambling. (60% of adults in lottery states play at least once a year.[34]) Politically, liberals value freedom in social matters and are attracted by the prospect of economic development in poorer areas. And many conservatives are uneasy with the behavior, but they generally work for freedom in economic matters and ultimately bow to business interests.[35]

Moreover, if gambling is sinful by nature, then the first thing to say is that we need to start with convicting those in the church. We shouldn't participate in office pools or raffles; we shouldn't play bingo, enter sweepstakes, or play scratch-off games at fast-food restaurants; we shouldn't use money to add a little excitement to our golf games; and so on.[36] If sinful, a failure to address it within the church, while simultaneously seeking its prohibition in the world, is simple hypocrisy.

That said, there is no Biblical injunction against gambling. Thus, one has to argue from Biblical silence—alluding to certain principles that can be associated with gambling and are sinful. The case here is that gambling is sinful to the extent that it: 1.) is motivated by greed and materialism; 2.) trumpets something-for-nothing (vs. a work ethic); 3.) promotes poor stewardship; 4.) relies on "luck" or superstition (vs. God's sovereignty[37]); and 5.) can be addictive and prohibitively costly.

While all of these are potential—or maybe even probable—concerns with gambling, they are not necessarily an issue. First, for many people, gambling is, at least in large part, simply a form of entertainment. What is the difference between dropping $40 at a horse track and paying $40 for an opera ticket? When gambling is treated purely as entertainment, the above concerns fade away.[38] Second, believing in superstition is not a prerequisite for gambling. Moreover, maintaining consistency on a concern about luck is difficult. Are we to eliminate the use of board games because they involve low to high degrees of luck? How would one judge investments that are based to some extent on luck? Third, addiction is a terrific concern, but is one willing to prohibit any substance or activity which is addictive and causes tremendous problems—virtually everything, but most notably tobacco and alcohol? The bottom line is that one can't Biblically condemn all gambling, but we can condemn addiction, poor stewardship, and gambling motivated by greed, superstitious beliefs, or a desire to get something-for-nothing.[39]

It also follows that the church should condemn similar personal investment strategies and business decisions—especially those within the church.[40] For instance, investing in the stock market can have many of the same characteristics—people motivated by greed, and so on. The futures markets can be treated as a legitimate hedging strategy or pursued as a speculative attempt to make big money quickly.[41] If one is consistent, the latter must be condemned as well.[42] Insurance is a reverse gamble—purposefully enduring a small loss to avoid a potentially large loss. But it can be very costly and pursued improperly if one doesn't trust God's sovereignty.

One can take this further with a few provocative parallels. First, most investments—from education to immigration to raising children to starting a new business—involve a substantial degree of risk with the hope for a strong payoff. Second, what are the odds that your vote in an election will make a difference. Isn't this bearing a small cost and hoping for a big payoff? And finally, perhaps even evangelism has some of the same features—a willingness to bear small costs, hoping for an eternal payoff—for oneself and especially for another.

Other Issues

Opponents of gambling often argue that it harms or even exploits the poor. Indeed, the poor spend a higher proportion of their incomes on lotteries.[43] But exploitation requires either a degree of fraud on the part of those running the gamble—or known ignorance or irrationality on the part of the gambler.[44] If fraud is involved, we should address this injustice—by law or through education. If there is no significant fraud, then we should educate gamblers about the odds and grant them the dignity of assuming their rationality.[45] Part of this inability to "understand" the decision to gamble is a failure to empathize. One may not understand why gambling is at all enjoyable—but who's to say why anything is enjoyable? Moreover, it may be a class issue to some extent—wealthy people not being able to imagine the impact of a given payoff on their lives and educated people looking down on this form of entertainment.[46] And contrary to another common claim—outside of fraud, gambling losses are *not* equivalent to taxation. Rex Rogers goes so far as to describe gambling as "robbery by mutual consent"![47] This erroneous conclusion either mistakenly elevates the level of coercion in decisions to gamble or diminishes the level of coercion with taxation. (And if they're opposed to this supposed taxation, are they also on the front lines in fighting true taxes on *all* of the working poor? See: chapter 10.) Finally, even if gambling causes some problems for the poor, are those problems as severe as those resulting from welfare dependency, our low-quality education system for the poor, redistribution from the poor to the non-poor, materialism/consumerism, and so on?[48] Where should our energies be focused?

Another common claim is that gambling fails to create (net) jobs—since it merely drains off economic activity from elsewhere.[49] This is a standard reasoning error in economics and politics which is easy to see with a few illustrations. Imagine any new business setting up shop. By definition, it will siphon off employee hours and customer dollars from other businesses. But clearly, the addition of another employment and shopping option is, on net, a good thing. And again, entertainment provides another useful thought experiment. When Steven Curtis Chapman comes to town, people purchase tickets to his concert, diverting resources from other uses—destroying economic activity in that locale. Should this then be prohibited? Finally, to the extent that gambling dollars are driven by tourism, then outside resources are brought into the area.

A more substantive argument is that gambling creates significant externalities for the surrounding community—that increased gambling leads to more divorce, bankruptcy, police and court costs, and so on. (Organized crime is often listed along with these, but it only follows government regulation or prohibition—by definition.) This is an empirical question for objective study—and one that should interest those on both sides of the debate.[50] Ideally, these costs would be assessed to those who participate in gambling—the individual who causes the cost, or more generally, through taxation on the activity. If these costs are large enough, one may perhaps be able to make a case for pursuing restrictions or even prohibition—but only on the basis of this argument. That said, one then opens the door to regulating any industry which has significant externalities. And more important, a Christian must be able to motivate a consistent LM effort in the face of the difficulties discussed here and in the previous two chapters. This seems extremely unlikely.

Conclusion

My discussion should not be construed as advocacy for gambling itself. And it certainly should not be taken as advocating any government involvement in gambling. For reasons we will develop in the next section of the book, government subsidies and artificial monopoly power are themselves unjust. (The only advantage of government involvement is that it makes taxation voluntary to a greater extent.)

What should be the church's non-legislative response? We should organize support groups, be active in one-on-one ministry, and provide benevolence (with discernment)—for gamblers and their families. But the Biblical and practical case for pursuing legislation is difficult if not impossible to make.[51]

Finally, consider that the world might view the church like we view the seamy side of gambling: its foundation is based on something-for-nothing (grace!); it looks like poor stewardship since we pay money and "get nothing back of value"; the poor voluntarily give the highest percentage of their income (or is it a tax?); and it diverts resources from job creation and other important economic activity. If we don't want people to regulate the ways in which we spend our money—on something the world views as folly, why would we seek to do the same to others?

IV. What Should We Do About the Public Schools?[52]

Many Christians are worried about the state of our nation's government-operated schools. The concerns range from specific subject material to overall quality. In response, many parents have decided to withdraw their children from government schools and place them in private schools or homeschooling. These options are certainly valid, and perhaps not exercised enough.[53] But for other (poorer) families, such options are prohibitively expensive.

The other popular strategy has been to battle within the government school system against other factions and their agendas. Hopefully, you'll recognize an uncomfortable similarity to other LM issues. If successful, Christians are able to *force* their preferences on others—rather than vice versa.[54] And whether successful or not, this method has some of the same costs we developed in the last chapter. Thus, this option is often unattractive and impractical, if not unbiblical. What should Christians do? Should Christians lobby for prayer in public schools? Should Christians fight for having creationism taught in addition to macro-evolution? Are there other options?

Prayer in Schools: Theory vs. Practice

First, there is the amusing but true observation that "as long as there are exams, there will be prayer in schools." Of course, students already have the right to pray in schools. It's just not at an organized time. Students can pray before, during, and after class; they can pray at lunch, at recess, or in study hall. Who is going to stop them? Moreover, there is no law to prevent Christians from praying for schools: "There is absolutely nothing that prohibits American Christians from bathing our principals, teachers, and students in prayer every day, except the will to do so."[55] And if this is so important, why don't Christians lobby for the same rules at their workplaces?

Second, the people pushing this agenda are the ones who are presumably most concerned about prayer. Unless they are hypocrites, they are already taking care of prayer for their children at home. Moreover, they should be concerned about teachers undermining their efforts at home—with prayers that are inconsistent with their own.[56]

Thus, this is not about prayer for their children. Instead, the goal must be to force others' children to observe a time of silence and perhaps to pray.[57] Unfortunately and ironically, this use of force would not be Biblical. Or perhaps proponents believe that having prayer in schools will legitimize prayer as an institution. Of course, this is misguided as well; prayer cannot be made more legitimate by forcing others to engage in it.

Third, some Christians have far too much faith in the role that school prayers have had in our nation's history. (As the old jokes goes: Congress starts each day with prayer. How much good has it done them?!) For instance, Bill Bright, the founder of Campus Crusade for Christ, referred to the 1963 Supreme Court ruling against government sponsored and initiated prayer as "the darkest hour in the history of the nation."[58] The group Concerned Women for America claimed that "removing prayer and the acknowledgement of God" was the "primary cause" of America's supposed disintegration.[59] Proponents of this view mistakenly attribute causation to what are only correlated events. Following their lead, we could argue that adding "one nation under God" to the Pledge of Allegiance in the 1950's is the root of every contemporary evil. Moreover, even the correlation is weak, given how slowly the Supreme Court decisions translated into practice.[60] At most, prayer taken out of the schools is one of many competing hypotheses for explaining America's troubles.

Fourth, imagine what an organized prayer time would be like. On paper, it might work well; in reality, it would be another story. There is a crucial difference between theory and practice. Liberals make this mistake in the economic realm; conservatives make the same mistake in the social realm. Do you want just anybody leading a prayer time? As Bob Briner notes, "We seem to have a Norman Rockwellian vision of a godly teacher, standing in front of a class with uplifted eyes, praying, while the students bow reverently."[61] Proponents of prayer in schools should consider whether the world would be a better place with an agnostic or a culturally Christian teacher leading a lukewarm prayer to an emasculated divine being in front of a captive audience.[62]

In discussing the related example of religious observances in the public square, Stephen Carter notes that "The symbols of the faith, when incorporated into civil religion, are inevitably drained of their significance. One sees this in the celebration of Christmas, which has essentially become Santa's Day...Christianity gains nothing from a secular observance of Christmas, and we might be better off shielding our children from the commercial monster that the holiday has become rather than endorsing it in the name of preserving a public role for the faith."[63]

A thought experiment is also helpful here. God wants us to worship Him and devote our financial resources to Him. But would it be within God's will to have the government mandate church attendance and tithing? Of course not. He has revealed this by His decision not to mandate our worship of Him; God gave us "free will." Why should we substitute human government edicts for God's decision within divine government to allow freedom? The same is true of mandating prayer in the schools.[64]

Moreover, this would encourage children to believe they are Christians because they perform a religious activity. Is anything more devastating to true evangelism?

I once met an evangelical pastor in Switzerland where a proportion of one's personal income tax goes to the denomination of the taxpayer's choice. He said it was exceedingly difficult to address the different groups in his audience—the true believers, the seekers, those who thought they were Christians because they had paid their dues, and so on. Is there anything more difficult than trying to witness to someone who already thinks they're a Christian? Why would we want to do anything to increase that number?

Of course, there are many other issues to debate about the government schools. For example, "They teach evolution as if it provides a comprehensive scientific explanation for the development of life."; or "They shouldn't teach that material in sex education or they shouldn't teach it in Xth grade." And there are a number of general educational concerns: overall quality of education, violence in the schools, the use of phonics, old vs. new math, how much to focus on self-esteem, teaching meditation techniques, the use of corporal punishment, and so on. What is the best way to deal with these concerns?[65]

Monopoly vs. Competition and The Importance of Freedom (Revisited)

Think of how most markets function. Producers try to provide goods and services that people want to purchase. Producers seek to make their product as attractive as possible—by providing high quality, low prices, better hours of operation, a more pleasant atmosphere, etc. In addition, they try to find niches where they can attract specific sets of customers. In all of these areas, they have an incentive to outperform each other in an attempt to win more customers—to innovate and improve, both in terms of the product itself and how it is sold. Consumers benefit from this competition through the availability of the best possible combinations of price and quality.

However, these behaviors are dependent on what economists call "market structure"—whether a market is dominated by one producer or whether there are a few or many producers competing. Clearly, the above scenario can change dramatically if a producer has substantial "monopoly power" over its customers. As competition diminishes, a producer does not have to worry as much about quality, price, or other consumer preferences. These concerns are extended in socialism or if a monopoly is run by the government.

For the sake of illustration, let us imagine that restaurants switch from a competitive market to a government-run monopoly. This could be accomplished by passing a law that says people must eat at the government-run restaurant in their neighborhood. All taxpayers will pay for the operation of these restaurants and if they choose to eat elsewhere, they will still pay taxes and then pay for their meal at a "private restaurant."[66]

What results do we expect to see in this hypothetical market? With a captive audience, the manager of the restaurant does not have much of an economic incentive to provide high quality food or to worry about costs (since the money comes out of the deep pockets of acquiescent taxpayers). Moreover, the manager may be relatively unconcerned with the preferences of many of his customers: "I'm going to serve Mexican food whether they like it or not." And the poor will be in the worst position since they will be most unable to opt out of the public restaurant system.

This analogy aptly describes our market for education. (Actually consumers of education are in a more unseemly position because homeschooling is a much more difficult option than "homecooking.") We will spend more time on the quality and cost issues in the "legislating justice" section of the book. But for our purposes here, the key issues are the lack of consumer choice and the subsequent lack of concern by producers to fill niches or respond to consumers.

Independent of whether Mexican or Chinese food is "right or wrong," the point is that, by definition, people will not enjoy being forced to eat food they don't like. The same is true of prayer in schools or not, types of sex education, school for nine vs. twelve months, and so on. Some, perhaps even a majority, will be forced to consume a type of food—a menu of social options—that they will not find palatable. Note also that only those wealthy enough to pay taxes and private school tuition will have much choice in their menu.

The solution to our hypothetical restaurant problem is easy. Simply allow competition to reassert itself in the market for restaurants and the desirable producer incentives will reappear. People who want to eat Italian food or burgers would then have those options.[67] Is the same thing possible in the market for education?[68]

Educational Choice, Vouchers, and Tax Credits

While Christians are distraught that X is taught in government schools, the crucial issue is that most parents do not have much flexibility in choosing a school. The key question is: Should one fight within the (monopolistic) system or fight to change the system itself? If morals are going to decline, fighting within the system is *by definition* a losing battle. Further, this method closely resembles LM and is fraught with the costs discussed in the last chapter.[69] A far superior solution is to work to end the monopoly that, ironically, Christians helped to create at the end of the 19th century.[70]

This can occur by empowering parents with "educational choice." A small step in the right direction would be to allow parents to send their children to the government school of their choice. This would be akin to the U.S. Postal Service—the government still runs the operation, but at least you're not forced to go to the branch in your neighborhood. (While an improvement, one should note that the Postal Service is not typically held up as a paragon of efficiency or addressing consumer preferences.) The problem which remains after instilling "choice" is that we still have a producer with tremendous monopoly power (who also happens to be the government). Thus, without more substantial reform, we are still uncomfortably close to a deadly combination of socialism and monopoly—the two ugliest economic institutions.

A better option is to empower parents to purchase education in a competitive market through "educational vouchers"—a coupon of some amount (e.g., $4,000) to be used toward the purchase of education services for one's children.[71] Given that many private schools have tuitions of less than $4,000, most parents would be able to send their children to a variety of schools. Then, the market for education would resemble the market for food where we empower poor people to make their purchases with food stamps (vouchers) while allowing private markets to produce the food and operate the grocery stores.[72] Educational vouchers could be given to families in the lower and lower-middle classes or to all families with children. In lieu of the current $8,000 per student that taxpayers cough up to fund each student in government schools, parents would have more choices for their children—and at a much lower cost to taxpayers.

There are two other reform possibilities. "Charter schools" use public money to operate public schools (i.e., taxpayer funding goes to the school vs. the parents), but with fewer regulations and different governing bodies (e.g., universities). State and local governments maintain degrees of control, but provide degrees of autonomy as well. "Tax credits" also hold considerable promise. These are especially popular because they involve the lowest degree of government attachment. But if tax credits go to parents who spend money on their own children, the policy disproportionately benefits high income earners, making it politically unattractive while simultaneously leaving in place most of the inequities and inefficiencies of the current system. Alternatively, tax credits could be given to people who charitably donate money to finance scholarships for other children, especially the poor. Tax credits of this type would be as effective as vouchers and cleaner, but funding would be much more limited.[73]

With increased competition, the cost of education to taxpayers would decrease dramatically, quality would increase, and parents would have the freedom to choose from a much wider range of educational options for their child. Evangelicals could have creationism and prayer in school; humanists would get their evolutionary theories and attention to self-esteem.[74] All would be happy— except the producers under the status quo (who would lose their monopoly power) and those who wish to force their "social menu" on others. This explains the education establishment's rabid opposition to such plans—something we'll discuss in greater detail in the next section of the book.[75] In any case, protecting monopoly power and forcing a "social menu" on others are not attractive options for Christians.

Bringing Glory to God...

Another relevant feature of these markets is that many non-Christian parents share these and other concerns about government schools. Politically active conservatives have pounced on these similarities to form allegiances to do battle within the monopoly. But these same points of agreement allow a more competitive market for education to be very attractive as well—and an opportunity to glorify God and easily share the Light with non-believers.

Imagine if Christians fought for competition in the market for education. If successful, they would be free to have their kids taught as they pleased. They would achieve a solution that promotes higher quality education at a lower cost to taxpayers. The competition would encourage innovation by the producers of education—in dealing with a diversity of challenging kids. Christians would establish additional excellent schools—and as happens now, some non-Christians who value education would voluntarily enroll their kids in those schools, independent of whether the Bible was taught or not. Most important, vouchers would release inner-city children from their bondage to government-run fiascos that are better at producing illiteracy, dropouts, and violence than education.

Of course, there are also non-legislative solutions. First, Christians can choose to operate more private schools in competition with the status quo. They would be at a tremendous competitive disadvantage (outside of subsidies from the church). Even so, Catholics in particular are renowned for their provision of high-quality, low-cost education. Second, churches and individual Christians can fund private voucher efforts. In virtually every large city, there are funds established for poor people to obtain a voucher to send their kids to the school of their choice. While expensive, it is still an excellent investment in the life of a child.

Christian political activists have shown a remarkable lack of creativity and insight when dealing with this issue. We have trusted education to a government-run entity with tremendous monopoly power. Fighting within the government school monopoly is remarkably unimaginative, impractical, selfish, and not Christ-like. If we put our energy into defending the rights of the poor to receive a decent education, we would accomplish that and so much more—all to the glory of God, not the State.[76]

A Brief Application to Cable Television

Likewise, evangelicals often complain about television, voicing concerns about the content of TV shows. What are the options? If our concern is merely for our families, we could choose to sacrifice by getting rid of the TV or enforcing household rules about watching it. But instead of quietly bearing those costs, Christians often raise a ruckus. God never promised us a free ride as Christians, and too often, protest amounts to Christians not being willing to bear those costs.[77]

But what if one is also concerned for society? Again, protest seems to be our only tool. Another option is to lobby to end local government's monopoly provision of cable television services. In almost all communities, local governments have awarded monopoly franchise rights to one cable company. Technology exists that would allow multiple companies to compete in most markets. The resulting competition would allow consumers to gain power. Subsequently, we would expect prices to fall, quality to rise, and service to become more flexible.

With a sizable bloc of Christians and other "concerned parents" as a niche, at least one of the cable companies would respond to the tastes of a segment of its market and provide the desired service—whether a set of "family-friendly" channels or complete flexibility in choosing channels. As with education, Christians could reach their primary goal and others by merely working to end local government's exclusive arrangements with a single supplier.

A Closing Thought on Private vs. Public Advocacy

I have established a clear case against Christian advocacy of "legislating morality" (LM). One cannot develop a positive case for LM from the Bible. Moreover, it is inconsistent with Christ's ministry and fraught with numerous practical costs. That said, there are some nuances within this realm; I have touched on them throughout, but they also require a separate discussion.

For instance, this is not a call to actively advocate gambling, but rather a call not to fight efforts to legalize gambling. This is not a call to vote in favor of anti-sodomy laws, but merely that a Christian should not actively advocate the prohibition publicly. And when considering boycotts, we need to be as conscious as Paul was in discerning how our public behavior will be interpreted by non-believers.

Similarly, the issues become somewhat more gray as we distinguish between what is appropriate for Christian laypeople, churches, and preachers. But as William Smith notes, "self-restraint [in this arena] will keep the church on message and on mission."[78] Christians—individually and corporately—have more important things to do; the costs of LM are too high and the benefits are dubious. In general, it is not an appropriate method for Christians to use.

Chapter 8:
Why and How Christians Should Legislate Justice (Part 1)
The Biblical Case for Legislating Justice

In the previous section of the book, I established a Biblical case against legislating morality—using the law to restrict consensual activities between adults. Moreover, I provided numerous practical reasons why such an approach is impractical and unlikely to allure souls or bring glory to God. In sum, legislating morality is rarely if ever an appropriate tool for Christians to use.

However, the Christian life is not just a matter of ending sinful practices, but replacing them with godly behaviors. Romans 6:13 teaches us: "Do not offer the parts of your body to sin, as instruments of wickedness, but rather offer yourselves to God...as instruments of righteousness." In Ephesians 4:25-32, Paul lists a series of behaviors Christians should not do and follows each with a behavior we should do instead. As such, we concluded the last section with some appropriate and practical alternatives to legislating morality. But are there other possibilities in the political arena? One candidate is to legislate against acts of "injustice"—defined as when one party directly harms another.[1]

What Does the Bible Say About Justice?
We worship a God of justice and righteousness.[2] In fact, Psalm 89:14 tells us that righteousness and justice are the very foundations of God's throne. We worship a God who does not show favoritism[3], a God who repeatedly condemns oppression[4], a God who defends the poor and needy in the face of affliction and oppression.[5]

As a result, the leaders placed in positions of authority by God are instructed to judge between the rich and poor fairly.[6] They are not supposed to oppress others, but are to establish "rules that are just."[7] Moreover, they are to enforce these rules and promote justice—"for he does not bear the sword for nothing"; the resulting outcomes would then be appropriate.[8] As an example of a theocratic king representing the government of God, David did what was "just and right"—at least early in his reign.[9] And I Kings 3:9-11 says "the Lord was pleased that Solomon had asked for...discernment in administering justice." The Queen of Sheba later told him that God had made him king to "maintain justice and righteousness."[10]

That said, Solomon warned, "If you see the poor oppressed...and justice and rights denied, do not be surprised at such things."[11] But counter to the world's norms, believers are not supposed to show favoritism.[12] We are supposed to defend the poor, the needy, and the defenseless.[13] In numerous passages, we are instructed not to oppress others.[14] We are encouraged to do good, to be generous, and to lend freely.[15] Moreover, we are told that God values justice over rituals of sacrifice, and thus, that we should "follow justice and justice alone."[16] Other passages also point to justice as a top priority: Proverbs 16:8 says "Better a little [gain] with righteousness than much gain with injustice" and the very purpose of the book of Proverbs as defined in 1:3 is to do "what is right and fair."

Further, Scripture often equates the seriousness of these issues with carnal sins.[17] In discussing the "sin of Sodom," Ezekiel 16:49-50 lists arrogance, being overfed, and having no concern for the poor and needy, along with the more oft-cited "detestable practices." And given its reference to Sodom and Gomorrah, Isaiah 1:10-17 places a greater emphasis on shedding blood and oppressing the poor than on carnal sins.

In addition, Scripture often defines the pursuit of justice as an issue of character: "The righteous care about justice for the poor...when justice is done, it brings joy to the righteous" and "the righteous give generously."[18] "The wife of noble character" in Proverbs 31:20 "opens her arms to the poor and extends her hands to the needy." Proverbs also relates our behavior toward others to our attitude toward God: one "who oppresses the poor shows contempt for their Maker, but whoever is kind to the needy honors God"; and "he who is kind to the poor lends to the Lord."[19] But Micah 6:8 probably best sums up what God wants from us: "To act justly and to love mercy and to walk humbly with [our] God."

We worship a God of perfect justice and righteousness who graciously stoops down to form relationships with us. Thus, believers should treat others with dignity, respect, and justice.[20] But we worship a God of perfect morality as well and we found that legislating morality was an inappropriate tool for Christians. Is legislating justice any improvement? At first, it would appear that we run into similar impediments. As noted earlier, the Christian pursuit of government to reach divine goals is not prescribed by the Bible. Christians are called to pursue God's standards of morality but should not use the law to coerce non-believers to adhere to that code. Is legislating justice any more Christ-like?

How Did Christ Deal with Injustice?

Not surprisingly, Christ perfectly manifested God's justice and righteousness in his days on earth. Jeremiah had prophesied that Christ would "reign wisely and do what is just and right."[21] Christ's ministry was largely centered on reaching the poor and those outside of power.[22] Christ was critical of the Pharisees for giving a tenth of their spices but failing to follow "the more important matters of the Law—justice, mercy, and faithfulness."[23] As always, Christ's life stands as the epitome of perfection, balancing a passion for not only conviction and compassion, but justice and righteousness as well.

In addition, Christ suffered tremendous personal injustices—greater than anyone will ever endure. He was rejected by the masses and deserted by his disciples. He overcame the petty traps of the Pharisees and the nearly incessant failure of the disciples to understand even his simplest points. And in the greatest single injustice in human history, perfection was placed on a cross to die an excruciating and undignified death. "He who was without sin was made sin for us."[24]

As Isaiah 53:3-7 notes, "He was despised and rejected by men, a man of sorrows, and familiar with suffering...he was pierced for our transgressions, he was crushed for our iniquities...he was oppressed and afflicted, yet he did not open his mouth; he was led like a lamb to the slaughter." In all this, he never defended his own rights, never took revenge, never sought to remedy the injustices done to him. His primary response is recorded at the place of the greatest injustice done to him, the crucifixion: "Father, forgive them, for they do not know what they are doing."[25]

In contrast, we are often too quick to defend ourselves and to become angry about injustices done to us. While understandable, it is not the Biblical prescription for dealing with the wrongs we encounter. And ironically, we often complain about punishment even when we have done wrong. But as Lamentations 3:39 notes, "Why should any living man complain when punished for his sins?" Similarly, I Peter 2:20 asks "But how is it to your credit if you receive a beating for doing wrong?"

As Peter continues, he shifts to godly behavior: "If you suffer for doing good and endure it, this is commendable before God. To this you were called, because Christ suffered for you, leaving you an example...when they hurled their insults at him, he did not retaliate; when he suffered, he made no threats." We are promised trials, suffering, and persecution. The godly response to these was modeled by Christ—to overlook injustices done to us, to love and forgive unconditionally.

In stark contrast to the injustices done to him, Christ was far less tolerant of injustices done to others. In Luke 4:18, Christ quotes Isaiah to describe part of his mission—"to release the oppressed."[26] Mark 10:14 records Christ becoming "indignant" when the disciples tried to keep the children away from him. In Matthew 18:6, Christ promised severe punishment for one "who causes one of these little ones to sin." When the Pharisees were bothered that he healed a man on the Sabbath, Mark 3:5 records that he "looked around at them in anger and [was] deeply distressed at their stubborn hearts." Concerning his numerous healings on the Sabbath, Christ flaunted these miracles to show that loving others often runs counter to religious tradition and the norms of the status quo and should be pursued independent of the costs.

The Gospel accounts of Christ clearing the Temple combine his anger when a.) the rights of the relatively powerless were violated by the powerful; and b.) when God's name was maligned by the behavior of religious people.[27] The religious leaders had allowed the money-changers and "those who sold doves" to turn the temple into "a den of robbers."[28] To "rob" the people, customers must have been forced to buy doves at too high of a price. (If the doves were sold at reasonable, competitive prices, the vendors would have been merely providing a valuable service.[29]) As with government today, the religious leaders may have sold exclusive rights to operate in the temple area, allowing those vendors to exploit the resulting monopoly power by charging high prices and providing unfavorable exchange rates—thus, "robbing" the people.[30] In particular, since doves were the usual offering of the poor (Leviticus 5:7), the effects of religiously-sanctioned monopoly power would have been disproportionately borne by the poor.

Ephesians 4:26 instructs us not to sin in our anger. This implies that anger is appropriate at times. Then, the questions become whether the anger is legitimate (in defending God's name or others vs. defending ourselves) and whether the subsequent responses are legitimate as well. Christ points the way by showing that becoming angry can be appropriate against injustice—in defense of the rights of others, especially the powerless. But what types of legislating justice are appropriate means to godly ends?

Legislating Justice vs. Legislating Morality

Why is the pursuit of justice for others different than the pursuit of morality for others? Biblically, we can see that Christ verbally defended the rights of others in matters of justice but did not restrict the freedom of unbelievers in matters of "social morality." We also saw earlier that attempts to legislate morality are fraught with unfortunate costs.[31] In contrast, attempts to legislate justice—especially if done effectively—have a number of beneficial by-products. First, by legislating justice, Christians set themselves apart as "servants" by seeking to minister to others, putting the needs of others first, defending the defenseless, and so on. As Carl Henry argues, "When Christian believers become thus involved in the struggle for justice, the world may recognize in a new way the presence of regenerate realities."[32] In other words, it is easier to be seen as "the light of the world."

Second, to the extent that Christians are critical of injustices, those who benefit from, or are responsible for, the injustices are usually the only ones who will view our efforts negatively. For example, if the poor are being exploited in some way, arguing against the injustice is likely to raise the sympathies of objective observers, not rankle them.[33] Unlike "legislating morality" (LM) issues, the problems with "legislating justice" (LJ) issues are obvious, even to non-Christians. Pursuing justice is easier to motivate and can more easily bring glory to God.

Third, the pursuit of justice gives Christians an opportunity to be *for* something. Unfortunately, we are more often known for what we are against. Likewise, effective preaching centers on what is great about Christ more than what is wrong with the world. Note also that Scripture records that Paul preached Christ and the gospel of grace, not immorality in the world.

Fourth, outreach ministry often targets "felt needs." Likewise, attempts to administer justice usually address the "felt needs" of those whose rights are being violated. The oppressed are often aware of how their opportunities have been reduced. To work with "felt needs" first is bound to be more effective than any effort concerning "*not* felt needs"—in particular, seeking to restrict consensual behaviors.[34]

Fifth, even if one wants to grant that the pursuit of legislating morality has some merit, legislating justice is undoubtedly a far greater pursuit. Reaching for "God's best" as opposed to what is merely "good" is a crucial and continuous battle in the Christian walk. In this context, is God more glorified by Christians seeking laws against sodomy and gambling or by Christians pursuing effective reform in education and welfare? Likewise, if one insists on supporting efforts to legislate morality, he will be unable to effectively refute a "Biblical case" for socialism, high taxes on income or consumption, or general government activism in economic arenas. If the use of government force is appropriate to reach morality goals, it is arguably as appropriate to use force to redistribute wealth, require military and community service, and so on.

In sum, as we seek to emulate Christ, although we should be careful about our choice of particular methods, we can be confident that defending the rights of others— using government as a tool—can be a noble pursuit.

Poverty vs. Oppression

Ron Sider's *Rich Christians in an Age of Hunger* is perhaps the most famous book among those who actively seek to "legislate justice."[35] Sider is particularly effective in pointing to God's concern about oppression and our failure to care for the poor.[36] However, he repeatedly equates poverty with oppression. This is definitionally false and causes him to interpret Scripture in a misleading manner. For instance, he cites the Israelites, but ignores that in the Wilderness, they yearned for what they no longer had—the leeks and onions (standard of living) of their bondage in Egypt; in slavery, they had certainly been oppressed, but were not destitute. Moreover, Scripture often mentions "the poor and the oppressed"; thus, the two terms are often connected.[37] However, since Scripture repeatedly distinguishes between "the poor" and "the oppressed," there must also be a difference between the two terms. In addition, Sider assumes that the rich usually oppress the poor to gain their wealth. Although certainly true in some cases—and prevalent in Biblical times, it is far from universal today. His conclusions explicitly make both mistakes—for example, that "The rich neglect or oppose justice because justice demands that they end their oppression and share with the poor."[38]

Webster's Dictionary defines "oppression" as "to keep down by the cruel or unjust use of power or authority; to trample down; the imposition of unreasonable burdens...[through] excessively rigorous government." In other words, oppression stems from a use of force which makes others worse off. (For example, James critiques those who withhold wages rather than criticizing the wage rate itself.[39]) By definition, this occurs much more frequently in political markets than in economic markets.[40] Economic markets feature mutually beneficial trade; political markets involve the use of government power to make some better off at the expense of others.[41] Ironically, those on the Religious Left end up endorsing tools of oppression to supposedly end oppression. Unless the ends somehow justify the means, this is not a tenable position.

To the extent that oppression occurs, it is certainly wrong. However, the primary causes of poverty are poor decisions by individuals and poor policies by those individuals' governments. Thus, Christians should seek to educate people about the consequences of their decisions and fight against unjust policies.

Poverty vs. Wealth[42]

Some on the Religious Left argue that wealth is inherently evil—or at least, in Ron Sider's words: "very dangerous"—and as a result, promote self-poverty instead.[43] Fortunately, Sider argues that poverty and suffering are not inherently good. They are unpleasant consequences of sin—by individuals who invite trouble on themselves, and by others (including government) who cause trouble for the poor. Likewise, Scripture teaches that money in and of itself is not evil. I Timothy 6:10 warns about "the love of money," not money per se.[44] Eight verses later, Paul promotes the proper use of wealth: "to do good, to be rich in good deeds, and to be generous and willing to share."[45]

A number of Biblical heroes were wealthy, including Job—both before and after his trials and tribulations. And when people note the wealth of the rich man in his story with Lazarus, they often forget that the third person in the story, Abraham, was also wealthy and in Paradise. In discussing this story, Robert Sirico quotes Augustine—if the rich man "had shown mercy to the poor man...he himself would have deserved mercy...if the poor man's merit had been his poverty...he surely would not have been carried by angels into the bosom of Abraham...it was not poverty in itself that was divinely honored, nor, on the other, riches that were condemned, but that the godliness of the one and the ungodliness of the other had their own consequences." Sirico then concludes: "If Lazarus had been wicked and poor rather than righteous and poor, his eternal fate would have been the same as that of the rich man...The real issue, therefore, is not the size of our bank accounts but the state of our souls."[46]

Moreover, although Christ became "poor for us"[47] (relative to his status in Heaven), he did not live in poverty (relative to his contemporaries). He never identified himself as poor, and in fact, was an artisan, probably earning a middle-class income. His lifestyle brought charges of him being a "drunkard and a glutton."[48] He even praised Mary for pouring expensive perfume on him—much to the chagrin of Judas.[49] And his followers maintained and used their wealth to help his ministry and support the Early Church.

Part of the confusion about God's view of material wealth is that God frequently rewards obedience with blessings. This is taught explicitly in the Law.[50] And although the connection becomes more tenuous throughout the Old and New Testaments, living life by "God's rules" is generally a way to avoid trouble, if not to prosper financially. That said, material wealth is not necessarily a sign of obedience. In the context of oppression, wealth can be gained through the use of force, theft, and bribes. Moreover, God expresses a special concern for the poor and Christ's teachings seem to favor the poor.[51]

But the way in which people gained wealth in that day was vastly different than today. John Schneider writes that "We now know beyond controversy that modern high-tech economies do not work in the same way that the ancient orders did...Nor do they work in the ways that the capitalism observed by Wesley, Marx, and Weber did...[It] works primarily by means of the creation of wealth, not by its seizure from others."[52] Thus, our response to wealth must be different as well. Schneider argues that this theological response should be based on the doctrine of the creation (how to use resources wisely) and the Exodus (a focus on freedom from oppression and poverty in a land of "milk and honey").

In an excellent chapter on poverty and wealth from a Christian perspective, Dallas Willard's starting point is that "Possessions and money cause uneasiness today in the minds of many sincere Christians. It is not just that they fear failing in their clear responsibilities to help others with the goods at their disposal. Rather, they are haunted by the more radical thought that their service to God would be better if they were poor—or at least if they owned nothing beyond what is required to meet their day-to-day needs. They are troubled by the idea that the very possession of surplus goods or money is evil."[53]

But Willard points out that "frugality" is not about the possession of goods, but their use. Watchman Nee notes that from the spoils of their exodus from Egypt, the Israelites put some money into building the Tabernacle, but some money into building a golden calf.[54] It's not what we have as much as how we use it. Putting it another way: there's a big difference between a million dollar salary and a million dollar lifestyle. Further, the possession and use of wealth are to be distinguished from "trusting" in wealth. In a word, we can possess wealth without using and trusting it; use wealth without possessing or trusting it; and trust wealth without possessing or using it.[55]

On one hand, Christ *commands* the "rich young ruler" to sell *everything* he has. But in the next chapter of Luke, Jesus eats with a rich man, Zacchaeus, who responds in faith by *voluntarily* giving *half* of his possessions to the poor.[56] In a word, the point is that God calls us to be wise stewards with the time, talents, and treasure with which He has blessed us. As such, "being poor is one of the poorest ways to help the poor."[57] As Willard concludes: "Possessions and use of them will occur...to assume the responsibility for the right use and guidance of possessions through ownership is far more of a discipline of the spirit than poverty itself. Our possessions vastly extend the range over which God rules through our faith."[58]

"Poverty" vs. True Poverty[59]

All statistics are a "proxy" for the state of the world they attempt to measure—an attempt to reduce a complex topic to a set of numbers which can be more easily digested while still accurately reflecting what they represent. The "poverty rate" is an oft-cited statistic which measures the number of people who live in households with an income below the poverty lines established by the government. (The poverty lines differ by household size.)

Unfortunately, the poverty rate has a number of substantial flaws. First, the standards—the poverty lines established by the government—are themselves arbitrary. (The original, somewhat-arbitrary poverty lines[60] have been adjusted each year by another proxy, inflation, to keep up with changing costs of living.) Perhaps "true poverty" begins at a lower or higher income level. In any case, we take the validity of the government's numbers on faith.

Second, the measurement of household income— *measured cash income in a single year*—is flawed and not necessarily a true reflection of a household's financial well-being. Not all income is *measured*; some is not reported to the government as people seek to avoid criminal prosecution, income taxes, or the reduction of means-tested government benefits. The government only looks at *cash* income, ignoring in-kind (non-cash) transfers. Since this covers much of what the government provides to the poor (health care, food stamps, housing vouchers, etc.), the statistic is a better reflection of dependence on government than on the poor's standards of living. In addition, the government only looks at *income*, not wealth. It is conceivable that one can have substantial wealth with little income. And this measurement of income is only *in a single year*. Thus, it fails to account for changes in income over time— particularly those which typically come with job experience. Young people often start with low incomes (including those in graduate school), but eventually do quite well for themselves.[61]

All of this is not to question the existence of poverty—but merely to point out that the poverty rate is substantially flawed as a statistic. The numbers should be taken with somewhere between a pinch and a shaker of salt, especially when making comparisons across demographic groups or over time.

Poverty vs. Income Inequality

The "income distribution" is another popular statistic which shares the flaw of looking at statics rather than dynamics. It reports the amount of income earned, for instance, by the highest 20% or the lowest 20%—in a given year. This statistic reveals that the rich earn more money than the poor. Surprise! It also indicates that in recent years, the highest 20% have been earning more and the lowest 20% have been earning less. From this, people have inferred that "the rich are getting richer and the poor are getting poorer." But since the statistic only measures income in a given year, this is not a reliable inference; the poorest 20% in one year are not the poorest 20% the next year. As such, we need a statistic which reflects "income dynamics"—what do the highest/lowest 20% from five or ten years ago earn today? In particular, do people have the opportunity to earn higher incomes over time? If not, then this is a matter of injustice. But in fact, the data suggest that the rich are getting richer and the poor are getting much richer.[62] While injustices exist in our economy (more later), the bottom line here is that we live in a class system, not a caste system.

Moreover, income inequality is a natural result of the mutually beneficial trades within a market economy— as some individuals are able to earn higher incomes by pleasing more people than average. Why is this a problem or something to be remedied? On the other hand, if the inequality stems from oppression, then the injustice should be vigorously opposed. Note also that some inequality is the explicit will of God: we are all created differently; the heavenly bodies all have different kinds of "splendor"; and there will different rewards for believers in heaven.[63]

Finally, why is income inequality necessarily a problem? For example, we might be able to eliminate poverty and injustice, but we cannot eliminate income inequality.[64] And focusing on equality could easily feed envy and materialism. As John Boersema argues, "Thus, rather than accepting the secular economic goal of an equitable income distribution, our goal should be to help those who are unable to adequately take care of themselves—the economically weak and marginalized."[65] Isn't dealing with poverty and injustice the more important goal?[66]

Competition vs. Monopoly

Competitive markets have many buyers and sellers; a monopoly is defined as a single seller. In practice, the term monopoly is not very useful, because it fails to distinguish between single sellers whose product or service has few or many close substitutes. For example, the extent of "monopoly power" is very different between the electric company and Coca-Cola. Both are the sole suppliers of their product in the market, but there are few close substitutes for the electric company's product (e.g., candles) and many close substitutes for Coca-Cola (e.g., other soft drinks, or more broadly, any other beverage). Thus, it is the *degree of monopoly power* that is the key to explaining and predicting market outcomes.

Limited monopoly power for producers translates to a highly competitive market. And in such settings, producers are forced to work hard to please consumers— in terms of price, product and service quality, filling specific customer niches, and so on. If they fail to do so, there are innumerable other producers who will be willing to do so—to increase their incomes, to put more bread on their own tables. Thus, competition has tremendous benefits for consumers, harnessing producers' self-interest in a manner that is efficient for society as a whole. But if competition is scarce, then consumers are more at the whim of producers who do not have to work as hard to satisfy their customers.[67]

A recurring theme in the next two chapters will be the use of government activism to limit competition—to benefit producers at the expense of consumers. No one likes competition for the things they sell; it should not be surprising to find people using government to restrict that competition. Unfortunately, neither the method nor the outcome is just.

One other thing troubles Christians about competition: it brings to mind rivalry and "cut-throat" business practices rather than cooperation. Although true to some extent, remember that in competitive markets, winning customers away from another firm is usually done by competing to serve customers more effectively. And ironically, economic activity is largely marked by cooperation—people engaging in voluntary, mutually beneficial trades—from people buying goods or services from firms, to workers renting their labor services to those firms. (When people complete a market transaction, they often say "thank you"!) Finally, consider that we all compete in various areas in life—from trying to win a board game, to competing to fill a job opening, to "competing" against standards of conduct. Even Paul talked about the merits of competition done well: "Run in such a way as to get the prize. Everyone who competes in the games goes into strict training..."[68] The bottom line is not *that* one competes, but *how* one competes.

Capitalism vs. Socialism

The empirical debate about socialism as an economic system has largely been resolved. As Clark Pinnock argues, "No one could be attracted to socialism on empirical grounds because evidence of its successes does not exist."[69] At least for Christians, the practical issues run deeper since socialism fails to ably address poverty.[70]

The ethical debate about capitalism is more interesting. Unfortunately, its opponents often have a "conception of capitalism [that] does not rise above caricature."[71] For instance, Sider says that capitalists "worship Mammon by idolizing economic efficiency and success."[72] James Haltemann writes that "the driving force behind capitalism is inequality—the dream of making more money than other people...a capitalist intends to die as unequal as possible."[73] Critics constantly conflate consumerism and capitalism—or otherwise misdefine it by ascribing moral values to it that are, in fact, optional.[74] But there is nothing inherent about capitalists worshipping Mammon or being driven by envy, covetousness, and greed.[75] Capitalists are merely those who invest their own time, effort, and money into a venture to earn an income—for anything from entirely selfish to entirely noble ends.[76] They provide physical and human capital for investment opportunities. Such activities create jobs and promote the economic well-being of others—certainly a worthy and even noble pursuit.[77]

And outside of using political markets, most behavior in economic markets is voluntary, mutually beneficial trade. As Robert Sirico comments on the parable likening the difficulty of a rich man getting into heaven to a camel going through the eye of a needle: "There was good reason for thinking this in pre-capitalist times because people acquired [massive] wealth by plundering their neighbors. The rise of capitalism, however, made it possible for people to become wealthy not by stealing from their neighbors, but by serving them."[78]

Thus, one of the advantages of capitalism is that it effectively harnesses self-interests.[79] If one is lazy or unloving in general—or not in the mood to do the right thing on any given day—the market typically provides a financial incentive to work hard and to treat people well anyway. If I fail to do so, I will drive away customers, irritate my boss, and so on. Thus, free markets cultivate a number of virtues; they encourage stewardship, sacrifice and servanthood.[80] "The nature of modern capitalism is normally to reward and encourage good ethical behavior in doing business. Of course, it does not guarantee good moral behavior, nor does it invariably punish bad behavior. No order of freedom can guarantee as much."[81]

Many advocates of government activism point to the supposed "injustices of capitalism."[82] But many of those outcomes are not from capitalism (pro-market), but mercantilism (pro-business)—the use of government to support privilege, restrict competition, and enhance interest groups' incomes at the expense of everyone else.[83] Sider even confuses capitalism with socialism. He argues that Zacchaeus had been "enmeshed in sinful economic structures" when in fact, he was a tax collector—an agent of the State![84] Other times, attributing worrisome outcomes to capitalism is more accurate, but the use of government as an alternative is greatly romanticized.[85] In a practical sense, the comparison of free market outcomes should be to the government alternative, rather than some unreachable utopia.[86] As Daniel Klein has said: "Some folks are dissatisfied with free enterprise if it doesn't work perfectly, and satisfied with government if it works at all."

Beyond semantics, the supposed arguments against capitalism are actually damaging in that they focus on the wrong issues. And equally troubling, such a mindset is then used to pursue socialism and government activism with its inequities, inefficiencies, and forced redistribution. Capitalism is simply about the freedom for people to do what they wish with their property and their life—unless it directly impinges on another's freedom to do the same.

All this is not to be taken as a blanket endorsement for all that capitalism can represent. In Galatians 5, Paul defends freedom but then argues that this freedom should be used to serve others. So too, ideally, the freedoms within capitalism should not be taken as license by individuals to ignore mercy and grace in their dealings with others. But that still leaves us with the question of whether government activism is an ethical and practical improvement over markets in any given context. In sum, don't expect too much from capitalism or democracy.[87] Recognize their limits, but weigh their merits against the available options. And remember that the focus in this book is on the limits of what Christians can do with government activism rather than the efficacy of markets per se.

A Note on Past Attempts to Legislate Justice

Some Christians have been very active in this arena. Unfortunately, in many cases, their proposals have been ill-advised. These poor policy prescriptions stem from elevating ends over means, and emphasizing compassion and zeal over an accurate understanding of how economic and political markets actually function.[88] Choices often involve pitting the heart against the head;

too often, activists have opted for the heart as the more spiritual choice.

In describing this dilemma, Os Guinness draws an analogy to the Tin Man in *The Wizard of Oz*. In one scene, Scarecrow reasons, "I shall ask for brains instead of a heart; for a fool would not know what to do with a heart if he had one." But the Tin Man replies, "I shall take the heart; for brains do not make one happy, and happiness is the best thing in the world."[89] Of course, the optimal strategy is to use one's heart and brains, with zeal and knowledge, to love the Lord our God with our heart *and* our mind.

I have provided a strong case for legislating justice. But if legislating justice is an appropriate tool, what would constitute a godly agenda for justice and which prescriptions will have the intended results?[90]

Chapter 9:
Why and How Christians Should
Legislate Justice (Part 2)
Explaining Redistribution to the Non-Poor[1]

A vast array of government policies redistribute income in a variety of product and labor markets. Many of these redistribute income to the non-poor at the expense of the poor. Presumably, these efforts are not designed to hurt the poor; their harm is merely a by-product or an indirect effect of policies with other goals. But why do these policies exist? And what are the mechanisms within public policy that people use to accomplish their goals?

Political vs. Economic Markets

Transactions in economic markets involve A giving money to B in exchange for goods or services. For instance, I might purchase a pizza from a restaurant or agree to work for someone in exchange for wages and fringe benefits. Transactions in political markets involve C taking money from A to give to B. For instance, Congress might increase taxes in order to pay for a new government program. Or Congress might prevent foreign suppliers from selling their products here, increasing prices for consumers and benefiting protected domestic firms.[2]

How are these two transactions different? First, political markets are coercive; money is forcibly taken from A and given to B.[3] Economic markets are voluntary; A willingly gives his money to B. Second, political markets make two parties better off (C and B) at the expense of somebody else (A). Economic markets feature "mutually beneficial trade" where both parties (A and B) expect to benefit.[4] Third, political markets transfer wealth from one party to another; economic markets create wealth since both parties benefit from the trade.[5] Fourth, political markets necessarily involve an unproductive third party, the "middleman" (C)—a bureaucrat or politician who must be paid a salary.[6] Another inefficiency is that it is unlikely that C will spend A's money as well as A would have spent it. Fifth, in economic markets, it is in the self-interests of producers to please their customers. Even in the completely selfish pursuit of greater income, producers typically benefit others by seeking to serve them more effectively. In political markets, self-interested "producers" and "consumers" have an incentive to develop more sophisticated ways to redistribute wealth.[7]

The Politics of Redistribution

Despite the public's focus on welfare programs for the poor, the bulk of government's redistributive efforts are actually targeted elsewhere—to help other "special interest groups" whose members are typically in the middle and upper classes. They encourage government to intervene and redistribute income away from the general public through higher taxes or higher prices. How does this work and why do people tolerate it? To help explain this, we will use a simple, hypothetical government program where a total of $280 million is taken from 280 million citizens through taxes to give to 10,000 people. The cost to each person would be a dollar; the benefit to each recipient would be $28,000.

First, think about those paying for the program— the general public. The cost for a family of four would be four dollars per year or $.33 per month. Who would notice such a minor expense? Now imagine that instead, the four dollars are extracted through slightly higher prices for something bought throughout the year. Who would notice the higher price and attribute its cause to the government program? These costs would be extremely subtle. Further, even if one did notice the additional cost, who would devote time and energy to oppose the government program? Only the most outraged would bother. In these matters, the public is usually "rationally ignorant and apathetic"—ignorant because they typically fail to see the small and subtle costs imposed upon them, apathetic because the expected benefits of taking action are easily outweighed by the costs, and rationally so, because the small-per-person costs are not worth the time and effort required for individuals to learn about them and to pursue their removal.

Now, consider those receiving the transfer. As opposed to the apathetic general public, this group will be "especially interested." There is probably no other public policy issue that they will care about more. They have an incentive to 1.) be selective with or to twist information in any public debate; 2.) create compelling stories for why the redistribution should occur; and 3.) support those in government who make the transfer possible through a bloc of votes, campaign contributions of time and money, or even bribes.[8]

In sum, members of the special interest group receive sizable benefits. Another small group that facilitates the transfers—politicians and bureaucrats administering the program—reaps obvious benefits as well. And there is a large group—the general public—whose members absorb relatively small and subtle costs. The latter group hardly notices the loss while the first two groups pursue such intervention with great vigor.[9] This is mutually beneficial trade between government officials and the special interest group—at the expense of the general public.

Note also that the recipients don't have to be needy or deserving in any sense; the mechanism is equally adept at transferring wealth to Bill Gates or to a homeless man. In fact, many of the redistributive schemes transfer money from the poor to the non-poor. For example, consider Social Security. Its taxes are regressive since they are not imposed above a certain income level. Its benefits are also regressive to the extent that those with lower income typically die sooner. (On average, black males actually earn a negative rate of return on their "investments" in the system.[10]) Assuming today's workers will be paid benefits when they retire, the poor and lower-middle classes have been forced to put most of their nest eggs into a "retirement plan" that yields, on average, a 1% rate of return. All of this makes Social Security reform an ethical as well as an economic and political issue. And deficit financing yields benefits for recipients today at the expense of the unborn who will bear the burden of that debt tomorrow. As Jonathan Rauch notes, "politicians and lobbies look to transfer money from a group that won't organize to defend itself...out of the mouths of babes and into the mouths of interest groups."[11]

James Schlesinger aptly describes the goal of this game: "to extract resources from the general taxpayer with minimum offense and to distribute the proceeds among innumerable claimants in such a way as to maximize support at the polls. Politics...represents the art of calculated cheating—or more precisely, how to cheat without being caught."[12] As such, politicians and interest groups look for ways to transfer wealth while making the costs as invisible as possible.

Legalized Theft and the Legitimate Use of Force

The first problem that often comes to mind after reading a pointed description of political market activity is that it seems to violate the 8th Commandment.[13] "Since government produces no goods, it can distribute only what it takes from others. This process is indistinguishable from theft."[14] As such, Libertarians consistently describe taxation for most types of government spending as "legalized theft."[15]

As Robert Heinlein asks, "under what circumstances is it moral for a group to do that which is not moral for a member of that group to do alone?"[16] Is theft appropriate as long as it's accompanied by a majority vote? In the late 19th century, President Grover Cleveland aptly described what was then a more dominant ideology: "I will not be a party to stealing money from one group of citizens to give to another group of citizens, no matter what the need or apparent justification."[17] And with the proliferation of government activity over the last 40 years, Herbert Schlossberg notes that "it requires unusual decadence for an entire population to acquiesce in mutual pick-pocketing, to allow itself, that is, to be bribed with its own money."[18] It seems odd that we would invoke on ourselves what David wished for one of his enemies: "May strangers plunder the fruit of his labors."[19]

In criticizing attempts to "legislate justice" through government redistribution, David Chilton argues that "The mark of a Christian movement is its willingness to submit to the demands of Scripture...'You shall not steal,' for instance...must not be relativized on the mere excuse that the thief has no bread. It must not be transgressed with the spurious rationale that the thief should have been given bread in the first place." As before, to pursue any goals with ungodly methods is not an appropriate option.[20]

Doug Bandow argues that "the political process has become a system of legalized theft, with personal gain rather than public interest becoming the standard for government action."[21] This use of force cannot be motivated from a Christian perspective, unless the government spending is for the "general interest" or the "common good"—a narrow set of examples when economic markets do not function well (as with pollution and national defense).[22] But it's not even clear whether Christians should vocally endorse even those efforts. And certainly, Christians should eschew the use of government to appropriate funds from the general public to benefit "special interests" or especially, themselves.[23]

Bribes and Justice

As noted earlier, special interest groups use money and blocs of votes to influence outcomes in political markets. In less-developed countries, the stereotype of these transactions is political graft on a national scale, or the $20 paid to a customs officer to make his inspection less thorough. In the United States, bribes are less frequent—or at least, more subtle. Cases of excessive corruption are prosecuted on occasion. And a provision in campaign finance laws that allowed retiring U.S. representatives to pocket excess campaign contributions in 1992 was uncomfortably close to bribery. But for our purposes, we will focus on the most prominent type of legal, political influence still in effect—campaign contributions and interest group voting support for elected representatives. Of course, taking campaign contributions and pursuing votes are not inherently evil per se. But to the extent that they influence justice negatively, they are a cause for great concern.

The most quoted scripture on money is I Timothy 6:10—"For the love of money is a root of all kinds of evil." Clearly, the worship of money by special interest groups and politicians has the potential to cause tremendous problems in terms of justice. Lysander Spooner argued that wars of conquest carried on by government were the greatest of all crimes, but that "the next greatest crimes committed in the world are equally prompted by avarice and ambition...not so much by men who violate the laws, as by men who, either by themselves or by their instruments, make the laws; by men who have combined to usurp arbitrary power...and whose purpose...is by unjust and unequal legislation, to secure to themselves such advantages and monopolies as will enable them to control and extort the labor and properties of other men..."[24]

More specifically, the Bible is active in condemning bribery. Proverbs 17:23 says that "a wicked man accepts a bribe in secret to pervert the course of justice." In the Law, the Israelites were told not to "accept a bribe, for a bribe blinds those who see and twists the words of the righteous."[25] In establishing Israelite government under God, the selection process for judges included that they should "hate dishonest gain."[26] I Samuel 8:3 notes that Samuel's sons "turned aside after dishonest gain and accepted bribes and perverted justice." In contrast, Samuel's farewell sermon included his declaration and the people's affirmation that he had not cheated or oppressed anyone, and had not taken any bribes.[27]

Two of the prophets do perhaps the best job of explicitly tying together the themes of bribery and justice. Isaiah 1:21,23 says "See how the faithful city has become a harlot! She once was full of justice; righteousness used to dwell in her...[now] your rulers are rebels, companions of thieves; they all love bribes and chase after gifts." And in Amos' treatise on justice, he accuses the people, and especially, the leaders: "You trample on the poor and force them to give you grain...I know how many are your offenses and how great are your sins. You oppress the righteous and take bribes and you deprive the poor of justice in the courts."[28]

Psalm 94:20 asks "Can a corrupt throne be allied with [God]—one that brings on misery by its decrees?" To the extent that our political system is supported financially and electorally in ways that pervert justice, to the extent that our political markets are corrupt and responsible for policies that promote misery, we need to repent and defend those who are oppressed.

The Importance of "Good Stories"

Even with the influence exerted by interest groups in terms of votes and money, perhaps it is still difficult to imagine how the general public would allow this game to take place in a democracy. One key is the diffuse and small per-person costs borne by the general public. The other key is the development of "good stories"—compelling reasons (at least on the surface) given by proponents of a government program as to why promoting their specific interests is supposedly in the best interests of the country. Likewise, Ambrose Bierce defines politics as "a strife of interests masquerading as a contest of principles; the conduct of public affairs for private advantage."

But "good stories" lack objectivity by definition. For instance, in the private sector, should one blindly accept negative remarks about companies from their rivals? Likewise, by nature, those who support a government policy will tell the public about its benefits while ignoring or downplaying its costs. Similarly, when two people run for political office, each one has an incentive to talk about his strengths and his opponent's weaknesses, the benefits of his policies and the costs of his opponent's proposals.[29]

To be successful, the interest group's stated reason cannot be "We want the government to increase your product prices (or taxes) because we want higher incomes." People would find this outrageous. The question then is how do you convince the general public to accept and even vote for and enjoy the government reaching into their wallets?[30] With a "rationally ignorant" public, the story needs a kernel of truth or logic, but not much more. Specific rationales will be covered in the next chapter, but I will discuss the general categories here.

Two of the most popular reasons are spoken concerns for the best interests of consumers and appeals to nationalism or other emotions. The first category consists of supposed concerns about the safety or quality of a good or service. This leads to calls to restrict some sellers from entering a trade. Ironically, one rarely hears consumers testifying about the need for such intervention; almost always, it is incumbent firms seeking protection from outside competition that speak on behalf of such proposals.[31] Appeals to emotion are also popular. Through the years, we have heard about the need to "save the family farm," to provide a "living wage" (a higher minimum wage), and how free trade will "cause all of our jobs to go overseas." Such rhetorical devices are immensely useful in the appropriation of wealth from a rationally ignorant general public to special interest groups. But as Schlossberg notes, "Justice has little to do with the process, except to serve as a cover."[32]

The Job Creation/Destruction Myth

Perhaps the most frequent "good story" is that government activism preserves jobs. But we all know "There's no such thing as a free lunch." In this context, everything government spends must be paid for through some type of taxation—higher current taxes, higher future taxes (deficit spending and debt), or inflation taxes (printing money to pay bills, making current money worth less). Of course, government often defers costs into the future (deficit financing) or makes them less visible (inflation). But to simplify things, assume that government programs are paid for with current taxes. Our $280 million program will create 10,000 jobs. Meanwhile, government has taken $280 million away from taxpayers. As a result, jobs are destroyed as people spend and invest $280 million less. At best, government's activism amounts to a "shell game": government creates (or subsidizes) $280 million worth of jobs in the public sector while destroying $280 million worth of jobs in the private sector.[33]

In fact, given the probable inefficiency of the newly created jobs (since they are subsidized or in the public sector), government will almost certainly destroy more than it creates. An extreme case would be to pay people to dig holes and fill them up again; jobs are created, but nothing useful is produced. Even in a best-case scenario, the bottom line is that government redistribution cannot create "net" jobs; it can create jobs through spending programs, but will destroy more through the subsequent taxation.[34] As Dave Barry notes sarcastically: "When the government spends money, it creates jobs; whereas when the money is left in the hands of taxpayers, God only knows what they do with it. Bake it into pies, probably. Anything to avoid creating jobs."

Taking money from the general public—whether through higher taxes or higher prices—creates some jobs, but destroys more. So why are these policies so popular? The created jobs are relatively obvious, whereas the destroyed jobs are quite difficult to see. They are eliminated one dollar at a time (the amount taken from each citizen) and in many different industries. Who would attribute a particular job loss to the tax or price increase?[35] But the fact of the matter is that you cannot take from X and give to Y and create anything on net.[36]

Government can redistribute income in a variety of ways. Direct redistribution to the non-poor is usually not politically popular.[37] Thus, politicians typically use indirect methods to transfer income to special interest groups. The most frequent indirect method involves restricting competition.

There is *Always* an Incentive to Restrict Competition

The story begins with the desire of a business to sell more products at higher prices and to obtain greater profits. But since most markets are rather competitive, efforts to increase prices are frustrated by other businesses undercutting their price and luring their customers away.

As a result, firms often try to form voluntary associations that restrict output, allowing incumbent firms in the industry to charge a higher price.

But once the firms have colluded to restrict output and increase prices, there is then an incentive to cheat on the cooperative agreement. It is now in each firm's best interests to produce and sell a few more units since those would be very profitable—units for which the market price significantly exceeds the cost of production. In addition, outsiders see an especially profitable opportunity and may decide to enter the market. If some of the firms cheat or if challengers enter, then we return to the competitive outcome we had before; the attempt to increase prices and profits will be thwarted.

Usually, a cartel is unable to effectively monitor and enforce a collusive agreement. If cheaters cannot be inexpensively policed or if new competitors cannot be kept out, the agreement will fall apart. This is why so few voluntary cartels work.[38] This outcome is almost a given—if not in the past, then certainly today in wealthier countries, as increased transportation and communication technology have allowed consumers much larger markets and diminished the monopoly power of any individual firm.

Because they are usually unable to collude on a voluntary basis, interest groups turn to government because it has the coercive power necessary to enforce such agreements. In the words of Walter Williams, "Free market competition is the most stringent, unyielding form of regulation there can be. That's precisely why so many sellers fear and abhor the free market...their common desire is to use government to lock out potential competitors—whether by import tariffs, minimum wages or airline regulation."[39] The use of government to restrict competition will be a prevalent theme in the next chapter's examples.

Although this mechanism is more subtle than direct redistribution, the results are the same. Interest groups engage in trades with politicians to restrict their domestic and foreign competition and to allow them to increase prices and thus, their income—at the expense of the general public. (Ambrose Bierce defines "tariffs" as "a scale of taxes on imports, designed to protect the domestic producer against the greed of his consumer.") The benefits are concentrated; the costs are diffuse and even more subtle. Where can one find Biblical warrant to prevent people from buying and selling legitimate goods and services—or artificially increasing their price? The mechanism is force; the method and the outcome are unjust.[40]

An Example

Before we continue, it will be helpful to illustrate these principles by thoroughly describing a real-world example—price supports (a government-mandated, artificially high price) and import restrictions in the market for sugar to protect domestic producers from foreign competition. The resulting domestic price of sugar typically doubles the world price. As always, protected producers benefit from restricted competition and consumers are hurt by having to pay higher prices.

Although the average family doesn't buy many bags of sugar in a year, the more significant cost is that any product that contains sugar will also be more expensive (soft drinks, cake mixes, cereal, etc.). So, consumers are "nickel-and-dimed" to death at grocery stores by higher product prices—$25 per year for the average family of four and $1.9 billion for the entire country.[41] Jobs are destroyed because consumers have less disposable income. The poor are disproportionately harmed because a higher proportion of their budgets are devoted to food.

Moreover, domestic firms that use sugar (especially as a primary input) are placed at a competitive disadvantage with foreign companies who have access to low-cost foreign sugar. Citing higher sugar prices, Brach's Candy closed a plant in inner-city Chicago and moved overseas. Many other jobs in industries that use sugar have been lost as well. And what about foreign producers? Producers from countries like Haiti are told they cannot sell their goods in our markets. It is unjust to forcibly deny market access to producers from any country— especially one whose people have an average income of $1,000 per year.

What about the politics of this redistribution? The subtlety is stunning. Who understands that they pay more for a six-pack of soda because of our nation's sugar policies? Who knows that jobs are lost in firms that use sugar as an input? While the costs are diffuse and extremely difficult to see, apparently the beneficiaries understand the game. The average sugar cane plantation received an extra $235,000 in 1991; in response, interest groups for sugar farmers spent $1.7 million in 1990 defending their subsidy in the farm bill.[42] Even corn producers made contributions since corn syrup (as a substitute) also benefited from the restriction in competition.

Prospects for Reform

The principles developed here are responsible for the bulk of all government policy. They explain why policies exist in a democracy, even when the costs to society outweigh the benefits and the number of losers far exceeds the number of winners. The key is that the costs of these policies are small-per-person, diffuse, and very subtle.[43]

To implement reform, from our earlier framework, one needs to persuade A, B, or C that these transactions are inappropriate. Education about the workings of political markets—making the subtle costs more obvious—would be helpful. Many people who bear the costs do not understand the cause and effect of government activism. Moreover, many beneficiaries never make the connection that the government activity requires force that makes somebody else worse off. And many politicians do not understand the full ramifications of the policies they promote.

Electing people who believe that such redistribution is inappropriate would be helpful. But that probably requires that a majority of the public has the same belief—a daunting task within today's dominant ideology: a strong belief in, and an idolatry toward, government.[44] Gary North says this will require a "moral conversion," and concludes that "every culture rests on moral presuppositions. The culture of state spending rests on a false one: the belief that the state is a morally legitimate instrument of coercive wealth redistribution... The culture of spending must be shown to be the moral low ground, not just an inefficient solution to (our economic) problems."[45]

As such, Christians need to be willing to relinquish the fruit of their political market transactions. Former Rep. Fred Grandy noted that the public is "torn between their addiction to bacon and their aversion to pork."[46] When we are receiving government subsidies out of the pockets of others, we need to reconsider our attraction to bacon. As Thomas Sowell said, "If you have been voting for politicians who promise to give you goodies at someone else's expense, then you have no right to complain when they take your money and give it to someone else..." While our assistance from government always "seems different," we should note that one man's "deserved" subsidy is another's tax loophole.[47]

Moreover, Christians need to have the passion of God toward the poor and the methods of Christ and the Bible in dealing with oppression and injustice.[48] In this context, Christians need to be willing to stand up in the public square—especially for the poor who are disproportionately harmed by so many forms of government activism. When we fail to do so, "justice is driven back, and righteousness stands at a distance; truth has stumbled in the streets, honesty cannot enter...The Lord looked and was displeased that there was no justice. He saw that there was no one, he was appalled that there was no one to intervene."[49] We need to respond to God's call to promote justice and righteousness. Isaiah 58:9-10 promises that "if you do away with the yoke of oppression...and if you spend yourselves in behalf of the hungry...You will be like a well-watered garden, like a spring whose waters never fail."

The Desires of the Status Quo

Probably most important, in each case, Christians will need to have zeal, wisdom, and courage to stand against a status quo that will fight all attempts at such reform. "When justice is done, it brings joy to the righteous but terror to evildoers."[50] We can take comfort in that Christ's ministry was one long battle against the religious and social conventions of his day. Exodus 23:2 instructs: "Do not follow the crowd in doing wrong...do not pervert justice by siding with the crowd." As Christians should be well aware, those who hold to the truth are often in a small minority. As J. Vernon McGee once noted: "Sometimes majority opinion means a lot of people going the wrong direction." We need to be steadfast in going the right direction, pursuing the things of God.

Scripture is replete with stories about how the economic, political, social, and religious establishments often sought to maintain the status quo with the use of force. For example, Acts 19:23-40 records "a great disturbance about the Way." Paul's preaching in Ephesus led to concerns that he was hurting the idol-making business—that their "trade [would] lose its good name." The primary concern: the loss of income. The good story: "the temple of Artemis will be discredited." The tool: the threat of violence, although Paul had "neither robbed temples nor blasphemed [their] goddess." Paul's preaching made the general public better off at the expense of the status quo. As a result, he faced terrific opposition from the establishment.[51]

Christ's ministry threatened the power of the religious leaders of his day as well, eventually resulting in his crucifixion. Even after his death, Matthew 28:11-15 records a bribe to the guards at the tomb in order to try to protect the status quo. And perhaps most noteworthy, in arranging the greatest act of injustice in history, Christ was betrayed by Judas to the chief priests and the officers of the temple guard—in a political market, to be taken by force, all for a bribe: 30 pieces of silver.[52]

Chapter 10:
Why and How Christians Should
Legislate Justice (Part 3)
Ending Redistribution to the Non-Poor

The Scriptural principles and the redistributive mechanism described in the previous chapter can be illustrated in innumerable markets. Special interest groups enhance their incomes by persuading politicians to impose small-per-person costs on the general public. Sometimes, these benefits come from direct redistribution. More often, the gains are in the form of higher prices resulting from restricted competition. The purpose of this chapter is to describe some of the more important examples— important either because of their overall impact or their impact specifically on the poor. In a word, it is difficult to imagine any Biblical justification for the means used and the ends achieved in this chapter.

I. Making the Essentials more Expensive: Higher Prices for Food and Clothing[1]

Farmers vs. the General Public:
Farming the Government and its Taxpayers
    Although full-time farmers have income and wealth well above the national average, they have been among the most active in using political markets to increase their incomes.[2] The resulting government programs redistribute income from the general public to the non-poor. Sometimes, the redistribution is direct— through the tax code. Taxpayers have subsidized farmers' production costs through direct payments, reduced interest rate loans, and defaults on debt.[3] In 1986 and 1987,

government payments to farmers actually exceeded their earned income.[4] In 1994, agribusiness received $29.2 billion in direct subsidies.[5] (This compares with a combined $50 billion spent for food stamps and AFDC that year.) Looking at individual programs: from 1995 to 1998, taxpayers subsidized $5.5 billion of the $8.9 billion farmers paid for crop insurance; and over and above that, emergency aid to farmers totaled $25 billion from 1998 to 2000.[6] (This last sentence alone resulted in a tax burden of nearly $460 for the average family of four.) Sometimes, the redistribution is indirect—consumers pay higher prices through price supports and restricted foreign and domestic competition. This is especially painful for the poor who spend a disproportionate amount of their incomes on food and for foreign producers who are denied access to the world's wealthiest market.

By itself, an artificially high price leads to a surplus since suppliers produce more and consumers purchase less at the higher price. To prevent the surplus, government must limit domestic and/or foreign suppliers. For example, under penalty of law, one needs a license to grow and sell peanuts in the United States, and since 1953, trade restrictions have only allowed companies to import two peanuts per American per year.[7] If the surplus is not prevented, it must be destroyed, stored, given away, or its purchase subsidized. In addition, between 1937 and 1992, by law, as much as 40% of the orange crop was destroyed, fed to livestock, or exported to increase domestic orange prices.[8] And nearly 72 billion pounds of dairy product were prohibited from coming to the market between 1986-1993 to keep prices higher.[9]

As James Bovard notes, "no price is too high to help Americans avoid the curse of cheap food."[10] Another irony is that "family farmers"—the supposed beneficiaries for such policies—receive disproportionately little of these subsidies, often doing harm to those the policy is said to help.[11] And our assistance to farmers does terrific damage to farmers in less-developed countries.[12] Is it moral to use government force to prevent suppliers from selling in certain markets? Are programs which redistribute money from consumers and taxpayers to wealthy farmers the epitome of justice? Policies which take from one group to give to another—especially when the redistribution is from the poor to the rich—can hardly be labeled righteous or just.

Textile Manufacturers vs. Consumers: The Emperor Has no Clothes

Despite the availability of clothing produced abroad, our textile industry is heavily protected from foreign competition—with more than 3,000 tariffs and quotas on clothing.[13] The government has estimated that this increases the average price of clothing by 58%; Gary Hufbauer has calculated that as a result, Americans pay an extra $25-30 billion dollars for clothing (about $400 per year from the average family of four).[14]

The outcome: significant redistribution to textile producers at the expense of consumers. The poor are especially harmed in that they spend a disproportionate amount of their incomes on clothing. And since many of the foreign producers are from less-developed countries, this policy harms the poor in other countries as well. Restricting competition in this arena tells the people of Bangladesh (average income of $1,200) to take their business elsewhere.

But Don't These Policies Save Jobs?

Yes and no. Government intervention saves the jobs of those protected from competition (or allows them to keep their wages artificially high), but it destroys more jobs than it preserves. The jobs saved are easy to see; but the jobs lost are more subtle. Higher prices and higher taxes diminish the disposable incomes of the general public. Thus, jobs that would have been created from the additional consumer spending and capital investment will not be realized. These job losses are more subtle since they occur in many different industries, a few dollars at a time.

This is merely a more complex version of the shell game described in the previous chapter. As before, the government redistributes from consumers to protected producers—special interest groups benefiting at the expense of all others. And since we are protecting an industry that is relatively inefficient, these restrictions promote the inefficient over the efficient. Thus, the country as a whole is worse off.

Consider a hypothetical example: Alaskan banana farmers. Imagine that Congress wants to "create jobs" and "end our dependence on foreign bananas." To accomplish this, they might subsidize the construction of greenhouses in Alaska with a $1 billion annual subsidy (for a "jobs program") and prohibit banana imports. While jobs would be created in Alaska, they would be destroyed elsewhere in the country as taxes and banana prices increase, thus decreasing disposable income. The created jobs would be obvious; the destroyed jobs would be subtle. Years later, if a few representatives tried to end the subsidy, one can imagine the opposition they would encounter: arguments about job destruction, accusations about a lack of compassion for banana farmers, and nationalistic concerns about becoming dependent on foreign bananas, and other "good stories" about everything from tarantulas to pesticides.

It is ironic that people understand that we benefit when individuals within our own country specialize and then engage in trade. For instance, would it be smart to erect trade barriers between states? "Free trade" with other countries simply takes this principle a step further. And why would we want to do to ourselves what we do to those that we punish with trade sanctions (e.g., trade embargoes with Cuba and Iraq, and divesting from South Africa)? Moreover, we typically understand that discrimination against buyers or sellers harms both parties, but trade restrictions are a mandated form of discrimination. Consumers and foreign producers are harmed by government preventing exchange (with quotas) or increasing the price of foreign-produced goods (with tariffs). Restricting trade and foreign investment may help certain groups, but hurts the country overall. Is this use of force a just method? Does it achieve godly goals?

Protected Producers vs. Consumers and Taxpayers

Our government shelters a wide variety of domestic industries: cars and steel, wine and cheese, dolls and the clothing that dolls wear, and so on. In total, Hufbauer estimates that U.S. trade barriers cost American consumers $80 billion per year (about $1,200 for the average family of four).[15] Although these other policies do not harm the poor as much, they are still relevant in the context of a discussion of justice.

Remember that interest groups receive concentrated benefits at the expense of the general public who bear small and subtle costs. As Ron Sider notes, "(import) restrictions are maintained mainly because their removal would threaten the interest of certain well-organized and politically entrenched groups."[16] No matter how good the rationale or how supposedly "unfair" another country's trade policy, producers *always* have an incentive to restrict competition. Protected producers are better off while other firms face higher input prices, consumers pay higher prices, workers pay higher taxes, and other countries are told to take their business elsewhere.[17]

Of course, even if one still supports protectionism in any given context, one should still acknowledge the redistribution of income that occurs and its impact on the poor. But Christians should ask themselves whether the use of government for these purposes promotes or impedes justice. Finally, it is sad that the public is so bothered by unearned transfers to the poor while it mostly ignores the larger welfare programs our government operates in support of special interest groups. And it is ironic that the public is concerned with the poor becoming dependent upon welfare programs. From the protests which arise whenever reform is suggested in these arenas, it appears that the addiction to welfare programs for the non-poor is at least as strong.[18]

II. Locking Unskilled Workers out of Labor Markets[19]

Those who sell products prefer higher prices and sometimes use political markets to reach that goal. The same is true of those who rent their labor services. As such, these interest groups lobby to make their competition more expensive (and thus, less attractive) or to lock them out of labor markets altogether.

Unfortunately, because the rhetoric surrounding these issues sounds good, the general public accepts a host of labor policies that limit labor market opportunities for the relatively unskilled, and thus, harm the poor.

Making One's Labor Competition More Expensive

One way to increase the demand for my labor is to increase the price of my competition. But I cannot force my competitors to charge more for their services—unless I can persuade the government to mandate the higher price level. For instance, if Burger King lobbied for a law that all Big Macs would be sold for at least $3, Burger King would benefit from people buying fewer Big Macs and presumably more Whoppers. In this section, we will cover three examples of laws which make certain groups of workers artificially more expensive.

The Minimum Wage[20]

A competitive labor market ensures that I will be paid comparably to what I can produce: if a firm paid me more, it would be charity; if the firm paid less, someone else would have a financial incentive to hire me—to pay me more and still make a profit from my services. (If a labor market is not competitive enough, this result may well not hold.[21]) Likewise, if the minimum wage is greater than my worth to a firm, I will not be offered a job. Why would a business want to pay $7 per hour to someone who can only produce $6 per hour worth of output?

Intuition tells us that as the price of something goes up (all other things equal), consumers will decrease their purchases of that product or service. To some extent, they adjust by switching to close substitutes that have become relatively less expensive. The same is true for businesses.

If the price of unskilled labor increases, firms will want less of it and will substitute toward other inputs— relatively skilled labor, automation, and so on. As with farm policies, artificially high prices create a surplus in the market—here, unemployment for unskilled workers.[22] Sadly, increased minimum wages—at the federal, state, and local levels (often labeled "living wages"[23])—are a top priority for those on the Religious Left.[24] But increasing the price of unskilled labor *above the market-determined wage* is a mixed blessing for the working poor. (If the minimum is set below the market wage, then the law has no impact and is a non-issue, except for its use in political rhetoric.) When the law lifts a minimum wage above the market wage, some unskilled workers will benefit at the expense of those who lose their jobs. Instead of "economic justice," many of the unskilled are locked out of the labor market.

The minimum wage is especially troubling because it harms the very people it is supposed to help. It is a significant barrier to entry for teenagers and members of many minority groups whose skills are often relatively low. Moreover, it limits opportunities to acquire the training and experience that accompany any type of job— the skills that are so important for those with so few skills. The unemployment statistics support the contention that teenagers and minorities are especially harmed by the minimum wage. In 1999, compared to a national average of 4.2%, for 16-19 year-olds, white unemployment was 12.0% and black unemployment was 27.9%.[25]

It is truly unfortunate that full-time minimum wage workers trying to support a family have such low incomes[26], but increasing the minimum wage is not the answer. If the government wants to help the unskilled in a more practical and ethical manner, it can reduce state income or Social Security taxes on low-income earners (more later), provide a wage subsidy for firms who employ unskilled workers (as with many welfare-to-work programs), and subsidize workers through the tax code (as with the Earned Income Tax Credit). All of these methods have modest shortcomings, but at least they avoid locking the unskilled out of labor markets.

"Prevailing Wage" Laws

These state and federal laws—also known as Davis-Bacon or "comparable worth" laws—are a minimum wage mandated for many public works projects. As a result, workers must be paid at least the "prevailing wage"—typically, the local union's wage rate. One problem is that these laws artificially increase the cost of government-provided infrastructure by more than $1 billion per year (about $15 from the average family of four), redistributing income from taxpayers to union members with above-average incomes. Another problem is that they restrict competition from, and artificially limit opportunities for, relatively unskilled labor.

Unions avidly pursue and defend such laws, so we can infer that these laws promote their well-being. If non-union workers—who are typically less-experienced and relatively lower-skilled—are allowed to compete on the basis of price, they may get the job. But if the price is mandated to level of the union wage, the game is over—union workers will always be chosen. The purpose of these laws is to preserve the status quo, to protect the incumbent from the challenger, to promote union workers over non-union workers. And ironically, these laws often prevent inner-city residents from working on inner-city construction projects.

Finally, these laws are discriminatory for the same reason as the minimum wage—they restrict relatively unskilled labor that happens to be disproportionately minority.[27] But unlike the minimum wage, the origins of this law were overtly racist. For instance, in debate over the bill, Rep. Clayton Algood said "that contractor has cheap colored labor...and it is labor of that sort that is in competition with white labor."[28] These laws (and a minimum wage) also exist in South Africa as part of the strategy to keep relatively unskilled blacks from competing for white union jobs. It is ironic that we condemned South Africa for apartheid while using the same policies and getting the same results. Independent of motives, the outcome is the same.

Mandated Benefits

Concerning the minimum wage, people often ask "who isn't worth $6 per hour?" But they forget that firms must absorb other costs when hiring workers, including many other government mandates. The problems with the minimum wage also apply to other employer mandates— Social Security "contributions," unemployment insurance, workmen's compensation, family leave, and so on. For example, the Mackinac Center for Public Policy has estimated that "for a worker making $22,000 a year, an employer kicks in an additional $2,640 annually for the various government mandates."[29] Again, these are particularly harmful to low-skilled workers. (Proposals to mandate employer-provided health insurance would be disastrous in this regard.) A firm simply will not (routinely) compensate a worker more than he produces.

All of these policies sound like they promote "justice." In fact, many Christians have actively advocated these prescriptions. But instead, these policies use an ungodly method and are detrimental to many of those they purport to help. Labor unions are clear beneficiaries, using government to restrict competition from other forms of labor—through higher minimum wages, Davis-Bacon laws, and mandated-benefit laws—as relatively unskilled labor is priced out of the market. Indeed, unions are the main proponents of these laws. Why would unions lobby for benefits or wages they are already paid? Perhaps they are charitable, wanting to benefit others who do not pay union dues. Or perhaps they seek to restrict some of their labor competition by increasing its price.[30]

Eliminating Labor Market Competition

In addition to making my competition more expensive, I will earn a higher income if I can eliminate some of the competition altogether. Labor unions and other interest groups use the government to do this with mandatory occupational licensing, restrictive trade policies, and explicitly pro-union legislation.

Mandatory Occupational Licensing

One way to restrict entry into a field is to require a permit or license to work in a particular occupation. With fewer legal practitioners, consumers pay higher prices while those with licenses have higher incomes. With these artificial barriers to entry, incumbents are protected from a set of potential challengers. As a result, the *relatively* unskilled face fewer labor supply options. Again, many minorities and the poor in general are especially harmed. As before, a special interest group extracts concentrated benefits from the general public which bears diffuse and subtle costs.

To make a restriction more palatable, advocates need to find "good stories" that make it seem as if mandatory licensing will benefit consumers—to improve quality or safety.[31] But it is easy to support the contention that those who pursue licensing primarily have their own interests in mind: suppliers always have an incentive to restrict competition; licensing arrangements are usually the result of lobbying by producers, not consumers; violations of licensing laws are almost always reported by producers, not consumers; and the incumbents inevitably seek "grandfather clauses," exempting themselves from the new standards. (If concern for the consumer was paramount, all practitioners would have to comply with the higher standards.)

Licensing causes problems only when it is mandatory. In the absence of mandates, one would still see licensing of some sort in many fields, serving as a signal of quality. But in that case, consumers would still have the freedom to legally choose someone who was unlicensed, and workers would have the option to avoid the licensing process if they could otherwise illustrate their competence. For example, if you want assistance with your tax returns, you are not required to use a certified public accountant (CPA) and you do not have to pass the CPA exam to file tax returns for others.[32]

Some of the most unfortunate examples of this occur in transportation (cabs and vans) and cosmetology. (For example, if you operate in these markets without a license, you can be fined or imprisoned.[33]) These jobs would normally be quite attractive to the poor and relatively unskilled, since the set-up costs and requisite skills are minimal. But despite small natural/economic barriers, the artificial/political barriers are large and often prohibitive. Removing opportunities from some producers and consumers to protect other producers from competition is hardly righteous or just.

There are also restrictions in the labor market for health services. Nurse practitioners and physicians' assistants are restricted from providing the care they gave to our soldiers in the Vietnam and Persian Gulf wars. If their efforts were good enough for our soldiers, why aren't they good enough for other citizens? The answer is that these policies are a successful effort by the AMA to restrict competition.[34] The result is higher health care costs and reduced employment options for the relatively unskilled.

Other Pro-Union Legislation

A labor union is simply a cartel in a labor market.[35] As with a cartel in a product market, suppliers have an incentive to collude and restrict quantity in order to get higher "prices"—here, higher wages and other compensation. But with union labor costs artificially high, potential non-union entrants have an incentive to enter the market and underbid the incumbents. Thus, like virtually all other cartels, unions would be unable to gain above-market wages and compensation without government help in restricting competition.

The government has enforced and strengthened these cartels in a number of ways. With the National Labor Relations Act of 1935, unions gained substantial bargaining strength in dealing with firms. And the fact that only about one-third of the states have "Right-to-Work" laws increases the monopoly power of unions. In the absence of these laws, all workers in a company must join the representing union *and* pay full dues. The historical union penchant for violence is simply a variation on the theme of using force to restrict competition. Physical harm (or the threat of it) serves to make non-union members think at least twice before competing for a union job or replacing a striking union member. In order to be effective, a union must prevent non-union workers from taking very attractive jobs.

Taken together, this is an agenda to restrict competition for union labor, allowing them to pocket greater incomes.[36] An upper-middle income group receives indirect income transfers from the general public. Relatively unskilled labor is prevented from competing and earning income in various labor markets. As always, the benefits are concentrated and go to a relatively small group that supports its politicians with a solid bloc of votes and significant campaign contributions. The means and ends hardly constitute an agenda for justice.[37]

III. Improving the Equity and Efficiency of the Tax Code

As commonly proposed, a flat tax would apply a constant (lower) tax rate to all types of income above a certain level—allowing for large personal deductions for taxpayers and their dependents. Other than that, only deductions for home mortgage interest and charitable donations would possibly remain. No one knows exactly what level of flat tax rates and personal deductions would allow the government to raise as much money as the current tax code. There is also considerable speculation about how much a flat tax would spur economic growth. In any case, Christians should embrace substantive reform in payroll taxes and state income taxes. Clearly, reforming the tax system would have many advantages for the economy and especially for the working poor.

First, a flat tax would be much more efficient. Preparation for April 15th would be far easier, saving time and money. The instruction packet for the 1040 form estimates that the average person requires more than 16 hours to file a 1040 with itemized deductions. With a ten-line tax form, we would eliminate most of the 5.4 billion hours Americans currently waste in completing their tax returns.[38]

Lowering the marginal tax rates on income would also spur productive behavior, and thus, encourage economic growth. Those who face lower tax rates are likely to work harder and innovate more aggressively since they can keep more of the fruit of their labors. And a flat tax would end federal income tax on more of the lower-middle class and further diminish the "welfare dilemma"—government would no longer reduce their rewards for work through income taxation, and thus, fewer people would find welfare as tempting.

Second, in many ways, a flat tax would be far more equitable than the current system. It would end the "marriage penalty"—a higher tax rate on some married couples than if they were single. In addition, more lower-middle-class workers would be removed from the tax rolls altogether. Under most proposals, families of four with incomes below, for example $30,000, would be exempt from federal income taxation. (Actually, at present, relatively few people pay very much in income taxes.[39]) Further, it would be more equitable since all people would be treated equally—taxed at the same marginal rate.

Although some of the wealthy would pay less in taxes, many would pay more. Recent history illustrates this concept well. In 1981, marginal tax *rates* on the wealthiest fell, but the proportion of total tax *revenues* from the wealthy increased; in 1990 and 1993, tax rates on the wealthy rose, but the proportion of tax revenues from the wealthy declined. Why? Largely because they changed their behavior in response to modifications in the tax code.[40] Is the goal to have higher tax rates *on* the rich or to collect greater tax revenues *from* the rich?[41] Moreover, a flat tax would limit redistribution to the non-poor through the government's use of subsidies and other loopholes in formulating tax policy.[42] And it would end the indirect redistribution to accountants and lawyers resulting from an unnecessarily complex tax code.

If a flat tax becomes more popular, we can expect to hear reasons why it would be bad for the country. As always, special interest groups will emerge to defend the status quo, protecting their interests by trying to persuade us that useful reform will be harmful.[43] In any case, the efficiency, equity, and sheer simplicity of the flat tax would make the inevitability of Uncle Sam reaching into our wallets far less painful.

Likewise, Christians need to decide whether it is appropriate for them to defend *their* subsidies in the tax code—any benefits they might receive as members of an interest group, and more generally, deductions for home mortgage interest and charitable contributions. For reasons we will cover later, substantive welfare reform would be easier maintaining the latter. But the home mortgage interest deduction is strictly a subsidy, largely pocketed by relatively wealthy home-buyers.[44] As Jeremiah 6:13 warns: "from the least to the greatest, all are greedy for gain; prophets and priests alike all practice deceit." Are we willing to surrender our subsidies?

Although federal income taxes receive the bulk of the public's attention to taxation, it turns out that state income taxes and Social Security payroll taxes also have a major impact, especially on the working poor. Note, first of all, that the Social Security and Medicare taxes are a flat tax (7.65%), but without any income exempted at lower income levels.[45] If a flat tax is appropriate in that context, why not also with respect to income taxes? Actually, the Social Security tax (6.2%) is clearly worse than a flat tax because no income is exempt and the amount of income taxed is capped (at $80,400 in 2001).[46] Thus, the first dollar earned is taxed at 7.65% and high income earners only have a portion of their incomes taxed.[47] Instead, for the equity and efficiency reasons detailed above, it would be far better to provide a sizable income exemption for the working poor and remove the income cap from the wealthy.[48]

Likewise, a number of states impose income taxes on the working poor. Of the 42 states with an income tax, 19 impose them on those at the poverty line.[49] Alabama imposes taxes on working families with the lowest incomes[50] ($4,600); Kentucky imposes the largest burden on a working family at the poverty line ($596 on a 2001 income of $18,104 for a family of four). In total, even though a family at the poverty line would pay no federal income taxes, they would pay $1,386 in Social Security and Medicare taxes and, in Kentucky, $596 in state income taxes—more than $165 per month![51] Another key issue is sales and excise taxes which are typically "regressive" (imposing a higher percentage tax on those with lower incomes). Although less obvious than income taxes, sales taxes are sufficiently large enough to vault others states above Kentucky in terms of total taxes imposed on the poor. Washington heads this list, taking 17.6% of the poor's income in taxes.[52]

Flat state and federal income taxes with sizable exemptions, the elimination of the Social Security tax for those below the poverty line, and the reduction or elimination of sales taxes would greatly promote freedom and justice—two prominent Biblical themes. It would reduce the reach of government and it would eliminate much of the political market activity surrounding the tax code. And notably, it would emulate the Old Testament concept of the tithe. As Joel Belz points out, "it's noteworthy that God never established one tithe for the wealthy and another for the poor and common folk. The rate was the same, and we can assume that God considers that as just."[53]

IV. Education: Dumbing Down Students and Taking Taxpayers to School[54]

College students at public universities receive vast subsidies in the form of reduced in-state tuition rates. In 1996, the average tuition at state colleges was less than $2,100 while the average expenditure per student was about $10,800.[55] In addition, many students have access to a variety of student grants and subsidized loans. Proponents usually argue that these subsidies enable economically disadvantaged young people to have an opportunity to more easily attend college. While true in some instances, the low quality of public elementary and secondary education for most poor families makes concerns about college attendance seem misplaced. In fact, these subsidies are mostly pocketed by the middle and upper classes whose kids constitute the bulk of undergraduate and graduate students at public universities.[56] Thus, subsidized tuition and loans usually amount to an income transfer to people in middle and upper income brackets.

Perhaps the largest policy issue facing America today is the monopoly power of public education providers at the elementary and secondary levels. As we detailed in chapter 7, the current system is akin to being forced to eat at the government-run restaurant in your neighborhood. As a result, consumers often have an unpalatable menu of social issues shoved down their throats. But here, our focus is the subsequent low quality of education available to the poor and the injustice of the redistribution which occurs in this market because of its artificially high cost. (Those who operate government-run schools with tremendous monopoly power may not respond to the incentives inherent in such a system—but we're certainly asking for trouble with this institutional arrangement.)

Government monopolies are not typically paragons of virtue with respect to efficiency, productivity, and consumer satisfaction.[57] In this context, government schools often provide a service which is high-cost, low-quality, and relatively unconcerned with innovations in teaching. Concerning quality, it is amusing and noteworthy that public school teachers send their kids to private schools at more than double the national average.[58] This is analogous to an employee refusing *free* products or services at their place of employment—to pay full price for an expensive product elsewhere.

As before, the monopoly power enables protected producers (those working in the government school system) to benefit at the expense of consumers (students and parents) and taxpayers. In essence, such a system is as much (or moreso) about employing adults than it is about teaching children. Public sector unions are able to dig into the relatively deep pockets of taxpayers, imposing small per-person costs on a large population while avoiding competition and taking home higher salaries. As a result, in 1999, the cost per student in public schools was $8,092, whereas private school costs average $4,983.[59] (New York, New Jersey, Connecticut, and Washington D.C. all spend more than $11,200 per student.[60]) Overall spending was $382 billion—about $5,400 in taxes from the average family of four.[61]) Thus, as a rough estimate, the increased cost of the government providing schools instead of the private sector is as much as $115.5 billion per year ($1,650 in federal, state, and local taxes from the average family of four).[62]

Beyond the redistribution through the tax code, the big losers in this game are the students, particularly those whose parents cannot afford alternatives to the government schools—most notably the low-income, inner-city poor.[63] If schools are bad in the middle-class suburbs, most parents can afford to send their children to private schools. But this option is largely unavailable to those in the inner city. With more control over the market, inner-city government schools have a "captive audience." The subsequent low quality is predictable and a supreme injustice. As Ralph Reed wryly notes, "In the 1960's, George Wallace stood in the schoolhouse door to keep minority children out; today it is liberals who stand in the schoolhouse door to keep them in. They oppose efforts to provide school choice to those who are trapped in schools that are war zones."[64] The easiest way to ensure a lifetime of abject material poverty is to provide someone with a ninth-grade education and send them out into the world.

The current system also increases spiritual poverty by producing minds that are ill-equipped to think and discern truth.

Of course, there are many difficult problems within inner-city schools. But ending the government monopoly with educational vouchers for the poor and lower-middle class (or tax credits to support charitable scholarships for the poor) would be an easy way to make a big difference.[65] In a nutshell, through vouchers, the poor would be empowered to go to the private or public school of their choice. (At worst, they would be just as well off since they could simply choose to remain in their current situation.) Increased competition would provide better incentives for producers. And under a voucher system, taxpayers would save thousands of dollars for every student who uses the voucher.

Vouchers are not an abdication of government responsibility in the market for education, but merely a recognition that government should empower parents to obtain schooling for their children, not operate the schools.[66] We make the same distinction with food stamps—government empowers people to buy food, but doesn't operate the grocery stores.[67] Other reforms might work, but it seems unlikely. It is improbable that one can tinker with a socialistic monopoly in a world of original sin and obtain optimal results. With vouchers, we introduce the incentives of a private sector, market-based, competitive system. We would allow the inner-city poor to escape the monopolistic, socialistic, high-cost, low-quality system that nearly promises them a life of poverty. This would improve educational quality, lower taxes, promote innovation and flexibility in education—and if the effort is led by Christians, bring glory to God.[68]

If we became advocates of substantive educational reform, Christians could be responsible for ending slavery of another sort—the children of the poor in bondage to pathetic schools and having to endure the subsequent low standards of living.[69] We would be defending the rights of others—inner-city children who deserve a better education and taxpayers who are currently shouldering too large of a burden for that education.

That said, Christians need to count the costs of fighting the status quo. As always, one should expect interest groups and their politicians to fight reform tooth and nail. In fact, they would be the only ones to lose. (Sadly, the elected officials who vote against educational vouchers frequently send their own children to private schools.[70]) If these are battles worth fighting, understanding the mechanism by which redistribution takes place is the key. Until the costs of government intervention become easy-to-see, the protesting screams of passionate defenders of the status quo will carry the day. As a matter of justice, Christians should not be deterred from fighting for the rights of others—especially the poor.

Chapter 11:
Why and How Christians Should Legislate Justice (Part 4) Redistribution to the Poor— Ethical and Practical Concerns

A Call to Government?

Substantial zeal for the plight of the poor and an avid faith in government have led many Christians on the Religious Left to embrace government activism in economic matters.[1] Although this view has become less prominent with the recent failure of socialistic economies and a growing disenchantment with current domestic policies, the desire for—and pursuit of—government solutions remains prevalent.

This advocacy is primarily based on two beliefs. First, there is the general perception that socialism is "less harsh" than capitalism and that government interventions are necessary to "smooth the rough edges" of free markets. Although market outcomes are often troublesome—business failures, displaced workers, and so on—it is doubtful that political markets are any substantive improvement over economic markets, especially toward the poor.[2] As we have seen, interest groups are rather adept at subtly redistributing money from the general public, including the poor. Second, many infer from Scripture that government activism—in particular, redistribution to the poor—is an appropriate or even the optimal means to pursue "economic justice." On the surface, there would seem to be an effective argument for this belief: the people of Israel and the early church lived under a system which resembled socialism.[3]

From the Old Testament, Deuteronomy 15:7-10 instructs: "If there is a poor man among your brothers...be openhanded and freely lend him whatever he needs. Be careful not to harbor this wicked thought: "the seventh year, the year for canceling debts, is near," so that you do not show ill will toward your brother and give him nothing...Give generously to him and do so without a grudging heart." Although this speaks primarily of lending, it also implies outright gifts, given the command to retire unpaid debts every seven years. Exodus 22:25 directly instructs the Israelites to "charge no interest" on loans to the "needy."[4] Leviticus 19:10 is even more explicit: "Do not go over your vineyard a second time or pick up the grapes that have fallen. Leave them for the poor and the alien."[5] Leviticus 25 describes the "year of Jubilee" when indentured servants were to be released from their obligations and property was released to its original owner (equitably determined by God when the land was first apportioned).[6]

From the New Testament's description of the early church, Acts 2:44-45 reports that "all the believers were together and had everything in common. Selling their possessions and goods, they gave to anyone as he had need." This sounds remarkably similar to the famous statement by Karl Marx: "From each according to his ability, to each according to his need." Acts 4:32-35 continues: "No one claimed that any of his possessions was his own, but they shared everything they had...There were no needy persons among them. For from time to time those who owned lands or houses sold them, brought the money from the sales and put it at the apostles' feet, and it was distributed to anyone as he had need."[7] In II Corinthians 8:14, Paul encourages financial support of the impoverished church at Jerusalem: "At the present time your plenty will supply what they need, so that in turn their plenty will supply what you need. Then there will be equality..."[8]

Christ's teachings also point to helping the poor and needy. In the "Parable of the Good Samaritan," Jesus described the call to love our neighbor—in this case, a man who was robbed and beaten within an inch of his life.[9] Two religious leaders passed him by, but a Samaritan stopped and rendered aid. He brought the victim to a nearby town, paid for two months of lodging, and promised to return and pay for any other expenses. Christ closes the parable by encouraging his audience to deal with its "neighbors" in the same manner.[10]

We worship a God who helps the needy and instructs His followers to do the same. Moreover, the early Christian church—often used as a model for the contemporary church—lived out socialism of a sort; income and wealth went into a common pool to be distributed by their leaders as necessary. It is easy to understand why some have interpreted these verses as a call to pursue socialism or government intervention—the idea that government should be a "good Samaritan" to those in need.[11]

However, there are two crucial distinctions between these examples and a Biblical call to pursue government activism of this type. First, they describe voluntary behavior; in contrast, government intervention is coercive by definition.[12] Advocacy of government activism in welfare policy requires that one endorse forcibly taking money from one party to give to another.[13] Note also that there is a fine line here between a moral duty to assist and a moral right to receive assistance. To say that Christians have an obligation to give to the poor is not to imply that the poor have a right to a Christian's possessions.[14] Further, there is no implied right for Christians (or others) to take money from others to give to the needy. Second, the Israelites and the early church were local efforts on a relatively small scale where socialistic (communal) living can be more effective. In contrast, government activity is often non-local and is almost always conducted on a large scale. In a word, the Bible does not advocate greater government involvement, but instead, greater personal involvement from Christians.

The "Good Samaritan's Dilemma"

Short-run financial assistance can promote long-term dependence. Franklin D. Roosevelt was concerned about this aspect of welfare: "Continued dependence upon relief induces a spiritual and moral disintegration fundamentally destructive to the national fiber. To dole out relief in this way is to administer a narcotic, a subtle destroyer of the human spirit."[15] Those who have worked with the long-term dependent will recognize this as an atrophy of decision-making capability, confidence, and self-esteem. Similarly, many parents are cautious about buying candy for their children because they know the purchase may have long-term implications. Rules against feeding bears in national parks are based on the same principle. Distinguishing between those who will and will not respond well is crucial to providing effective assistance. Thus, uniform giving is unlikely to discern motives and specific needs. In short, it can be a significant challenge to help people in the short-run without hurting them in the long-run.

Of course, not all recipients become addicted to aid. But dependence becomes more likely as assistance increases in amount, uniformity, or length of time. In the context of welfare, certainly there are those who will voluntarily work despite high benefit reduction rates, receiving little financially from the fruits of their labor. Likewise, the early church, some communes, and kibbutzes in Israel are groups based on voluntary socialistic principles. But participants in these groups are driven by more than economic incentives.

Even in these special cases, incentive problems are still present. Again, the example of the early Christian church is instructive. Acts 5 relates the story of Ananias and Sapphira, a couple who voluntarily sold a piece of property and claimed to give the entire proceeds to the church. Instead, they kept part of the money for themselves. By lying to the apostles, the couple responded to the economic disincentives at the expense of their stated religious beliefs. The same tension is evident throughout Paul's letters to the early churches. Paul encourages work, condemns laziness, and discourages financial dependency on others. His most famous comment on this topic: "If a man will not work, he shall not eat...[They should] settle down and earn the bread they eat."[16]

In sum, providing financial assistance can easily have detrimental short-run and long-run implications. The Bible does not endorse governmental welfare efforts, blanket solutions for disparate problems and motivations, or indefinite assistance to those capable of supporting themselves. Instead, the Bible encourages Christians to voluntarily help the poor with individually-tailored solutions designed to empower recipients to lead productive lives.

The "Welfare Dilemma"

Before we compare government and charitable efforts to help the poor, we need a framework to understand the problems associated with redistribution to the poor in general. To begin with, the variables in a generic government welfare program are: (1) a maximum benefit level (with no earned income); (2) a "dollar cut-off point"—when earned income becomes high enough that benefits are eliminated; and (3) a "benefit reduction rate" as earned income increases. (For now, assume that assistance is given indiscriminately and indefinitely.) The idea behind the benefit reduction rate is that recipients will need less financial assistance as their earned incomes increase. Unfortunately, the subsequent problem is that reducing benefits necessarily diminishes the financial incentive to get off welfare—thus, decreasing incentives to work, form a family, save money, and so on.[17]

Today, the poor are eligible for a variety of "means-tested" welfare programs that are tied to (low) income levels and household status: Medicaid, housing vouchers, food stamps, and so on. The relevant benefit reduction rate is the sum of the rates for all of the programs for which a recipient is eligible. In practice, the loss of benefits (especially government-provided health insurance), combined with income and Social Security taxes, child care costs, and so on, often makes work prohibitively costly.

Why not lower the benefit reduction rate to provide better incentives? To do so, one would also have to decrease the maximum benefit level or increase the cutoff point. Unfortunately, these options are also unpalatable. The dilemma is that policymakers need to 1.) provide a benefit level high enough for the truly needy to survive; 2.) establish a dollar cutoff point for benefits that is low enough to avoid extending the disincentives and costs of the program well into the middle class; and 3.) determine a benefit reduction rate low enough to limit work disincentives. With a welfare policy that renders assistance indefinitely and indiscriminately, it is impossible to reach all three goals at the same time. As such, welfare efforts of this type—a summary of our government's pre-1996 efforts—do not hold any satisfactory answers.[18]

Fortunately, with the welfare reforms in 1996, government efforts have departed somewhat from bureaucratic and federal efforts providing indiscriminate and indefinite assistance. Moreover, with the "Charitable Choice" provision of the 1996 reform, religiously-based programs are not supposed to be discriminated against in favor of secular programs.

Why Emphasize Voluntary, Private Charity vs. Coercive, Government Welfare?

For God

As we have discussed throughout the book, the Bible portrays a God of freedom. He wants us to praise and glorify Him of our own volition. What is the value of coerced praise and righteousness? He gives us free will—to do right or wrong, to follow Him or to disobey. In fact, moral decisions require the freedom to make those decisions. Likewise, the Bible encourages voluntary giving; coerced giving is not particularly glorifying to God. To support the poor, charity voluntarily given out of love trumps taxation involuntarily "given" out of fear. Going back to Acts 5:4, Peter makes it clear that Ananias and Sapphira's offering was not compulsory: "Didn't it belong to you before it was sold? And after it was sold, wasn't the money at your disposal?" Even the Old Testament prescribed that offerings for the Tabernacle were to be "from each man whose heart prompts him to give."[19]

The Bible's most famous comments on this subject are Paul's writings in II Corinthians 8-9. Paul speaks of "rich generosity," "eager willingness," "eagerness to help," and "a generous gift, not as one grudgingly given." Describing the charity of the Macedonian church, Paul writes: "They gave as much as they were able, and even beyond their ability. Entirely on their own, they urgently pleaded with us for the privilege of sharing in this service..." Advising the Corinthians, Paul concludes: "Each man should give what he has decided in his heart to give, not reluctantly or under compulsion, for God loves a cheerful giver." The charitable efforts of the early church fully preserved personal property rights and relied on voluntary efforts to redistribute to those in need.[20] Even Christ's feeding miracles created wealth rather than merely redistributing it.[21] In contrast, government activism compromises freedom (and thus, virtue) by the forcible redistribution of income. How much is God honored by us voting to take our neighbor's money to care for the needy?

Moreover, if we do not mandate contributions within the church, why should we advocate using instruments of force on the world? Paul explicitly did not "command" that the Macedonians give (II Corinthians 8:8); why should we advocate taxation which commands all to give? In fact, God's call to justice and the prescribed mechanisms for redistribution apply only to the individual Christian and the Church, not to society as a whole. When Christians respond to this call, the church's impact as "light in the darkness" can be especially powerful. A pagan emperor, Julian the Apostate, noticed the transformed lifestyles of Christians in this context: "the godless Galileans [Christians] feed not only their poor but ours also."[22] Perhaps the bottom line is that when Christians use the State as a tool, some glory may go to God, but more is likely to go to the State.

For Others

To the extent that voluntary efforts are able to meet needs, there are many reasons to believe that such assistance tends to be more beneficial to recipients. One factor is that bureaucrats have different incentives from those who help the poor voluntarily. Bureaucrats are often more interested in expanding their budgets than in helping people per se—a mindset of "when in doubt, give it out." When bureaucrats use our money to help others, it is unlikely they will spend it as carefully as we would. Such indiscriminate giving enhances fraud and is not helpful in the context of the Good Samaritan's Dilemma. Moreover, intimate concern for recipients seems less likely in a more centralized, large-scale program since the aid is more impersonal. "The State moves through machinery while the individual and the group move through the hand-clasp and the heart-throb."[23] In contrast, pre-20th century efforts were often centered in the church where members responded to Biblical imperatives to help the poor. In general, volunteers, giving their own time and money, are people who care more deeply about the poor.

From a Christian perspective, government programs are also wrong-headed in that they promote idolatry of, and dependence on, the State. Taxpayers look to the State to solve yet another social problem, and of course, recipients are led to rely on the State. In other words, the use of tax monies to render financial assistance to the materially poor may increase moral poverty in both the donor and the recipient. The donor has a diminished sense of obligation to his fellow man and is divorced from the process of helping the poor.[24] The recipient is left with a system which often fails to respect the dignity of the human person and fails to promote values that would allow one to rise from material and spiritual poverty.

Most important, government programs naturally fail to place any emphasis on spiritual issues. Without a spiritual component, material recovery is less likely and spiritual "recovery" is ignored.[25] For this reason, if no other, Christians should be leery of government activism, and instead, should be personally active in this arena. As Herbert Schlossberg notes: "'Serving the poor' is a euphemism for destroying the poor unless it includes with it the intention of seeing the poor begin to serve others, and thereby validate the words of Jesus that it is more blessed to give than to receive."[26]

Finally, to the extent that welfare programs move to the private sector, we improve the well-being of taxpayers. Of course, taxes would decrease in the short-term. (The average family of four pays nearly $6,000 in taxes to support current efforts.[27]) But in addition, to the extent that Christian charity would be more effective than public welfare, our efforts would result in more productive citizens instead of perpetuating a government system that can only promise massive, long-term redistribution.

For Ourselves

In the story of the "rich young ruler," Christ tells the man to sell everything and give it to the poor.[28] Not only was Christ's injunction a precondition for the man to follow Him, it was also in the man's best interests to do so. Although money may not hold the status of an idol in our own lives, God still instructs us to care for the poor and needy. If God says so, by definition, it must be in our best interests—with respect to earthly ramifications and/or heavenly rewards.

From another angle, it is what God expects from us. As Geoffrey Brennan asks about Matthew 25: "Will it, I wonder, be any response to Christ's charge to visit prisoners, or feed the hungry, to respond: 'Well, no Lord, I didn't. But I did pay my taxes, and I did vote for prison reform and food stamps'? Will it be adequate to respond: 'Well, no. But I made those other guys do it?'"

Of course, you may not be called to lifetime ministry with the poor or to a life of self-imposed poverty. But Christians should prayerfully consider this mission field as well—at least on a part-time basis. The needs are as diverse as our gifts. Our God-given talents can be harnessed by the Spirit for charitable efforts. Different ministries within the church allow for specialization and teamwork. The key is giving of ourselves, becoming involved in individual lives, loving others, and glorifying God.

Civil Society and Culture: Why Local/Individual vs. Federal/Blanket Solutions?

For whatever reason, we live in a time where most people look first to government for solutions to a myriad of problems. Government is clearly equipped to handle certain tasks relatively well—areas where markets struggle to provide socially optimal outcomes, such as "public goods" (e.g., national defense, city streets) and "externalities" (e.g., pollution). But over the course of this century, government has increasingly become involved well beyond this scope and the results have been far less than optimal.[29]

There is an interesting correlation here: the size and scope of government have increased as other social institutions have diminished. One can interpret this as government rushing in to fill the needs abandoned by other social institutions or as government crowding out the efforts of these institutions. In any case, in the context of poverty—where government efforts have resulted in unsatisfactory outcomes and where other social institutions have a record of past and present success— these other social institutions should be relied upon and encouraged to do more.

The sum of these voluntary, social institutions is referred to as "civil society." These organizations range from professional to religious, from familial to community, and from civic to advocacy.[30] In each case, they address important social concerns—ranging from entertainment to raising children. In the context of helping the needy, it should be clear that voluntary organizations—especially churches—play a significant role today and could provide a more substantive role in the future. In fact, in our inner cities—with their moral and material poverty—churches are often the only remaining vestige of civil society.

The idea that it is useful to have a range of institutions to provide for a variety of needs—and a bias toward having those needs met in as local a setting as possible—has a number of labels. Catholics call it "subsidiarity"[31]; Protestants (particularly Reformed) call it "sphere sovereignty"[32]; in secular/political terms, it is referred to as "federalism." In a word, it is the idea that individuals should have their needs addressed through the most local method that is effective. Family should provide for and take care of its own; if that is not sufficient, then extended family should step up. As Paul wrote, "If anyone does not provide for his relatives, and especially for his immediate family, he has denied the faith and is worse than an unbeliever."[33] If that does not work effectively, then local, voluntary organizations should become involved; and so on. In sum, "A community of a higher order should not interfere in the internal life of a community of a lower order, depriving the latter of its functions, but rather should support it in case of need..."[34]

The arguments for this are both moral and prudential. The Bible emphasizes individual responsibility and ministering to people on a one-to-one basis. In Genesis 2:18, God shows intimate concern for Adam in noticing his subjective feelings, observing that "it is not good for the man to be alone." And Christ had individual prescriptions for the people with whom he dealt. Among those who need assistance, "the one thing they lack" may vary considerably. Thus, Christians should focus their energies on working with the poor directly. As Francis Schaeffer said, we should avoid giving more power to the "monolithic monster of a bloated state" and instead emphasize the "compassionate use of accumulated wealth."[35] The focus should be on individual action, not invoking the powers of the State.

When local, voluntary organizations are able and willing to meet needs, they have a number of other likely advantages. In most cases, local, voluntary organizations are more likely to recognize, address, and meet physical and especially emotional and spiritual needs; they are more likely to render assistance in a way that upholds the dignity of the human person—for both the donor and the recipient; and their activities will work to enhance community.[36] (Of course, depending on the context, different elements of civil society will be more or less effective.) It is often easier for them to monitor the behavior of recipients and to discern true need; fraud and long-term dependency (the Good Samaritan's Dilemma) become less likely. In contrast, when aid is distributed from a distance, aidgivers are less able to discern between those who will use welfare as a hammock rather than as a safety net. Moreover, intimate concern for recipients seems less likely in a more centralized, large-scale program since the aid is more impersonal. And to the extent that guilt is a factor, recipients are more likely to abuse a system that involves an impersonal donor rather than an individual with a face.

Instead, since government now does what individuals should do voluntarily, we are left with the current welfare system: "the ultimate in bureaucracy—an anonymous public supporting anonymous machinery supporting anonymous clients."[37] Without intimate knowledge of those we are trying to help, it is difficult to provide effective solutions. As Jim Wallis criticizes: "Liberalism became captive to large distant institutions and impersonal bureaucracies that are more concerned with control than caring, and the result became more dependency than empowerment."[38]

This view does not at all eliminate a role for government, but merely provides boundaries for its activities, identifies likely strengths and weaknesses of the actions of government and civil society, and establishes goals for the future. When lower-order organizations are unable or unwilling to assist, then government has an obligation to step forward and assist the needy. It follows from this view that the first line of offense in the poverty war should be the family. Although helpful in some situations, one would have to say that, society-wide, this first line is cannibalizing itself. Since the 1960's, divorce and especially illegitimacy rates have increased dramatically. Thus, not only are families today less capable of helping those in need, but they are in themselves, creating much more need. The obvious conclusion is that public policy and private efforts must target the efficacy of the family structure. Much more will be said about this in the next chapter.

Why Categorization and Discernment vs. Indiscriminate and Indefinite Giving?

Moving toward local and voluntary efforts would clearly be an improvement. But what is the "best way" to help the needy? Some need a helping hand; others need a push; some need a combination of the two. Some need transportation; others need child care; others need resume preparation or basic job skills. Only an approach that categorizes and discerns can hope to determine effective solutions. Local and voluntary efforts are more capable of providing these solutions because they are usually closer to the action.[39] As a government program becomes more centralized, it is less likely that a bureaucrat will be willing or able to categorize and discern. This is the most important consideration since indiscriminate and indefinite assistance—no matter who the aidgiver—is unlikely to be helpful. Well-designed assistance provides time, money, and individual prescriptions for individual problems.

Why is the Samaritan in Christ's parable an appropriate model for our acts of charity? When rendering assistance, the Samaritan was confident that the circumstances were beyond the recipient's control. The key was local involvement along with the use of categorization and discernment. The Samaritan knew that disincentives were not likely to be a problem in this case; fraud and long-term abuse were unlikely.

Marvin Olasky documents that pre-20th century charitable organizations frequently used "work tests" to separate out the truly needy from the lazy: men chopped wood and women sewed to earn their keep.[40] These "tests" allowed discernment and taught good work habits.[41] Further, since the fruits of their labor were donated to the *truly* needy, it drew a clear distinction between the able and the helpless. Taken together, work tests and confrontation serve to minimize the Good Samaritan's Dilemma.[42] Olasky notes that this "tough love" was often counter to an initial instinct to provide unconditional assistance. Leaders in the charitable movement had to encourage their new volunteers to stifle the impulse to provide immediate aid.

Without discernment, well-intentioned aid could actually harm a recipient. Or as Ron Sider asks, "Is justice rather than continual charity the result?"[43] Categorization and discernment identify specific solutions to specific problems; they provide self-control mechanisms for those who want to end their dependence on the dole; they teach aid recipients that they can help those who truly can't help themselves. Finally, categorization and discernment provide more vision and hope for those who are trying to help.[44]

Notably, three times in I Timothy 5, Paul says to help those who are "*really* in need," implying that some in the early church were more "in need" than others. Paul was teaching against the incentive problems inherent in any charity or welfare program. Implicitly, he was encouraging an increase in monitoring and discernment to stem the tendency to take advantage of others' charity.

And when did Christ give people food? Notably, one of the first things we read about in Christ's life is how he withstood the temptation from Satan to turn stones into bread. Likewise, throughout his ministry, he mostly refused to use his powers to feed the masses. On the two occasions where Scripture records feeding miracles, the people had listened to his preaching all day and were not in a position to acquire food. In a word, the Good Samaritan's Dilemma was minimal.

Christians who have a passion to care for the poor often recite Matthew 25: "When I was hungry, you gave me food; when I was thirsty, you gave me drink..." But as Olasky notes, indiscriminate giving can be sinful: "Giving is morally neutral...It depends on what is being given and where the giving is going...Christ does not include in his list of commended charitable acts: 'when I was strung out, you gave me dope...when I abandoned my family, you gave me a place to stay and helped me justify my actions'...If we take Christ's word seriously, then giving money that goes for drugs is akin to sticking heroin into Jesus' veins."[45]

The term "charity" itself comes from the Greek word, *"charis"*—which can also mean gift, grace, and love. The implication is that charity is indeed a gift, not a right—and it must be something good, not just random assistance. Thus, the optimal approach is working with people one-on-one, with assistance tailored to the individual, requiring changed behaviors, practicing tough love, and ultimately, leading people to form or deepen a life-changing relationship with Jesus Christ. None of this is an excuse to avoid helping people, but a call to help, and to help properly. "Let no close-fisted brother hide behind our words, and find in them an excuse not to give at all. What is censured is not giving too much, but giving in the wrong way."[46]

The Nature of Work

The Bible emphasizes the inherent value of work. At the very beginning, even in Eden, Adam and Eve were given work to do in the Garden that was meant to be a blessing. Adam was told to name the animals; Adam and Eve were told to be fruitful and multiply, to exercise dominion over creation, and to care for the land. Moreover, we know that we have been made in the image of a Creator God—a God who finds joy in building and producing, adding value and creating things of value. (In fact, John 5:17 tells us that God is still "working.") Thus, work is defined in a broad sense as anything that creates or adds value. And God intends for us to share His joy— by creatively working and producing, creating, re-creating, and pro-creating in His image.[47] Solomon wrote that "the sleep of a laborer is sweet, whether he eats little or much." Likewise, work is meant to bring us satisfaction and contentment. In a word, God hopes to redeem our work at the foot of the Cross through the empowerment of His Spirit.

Moreover, God condemns sloth and holds us accountable for the work that we do.[48] The Parable of the Talents illustrates that the "good and faithful servant" is commended for putting his resources to work in an effective manner and rewarded by being given more resources over which to exercise his stewardship. In contrast, the "wicked, lazy, worthless servant" is condemned for his failure to take action and to invest his resources prudently—and is punished by having the resources taken away.[49] Thus, public policy and private charity need to make work more attractive and remove barriers from those who wish to engage in productive work.

Note that the Old Testament practice of "gleaning" provided material assistance for the poor and needy, but required work from the recipient. Similarly, Paul's "rule" in II Thessalonians 3:10—"If a man will not work, he shall not eat"—explicitly recognizes the importance of work for those who receive assistance and implicitly recognizes it for those who give assistance and the community as a whole. As such, work of some type should be at the center of efforts to assist the needy. Work can serve as a tool for categorization and discernment; work promotes dignity, develops self-esteem, and builds skills; work allows us to fulfill our inherent need to create value. And it is eminently practical: as Henry Ford noted, "Chop your own wood and it will warm you twice."

A Call to Christian Ministry

Instead of relying on government, Christians are called to live in a radically new way. This includes our efforts to minister to the poor. But Christianity provides more than a moral code to which its believers should adhere. It provides a motive—the opportunity to love a God who wants relationship with us and to extend His grace to others. God provides the means as well, through the Holy Spirit indwelling in the heart of believers. Christ told his disciples: "I will ask the Father, and he will give you...the Spirit of truth. The world cannot accept him, because it neither sees him nor knows him. But you know him, for he lives with you and will be in you."[50] For believers, because "God sent the Spirit of his Son into our hearts...Christ lives in us" and "it is God who works in you to will and to act according to his good purpose."[51] As a result, II Corinthians 5:17 tells us we are "a new creation"—individuals changed by the power of God.

Of course, this requires our participation as well as God's provision. But without this enabling power, it would be like Tiger Woods instructing someone on how to play golf for months and then sending that student to play in the British Open. Despite the lessons, victory or even below-par golf would be unlikely. But if Tiger could play from within his student, the results would be very different. Instead of merely receiving instructions through "the law," Christians can be empowered to live this radically new life with a "new heart," empowered by Christ through the Holy Spirit.[52] Watchman Nee draws an analogy to grafting a branch from a good tree onto a bad tree in order to grow good fruit: "If a man can graft a branch of one tree into another, cannot God take of the life of his Son and, so to speak, graft it into us?"[53]

In sum, there is no relation between the Biblical call to Christians and the advocacy of government to help the poor. In fact, they are diametrically opposed: the use of government to reach certain ends is based on coercion; the change in behavior designed to accompany the Christian's "Spirit-filled life" is voluntary.[54]

Doug Bandow concludes that socialism and income redistribution are inconsistent with Christianity because they "exacerbate the worst of man's flaws. By divorcing effort from reward, stirring up covetousness and envy, and destroying the freedom that is a necessary precondition for virtue, it tears at the just social fabric that Christians should seek to establish."[55] Many Christians have pursued "social justice" and "substantial income equality" in both the domestic and international arenas. However, their prescriptions for politically organized redistribution are often impractical and more important, misinterpret the Biblical call to Christians.[56]

Chapter 12:
Why and How Christians Should Legislate Justice (Part 5)
Past Government Activism and the Poor— Money vs. Compassion

In the last chapter, we covered the theory behind the disincentives inherent in government welfare programs, noting that unfortunate long-term behaviors would become more likely as financial assistance increases in amount, uniformity, or length of time. But in practice, has this translated into a large or a small change in behaviors? For instance, if people inherently want to work (i.e., they will work for little or no financial reward), we would expect the effects to be minimal since people would not typically respond to the economic disincentives. In a word, it is useful to judge the results of the government's War on Poverty.

The War on Poverty

The roots of our current policies extend to the beginning of the 20th century. Welfare programs sprouted before the New Deal, but were rather limited until Lyndon Johnson's Great Society programs of the mid-late-1960's. Since then, although the per-person level of benefits for some programs has diminished at times, overall "social welfare" spending has continuously increased. Moreover, the cultural stigma attached to "illegitimate children" and taxpayer-financed sloth have decreased significantly over the last generation.

Despite elevating standards of living for the poor, many people have come to believe that welfare is too costly for taxpayers (although, outside of expenditures on

Medicaid, it is a surprisingly small part of government spending) and that it is, on net, detrimental to the poor—at least in the long-run. "Poverty today is too often accompanied by social pathologies, deep corrupting vices, and a smoldering despair that Great Society welfare services do little to alleviate, and perhaps much to exacerbate."[1] Following our concerns about the Good Samaritan and Welfare Dilemmas in the last chapter, it should not be surprising that work and family disincentives have borne bitter fruit—in particular, reduced labor force participation and increased illegitimacy rates.

In the late 1960's and early 1970's, social scientists ran a series of experiments to compare the behaviors of a group that received welfare benefits and a "control group." For the longest and best-run efforts, the results were stunning. In particular, the behavior of young males changed dramatically: those who were married reduced their hours worked by 33%; singles decreased theirs by 43%. The experimental group also experienced longer periods of unemployment and 40% more marriage dissolutions.[2]

Moving to the "real world" impact of the War on Poverty, Charles Murray describes the resulting decrease in labor force participation rates after the late-1960's as the "first-ever large-scale voluntary withdrawal from the labor market by able-bodied males."[3] This statistic is even more troubling than high levels of unemployment since these people were not even actively looking for work. Further, if young people do not work early-on, they fail to acquire the skills they will need later in life to earn higher incomes. This outcome is clearly the opposite of one welfare policy goal—to promote long-term independence.

Concerning illegitimacy, one of John F. Kennedy's stated goals for welfare policy was to promote the "integrity and preservation of the family unit."[4] In stark contrast, the rapid increase in single heads-of-household over the last 30 years—particularly among the poor—is extremely troubling. The percentage of children born into black (disproportionately poor) two-parent households remained around 80% in every census from 1890 to 1960.[5] But this percentage fell from 72% in 1968 to 59% in 1980.[6] By 1994, fewer than 30% of births to black women were within two-parent households. Meanwhile, white rates fell from 85% in 1985 to less than 75% in 1994, nearly equal to the rate which motivated Patrick Moynihan to write about the "breakdown of the black family" in 1965.[7] (By 1999, the black rate had improved slightly to 31% while the white rate continued to slide—to 73%.[8])

Is this a matter of race or class? Murray argues that it is a class issue first—that the "rules of the game" changed for the poor who happen to be disproportionately minority.[9] To note, ignoring race, in 1991, women with a high school education or less were responsible for 82% of illegitimate births in the U.S.; women with family incomes under $20,000 were responsible for 69%.[10] Further, 44% of births to white women living below the poverty line were illegitimate; for those above the poverty line, the rate of illegitimacy was only 6%.[11] As Duncan and Hoffman state: "national data still support the claim that schooling and delayed child-bearing are sufficient for most women, black and white, to avoid poverty."[12] When women are paid if they're unemployed and not married to an employed male, we shouldn't be surprised to find an increasing occurrence of such situations. Illegitimacy is increasingly influenced by cultural factors, but is largely an issue of poverty and the policies that affect the poor.

Ironically, these trends either began or became worse just as the programs of the Great Society were substantially funded. Murray notes that the outcomes run counter to what one might have reasonably expected— that great gains against poverty were on the horizon. There had been substantial progress against poverty throughout the 20th century, government was now "serious" about ending poverty, the civil rights movement was well underway, economic growth seemed secure, job training programs had been established, and so on.[13] Victory in the war against poverty seemed to be only a matter of time.

One could claim that the timing of these changes was coincidental, but Murray argues that after the fact, the results were not particularly surprising. The poor simply responded in a rational manner to the incentives of the new programs. Unfortunately, policymakers had assumed that people would naturally want to work and marry, and that the poor and the non-poor would behave identically given similar financial inducements. But it is easy to imagine how $12,000 in welfare benefits might be viewed as a safety net by someone from the middle class and as a hammock by someone who is poor. The key is that the inducement is the same in absolute dollars, but rather different relative to what each can earn in the labor market.

Given the work disincentives and the subsidization of undesirable behaviors, Murray concludes that, despite the good intentions, the reforms of the Great Society were "a blunder on purely pragmatic grounds" and "wrong on moral grounds."[14] The "rules of the game" were changed for the poor in ways that hurt them, especially in the long run. As such, Christians should be sobered by a concept that appears 24 times in I and II Kings—that the Israelite leaders "caused Israel to sin" (through idolatry and so on).[15] Although God holds individuals responsible for their actions, He apparently places some blame on leaders with bad policies. When the government taxes good behavior or subsidizes bad behavior, advocates of such policies may be reaping a stricter judgment.[16]

Battling the Status Quo

As with most other government programs, the growth of welfare was nearly inevitable—at least until its costs became obvious enough to a rationally ignorant and apathetic general public.[17] Political support comes from recipients, "compassionate" voters and politicians, and the bureaucrats who administer the programs. Government agencies are generally driven by the desire to maximize budgets, so bureaucrats always have an incentive to look for new constituents. In the context of welfare programs, this translates into generating greater "need" for income transfers. Until the general failure of the government's War on Poverty became obvious, the momentum was on the side of merely tinkering with the status quo, and of course, spending more money.

Left-wing activist Theresa Funiciello's cynicism toward the U.S. welfare system peaks when she argues that "while poor people have become poorer in the past twenty years, social work has become a growth industry [and has] prospered beyond anyone's wildest dreams... Welfare mothers wanted an adequate guaranteed income, which would have rendered many activities of social welfare professionals meaningless. The agencies wanted a guaranteed income, too; for themselves."[18] As before, bureaucrats and politicians benefit; whether taxpayers or the poor are better off is debatable. But as we have seen before, the status quo will fight substantial reform because they would be made worse off. In the context of welfare, charities with their noses in the government trough and bureaucracies (which will not want to yield control and budget) have been and will continue to be among the biggest impediments to reform.

This general principle is modeled by Judas in John 12:4-6 when he questioned the use of perfume to anoint Christ's feet, feigning an interest in the poor while he had his hand in the till. Judas put his own interests well ahead of those of the poor. Fittingly, Mark 14:10 records that this episode immediately preceded his betrayal of Christ. With improvements in welfare policy and compassion defined as "more spending," a still-strong faith in government's ability to fix social and economic problems, bureaucrats who defend their turf, and a mostly apathetic public, reforming the policies that directly affect the poor is difficult.

That said, the 1996 welfare reform—the "Personal Responsibility and Work Opportunity Reconciliation Act"[19] and its transition from AFDC (Aid to Families with Dependent Children) to TANF (Temporary Assistance to Needy Families)—has shown significant promise. With this dramatic change in policy, government efforts have moved from the federal to the state level, begun to get the private sector more involved, imposed a work requirement within two years, and an overall time limit of five years on recipients.[20] Welfare rolls have declined by more than half, unemployment has dropped, and illegitimacy rates have reversed a decades-long slide—even within a sluggish economy.[21] But some states have been lax in implementing reform, exploiting loopholes in the legislation.[22] What remains to be seen is whether states will choose to or be "persuaded" to improve their welfare efforts and whether the federal reforms will be extended.

Defining Compassion

In modern times, compassion has become a euphemism for "more government funding," whether in education, welfare, foreign aid, etc. But why is it usually taken as *axiomatic* that more money will help? As Dwight Lee has remarked, "the notion that compassion toward the poor requires favoring expansion of government transfer programs has achieved the status of revealed truth."[23] And how compassionate is it to spend other people's money or to promote long-term dependence among recipients? But in fact, indiscriminate giving can easily harm recipients in the short run or the long run. In Charles Murray's words, "When reforms finally do occur, they will happen not because stingy people have won, but because generous people have stopped kidding themselves."[24]

From his influential book, *The Tragedy of American Compassion*, one could argue that Marvin Olasky's most important contribution to the welfare debate is how he reclaims the moral high ground by properly defining "compassion." He notes that those who give money are often the stingy ones since they fail to give what is truly needed—time and personal involvement. Too often, writing a check is mislabeled charity because its primary accomplishment is in soothing one's conscience with indiscriminate giving.[25]

Although Olasky is critical of most government efforts, he repeatedly cautions that the key ingredient is personal involvement; a private charity dispensing aid indiscriminately is little improvement. "Change in poverty fighting is needed, but Americans need to be clear about the reasons for change. Governmental welfare programs need to be fought not because they are too expensive—although clearly much money is wasted—but because they are inevitably too stingy in what is really important..."[26]

There are a number of potential criticisms to these proposals. Bureaucrats will argue that only trained specialists can help the poor. Advocates for the status quo will claim that reformers "don't (truly) care" about the poor and only want to reduce their tax burdens. But aside from bureaucratic self-interests and widely disparate worldviews, a larger issue seems to be that many opponents of substantive reform lack the courage to risk allowing people to suffer in the short run to encourage their progress in the long run. Bill Bennett notes that "virtue by itself is no guarantee of right action, which requires more than good intentions. We need in addition both the wisdom to know what the right thing to do is, and the will to do it."[27] Or perhaps they're so focused on material goals that they are implicitly willing to make trade-offs with respect to dignity, self-actualization, and so on. In any case, too often, aidgivers are too short-sighted or do not have the will necessary to provide the tough love that would be truly compassionate.

Defining Poverty

Kristen Kraakevik draws a useful distinction between moral and material poverty. One can be morally and materially rich, morally and materially poor, morally rich and materially poor, or morally poor and materially rich. Because the government can only focus on material poverty, it is unable to address either combination that includes moral poverty. And unfortunately, "giving money to those who are materially poor has [had] the unintended consequence of increasing moral poverty in both the donor and the recipient."[28] The challenge then is channeling the morally and materially rich to financially assist the materially poor and spiritually challenge the morally poor.

Thus, spiritual or moral poverty is at the heart of both the problems of poverty and the best prospective solutions. The materially poor suffer from a combination of poor moral character and oppression by those with poor moral character. And despite tremendous material wealth—which could translate into means to address poverty—the non-poor largely ignore their moral obligation to be concerned for the needy. They focus exclusively on a narrow version of stewardship over their corner of creation and fail to understand that their position in this world is a product of their work as well as a gift from God.

It follows, then, that the non-poor have much to offer to the poor and much to gain for themselves. Selfless love on the part of the non-poor combined with a commitment to improve on the part of the poor can overcome both material and spiritual poverty. As Mother Teresa said, "I do not believe in class warfare but in class encounter, where the rich save the poor, and the poor save the rich." From pulpits to public policy, for the benefit of the rich and the poor, we must stir up hearts of compassion to find effective solutions to the myriad problems of poverty.

More than Money...

One part of Olasky's "compassion" argument is that "true" assistance requires more than money. To note, poverty in the United States today is not so much a matter of material deprivation as financial dependence on others and an inability to participate in the social order. The possibility of long-term dependence on welfare also points to the "non-money" issues associated with providing assistance. Likewise, Paul instructs the rich to give more than money: "Command them to do good, to be rich in good deeds, and to be generous and willing to share."[29] We need to recognize that ultimately, money alone can solve few of the issues of poverty.

But at least implicitly, welfare policies and charitable practices are often reduced to merely materialistic concerns. Although physical needs are important—and crucial up to threshold levels—they do not represent the sum of a Christian's hope for other people. Our goal should be to build others up according to their needs, to enable them to be all that God has designed them to be, to be productive, to pursue a life of dignity.[30] Policies and practices which enhance material well-being while diminishing dignity, independence, and self-actualization are, in fact, harmful to the human person.[31]

In addition, we need to recognize that indefinitely providing the poor with an adequate standard of living is not the ultimate (earthly) goal. The more compelling goal is to empower people to function without assistance, to end their dependence on others. A familiar adage comes to mind: "Give a man a fish and he'll eat for a day; teach a man to fish and he'll eat for a lifetime." We should be about the business of teaching people how to fish. Or as Olasky explains, "what America needs is not a safety net but a vast variety of small trampolines."[32] For example, the Law instructed loaners not to take a man's millstones as security for his debt.[33] God deemed it inappropriate to take away a borrower's means of production. The Egyptians asked Joseph for food *and* seed during the famine.[34] They were not only interested in short-run sustenance, but in providing for themselves as much as possible in the long-run.

Note also that the Old and New Testaments use many different words to denote poverty. The words most often imply "scanty means," not complete destitution. For example, Paul discusses the extreme "poverty" of the Macedonians, yet he describes their contributions as "rich generosity."[35] Indeed, it is more blessed to give than to receive—and in the case of the Macedonians, more blessed to give from their scarcity than to have received from someone else's plenty. Like the generous widow with her two mites, they were not living like kings, but were still in a position to give to others. Olasky notes that pre-20th-century "poverty warriors" used to make a similar distinction—between merely being poor and being a "pauper" who was completely dependent on others to survive.

Another implication of the Bible's multiple definitions of "poverty" is that there are many causes, and thus, many different optimal prescriptions for the plight of the poor. Again, money alone will probably not be sufficient. Sometimes the cause is oppression. In such cases, Christians should seek justice. Sometimes it is self-inflicted. Then, Christians should embrace categorization and discernment to try to bring about long-term change. In all cases, Christians should be quick to give them "the reason for the hope" we have in Christ Jesus.

In order to have a more comprehensive concern for the human person, one must acknowledge and address a broader range of poverties beyond the merely material—for example, poverty in the contexts of safety, self-actualization, ethics, and so on. If an individual is cared for in a material sense, but has no purpose in life, then their poverty has not been eliminated. If one has sufficient levels of food, clothing, and shelter, but behaves consistently in a way that is self-centered, then significant poverty remains.

Further, given a subsistence level of income, happiness is not closely related to additional income. We see this principle in everything from psychological studies that show little or no relationship between the two, to our own personal experience where "one can never have enough money," to the anecdotes of wealthy people that the most important dollar is the next one. Once people are beyond subsistence standards of living, there are more important components to well-being: character, joy, self-respect, self-actualization, peace, and so on.[36]

This line of thinking should come easily for Christians. Even in the Garden of Eden, Adam's situation is "not good" until a "suitable helper was found" for him; all the material goods in the world were not sufficient to resolve his loneliness. Proverbs 28:6 says it is "Better to be a poor man whose walk is blameless than a rich man whose ways are perverse." Charles Murray uses a thought experiment to illustrate the same principle: Would you prefer that your children be raised by poor people in Thailand with good values or by middle class people in America with poor values?[37] Unless one is barely surviving, there are more important issues than money.

Christ also made it clear that the gospel was about far more than money. He turned five loaves and two fishes into a meal for 5,000 people. But in Matthew 4, he turned aside Satan's first temptation—to turn stones into bread. Christ could have fed the world with miracles then or later. Why didn't he? Jesus answered, "It is written: 'Man does not live on bread alone, but on every word that comes from the mouth of God.'" He later endorsed the woman anointing his feet with a bottle of expensive perfume. Although Judas complained that the money could have been used to feed the poor, Christ said that the expenditure was appropriate. And his healings were spiritual and physical "empowerments" of a type—forgiving sins and curing medical maladies.[38]

Finally, beyond figurative and literal healings, short-term assistance, long-term empowerment, higher levels of self-actualization, and so on—from an eternal perspective, it is all for naught without the life-saving and life-transforming power of Jesus Christ. To focus on material needs alone is a travesty and a sin. Or as Tim Stafford notes: "Christ does not want his people to be only a thousand points of light...he has more in mind a thousand tongues of fire."[39]

Why do we focus so heavily on providing money? First, it is easier. In a busy, wealthy country, it is often "cheaper" to provide money rather than time. Second, it may be sufficient to relieve guilt. Although guilt may be a useful motive to begin charitable activity, it leaves no assurance that aid will be effective. Third, it seems to help on the surface. But as we have seen, to provide true assistance often requires a substantial investment in an individual's life. Fourth, we are inherently biased toward understanding and valuing blessings that are direct, immediate, and tangible over blessings that are indirect, delayed, and abstract. Fifth, from the aidgiver's view, "success" can be measured (although perhaps inadequately) in dollar terms. Since the mid-1960's, we have measured "compassion" by the amount of government spending on the poor and "progress" by fluctuations in the poverty rate. More than 35 years and a trillion dollars later, it should be evident that success in spending money does not equate to success in helping people improve their lives. Government welfare and private charity have too often preserved the body but killed the spirit.

The Importance of Marriage and Family

The decrepit state of our country's family structure continues to be our most important social ill. For example, children in single-parent households are 11 times more likely to experience persistent poverty than children in two-parent households; 73% of the former will fall into poverty (as measured by the government) at some point in their childhood while only 20% of the latter experience poverty.[40] Today, the sanctity and efficacy of marriage as an institution are routinely violated in two ways—people who should enter marriage given their relationship but fail to do so, and those who exit marriage too easily. Divorce and illegitimate births continue to marginalize families economically, to damage children in a staggering variety of ways, and to unnecessarily stretch our social resources. The result is shattered lives and broken community. Again, a Biblical and prudential view holds that family is supposed to be the first line of offense in the poverty war. Instead, the modern family is busy creating more problems for society through divorce and illegitimacy.[41]

The problems introduced by divorce (especially when children are involved) and illegitimacy are numerous. A single parent has fewer financial, physical, emotional, and intellectual resources to bring to bear on the very challenging job of parenting. A single parent loses areas where their spouse had a comparative advantage and where they complemented each other—as men and women in general, and as any two spouses in particular. The children have diminished relationships with both parents, lose a parental (typically male) role model, lose stability in their home life, lose the potential example of an effective marriage, and so on. With respect to illegitimacy, the impact on children is usually even greater. Absent adoption, the child is typically born into a patently unstable situation and primarily parented often by young single mothers who may also try to work. This level of immaturity and inattention can only rarely be in the best interests of the child.

Aside from the impact on children, divorce and illegitimacy cause damage to the institution of marriage, to individual lives, and to society as a whole. Moreover, if marriage is not a viable institution, then individuals pursuing their self-interests will look to end relationships quickly and move on to other relationships that are at least temporarily more satisfying. Thus, a significant probability of divorce or co-habitation introduces the likelihood of a cycle of impermanence in marriage. When illegitimacy becomes the norm in a community, these problems snowball, rapidly draining a community's resources and increasing the likelihood of extending this vicious cycle. In a word, a society where divorce and illegitimacy become typical is not beneficial for men, women, children, or society.

Within the church, as a generalization, divorce is the larger issue. Divorce continues to be prevalent in our country and in our churches, so much so that it is woven throughout the fabric of our daily lives. It has gone from a rare tragedy to a plague that affects everyone—at least indirectly. For every two marriages, one couple divorces; there are more than one million divorces each year; and our nation has the highest divorce rate in the world.[42]

Although addressed in the 1996 welfare reform legislation, little was done to pursue improvements in divorce rates, illegitimacy rates, and the formation of single-parent households. The focus of the church's internal and external ministry—as well as the next phase of welfare reform—need to aggressively deal with these problems (as possible).

A Note on Economic Laws and Biblical Tools[43]

Of course, Christian advocacy of government activism has extended far beyond welfare programs. In the late-19th century, Protestants transferred control of education to the government in order to more effectively proselytize an increasing number of Catholics.[44] In more recent times, the U.S. Catholic bishops and the National Council of Churches were among the most adamant supporters of socialism. Even today, in the name of "social justice," religious people fight against substantive welfare and education reform and advocate higher minimum wages, redistribution to the non-poor, and a host of other unfortunate policies.[45]

In addition to embracing unethical means to their spoken ends, Many of these prescriptions have been, in fact, detrimental to many of the poor. Thus, Christians with a concern for the poor need to work within "economic laws," whether these laws seem to be "fair" or not. For example, if the price of unskilled laborers increases, businesses will rent less of their services, increasing unemployment for that group. If we subsidize unemployment through welfare programs and unemployment insurance, we will find that it increases. Just as believing in God as we want Him to be is not appropriate, believing in the nature of man, economic dictates, and political realities as we want them to be, or as we think they should be, is not useful. We must accept them as they are. "Even setting aside the moral issues of whether such power ought to be used, and whether a more equal distribution of income is a prime moral end, one is confronted with the purely analytic issue of whether the end will be achieved..."[46]

The point is not to tell Christian leaders or laypeople to be silent on economic issues.[47] But concern for the poor must be supplemented with the reality of economic laws and human nature.[48] Blaise Pascal argued that "working hard to think clearly is the beginning of moral conduct." Again, one must "count the costs" before blindly implementing policy. Louis Brandeis warned about "men of zeal, well-meaning, but who lack understanding." Zeal and compassion are important, but understanding should be a prerequisite not an option for Christian policy prescriptions.[49] "To this end, we need a combination of supreme moral sensitivity and economic knowledge. Economically ignorant moralism is as objectionable as morally callous economism."[50]

Although the desire of the Religious Left to help the poor is admirable, the subsequent policy recommendations are often incompatible with reaching that goal.[51] For example, indefinite and indiscriminate giving can easily harm recipients. In I Corinthians 13:3, Paul says "If I give all I possess to the poor and surrender my body to the flames, but have not love, I gain nothing." In such cases, the poor typically gain nothing as well. Without understanding and true compassion, efforts to help the poor can easily be futile or misguided. In Mark 11:12-14, Christ condemns a fig tree that had plenty of leaves, but no fruit. Likewise, prescriptions for government activism often look good on the surface, but fail to produce fruit—and thus, should be condemned.

Aside from questions of effectiveness, another crucial issue is that Christians need to be sure that their chosen tools are Biblical.[52] Redistributing money from A to B through the tax code is coercive by definition— equivalent to "legalized theft." Do moral ends justify the use of immoral means? Note also that any government policy necessarily restricts freedom; instead, Christians should generally support policies that promote individual liberty. P.T. Bauer notes that government activism has other spiritual and moral implications as well: political markets and redistribution encourage people to "focus on man" and to be preoccupied with others' wealth. He argues that these policy prescriptions "legitimize envy and resentment."[53] Moreover, as Arthur Shenfield notes, socialism "treats men as pawns to be moved about by the authorities"—something less than the levels of dignity and free will that God wants us to have.[54]

Even though an emphasis on the poor is Biblical, this does not ensure that efforts to help will be either practical or ethical. It is often said that "the road to Hell is paved with good intentions."[55] This is certainly the case with most calls for government activism and many acts of "charity." In sum, while there is a Biblical call to assist the poor, the use of government to redistribute income is not sanctioned as a means to that end. This is not to say that Christians should aggressively battle all efforts to use government in this regard. In fact, given the church's questionable willingness and ability to step up to the plate sufficiently, a call for the complete and immediate revocation of welfare programs would arguably be sinful. Rather, we should condone effective efforts, condemn ineffective efforts, and be personally willing and eager to help the poor properly when possible.

Chapter 13:
Why and How Christians Should Legislate Justice (Part 6)
How We Can Help the Poor—Prescriptions

Poverty had no place in God's initial design. Adam and Eve were provided with abundant life, and even work was considered to be a perpetual blessing in the Garden. But after original sin, "economic death" entered the picture and we have been engaged in a battle with scarcity of time and resources ever since.

In Deuteronomy 15:4, Moses was hopeful when he said "There should be no poor among you, for in the land the Lord your God is giving you to possess as your inheritance, he will richly bless you." However, these blessings were conditional on the next verse: "if only you fully obey the Lord your God and are careful to follow all these commands I am giving you today." Of course, full obedience was not forthcoming and God's full blessings were not delivered. Interestingly, Moses seems to anticipate this by providing instructions on how to care for the poor throughout the rest of the passage. In Deuteronomy 15:11, Moses concludes "There will always be poor people in the land. Therefore I command you to be openhanded toward your brothers and toward the poor and needy in your land." In Matthew 26:11, Christ reiterates the same theme: "The poor you will always have with you."

The prophecies remain true today—in terms of *absolute* poverty, if not so much in the United States today, then in much of the rest of the world. Although economic progress has diminished absolute poverty, especially in relatively free economies— –it still remains a topic of vital concern in less-developed countries. Independent of private or public assistance, too many people do not possess threshold levels of life's necessities.

Of course, independent of advances against absolute poverty, *relative* poverty will always be with us—by definition. Although one can be concerned about varying degrees of income or wealth inequality, the larger issues would seem to be those of appropriate access to opportunities for life, liberty, and the pursuit of happiness. Too many people, even in a relatively wealthy country like the United States, do not have enough skills, character, and opportunity to live in accordance with the dignity of the human person.

The Bible also notes that people are poor for a variety of reasons—ranging from poor personal decisions and weak moral character to institutions that promote systemic injustice and oppression against the poor. In a word, poverty and suffering are unpleasant consequences of sin—by individuals who invite trouble on themselves and by others who cause trouble for the poor. Because of individual depravity and corrupt social institutions, people prevent themselves and are prevented by others from becoming what they could be—physically, mentally, and spiritually to the glory of God.[1]

I have argued that it is not appropriate for Christians to *pursue* government as a tool for income redistribution. This eliminates open advocacy of government welfare as an option, but still allows Christians to pursue a number of justice issues—when interest groups use government to make themselves better off at the expense of others, especially the poor. As such, Christians should seek to remedy unjust social institutions as detailed in chapter 9 and 10. As William Miller argues, if the Good Samaritan had come across men in a bad condition day after day, "would we not think that there was something deficient in his faith if he never thought to ask who was patrolling that road against bandits?"[2] Likewise, when government plays the role of roadside bandit—as, for example, with education policy— Christians should actively protest such injustices.[3]

In addition, Christians should focus on reducing individual depravity through evangelism and ministry. But as we noted in chapters 11 and 12, past welfare programs and charitable efforts have not been especially effective in helping the poor; long-run dependence is still a serious problem and spiritual concerns have often been ignored. The most effective efforts are local and voluntary, using categorization and discernment to address moral and material poverty. All that said, what else can Christians do to help?

What Else Can We Do?
Using Government (revisiting some old themes)
The previous line of argument should not be taken as a call for Christians to avidly oppose all government efforts to help the poor, but rather not to actively advocate taxpayer-financed efforts. Moreover, we should try to distinguish between those government efforts which provide long-term solutions to the problems of poverty and those which are merely short-term band-aids.

As such, work rules for TANF (Temporary Assistance to Needy Families— the old AFDC program) should be tightened further in states which have been lax. The welfare reforms spawned by the 1996 legislation were a strong start in encouraging people to transition from welfare to work; the "Personal Responsibility and

Work Opportunity Act" has lived up to its name in large part. But more can be done. While many states have had success in helping former welfare recipients make the transition from welfare to work, other states have run half-hearted programs. Finally, work requirements should be established for food stamps and public housing for non-elderly, able-bodied adult recipients.

All financial disincentives to become and remain married should be dropped—the marriage penalty in the income tax code and the implicit marriage penalty on all means-tested assistance programs. One should not be taxed at a higher rate because of one's marital status and the poor should not be encouraged to remain unmarried because the government will cut their benefits.

Education reform can play a tremendous role here as well. So far, in chapter 7, we saw how increased competition in the market for education would effectively deal with some stubborn social morality issues; and in chapter 10, we saw how increased competition would deal with the economic injustice of low-quality, high-cost government education. Here, think of education reform as a way to revitalize the urban core. As Jonathan Rauch argues, by breaking the link between home location and schools, "Vouchers are possibly the best desegregation and urban-renewal program that the United States has hardly ever tried."[4]

For one thing, producers in a competitive and revitalized educational system would strive to find more innovative ways to deal with the social ills described earlier. For example, education under a competitive regime would probably have longer hours and fewer weeks away from school—at least in the inner city. This should enhance educational quality, but would also provide a useful alternative for children in single-parent households with little supervision. Moreover, the presence of effective schools—and the ability to choose among schools—would give middle-class families a reason to stay in the inner city rather than escape—a strong reason when one considers the cost of a home. Schools could be at the heart of efforts to revive community, provide good role models, teach job and life skills, and instill morals and character. Children would be less likely to get pregnant, commit crimes, get involved with drugs or gangs. In a word, merely changing the funding mechanism—from schools to parents—could revitalize the inner city. Education reform is not just about education, but a matter of social policy as well.

Using Government (introducing some new themes)

There are other appropriate uses of government. As a matter of justice, we should encourage the government to pursue private instead of public "child support" when possible. This could include everything from tougher enforcement of child support laws to identifying the fathers of illegitimate children and encouraging mothers to pursue alternative sources of financial assistance. Our child support laws should be enforced and prosecuted as vigorously as bad loans and delinquent tax payments. In sum, fathers, families, and voluntary organizations should be the first to assist poor single mothers—not taxpayers and governmental bureaucrats.

To the extent that illegitimacy is a result of a relationship between an adult and a minor, we should advocate more avid prosecution of statutory rape laws. For example, in 1993, 27% of all babies born to 10-14 year-olds in California were fathered by adult men aged

20 to 24. Girls in high school had babies with men 4.2 years older than them on average; for junior high girls, the men were 6.7 years older.[5] In addition to bringing a new baby into a difficult situation, we are allowing predatory males to have their way with under-age girls.

In New York, former Mayor Rudy Giuliani proposed legislation that would have brought legal proceedings against mothers with babies who test positive for drugs at birth. And Connecticut has considered a law that would remove custody of children born to mothers who used drugs during the pregnancy. Although the merits of such measures are debatable, we should at least consider advocating strict probationary custodial terms for irresponsible mothers. As a matter of justice, Christians should stand against people who do harm to a third party, especially a baby. And of course, we should be willing to provide foster care and adoptions as positive alternatives.

Likewise, Christians should continue to encourage the government to liberalize its adoption and foster care policies. Too often, optimal arrangements are prevented by guidelines that encourage "race-matching" or by bureaucratic quibbling over jurisdiction. Cities often suffer from too many children and not enough parents; suburban counties tend to have too few children and an abundance of interested families. When cities do not allow those in surrounding counties to have access to these children, all are made worse off, except perhaps the bureaucrats who administer the program. And although a preference for race-matching is perhaps understandable, it is not appropriate to force a child into an orphanage, continued foster care, or a home with inferior parenting—to meet that preference.[6]

Each of these policies defends the rights of others (particularly the vulnerable) and clearly improve justice. But the Bible focuses on one-to-one ministry. What can we do—as churches and as individuals?

Extending Ourselves

Christians need to improve and extend their efforts at ministering to the poor—especially those within the church.[7] The church, in helping its own, should be a model to the world in helping people emerge from dependence, despondency, and depravity. As Tony Evans notes, "The primary job of caring for those in need was never intended to be a function of government. Can you imagine Paul going to Caesar and asking for a federal grant to fix the problems of poverty within the church in Jerusalem? God called the church to care for its own and set an example of compassion..."[8] Beyond activity within the church, we should also reach out to those outside of our communities as well—hoping that they will establish or deepen their relationship with God, but mostly, loving them as we walk as Jesus did. This is one way to practically follow the now-famous Prayer of Jabez—that we would "increase our territory" and our influence on the world around us.[9]

Moreover, Christian welfare recipients should reconsider the source of their income. The government forcibly takes that money from others to give to them—not exactly the epitome of following the 8th Commandment. Some are too lazy, failing to follow Ephesians 4:28's injunction "to steal no longer, but [to] work, doing something useful with his own hands." And the result of the income transfer is degrees of idolatry toward the State, depending on it for security and sustenance.

In helping the needy, churches need to go beyond merely providing food and clothing. Although cleaning out the pantry and the closets for the poor is admirable, it only begins to scratch the surface. For instance, with enough good teachers, volunteers, and administrators— and with building space which sits empty most of the week—churches could organize effective schools and child care services. We could provide transportation— everything from van service to selling old vehicles at a discount to people without a car. Other ministries should target the specific needs of the poor—everything from job search skills to offering them manual labor jobs. Tony Campolo suggests church sponsorship of "micro-industries" like cleaning businesses, moving companies, and so on.[10] In a word, the church should be active in helping people move from welfare rolls to the work force. Finally, direct financial assistance can meet short-term needs or pay bills. But again, this requires time and organization; to do it properly requires discernment and monitoring by the church and other local aidgivers.

The Windsor Village United Methodist Church in Houston provides a model example of these principles at work. In addition to an altar call, Pastor Kirbyjon Caldwell invites people to get involved in the church's ministries to write better resumes, enhance job skills, and so on. Beyond feeding the poor, Caldwell's vision has included "the Power Center"—a 104,000-square-foot complex with 276 employees that provides educational, medical, and entrepreneurial services for the lower-middle-class. The Center is able to create jobs, enhance skill formation, and promote economic as well as spiritual development. The ministry has also been extended to reach the lower-class and the homeless—providing job training, GED classes, medical facilities, and so on.[11]

For those who operate shelters, rules of conduct should be enforced, "categorizing and discerning" to promote more productive habits. A number of successful programs have mandated some or all of the following rules: no alcohol or other drug use, wake-up and curfew times, cooking and cleaning, education (at least through a GED), Bible studies and Chapel services, random drug testing, substance abuse programs when necessary, and classes in parenting, comparative shopping, and other "life skills." In sum, we should seek to empower those who are unskilled at life with a focus on accountability and personal responsibility. And of course, the bottom line is that this is an earthly means to an eternal end—establishing or deepening relationship with God and redeeming unprofitable lives.[12]

Assistance to "the homeless" needs to follow the same principles. Marvin Olasky encourages aidgivers to see if panhandlers really want help or just some money. He notes that many urban shelters provide cards with information about how to get food and shelter. Another option is to hand out gift certificates for food and gospel tracts as opposed to cash.[13] He reports a few experiments where many of these offers were not accepted. Even less popular were offers for work, counseling, or other assistance. But some people will accept help, and as Olasky notes, "Christians should be agents of change, not agents of small change."

Note also that the Bible promotes the inherent value of work. Adam and Eve were given work to do in the Garden. Solomon wrote that "the sleep of a laborer is sweet, whether he eats little or much."[14] And in particular, Paul's "rule" in II Thessalonians 3:10—"if a man will not work, he shall not eat"—implicitly recognizes the importance of work for aid recipients, aid givers, the church, and society. As such, work of some type should be at the center of efforts to assist. Work serves as a tool for categorization and discernment, promotes dignity and self-esteem, builds skills, and so on.

Beyond that, the issue is not just work, but consistent work—a work ethic. At Bethlehem Baptist Church in Minneapolis, church member Tim Gladder operates an offline assembly business called Masterworks out of a church-subsidized building. The goal is to help people get off of welfare and back on their feet. Gladder observes that "the key problem is not starting a job but staying with it...You can train people, but until they break this habit, training will be a waste. You have to break the cycle...It's so important to achieve some consistency at work; if they get it, that discipline carries over into other areas, so they'll stick with a lease, and maybe they'll even stick with a marriage."[15]

For those who feel called to more of a mission field, the "Urban Renewal Movement" has assisted more than 5,500 middle-class families in "immigrating" to the inner city. "By serving as role models and connecting the neighborhood to outside friends and family who can offer job leads, tutoring, and donated services, these individuals hope to help seed troubled areas with good neighbors."[16] Unfortunately, as Tim Stafford notes, "Today the darkest and most fearsome place many of us can imagine is not Africa, it is not India, it is far closer in miles and in heart. It is in the city where we live."[17] Indeed, our inner cities offer a fertile mission ground—to alleviate material and especially spiritual poverty.

A more moderate version of this strategy is a church, a Sunday class, or even a few individuals investing their time, talents, and treasure in troubled neighborhoods—partnering with churches in that area. Needs differ by area, but working with children (tutoring, Bible studies, recreation) probably tops the list every time. Given so many children living in broken homes with not enough healthy parental involvement, you can make an investment that will have an earthly and eternal impact.[18]

Business owners can help also. We noted earlier that in competitive labor markets, people tend to be paid comparably with what they can produce. To pay more is charity; to require higher pay by law (mandated wages and benefits) is to render unskilled people an unprofitable option for businesses. But in the book of Ruth, Boaz subsidizes the wage of hard-working Ruth by having his workers "pull out some stalks for her from the bundles and leave them for her to pick up."[19] In other words, he provided charity by supplementing her income. Likewise, as a form of (tax-deductible) charity, business owners can pay higher wages to their workers, particularly those with fewer skills. This strategy also reduces turnover, develops more consistency among workers, allows longer and deeper relationships to form, puts an emphasis on work rather than welfare, and gives glory to God through the charitable actions of the business owner.

Other times, it's a matter of businesses being sensitive to needs. South Shore Bank in Chicago works to provide loans to churches who do not meet all of the criteria for "wise investment opportunities." They have loaned more than $20 million to nearly 600 congregations in poorer neighborhoods. To be effective, this requires local involvement and knowledge, categorization and discernment—and either a passion to help the financially unlovely or a desire to fill an overlooked niche in the market.[20]

All of these have at least one thing in common— they require a greater commitment on the part of believers. In particular, simpler and more focused living would allow us more time and money to minister to others. But too often, we rationalize that we cannot afford the time, money, or effort. As Kenneth Kantzer notes, "The fact is, we really don't consider ourselves rich...We observe self-righteously that our next-door neighbor has many things we wish we had too; but we can't afford them. So we congratulate ourselves that we have learned to do without. We find it easy to justify our image of ourselves as disciplined and self-sacrificing."[21] Likewise, we could give more to the church and charity upon our deaths—amounts above and beyond the needs of our families. The bottom line is that if Christians are unwilling to live out their faith in a self-sacrificing way, they should not complain vociferously about the welfare state.

Bob Lupton takes the argument a step further: "Some of the most unneighborly residents are those [heavily] involved in their churches...I'm not saying these are bad neighbors. They're more like un-neighbors... isolated from their neighborhood...withdrawn from active, redemptive community participation...Yet engagement— not withdrawal—has always been the operative word of the Church."[22] Likewise, John Stott describes "rabbit-hole Christianity" as when our only encounters with the world are mad, brave dashes from one Christian event to another. This brand of Christianity will not be sufficient to address the physical or spiritual needs of the world.

Amy Sherman draws an analogy from Jeremiah 32 where God tells Jeremiah to purchase a field in Anathoth—a community near Babylonian-seiged Jerusalem, but behind enemy lines. "God is asking Jeremiah to invest in a neighborhood others have given up as lost...God is still in the reclamation business. He is still calling his followers to "foolish" investments. Impoverished neighborhoods in our communities are also behind enemy lines."[23] Can we also step out in faith to answer the call?

Individuals should prayerfully consider if some of these suggestions are something to which God is calling them. Start gradually or stretch yourself further. Churches can help by exhorting their people to serve and by acting as a clearinghouse for ministry information and opportunities.[24] In any case, believers need to be willing to risk more and to be more dependent on God. What is the purpose? To love others and to love God with all of our mind, heart, soul, strength, time, talents, and treasure—to bring glory to God and to win souls to Christ.[25]

But Would It Be "Enough"?

Given the enormous wealth in this country and the number of people who would claim to be compassionate—tens of millions of political "liberals" and followers of any religion, this country clearly has the capacity to assist the poor on a voluntary basis.[26] In addition, if government relinquished control over welfare, taxes would fall and disposable incomes would rise dramatically, enabling individuals to help others even

more. (The cost of welfare was $416 billion in 2000—
nearly $6,000 from the average family of four.[27]) We are
able, but are we willing? Has our current ability to be
compassionate atrophied too much? Has the government
controlled poverty relief for so long that the private sector,
and specifically the church, would not be willing or able
to respond adequately?[28]

One can only speculate, but we have historical
basis for believing that people are capable of supporting
the poor through private means. Olasky's research makes
clear that throughout the 19th century, private charities
were limited but effective.[29] With real incomes five times
higher than those at the turn of the century, we certainly
have the resources for a more far-reaching effort. And we
have recent evidence as well—whether floods, hurricanes,
earthquakes,   or   terrorist   attacks—that   people
overwhelmingly respond to others in need, at least in the
short-term.

Further, charitable giving by individuals has been
increasing more rapidly than income since at least the
1950's. From 1955-1979, donations increased by an
average of 3.1% per year (after inflation); charitable
giving by individuals in the 1980's ("the decade of
greed") increased by 5.1% per year.[30] Additional evidence
can be garnered by analyzing charitable contributions as a
percentage of personal income. From 1950 to 1964,
charity as a percentage of income steadily increased from
2.05% to 2.65%. From 1964 to 1980 (the beginning of the
Great Society programs to the Reagan administration),
government became more actively involved and charitable
efforts fell consistently from 2.65% to 2.1% of income. In
the 1980's, with the perception that government was
pulling back in its efforts to help the poor, charity again

increased steadily from 2.1% to 2.7% of income.[31] And "since 1995, when philanthropy represented 1.7% of GDP, giving as a share of GDP has steadily increased...[to] 2.1% in 1999."[32]

In terms of incentives for providing financial assistance to charitable concerns, the debate over the flat tax is relevant here as well—in particular, whether one should receive a deduction for charitable contributions. Although we would confidently predict greater contributions if the subsidy remained, one weakness is that we would be equally sure that people's motives would not be as pure. Another option has been proposed by Olasky and Sen. Dan Coats (R-IN): to provide tax credits to those who contribute to charities. Deductions merely reduce taxable income—and only for those who itemize deductions. A tax credit would reduce everyone's tax burden and be equivalent to allowing individuals to determine the destination of some of their tax dollars to the poor—a far stronger incentive than exists now with an income tax deduction.[33]

In any case, one might imagine that government intervention in providing financial relief for the truly needy could be replaced more than adequately by private efforts (at least some day). For the "not so needy," receiving assistance might become more difficult or might have stringent conditions attached. Perhaps that's not such a bad thing.

All that said, most people view a complete reliance on the private sector as "too risky" at this point. But at the least, we should move in that direction.[34] As such, we should choose local government involvement over state or federal efforts while encouraging private charitable efforts over public welfare programs. In public and private efforts, aidgivers should use categorization and discernment. In addition, the church and the private sector should be used in areas such as job training and helping people move from welfare to the work force. Finally, to the extent that the government remains in the poverty business, aside from those who are fully incapable of caring for themselves, there should continue to be time limits on one's ability to receive welfare benefits. Although choosing the length of time is somewhat arbitrary, this general approach has obvious advantages for dealing with the most dependent in our society: (1) it limits the ability to use welfare as a hammock instead of a safety net; (2) it allows us an opportunity to see voluntary efforts in action beyond the time limit—inarguably, the church would be capable of providing *this* level of assistance; (3) these local, individual, and voluntary efforts would be especially effective in dealing with this population, which is presumably the most challenging to help; and (4) as a result, welfare recipients would leave the "welfare culture" for an environment where categorization and discernment could better determine what a given individual needed.

The Prospects and Prospective Problems of "Charitable Choice"

"Charitable Choice" is a provision within the 1996 welfare reform that allowed faith-based organizations (FBOs) to provide services to the poor "on the same basis" as other (secular) providers, but without having to sacrifice their "religious character." In a word, it prevents the government from discriminating against explicitly religious organizations because they work from spiritual motives and have spiritual goals for their clients.[35] In theory, there is no reason why FBOs cannot work with the government to promote the needs of the poor. Given the overall effectiveness of churches in helping the needy, the intersection could be fruitful for everyone involved—the organization, the individuals within the organization, the government (taxpayers, politicians, and bureaucrats), and of course, the recipients of the assistance.[36] But in practice, there are a number of substantive concerns.[37]

First, there is an ethical issue to be considered with FBOs accepting public funding. In what contexts is it appropriate for an FBO to accept funds that have been coercively taken from taxpayers? The least acceptable alternative is for a provider to lobby for additional monies to be spent for their services—to advocate that more money be taken from taxpayers and given to them. At best, this is unseemly since the Church does relatively little to help the poor today. Why should we advocate forcibly taking money from others when we're not willing to spend our own money? A more acceptable alternative would be to lobby for funds already guaranteed to be spent within a governmental agency's budget. In other words, assuming the amount of money taken from taxpayers and spent by the agency as a given, one simply argues for the right to use that money, presumably in the most efficient way possible. The best alternative would be to take most or all of the coercive element out of the exchange of funds between taxpayers and service providers. This can be accomplished through tax credits for charitable donations. Given one's tax liability, the taxpayer can then have considerable discretion over how to allocate those monies. If FBOs are considered to be effective providers, then they will attract monies on a voluntary basis.[38]

Second, there is a constitutional balance to be maintained with private FBOs receiving public funding. Not surprisingly, good people disagree on what that balance should be.[39] On one hand, from an objective view, the most troubling situation would be when taxpayer funds are used to proselytize in a way that would seem, to secular society, to be outside the scope of "helping the poor." On the other hand, it should not be at all troubling for public monies to be used to support effective faith-based programs that have Biblical principles as a considerable part of their methodology and Christians as an integral (or even exclusive) part of the management and workforce of the organization. A key distinction would seem to be whether evangelization is the goal rather than a potential by-product of helping the poor. Again, tax credits have an advantage here in that it provides a more direct link between specific taxpayers and the organizations they would choose to voluntarily support.

Third, private sector charity that had been done well previously may become corrupted by an intersection with government.[40] FBOs might compromise their principles in order to obtain government grants. Or the desire for government grants may lure them from their original mission into areas that are not within their comparative advantages. Applying for government grants is a time-consuming process that may impose significant costs, especially on smaller FBOs—again, distracting them from their mission. In addition, small agencies may not be able to effectively handle a large influx of funding. And organizations may become dependent on government grants—ironically, in a way that mimics the dependency on government funding with which many of their clientele wrestle. Charitable organizations need to be aware of these issues—and as always, to count the costs.

Fourth, some degree of government regulation may follow government money in a way that would harm the ability of an FBO to provide services. In theory, there is no reason why this must take place. For example, the government provides food stamps to the poor but has not significantly increased its regulation of grocery stores. And the G.I. Bill allowed veterans to attend religious schools without increasing governmental oversight. That said, in practice, this is certainly a substantive concern. There are far too many examples of such encroachment by government to safely ignore this point.[41] And to be objective, it is certainly reasonable that some government oversight should be involved with taxpayer funding.[42] Likewise, if one gives money to someone, attaching strings is not outrageous. The key, again, is whether the strings considerably impede the work of the organization. Again, tax credits have the advantage of both separating government from the organization and increasing the links between individual supporters and the organization.

Considering all of the above, FBOs have a moral obligation to themselves, their supporters, and the people they serve to fully think through the short-term and long-term ramifications of accepting government money—in general and with respect to specific grants. Moreover, they should remain vigilant in making certain that government money does not have an adverse effect. In addition, FBOs should derive a formal mission statement and adopt a rigorous Code of Ethics at their earliest convenience (preferably prior to their acceptance of any public funds).[43] Many of these issues are of the "slippery-slope" variety and are ideally dealt with in a proactive, rather than a reactive manner. These decisions will always require wisdom and sometimes require courage—to turn down or to discontinue government funding.[44]

Three Biblical Examples in Closing

In I Timothy 5, Paul speaks of how to help widows. First, he says to give widows "proper recognition." The Greek word (*timao*) is also rendered "esteem, price, honor, or value." Again, we are to provide more than merely material support. Second, Paul also makes clear that the first line of charity is the family. He also lists some of the benefits of this activity—for Christians to learn how to put their religion into practice and to return the favor to those who raised them. Paul continues by saying that a failure to provide such assistance is to be "worse than an unbeliever"—a remarkably serious offense. If the family is not willing or able, the next line of charity is the church. Third, the local assistance on a one-to-one basis commanded by Paul follows our earlier prescriptions of categorization and discernment. Notably, Paul uses the phrase "really in need" three times in this passage—signaling that this was indeed a concern. Believers were to require something from widows in return for assistance, and different behaviors were expected from younger and older widows.

In I Samuel 30:21-25, David returns from leading 400 men in a successful raid of the Amalekites. Before the battle, 200 of his men "had been too exhausted to follow him," and stayed behind to guard the supplies. Afterwards, David decides to reward each of the 600 men equally. Some of the 400 did not like this arrangement, but David stood fast against them. First, note that David valued the efforts of those not directly involved in the fighting. Whether parents who stay at home with their children or people working hard but with few skills, we need to have the eyes of David for those who work but don't produce much in society's eyes. Second, he probably thought that their inability to fight was not a matter of shirking. Because of his "local involvement" and the use of discernment, he determined that the Good Samaritan's Dilemma was not an issue here. Third, he knew that victory had been granted by God's grace—and that to selfishly quibble over shares of the plunder would be absurd. We often fool ourselves, thinking our prosperity is solely the result of our own efforts. Although we might work hard, our talents and experience are a gift from God. Fourth, for those who had been involved in God's victory, the glory and excitement of that moment should have been enough reward. Instead, they were focused solely on the financial aspects of the victory. We also get caught up in material pursuits and underestimate the thrill of being involved in God's work and seeing the hand of God in action.

Finally, Acts 2:42-47 provides an account of the lifestyle of those in the early church. The passage concludes: "the Lord added to their number daily those who were being saved." Why was God moving so powerfully in this group? The passage notes that they were devoted to the apostles' teaching, fellowship, and prayer; they saw "many wonders and miraculous signs"; they praised God; and they lived selflessly: "all the believers...had everything in common...they gave to anyone as they had need." All of these are important to individual growth and a vibrant church. Are we devoted to loving God and loving others? Do we share of our time and our financial resources? Do we invest in others' lives?

If not, seeing God move in that setting would be a miracle indeed.

Appendix: What about Foreign Aid?[1]

Clearly, we are called to help the poor—not just here, but around the world. For instance, Paul collected money from the Greek churches for the church at Jerusalem. That said, foreign aid is not a viable option within a Christian political agenda; to advocate the use of government to take money from some to give to others is unbiblical. Moreover, there are a number of reasons why foreign aid is impractical.

First, the term itself is bothersome since it is assumed to be just that—"aid." For instance, Sider claims that foreign aid is necessary for growth: "Third World countries cannot do this by themselves. They need economic aid."[2] But it is a mistake to view foreign aid as a crucial factor in a less-developed country's (ldc's) economic development. Poor countries somehow experienced economic growth before the advent of foreign aid—if not, we would all still be in the Stone Age! And many countries have achieved recent economic success with little or no foreign assistance. Moreover, many countries that have received assistance for years and years remain in abject poverty. Clearly, foreign aid is neither necessary nor sufficient for emerging economic prosperity; at best, it is a secondary contributor to economic growth.[3]

Second, given the practical problems with domestic welfare, we have a moral responsibility to question the effectiveness of foreign welfare. Not surprisingly, the potential problems with foreign aid are very similar. If a country experiences economic growth, donor countries will be less likely to send assistance. Thus, the rewards for improving economic performance are diminished by definition. The "Good Samaritan's Dilemma" reappears here as well: short-run assistance may promote long-term dependence.[4] Thomas Sowell has observed that Africa (long a net food exporter) lost its ability to feed itself precisely when donor agencies began to "smother Africa with project aid."[5] Our foreign "assistance" may subsidize harmful government policies.[6] Finally, the difficulties with providing effective assistance become greater as one administers a program from further away; it is difficult to imagine international assistance efforts being any better than national efforts. Foreign aid can be effective, but as with welfare, it is fraught with practical difficulties.[7]

Third, in theory, foreign aid is meant to take money from relatively wealthy Americans to help poor individuals in ldc's. Again, the means to the end are not Biblical. And practically, one should note that foreign aid goes to ldc governments, not necessarily to poor people in ldc's. It is one thing to provide foreign aid; it is often an entirely different matter to provide assistance to needy people in ldc's. And to some extent, our "assistance" subsidizes the lifestyles of wealthy people. Foreign aid bureaucrats make our government workers look like paupers and the corruption of ldc leaders is legendary. Whether by negligence or deceit, our government's participation in such schemes is highly regrettable. As Gordon Hancock cynically notes: "the real trick, throughout the expropriation, is to maintain the pretense that it is the poor in the poor countries who are being helped..."[8]

It's not that we spent very much money on foreign aid ($13 billion in 2000; less than $200 per year from the average family of four).[9] It's that the means to the end— forcible redistribution of income—is not Biblical. And the means rarely reach the supposed ends. An ethical and more practical solution is "micro-lending"—private banks and institutions voluntarily making small loans to entrepreneurs in ldc's. The Grameen Bank in Bangladesh is the most famous example, having provided $2.5 billion in loans with a default rate of only 2%. They charge 18% interest on loans of up to $200 for businesses and $300 for houses.[10]

Finally, independent of providing foreign aid, Christians should advocate the elimination of our countless trade barriers against imports from ldc's.[11] When we use force to protect our industries from foreign competition, we prevent poor people in ldc's from improving their incomes by selling their goods here. Moreover, trade in economic markets is mutually beneficial—our consumers get lower prices and more choice.[12] Hypocritically, we lecture the world about freedom and capitalism while we lock them out of our markets. And ironically, the United States often provides foreign aid to countries while restricting their trade. James Bovard notes that "The federal government acts as if the United States is obliged both to help foreign nations and to prevent them from helping themselves."[13] Bovard then asks "Are we rich enough that we can afford to give...shiploads of handouts—yet so poor and fragile that we cannot allow them a chance to earn a few dollars honestly?" With freer trade, we help consumers here and allow people living in abject poverty in ldc's an opportunity to work and make themselves better off.[14]

By far, the most important issue for ldc's is "poor policy." Without the financial incentives to engage in productive behavior, domestic and foreign investment of capital and human capital will be unnecessarily limited.[15] The failure to provide strong private property rights, an effective judicial system, a stable monetary system, rule of law, low taxes and tariffs, relatively free trade and foreign investment—the institutions which are responsible for the prosperity of developed countries—has condemned too many people in too many countries to lives of abject material poverty.[16]

People in ldc's continue to languish in economic misery because their political leaders insist on avoiding these institutions of economic freedom. However, as we look into a future of ever-increasing globalization, countries that are relatively statist will continue to face increased competition and will find it increasingly difficult to maintain inefficient and unjust policies. The lesson for us in the United States, is that it is essential—both for the poor trying to emerge from poverty and for the non-poor to have more resources with which to help the poor—that our strong economic "institutions" be maintained and strengthened to promote growth for the economy and opportunity for individuals.

Chapter 14:
What About Abortion? (Part 1)
A Biblical and Historical Perspective

Many of my readers are deeply concerned about this issue. As such, a few points are in order. In particular, if this is the first chapter you have read, I firmly but politely ask you to turn back to the beginning of the book. Without the context of what I have written to this point, your understanding of this chapter will be unnecessarily limited. Further, if this chapter is your first stop, that may signal an idolatry toward this topic.[1] Although abortion is an important issue, it is secondary to the Gospel, God's name, and so on. And as described throughout the book, there are many public policy issues that impact things of eternal significance.[2]

Is Abortion an Issue of Legislating Morality or Legislating Justice?

On one hand, I have argued against legislating morality (LM)—restricting consensual acts between adults in which no significant, direct costs are imposed on others. There are no Biblical examples of using government to restrict such behaviors, especially among those outside the community of believers. And it is difficult if not impossible to imagine Christ using government for such objectives. Moreover, I presented a number of substantive practical concerns about using this tool. In sum, Christians should not use the force of government to promote a set of "Christian values" for non-Christians. On the other hand, I have made a significant case for legislating justice (LJ)—if justice is defined properly and if the tools used are Biblical and practical. LJ is different than LM for many reasons, but primarily because LJ can be based on God's passion for justice and Christ's example to defend the rights of others.

So where does abortion fit into this framework?[3] Abortion resembles a LM issue in that a woman voluntarily purchases immoral services from a supplier.[4] However, a behavior is a LJ issue if direct costs are borne by another party. If the fetus in the womb is "alive," abortion is a violence and an injustice committed directly against an innocent person. Thus, the key issue is whether the fetus is alive or not. This point should be intuitively obvious. Even the Supreme Court's infamous *Roe v. Wade* decision recognizes that if the fetus is alive, abortion would almost always be unjustifiable homicide.

In a word, abortion would be a LM issue except for the belief that there is a third party—one without a voice, one who is oppressed, an innocent who bears the ultimate earthly cost of death at the hands of others. If life begins before birth, there is sufficient reason for Christians to intervene using government as a tool to prohibit abortion—to defend the rights of another person. Of course, there are also a variety of possible non-government approaches. And as before, we will be concerned with whether specific proposals for government and private activism are Biblical and practical.

One other relevant point comes to mind. Abortion is clearly connected to LM when we talk about trying to reduce its frequency. We are attempting to prevent what are perceived to be mutually beneficial "transactions" between women and abortionists.[5] One should understand that demand for this service will not go away simply because it is made illegal. Moreover, as with prohibition of certain drugs, making something illegal merely reduces some problems while heightening others. Advocates of a constitutional ban against abortion (as well as more moderate proposals) should be sobered by this reality and the complexity of this issue. Likewise, the practical concerns with public advocacy in LM issues and the balance between conviction and compassion when preaching about LM issues are equally a concern in the realm of abortion.[6]

What Does the Bible Say About Abortion?

Nothing directly. There is no commandment, "Thou shalt not abort.", and there are no passages that describe anyone having an abortion. The Bible's silence on the topic is seemingly incongruent with the degree and passion to which we speak on this issue today. Of course, Christians can "argue from silence," but that must be done carefully.

Before we get to those arguments, it is important to wrestle with why the Bible says nothing directly about the topic. First, it is not that abortion was not practiced.[7] As Roy Ward notes, "we know that abortion was available in the time covered by the Bible—mostly via herbal recipes that were like a morning-after pill that caused a miscarriage."[8] Second, perhaps the Bible takes for granted that abortion is murder, and thus, there would be no need to talk about it separately. After we look at the Scriptural references, this will be a difficult position to hold. Third, given the seemingly eternal nature of the issue and the debate, perhaps this is too complicated for Christians to deal with effectively in a pagan world. To note, we observe that the world easily condemns murder, but somehow finds many types of abortion to be reasonable, at least for others to choose.[9] But of course, God calls us to many difficult beliefs and pursuits that often make the world angry—"the offense of the cross," justice and oppression, and so on.

Perhaps the Bible is unconcerned with abortion because it sends the unborn straight to the Father's arms.[10] "Surely the Lord's arm is not too short to save."[11] As Ezekiel 18:4 notes, "For every living soul belongs to me...the soul who sins is the one who will die." Given that children in the womb do not sin, they will be eternally in the presence of a perfect and holy God. This parallels Joshua's "holy war" in that the death of the pagan children was the most eternally compassionate possibility for those born into such a society.[12] This also fits one of God's general strategies—to grasp victory from the apparent jaws of defeat. For instance, when Cain murdered his brother, he simply made Abel the first person to be ushered into God's presence. And in the ultimate example, Satan strived to put Christ on the cross which led to Satan's defeat and the perfect manifestation of God's grace, judgment, and sovereignty.

In any case, if we want to claim that the Bible is highly relevant to our lives, we need to seriously consider its silence on this issue. As a result, we should at least rethink our position and approaches to abortion. And some of us need to reorder our priorities and reemphasize the things about which Christ talked much more.

Is Abortion Equivalent to Murder?

Clearly, abortion is a sin insofar as it is self-centered, careless about the sanctity of (at least prospective) life, does violence to a woman's own body, and so on.[13] But unless abortion implies direct costs imposed against another person, the political philosophy and practice developed in this book would classify the sin as LM, and thus, not properly the subject of Christian efforts to legislate.

In fact, many Christians argue against abortion based on the "spirit of the law"—that it is a type of murder. From this view, the sin is particularly heinous because the death is of one who has not committed any offense—what amounts to the shedding of innocent blood.[14] Murder is condemned early in Genesis as Cain is put under a curse for killing his brother Abel.[15] Genesis 9:6 signifies the seriousness of murder and provides a reason: "Whoever sheds the blood of man, by man shall his blood be shed; for in the image of God has God made man." The next verse instructs Noah to "be fruitful and multiply"—a goal that is more difficult to reach in the face of murder.

To connect abortion with murder, Christians invoke a number of passages to illustrate that life begins in the womb. For instance, Job says "Your hands shaped me and made me...Did you not clothe me with skin and flesh and knit me together with bones and sinews? You gave me life...Did not he who made me in the womb make them? Did not the same one form us within our mothers?"[16] In Isaiah 49:1, the prophet says "Before I was born the Lord called me" and, four verses later, that God formed him in the womb. And as Peter Leithart asks: "If God takes such care in forming unborn children, how dare we treat fetuses as blobs of disposable tissue."[17]

Of course, to assert that life begins in the womb (sometime between conception and birth) is not necessarily equivalent to life beginning at conception, and thus, is not sufficient to prove that all abortion is equivalent to murder.[18] But some verses more clearly point to life beginning at conception. Psalm 139:13-16 says "For you created my inmost being; you knit me together in my mother's womb...All the days ordained for me were written in your book before one of them came to be." The prophet Jeremiah describes his call from God: "Before I formed you in the womb I knew (or chose) you, before you were born I set you apart..."[19] And in Luke 1:31, the angel Gabriel describes Jesus before his conception.[20]

But there are at least three potential problems with using the "womb" verses as proof-texts for a Biblical stance that all abortions are equivalent to murder. First, these passages refer to historical events—the lives of heroes of the faith. Since in fact they had been born, the idea that God formed them in the womb is merely a given. Second, God is not constrained by time. Thus, we must be cautious in interpreting the meaning of time in these passages.[21] Third, although these passages can speak indirectly to abortion, one should note that their primary purpose is to speak to God's creative activity, foreknowledge, planning, and sovereignty.[22]

Similarly, Ward argues that predestination and God's sovereignty are the preeminent focus of the Jeremiah passage: "If you take it literally, Jeremiah existed before his mother and father conceived him because it says: 'before I formed you in the womb.'" Ward then notes that the view of the passage "is retrospective. Technically, the prophet Jeremiah was called in the 13th year of the reign of King Josiah...[but] Yahweh picked him out before he was conceived. From the point of view of the prophet, he is not somebody that was picked by Yahweh one day because Yahweh woke up and said 'I think I'll pick Jeremiah.' It's part of a plan. It's part of the way Yahweh works in history."[23] Ward then concludes, "This in no way suggests that Jeremiah was [alive] before he was born, but that the Creator knows things and people before they exist."[24]

Does A Person's Life Begin at Birth or at Breath?

In the Old Testament, the most prominent word describing a human being is "*nephesh.*" And the most important characteristic of a *nephesh* is its breathing. (Likewise, Scripture points to death occurring with the cessation of breath.) For instance, in Genesis 2:7, "the Lord God formed the man from the dust of the ground and breathed into his nostrils the breath of life and the man became a living *nephesh.*" In Genesis 35:18, Rachel dies as "she breathed her last." In I Kings 17:17-24's story of the widow at Zarephath, "her son became ill...grew worse and worse, and finally stopped breathing." Elijah asked God why he had brought tragedy "by causing her son to die" and then prayed that the "boy's *nephesh* would return to him." As a result, "The Lord heard Elijah's cry, and the boy's *nephesh* returned to him, and he lived." Another telling passage is Ezekiel 37:8-10, the prophet's vision of the valley of dry bones, where "*ruah*" is used for breath and life: "I looked, and tendons and flesh appeared on them and skin covered them, but there was no breath in them." God told him to "prophesy to the breath." He did and "breath entered them; they came to life and stood up on their feet..." Oftentimes, Scripture connects life (and death) to breath.

In the Septuagint (the Greek translation of the Old Testament), "*nephesh*" is translated as "*psuche*" which again means breath and life.[25] Another relevant word is "*pneuma*" which can be translated "breath," "wind" or "spirit" (all of which are unseen forces). In Luke 8:55, Jairus' daughter comes back to life as "her spirit returned." In all four of the Gospels, Christ's death is marked by him "giving up" his *pneuma.*[26] In Revelation 11:11, the two prophets are dead and then "a *pneuma* of life from God entered them and they stood on their feet." In Revelation 13:15, the first beast was dead, but then the second beast "was given power to give *pneuma* to the image of the first beast, so that it could speak and cause all who refused to worship the image to be killed."

Outside of Scripture, one would most reasonably define life as beginning at conception—although relatively weak arguments are available for the appearance of various "life signs," the viability of the fetus, or the birth of the baby. Some abortion advocates argue that an acorn is not an oak tree, a tadpole is not a frog, and a caterpillar is not a butterfly—and therefore, that a fetus is not a baby. But this is not helpful given that a baby is not a teenager or an elderly person either. Others claim that a fetus is only a "potential" human being. But they then leave unanswered (at least coherently) the question of why and how it is not an *actual* human being at that point. Likewise, they probably support laws against destroying the eggs of endangered birds. Some abortion opponents argue that once the fertilization process has begun, it is inappropriate to stop it. But this is not fully satisfying either since the egg and sperm separately—in the woman's body pre-conception—constitute an earlier stage of the same process.[27] (This can be a consistent position, but note that it implies that many types of birth control, by preventing what would naturally occur, are equivalent to abortion.) Others appeal to pluralism and respecting other people's opinions on abortion and the beginning of life and personhood. But Francis Beckwith notes that many people in the 19th century believed that slaves were not persons—and presumably the popularity of a belief does not validate it.[28]

In any case, a focus on physical manifestations of "life" necessarily ignores unseen "spiritual" manifestations. Are we right to assume that "personhood" begins, in God's eyes, at a time when there is some physical event or manifestation? "Anyone looking honestly...must conclude that Scripture has not clearly presented the exact moment when the soul is given."[29] Joel Belz argues that "the issue isn't really when life begins...The tough question for most people has more to do with when a unique human being gets his or her start. I would argue that even most pro-lifers have not settled that issue—and probably shouldn't have settled it if they have."[30] As John Henry Crosby notes: "the difficulty with the embryo is that it does not reveal itself as a person, a someone. It reveals itself as a living organism, but this does not make it a someone. The world is full of living organisms... Biology only captures the objective, thing-like side of human life. The crucial question of whether or not the embryo is a person, a someone, is not one that can be answered by pointing to scientific facts...The truth is that we really cannot know, at least with any demonstrable certainty."[31]

When does "life" begin? When does "personhood" begin?[32] I wouldn't bet my salvation—or even my savings account—on any answer.[33] The Bible is not totally clear on the question of the beginning (or end) of physical or spiritual life.[34] As such, in terms of seeking justice and given the costs of being wrong, it would seem that "far better safe than sorry" would be the best approach.[35] (Crosby notes, by analogy, that "No one, for example, would question that ignorance over the possible presence of people in a mine would entail a moral prohibition on blasting. It is self-evident."[36]) In sum, although a leap of faith with respect to the beginning of life and personhood is required, because life is sacred, Christians should advocate the most conservative standard.[37] But as Ward notes, "The Bible [by itself] should not be used to support a doctrinaire opposition to abortion."[38]

Marvin Olasky's *Abortion Rites: A Social History of Abortion in America*[39]

For those who are passionate about this issue, it is important to look at the history of abortion, its politics, and successful approaches to limit its practice. As such, Olasky's effort is indispensable. Many will be challenged by his historical insights. In his preface, this avid pro-lifer writes: "This is not a happy book. Since it cuts against established views and convenient villains on both sides in the abortion wars, I wonder whether many partisans will have the desire to read it. This is not the book I wanted to write...[but it is] important to tell the real story of mixed victories and defeats over the centuries, rather than spectacular, immediate turn-arounds."[40]

Olasky covers the history of abortion from colonial America to contemporary times. Into the early-19th century, Olasky says that infanticide was probably the most frequent way to kill unwanted and illegitimate children. Abortifacients were available and used on occasion, but there were relatively few abortions since late-term abortions were dangerous and pregnancy generally led to marriage.[41]

In the first half of the 19th century, the number of abortions increased considerably. Olasky points to increases in three categories of women: the "seduced" (seduction and abandonment became more frequent with urbanization and improved transportation), prostitutes (increased income and mobility for businessmen and poor means of birth control), and "New Agers" or "spiritists" (mostly married women with a religion of self-gratification). Olasky estimates that at the beginning of the Civil War there were 160,000 American abortions in a non-slave population of 27 million people.[42] Compared to today, this represents a lower percentage of pregnancies ending in abortion, but amazingly, a higher abortion rate per person.[43]

Early in our nation's history, "legislative action was not the first recourse when social problems arose. Much of the pressure on individuals was to come from family, church, or associations."[44] But as abortion became more frequent, "19th-century legislators were forced to come to grips with abortion, as the infant-killing method of choice gradually changed from infanticide (often with concealment) to abortion. The first state legislative response pinpointing abortion came in 1821."[45]

But legislating and enforcing strict abortion laws was extremely difficult. For a conviction, one needed to prove that there was a live unborn child at the time of the abortion and that death was caused by the abortion—a virtual impossibility.[46] Legislators refused to make abortion a capital crime and mandated little or no penalty for the women involved so that they might testify. Moreover, contemporary activists thought that most judges and juries would not convict if the penalties were too large; they believed that abortion was murder, but their primary goal was to put abortionists out of business. Olasky concludes that "These laws were not as effective as some of their champions hoped...But the goal was to contain abortion, to signal that abortion was out-of-bounds—and signal the legislatures did, by overwhelming votes."[47]

As the Civil War approached, social activists switched their attentions from abortion to slavery. "For better or worse, the priority for many Northern reformers became the evil down south rather than the evil in their own backyards."[48] To the extent that the church remained socially active, their focus was on the most vulnerable—young girls moving to the city—using preventative and follow-up measures: adoption, overt discussions of the physical and psychological effects of abortion, and one-on-one ministry with its commitments of time, attention, and money. Ironically, the greatest reductions in abortion were independent of political and social efforts. In particular, improved contraception (with the proliferation of vulcanized rubber) and New Age theology falling into disrepute (with the advent of the Civil War) were most responsible for the decrease.

Concerning more recent history, Olasky makes three claims that run counter to conventional wisdom. First, he states that abortion "broke through" in the first third of the 20th century, not the 1960's as is commonly asserted.[49] Second, he blames part of the problem on polarization and a failure to compromise in gray areas. For instance, in the debate about contraceptives (which were illegal from 1870-1920 in many states), conservatives argued that they should be legally available for married women only. But "those who saw the Bible as forbidding birth control even within marriage were determined" not to compromise on allowing others that freedom. As a result, moderates chose an ideological camp with liberals that led to eventual abortion victories.[50] (Likewise, C. Everett Koop argues that a similar failure to compromise in the late 1960's prevented us from having legal abortions today in only a few cases.[51]) Third, he identifies Sherri Finkbine's 1962 thalidomide baby, rather than *Roe v. Wade*, as the turning point for public perceptions about abortion. "Since the Finkbine's did not seem like murderers...the term fetus...began to replace the words 'unborn child'."[52]

Olasky concludes that pro-life forces have been wrong to assume that 1.) abortion was rare in the 19th century; 2.) tough laws greatly reduced the practice; 3.) doctors and ministers led the way; and 4.) the anti-abortion consensus remained intact until the 1960's.[53] "People fighting abortions applauded legislation protecting the unborn but they did not live by laws alone...people did what they could in their own spheres of influence."[54] More important, "anti-abortion forces examined the needs of populations disposed to abortion and found ways to keep some women from falling into the roles, situations, and beliefs that made abortion more likely."[55] And "opponents of abortion did not consider their job done when women decided not to abort. They hoped to find stable homes for children, whether through marriage of the parents or adoption by others."[56]

If Scripture and history are any guide, our primary answer to the problem of abortion should be to look for some support from laws, but to focus on ministering to individuals one-on-one with compassion, counseling, and increased efforts to adopt.

Chapter 15:
What About Abortion? (Part 2)
What Should We Say? What Can We Do?

As George McKenna wryly observes, "Abortion today is as American as free speech...with this difference: unlike other American rights, abortion cannot be discussed in plain English."[1] The kingdom of God and the cause of reducing abortion have much to gain from a higher level of forthrightness and honesty in the language of the debate. Christians should lead by example and encourage opponents to follow suit. This begins with level-headed public discourse and well-reasoned private conversations. Such grace-seasoned talk involves skills endemic to ministry—listening, empathy, sincerity, and love, but not at the expense of compromising truth.[2]

The Dialogue, the Rhetoric
A Few Pokes at Pro-Lifers
What We Say Improperly...
Christians need to avoid disproportionately scapegoating doctors and clinic workers. Regardless of the seriousness of the sin of abortion, we should treat both sides of this demand-supply equation equally. Unless women receive fraudulent information about abortion (through substantial omission or commission), they are moral agents who are fully responsible for their decisions.[3] Likewise, we need to recognize that it is not only women who want abortions, but the men who get them pregnant, the doctors and clinics who benefit financially, middle-class parents who want to avoid embarrassment, bosses who do not want to lose regular workers, and so on.

Christians need to recognize that many other people benefit from the status quo. In particular, prohibiting (or restricting) abortion involves sacking (or shrinking) an entire industry; any industry would fight such efforts. Others benefit from the abortion debate itself. As Jeffery Mercer noted, "Politicians have been able to use it to gain attention and support for their careers. Fundamentalists have been able to use it to browbeat and guilt people into conversion. Journalists and authors...have gotten lots of mileage out of this topic. Doctors make money from the procedure. And mothers get rid of what could have been a lifelong responsibility. It's a win-win situation for everybody. Who's the loser?"[4] Too often, Christians only see a few legislative battles rather than the bigger picture.

Christians should also recognize that the flip side of "there are so many abortions" is that many, many of your "neighbors" have had an abortion or are close to someone who has. "Forty-three percent of American women will have an abortion in their lifetime, if current rates are sustained."[5] A key question to consider: Would you talk the way you do about abortion if you knew someone within earshot had been involved in some way with an abortion? In fact, given the statistics, they likely have. Christians are called to season their talk with grace. Failure to do so is a sin and an unnecessary stumbling block.

What We Fail to Say...

First, Christians need to better understand why so many people moderately or staunchly defend abortion rights. One of the keys is one's starting assumptions about when life and personhood begin. If one firmly (or even not so firmly) believes that life begins at conception, then they will consider abortion to be murder. If one firmly believes that life begins at birth, then abortion will be viewed as anything from an elective surgery to the cessation of potential life. Given the starting assumptions, one's conclusions are not at all surprising. Therefore, if we seek to be persuasive, we must deal with the opening premises about when life and personhood begin. Ironically, pro-lifers hold the scientific arguments on their side with respect to the beginning of life—while pro-choicers downplay the science, hoping to transform the debate into something beyond the science.

But this doesn't fully explain the public's perception of abortion. In fact, many pro-choicers view abortion as murder or more vaguely, "the taking of human life," but still support its legality. Clarke Forsythe argues that this is, in large part, a pragmatic stance: this group "believes that criminalizing abortion would only aggravate a bad situation" and that "little can be done about the issue legally or politically." He is convinced that pro-lifers need to combat myths which make legal abortion mistakenly seem pragmatic—most notably, the assumed necessary prevalence and the supposed problems of so-called "back alley" abortions if the practice were to made illegal. For example, he notes that only 5,000 abortions were performed in California in 1968 (the first year it was legal there) and that in 1972, 39 women died from illegal abortions and 27 from legal abortions.[6]

Second, evangelicals need to understand that women with unplanned pregnancies often feel trapped.[7] Frederica Mathewes-Green summarizes that "Abortion is the solution, so to speak, of the problem of pregnancy," but then asks: "But when, and why, did pregnancy become a problem?"[8] She traces the answer through "two bad ideas"—that women should put career over child-raising and that women should be promiscuous.[9] As a result, "a high proportion of her sexual experiences are going to be in a context where the male partner feels no responsibility for a resulting child...Likewise, if she has adopted the idea that professional work is more important than child-rearing, pregnancy can seem a disaster to her life plans...This dilemma—simultaneous pursuit of behaviors that cause children and that are hampered by children—inevitably finds its resolution on an abortion table." With nearly 80% of abortions chosen by unmarried women, feeling "trapped" is a large part of the equation that needs to be addressed.

Commenting on the results of a study by the Caring Foundation, Paul Swope reports that "Women do not see any 'good' resulting from an unplanned pregnancy. Instead they must weigh what they perceive as three 'evils', namely, motherhood, adoption, and abortion...The primary concerns in [all] three options revolve around the woman, and not the unborn child. This helps to explain the appeal of the rhetoric of 'choice'. It offers the sense that women in crisis still have some control over their future."[10] As such, it follows that "The 'It's a Baby!' message, used alone can backfire...We're on her baby's side. Who's on her side? Abortion advocates."[11] It is crucial that we convince women in this position that we are working for their best interests.

Swope also provides some rhetorical and political advice within the context of his review of Press and Case's book, *Speaking of Abortion*.[12] For example, the authors find that pro-choice working class women often see the world as "us vs. them [those in power]." Swope notes that these women "are open to seeing abortion as a tool of manipulation by those in power." Unfortunately, "to date, the pro-life community has not convinced this group that it shares their interests...Pro-lifers are seen as one more upper-middle class group with an agenda." Swope also argues that pro-lifers should focus on real life stories that will make pro-choicers uncomfortable with abortion. "For vulnerable women in our modern culture, anecdote trumps abstraction and individual difficulties trump principle."

In sum, pro-choice Naomi Wolf describes abortion as "a desperately needed exit from near-total male control of our reproductive lives."[13] Pro-life Frederica Mathewes-Green describes it as "a tragic attempt to escape a desperate situation by an act of violence and self-loss."[14] Either way, pro-lifers must become more effective at communicating empathy with the primary decision-makers in abortion.

Third, Olasky cites our simple-mindedness and naivete in insisting that politicians support a constitutional amendment against abortion without asking them other relevant questions: Do you support a variety of less ambitious abortion restriction laws? Do you actively advocate laws that make adoption easier? Have you done anything in your personal life to promote adoption or stymie abortion? Do you defend the right to engage in acts of civil disobedience with respect to abortion clinics? Failure to ask these questions lets politicians off the hook too easily. In addition, a litmus test approach lends the debate a black and white context that is simply not real.[15]

Fourth, pro-lifers—and Christians in general—have not spent enough time thinking through cloning, embryo and stem-cell research[16], and the implications of in-vitro fertilization, contraception, etc. on society's perception of sex, procreation and the "sanctity of life."[17] These are difficult and inter-related topics that do not get enough attention.[18]

Fifth, pro-lifers now face another problem. Given that the most persuasive pro-life arguments (at least to the world) are based on surgical abortions after "life signs" have begun, the advent of RU-486 (Mifepristone or Mifeprex) makes these largely irrelevant. For better or worse, the practice of abortion will probably change dramatically with this pill's availability. Pro-lifers are unprepared to argue effectively *from the world's viewpoint* that life begins at conception. Moreover, pro-lifers will be far less able to stop this practice compared to the standard visit to a doctor's office or clinic. Christians need to give far more thought to the future of this debate.

One possible approach is to advertise that the RU-486 process is painful, lengthy, and far from failsafe—severe cramping and bleeding, at least three doctor's office visits, and still, a 8% likelihood of failure and thus, "surgical intervention."[19] Moreover, two women have died and others have become seriously ill from taking it.[20] And RU-486 loses much effectiveness after the seventh week of pregnancy—a time period which covers only one-third of all surgical abortions today—requiring precise dating of pregnancy duration.[21]

Another issue is the psychological costs of a "successful" RU-486 procedure—dealing with the slow death of a newly-conceived baby, contraction-inducing drugs to expel the fetus, and getting to see the outcome of the 92% "success rate." Perhaps the latter is *good* news in the long run: "No longer will abortionists be able to conceal from pregnant mothers the actual results of their procedure. The blood, literally, will be on each mother's hands."[22]

A Few Pokes at Pro-Choicers

First, pro-choicers who work at abortion clinics should be more candid with their clients and more consistent with their self-chosen title.[23] In a word, they should counsel women about *all* of their options, and if they perform an ultrasound, it should be shown to the prospective mother so she can make a more informed "choice." In fact, "choice" may not be the most appropriate word when 98% of women seeking counsel from Planned Parenthood choose abortion.[24] Moreover, NARAL wants to force hospitals to provide abortion services—even if doing so would violate its core beliefs. It appears that abortion rights advocates are "pro-choice only about some choices."[25]

Second, political liberals are fond of pointing to the selfishness of some conservatives and the supposed selfishness of many conservative policy stances. But ironically, in the context of abortion, "selfishness" is parked squarely in the liberal camp. If one listens to the rhetoric carefully, it is a clear example of putting one's own desires first.[26] And as Candace Crandall notes about "a woman's right to *control* her own body": "When one looks at the data today, noting that half of all women undergoing abortion in 2002 will be having at least their second, and that one of every five will having at least her third, a number of highly descriptive thoughts come to mind. 'In control' isn't one of them."[27]

Abortion rights advocate Naomi Wolf is highly critical of the language used to defend abortion: "Let us at least look with clarity at what [abortion] means and not whitewash self-interest with the language of self-sacrifice...Let us certainly not be fools enough to present such spiritually limited moments to the world with a flourish of pride, pretending that we are somehow pioneers and heroines and even martyrs to have snatched the self, with its aims and pleasures, from the pressures of biology."[28]

Another in-house critique comes from Christopher Hitchens: "It is a pity that...the majority of feminists and their allies have stuck to the dead ground of 'Me Decade' possessive individualism, an ideology that has more in common that it admits with the prehistoric right, which it claims to oppose but has in fact encouraged."[29] And George McKenna, commenting on Hitchens' essay, notes that "What struck him as ironic, and totally indefensible, was the tendency of many leftists suddenly to become selfish individualists whenever the topic turned to abortion."[30]

Third, it would be refreshing if today's abortion advocates understood and articulated how the political history of abortion in America is not helpful to the cause of "feminism." Margaret Sanger, the founder of Planned Parenthood, advocated the use of abortion for eugenics—in particular, with respect to controlling the population of minorities.[31] (Even today, African-American women are 2.6 times more likely to have an abortion.[32]) Moreover, Susan B. Anthony, Elizabeth Cady Stanton, Alice Paul, Mary Wollstonecraft, and other early feminist leaders were adamantly pro-life, even denouncing it as "the ultimate in the exploitation of women." Rosemary Bottcher goes as far as to label abortion "a betrayal of feminism." Looking back to its founders, she argues that "Human worth, in their view, was not based upon size (physical size had always been one supposed reason for male superiority), 'wantedness' (women were wanted only insofar as they could be controlled by men), or dependency."[33]

Fourth, let's "call a spade a spade." Aside from the frequent slip of identifying the fetus as a baby, there are more revealing, pre-meditated instances. As Gene Veith points out, although the "pro-choice position is taken for granted on TV, few characters in TV shows or even movies actually get abortions...Apparently, abortion and entertainment do not mix."[34] Why would abortion be "abhorrent" (the description of Henry Foster, an unsuccessful Clinton nominee for Surgeon General who had performed abortions) if it is only a surgical procedure? Or in Bill Clinton's words, why would one wish abortion to be "rare"? McKenna argues that Clinton "knows he is talking to a national electorate that is deeply troubled about abortion."[35]

McKenna makes a number of other interesting observations about pro-abortion rhetoric, comparing it to the pre-Civil War language that identified slaves as "persons" or "other persons" as opposed to "free persons."[36] Some other questions: Why don't we name abortion clinics after people? Why doesn't society honor abortionists and those who won abortion rights? Why should unmarried birth-fathers be forced to financially support a baby they don't want if they have no say over a woman's choice about that pregnancy—obligations without rights or a choice? Why do proponents insist on using euphemisms for abortion—"termination of a pregnancy," "reproductive health clinics," and so on? Why do proponents insist on using euphemisms for abortionists—"abortion providers" or "abortion doctors"?[37] As McKenna concludes, even "its warmest supporters do not like to call it by its name."[38]

Fifth, it would be nice to see self-proclaimed advocates of women at least occasionally discussing the dangers of abortion to women—in terms of physical, emotional, and psychological pain. Julius Fogel (a psychiatrist and ob-gyn who has performed more than 20,000 abortions) says: "There is no question...about the emotional grief and mourning following an abortion...Something happens on the deeper levels of a woman's consciousness when she destroys a pregnancy."[39] Dr. Janice Crouse notes that "so many women have these problems that they have earned a medical name: post-abortion syndrome."[40] Abortion is four times more deadly than childbirth and women who have an abortion are more likely to commit suicide.[41] Breast cancer, infertility, pelvic infection, ectopic pregnancy, subsequent premature births, and children born with cerebral palsy are also positively correlated with abortion.[42] How ironic for abortion advocates who used to trumpet the "health of the mother" as a reason for abortion. And how ironic for society as a whole. "In an era intensely concerned about health risks, the lack of public concern regarding abortion's effect upon women's health is inexcusable. The abortion industry remains largely untouched by the obligation to provide warnings that has been recognized in other contexts where health is at stake."[43]

Sixth, recent evidence indicates that in giving children abortions, Planned Parenthood has covered up violations of statutory rape laws. Life Dynamics recorded 614 conversations with workers at Planned Parenthood offices. In 516 of the conversations, employees agreed "to conceal or willfully ignore the felony sexual abuse of a 13-year old girl by a 22-year old man."[44] As a so-called advocate for women, wouldn't it be more appropriate for Planned Parenthood to defend female children's rights as well?

Finally, it would be refreshing if avid abortion advocates would let the public know if there are *any* cases when abortion is wrong. It would be encouraging if pro-choice advocates argued for full information about abortion and its consequences rather than merely selling the choice to terminate a pregnancy.[45] It would be consistent if they provided assistance to those who *choose* not to abort. Without doing these things—and without using honest language—they cannot even begin to approach the moral high ground on this issue.

In contrast, Wolf argues for the pro-choice position from what she labels a "paradigm of sin and redemption." She advocates freedom to choose with the reasoning and honest language of "between myself and God" as opposed to "between myself and my doctor" (the Supreme Court's *Roe v. Wade* language which voids the issue of moral content) and as opposed to "it's nobody's business" (revealing selfishness and seeking to sweep its moral content under the nearest carpet). As such, she says that for a woman "to use the word 'sin'...may mean that she thinks she must face the realization that she has fallen short of who she should be; and that she needs to ask forgiveness for that, and atone for it."[46] If abortion advocates can muster the same honesty as Naomi Wolf, one could hope for less division, more consensus, and fewer abortions.

Prescriptions for Christian Activism
Activism Outside of Politics

First, murdering abortionists is not approved by God and should not be sanctioned by the church. This is akin to my earlier remarks about pursuing godly goals with ungodly methods; the ends do not justify the means.[47] Other Biblical examples make this more apparent. Should the early Christians have murdered those who unjustly stoned Stephen to death? Note also that Christ's temple clearings must have been orderly and legal given that anything else would have provided a clear pretext to arrest him. And at a practical level, law-breaking and *uncivil* disobedience make things more difficult for other pro-life activists as well as for spreading the Gospel.

Second, the continued merits of another popular tool—civil disobedience—are debatable. In general, civil disobedience in this and other areas can be defended Biblically.[48] But that does not assure that its practice is always appropriate or practical. "Everything is permissible...but not everything is beneficial."[49] In particular, given the context of early-21st century America, the peak of its usefulness has probably passed. This is not to say that this method is always ungodly, but at least, that we should consider other alternatives.

One option—and an increasing popular strategy—is to locate crisis pregnancy centers next door to abortion clinics. Frederica Mathews-Green makes another suggestion:

> It could be argued—and I find it persuasive—that there's nothing you can do outside a clinic that looks good...the one exception I would make is my friend Mariam Bell. She works for Child Health

USA, the child-abuse agency. She's been married for 20 years, has never had kids, and desperately wants to adopt. For the last five Saturdays, at a clinic in Alexandria, VA, she's set up a folding table with a lot of helium balloons, coffee, donuts, and a big banner that says, 'CHOOSE ADOPTION'...She gives out a folder that has a lot of information in it, plus profiles of herself and other couples who want to adopt. So, the woman who drives away from there can read about them and look at their pictures and perhaps decide for a private adoption.[50]

On most social issues (and on abortion in particular), Christians need a more positive, creative, and proactive approach: "PR is always a problem. In the early days of Christianity...the church also built orphanages and hospitals and established and upheld marriage and fidelity, to better cherish the least, the last, and the helpless."[51] We can create more alternatives for pregnant women and advertise their services more effectively. We can offer free ultrasounds and otherwise lower the cost of obtaining accurate information.[52] We need to express both conviction and compassion toward women who become pregnant outside of marriage, minister to those who have had abortions[53], teach sex education and abstinence, and advocate greater punishments against rape and statutory rape. Most of all, we need to preach the Gospel and the life-changing power of God's grace. Instead, we are often short on love to those who give birth to their child and short on forgiveness to those who don't.

Third, Frederica Mathewes-Green argues that one-on-one personal attention for pregnant women is the most vital issue in preventing abortion.[54] When researching her book, "woman after woman told me that the reason she'd had an abortion was that someone she cared about told her she should."[55] When she asked them what they needed to bring the pregnancy to term, they repeated told her, "I needed just one person to stand by me." She concludes that "individual, personal care for pregnant women is a very, very good idea." This takes us back to the principles of effective charity—the importance of local, voluntary efforts using categorization and discernment.

Fourth, although the bumper sticker slogan "Every Child a Wanted Child" is not relevant to the ethics of abortion, we need to be more responsive to the spirit of its argument.[56] There should be a waiting list of potential adoptive parents for every type of child. In a word, if pro-lifers were given the option, would they be willing to convert all abortions into adoptions or at least provide financial, emotional, and spiritual support to expectant mothers?[57] There are about 1.3 million abortions per year, but only about 130,000 adoptions each year—and only 80,000 of these are outside of one's family.[58] As individuals, are we merely yelling on the sidelines or are we willing to support the courageous decisions to give birth, and perhaps, to put the child up for adoption? Are we willing to make sacrifices in our standard of living to provide life to another child? Are Christians willing to forgo having a second or third natural child in order to adopt one or two other children?

If not, those who claim an immense passion for this issue but are unwilling to sacrifice should simply shut up (at least vocally and publicly). If a Christian is unwilling to bear a significant cost for the unborn, then he should quit arguing that it is such an important issue. If abortion matters *so* much, we should be willing to take appropriate (and personally costly) steps. To paraphrase Christ in John 8, "whoever among you has ever adopted a child or helped a reluctant young mother, let him be the first to protest." As with the Pharisees, many will leave, but those who remain will be credible to the outside world.

Political Activism

The fact that the majority of the public is troubled about at least some types of abortion implies that some limited legislative victories may be within reach. We should seek to legislate where moderately easy victories are possible.[59] A recent example is the "Born-Alive Infants Protection Act" which established (legally) that a baby has a right to life. (Planned Parenthood fought this vociferously, saying that it works toward over-turning *Roe v. Wade*.) Another recent step was the Bush administration decision to classify fetuses as unborn children in order to extent prenatal care to low-income women.

Beyond those examples, it seems likely that pro-lifers could encourage a number of state and federal legislative restrictions against abortion, including the illegality of abortions after viability; "partial-birth abortion" (the "dilation and extraction" technique— D&X); the "dilation and evacuation" method (D&E) where children are torn apart in the womb and then removed[60]; fetal protections laws such as the Unborn Victims of Violence Act[61]; the elimination of public funding for abortions and for organizations that perform them; giving health care providers and insurers the right to refuse to perform, pay for, or counsel for abortion; waiting periods[62]; and informed consent laws[63] and parental consent laws for minors.[64] Such a strategy works for good directly[65], puts the opponents on the defensive, and keeps the question of abortion relatively fresh and in front of the public. Moreover, we should be especially active in lobbying to ease adoption and to condemn racial discrimination in adoption.

But currently, Christians may be expecting too much from politicians—especially in looking for a Constitutional amendment to protect the unborn—whether from idolatry or naivete.[66] Part of the problem is the prevalence of lip service in the face of political reality.[67] Moreover, as Olasky notes "Legislation does little without enforcement, and enforcement does not happen without community consensus."[68] Our first priorities should be putting our house in order and persuading the public about the truthfulness of our position.

McKenna adds that the current political alignments are not favorable for action against abortion since "Democrats are pro-choice politically and Republicans are pro-choice philosophically (since they are the party of 'individualism')." Ironically, McKenna argues that the most fertile soil for pro-lifers may soon be the liberal wing of the Democratic party. "Republicans emphasize the role of government as a neutral rule maker that encourages private initiative and protects its fruits...Democrats emphasize the role of government as a moral leader that seeks to realize public goals unrealizable in the private sphere."[69] As evidence, he notes that if one substitutes abortion for racism in liberal speeches, the effect is the same. Regardless of which party is most friendly to the unborn, Christians need to be effective in bearing others' burdens privately and in debating this topic publicly.

Judicial/Legal Activism

Christian lawyers should seek to prosecute cases of abortion malpractice. It is difficult to argue against one who is defending the rights of unjustly injured women. For example, a law firm in Louisville, KY has litigated abortion malpractice cases.[70] Their past lawsuits include women who nearly bled to death, women with perforated cervixes, those unable to bear children in the future, and four deaths. Another group, Life Dynamics Inc., has established a network of 600 lawyers nationwide and has assisted in at least 90 such malpractice cases.[71]

But currently, Christians are expecting too much from the courts, especially the Supreme Court in focusing so much on trying to over-turn *Roe v. Wade*. First, note that such a position at least implicitly overstates the impact of *Roe v. Wade*—which was arguably more effect than cause, and more about the Court reflecting social change than changing society through judicial activism. Between 1967 and 1973, 18 states had already liberalized their anti-abortion laws, causing the frequency of abortion to jump dramatically, to more than half of a million cases.[72] Other states would have probably followed, with the country eventually reflecting the diversity of majoritarian beliefs about abortion in each state. The number of abortions increased more given *Roe v. Wade*, but given the cultural changes and the legal changes at the state level, abortion was almost certainly going to increase dramatically in the 1970's and 1980's anyway.

Second, in any case, over-turning *Roe v. Wade* is apparently not practical legally. (This is not an area of any expertise for me, so I'll simply relay my impressions of the debate.) Robert Bork argues persuasively against one approach—attacking *Roe v. Wade* as a violation of the 5th or 14th Amendments. The crux of his argument is that "It is impossible to suppose that the states ratified an Amendment they understood to outlaw all abortions but simultaneously left in place their laws permitting some abortions."[73] Antonin Scalia and Paul Linton argue persuasively that over-ruling *Roe v. Wade* on the basis of "personhood" litigation is likewise doomed to failure. Although avidly pro-life, Scalia writes that he would not vote to invalidate a law that permits and forbids abortion on demand "because the Constitution gives the federal government (and hence me) no power over the matter."[74] Linton adds that "it should be clear that no member of the Court—past or present—believes that the unborn child is a 'person' as that term is used in...the 14th Amendment."[75]

Third, in any case, over-turning *Roe v. Wade* is not practical culturally. For one things, the end of *Roe v. Wade* would throw the question back to the states where "the pro-life cause would lose more battles than its proponents contemplate."[76] Aside from changing the law, the larger issue is changing hearts. It is to that point that we now turn.

The Need for Persuasion

As Mathewes-Green notes, "the pro-life movement has succeeded in keeping people uncomfortable with abortion but not in translating discomfort into a firm will to oppose it."[77] And this is a crucial matter; the pursuit of legislation independent of persuasion is impractical. In a word, we need to recognize that public sentiment—driven by improved cultural morality, or far better, by spiritual revival—is essential to winning this issue in the long run. In this regard, McKenna quotes Lincoln on slavery: "public sentiment is everything...with it, nothing can fail;

against it, nothing can succeed. Whoever moulds public sentiment, goes deeper than he who enacts statutes, or pronounces judicial decisions." Or as Ludwig von Mises put it: "Whoever wants to see the world governed according to his own ideas must strive for dominion over men's minds. It is impossible, in the long run, to subject men against their will to a regime that they reject." This is not to say that we should do nothing until public sentiment changes, but we should focus on earnestly trying to persuade others about our view.

Frederica Mathewes-Green looks back to cultural change on another issue to find hope for pro-lifers. "Our great-grandparents embraced some values that today we readily recognize as negative and damaging. These attitudes were broadly accepted and celebrated in popular entertainment, much as reckless sexual ideas are today, yet over time they were gradually exposed, discredited, and discarded." To make her point, she then provides examples of drunkenness, alcoholism, male adultery, and women being "routinely slapped and physically degraded"—which are glorified in prominent movies from the 1930's.[78] She concludes that "What was sophisticated now looks juvenile and self-destructive. And some day, God willing, irresponsible sex and its handmaiden, abortion, will look the same to our descendants." There is already some evidence of this in the younger generations. In any case, Truth will eventually prevail. The pace of change is not as quick as one might want, but the direction of change can be correct, especially if we're strategic and aggressive but patient in putting forward the truth.

Comparing the anti-abortion movement to the anti-slavery movement, David Smolin provides another reason for patience. He notes that slavery and race divided the nation geographically and represented more strongly entrenched economic concerns. "Although abortion rates and attitudes vary geographically, we can expect no fundamental geographic division and no literal civil war to resolve the issue. We are unlikely to get abortion right until we come closer to getting things right on broader matters of culture."[79]

As such, McKenna argues that the emphasis of pro-lifers "should be on making it clear to others why they have reached the conclusions that they have reached. They need to reason with skeptics and listen more carefully to critics. They need to demand less and explain more." Or as James 1:19 counsels us: "Be quick to listen, slow to speak and slow to become angry." McKenna then notes that "there is a patient philosophical response...but it finds no purchase in a mass media that thrives on sound bites. There is also a primal scream—'Murder!'—that is always welcomed by the media as evidence of pro-life fanaticism." Finally, he asks a crucial, but hopeful question: "Is there a proper rhetorical response, a response suited to civil dialogue that combines reason with anger and urgency?"

There are a number of approaches to take in this regard. The starting point of the debate must center on what constitutes "life" and "personhood"—perhaps not as a religious question, but as a fundamental moral question. "The theme of choice without reference to the object of choice is morally empty." Does life begin at conception, with "life signs," with viability, or at birth? Does one become a person when biological life begins or later—and why? These are the questions whose answers largely define the debate.

Moreover, we need to point to the inherent selfishness of the pro-choice position and the implied selflessness of the pro-life stance. And we should more fervently discuss the dangers of abortion to women, bringing into question the implicit pro-choice assumption that an abortion improves a woman's situation. Many people could be persuaded that women are often made worse off by an abortion—that it removes one burden to add other, larger problems: guilt, physical and emotional trauma, and so on.

We should be more aggressive about displaying the gruesome results of surgical abortions with advertisements and so on (as the National Right to Life Educational Trust Fund and others have done).[80] CBS's "60 Minutes" showed Dr. Jack Kevorkian performing an act of euthanasia; why not also produce a documentary on "partial-birth abortion"? If we present the facts on abortion, people are likely to come to their own conclusion that it is a revolting practice. Let's aggressively expose the darkness of ignorance with the light of truth and see how people respond.

As Wolf notes, "'Abortion stops a beating heart' is incontrovertibly true. While images of violent fetal death work magnificently for pro-lifers as a political polemic, the pictures are not polemical in themselves: They are biological facts....How can we charge that it is vile and repulsive for pro-lifers to brandish vile and repulsive images if the images are real? To insist that the truth is in bad taste is the height of hypocrisy."[81] Or as Hitchens says, "Anyone who has ever seen a sonogram or has spent even an hour with a textbook on embryology knows that the emotions are not the deciding factor. In order to terminate a pregnancy, you have to still a heartbeat, switch off a developing brain and, whatever the method, break some bones and rupture some organs."[82] Civilized people will be horrified by the evidence. If not, our society is in deeper trouble than even Christian pessimists think. But if so, the tide of the debate could change quickly.

From the other angle, we should more aggressive in showing the living baby in the womb and talking about what we know about their development in the womb—to prospective mothers and to society as a whole.[83] Images can be very powerful and could quickly change the tenor of the debate. Of particular note is new ultrasound technology. New "3-D" machines provide images that can be rotated so that doctor and patient can see the baby from every angle. General Electric has developed so-called "4-D" ultrasound which allows a baby to be seen in motion. And there is a growing market for consumers, aside from the use of ultrasound for health issues. Fetal Fotos, Inc. has ten locations across the country where pregnant women can buy baby (in the womb) portraits; and Before the Stork offers a "trimester package" that allows parents to keep track of their child's growth in the womb.[84]

Of course, some of this requires that Christians pay a price to finance such projects. Are we willing to bear these costs or will we stick to yelling from the sidelines? After all, talk is much cheaper than substantive action.

The final issue is the debate within the pro-life camp about the opposing strategies of containment and no compromise: whether to pursue cultural remedies (abstinence and adoption), pass moderately restrictive laws, and use persuasion—or to focus politically on passing a constitutional amendment making abortion illegal.[85] Given the importance of persuasion to long run success and given the historical limitations of legislation in reducing abortion, it would seem that a gradual approach would be best, at least in the context of early-21st century America.

As Olasky notes, the goal is not to pass laws against abortion, but to reduce the number of abortions. A policy of containment promises small victories and emphasizes positive pro-life alternatives. One can still pursue laws, but as a secondary tool. Olasky argues that the Soviet Union was defeated with a similar strategy. And he cites the success of Mothers Against Drunk Driving (MADD). Are its efforts "depressing, even though the effort does not stop most of the 50,000 vehicular homicides that occur annually?...Containment can lead to rollback." We could then celebrate that "in a fallen world, many were saved."[86]

Perhaps Norma McCorvey, the most prominent symbol of contemporary abortion, and her conversion to Christianity serve as an indication of the power of this strategy and provide a foreshadowing of things to come.[87] In 1995, she left a lifestyle of drugs, lesbianism, and work at an abortion clinic to embrace the cross of Christ. "...These pro-life folks were getting harder to hate...One day in Dallas, Miss McCorvey said she'd like to get some ice cream, so the Mackeys went...Emily hung on Miss McCorvey the entire time...[One day] Norma got a crank call, and had told the caller she'd see her in hell. At that point, Emily informed Miss McCorvey that she didn't have to go to hell; that if she'd ask forgiveness and repent, God would forgive her. The seven-year-old told the national abortion icon that they could pray 'right now'." Soon afterward, McCorvey professed her faith in Christ— because of the heart and hands of a child.[88]

Chapter 16:
The Conclusion of the Matter—
Defining and Pursuing True Freedom

The life of Daniel provides perhaps the best guide for how Christians are to deal with government. Much of his career was spent working with thoroughly pagan regimes. In Daniel 1, he distinguished between the parts of the Babylonian training routine which were merely cultural and those which were a matter of holiness. In the former, he was, as Paul, "all things to all people"; in the latter, he refused to compromise. In Daniel 3, his three friends refused to obey a law which legally required them to sin—to bow down before Nebuchadnezzar's idol.[1] In Daniel 6, he refused to observe an edict from Darius which legally required him to sin—by forbidding prayer to God. In each case, obedience to God superseded obedience to the state; one must choose the authority of God when it conflicts with the authority of man. As Alexander Solzhenitsyn said, "When Caesar, having exacted what is Caesar's, demands still more insistently that we render unto him what is God's—that is a sacrifice we dare not make."[2]

Interestingly, despite Daniel's prominent position, we have no record of any instances when he advised kings in a way that would be consistent with the political agendas of today's Religious Left or Religious Right. It is difficult to imagine him trying to persuade the kings to put an end to gambling or to equalize the income distribution in the kingdom. In fact, we have no account of him speaking about matters of government—even when Nebuchadnezzar built an image of himself.[3] We can also be certain that Daniel had to continuously endure sinful policies and the immoral behavior of others. In sum, Daniel allowed others to sin and he did not even interfere with laws that encouraged others to sin, but he did not allow the state to effectively limit his personal relationship with God.

As such, for Christians, the larger issue is what we do with whatever political freedoms we have. Independent of the importance of the issues raised in this book, our primary concern is to obey and glorify God in whatever circumstances we face—whether capitalism or socialism, plenty or want, pleasure or pain.[4]

Daniel set the standard for Christians in another important way. He was "serious about the work of statecraft, but he was even more serious about being known as a servant of God, determined to follow God's precepts no matter what the cost."[5] He had studied the theory and practice of government; he understood the role of government within his theology of God. Most important, he was a man of tremendous integrity who handled his affairs with wisdom and tact. When his enemies were looking for dirt on him, "they could find no corruption in him, because he was trustworthy and neither corrupt nor negligent."[6] We are quick to judge corruption, but we are called to avoid negligence as well. In the context of public policy, this requires study and discourse about the role of government in God's economy.

As Daniel, we are to distinguish between cultural, personal, and Biblical issues. In our relationships with others, we are to understand that the art of politics requires flexibility, insight, and discernment. As such, Ralph Reed argues for "the importance of being politically sophisticated—of knowing that there are times to fight harder, times to speak loudly, times to say nothing."[7] But even if we occasionally embrace government as a tool, we are commanded by God not to put our dependence, our security, and our deepest hopes in anything except Him. This includes government. To fail in this regard is idolatry. As Reed illustrates, this is a sobering, but freeing realization:

> Unlike some of our predecessors, our deepest hopes for restoring and renewing America do not rest solely on our political involvement. In fact, though it may come as a surprise to some, I believe there are strict limits to what politics can accomplish...That is not a limiting admission but a vital affirmation. It is an affirmation of Christ's pronouncement that 'my kingdom is not of this world'. Only after we acknowledge how little government and politics can accomplish are we free to roll up our sleeves and enter the fray with a realistic view of what politics can achieve...what America needs is not political revolution but spiritual revival.[8]

Unfortunately, this is often difficult to believe. Despite its failings, government can be so effective at changing external behavior. And it is very tempting to reach for weapons that are powerful. However, our criteria for righteousness are not power and earthly effectiveness, but instead, the word of God and the ministry of Christ. As Bob Briner notes, "To think that we can change the course of history through politics is folly. To think that we can change the hearts of men by anything other than Christ is blasphemy."[9]

Joel Belz comments on another reason why the temptation to believe in and depend on government is strong: because so many others take the political route.

Christians respond to peer pressure as we watch our opponents and those within the church grasp for the instruments of political power. Belz also looks deeper and points to "an embarrassing reason deep within us that also prompts us to fall for the political temptation—that we don't really believe in the unique dynamic that powers the kingdom of God. We don't ultimately trust the God whom we so glibly profess."[10]

As one secular author, P.J. O'Rourke, realizes: "We can't vote our troubles away...we can't give fifty dollars to the Sierra Club, read Douglas Coupland, and sing the Captain Planet theme song and set everything right. Instead we have to accept the undramatic and often extensively boring duties of working hard, exercising self-control, taking care of ourselves, our families, and our neighbors, being kind, and practicing as much private morality as we can."[11] This sounds remarkably similar to the ministry we are called to in Christ. In Matthew 5:13, believers are called to be "the salt of the earth." Unlike the political process—whose means and ends are obvious—Christian ministry involves a subtle and nearly invisible cause-and-effect, quietly penetrating that which is to purified, preserved, or flavored.[12]

Just as Christ was tempted by his disciples and Satan, we too are tempted to pursue political means to godly ends. But we are in a cultural and spiritual war; it cannot be won through political means. In practical terms, the pursuit of politics is akin to bringing a knife to a gunfight. In Biblical terms, the extension of government is often an inappropriate method. The ultimate answer is not better public policy, but spiritual revival.

The Government of God

The Bible describes a number of political systems ranging from oppressive dictatorships to anarchy. Israel was ruled by judges, kings, and foreign leaders with a wide variety of leadership philosophies; the early church flourished under Roman role of different types. We have already discussed the difficulties associated with human kings which were prophesied in I Samuel 8 and experienced repeatedly by the people of Israel.[13] Before that, governance by judges was established by Moses after he received administrative advice from Jethro.[14] As a result, Moses instituted a judicial system that featured a hierarchy in which capable men were chosen to be judges over "thousands, hundreds, fifties, and tens." These leaders were to be men who feared God, were trustworthy, and who "hated dishonest gain" (bribes). Over them, God ruled through Moses.

Given the importance of both freedom and local governance in God's economy, Willard argues that the "judges government" was a foreshadowing of what Christ's reign on earth will look like: "the rule of God is to be a government by grace and truth mediated through personalities mature in Christ. It will not be by force, but by the power of truth presented in overwhelming love."[15] Although the judges' decisions were binding, ideally they were voluntarily accepted—as opposed to the more coercive and capricious nature of standard human government. Willard then concludes that an "inability to conceive of [government] other than by force merely testifies to our obsession with human means for controlling other people."[16]

Willard also has a rare interpretation of the twofold statement "everyone did as he saw fit" in the book of

Judges.[17] "Many today who read that...think that something terrible was covered by that phrase. But to do as one pleases is the ideal condition of humanity, what is often called 'freedom', and does not imply wrongdoing at all."[18] Independent of his interpretation of these passages, it is certainly true that freedom can be badly abused, but that it is not inherently evil. To the contrary, freedom is at the root of God's ideal for the world as well as a necessity for free will and the existence of virtuous and sinful actions by individuals.

As Galatians 5:1 proclaims: "It is for freedom that Christ has set us free!" But Paul immediately follows his "declaration of independence" with a warning: "Stand firm, then, and do not let yourselves be burdened again by a yoke of slavery." There are a variety of yokes we can strap on our backs: bondage to the law, addictions to carnality and license, subservience to government, and so on.[19] We are to avoid each of these—for our own good, for the good of others, and for the glory of God.

With freedom in hand, the question is then what one does with it. With freedom, one has both greater responsibilities and opportunities. Paul instructs "the free" in Galatians 5:13: "You, my brothers, were called to be free. But do not use your freedom to indulge the sinful nature; rather, serve one another in love." This is the ideal use of our Christian freedom—to self-govern properly, to more fully obey God and love others.

To the extent that freedom is properly used, government is not necessary to regulate individual actions, or perhaps, even collective actions.[20] As Paul wryly concludes about the "fruit of the Spirit" (love, joy, peace, patience, etc.): "Against such things there is no law." And if freedom is not properly used, restricting freedom is an option that promotes order, but can only imperfectly teach virtue.

In fact, freedom is necessary for virtue. And some degree of virtue is necessary to allow freedom. A well-founded society needs both. Cultural and social norms, outside of Christianity, can use peer pressure to imperfectly simulate the ideal. But only Christianity can change the heart in a way that allows the ideal to be realized. As Kevin DeYoung argues:

> If freedom is the ability to act free from external compulsion, then the restraining influence of religion is what preserves freedom. To be sure, fear masquerades as an efficient restraint, but it is a pseudo-restraint. Restraining fear is like damming a river: it works for awhile but only by forcing the river to do what it does not want to do. Eventually the dam will break and the restraining efforts will only have exasperated the problem. Religion's restraint is different. It does not dam the river; it changes its course and then allows its free flow. Fear can change a man's actions, but only religion can change his nature.[21]

In a word, fear does imperfectly through external compulsion what the Spirit-filled life does more completely by internal transformation.

Thus, the theme of Biblical freedom also puts any legislative agenda into its proper perspective. All political agendas pale beside the need to tell people about the Gospel, to allow them the opportunity to pursue life more abundant, to be "redeemed from their empty way of life," to know a peace that passes all understanding, to experience an unconditional love that knows no end—in a word, to experience "true freedom."

Without Christ, "true freedom" is impossible. As Stanley Hauerwas notes, "Freedom is the great illusion. There are no free people. Everyone is enslaved to something. The goal of faith is to make you enslaved to the right stuff. We are amused at these people running around talking about how free they are. It just means they are so dumb they don't know they are being jerked around by their parents, Wall Street, and the government. Christians exist to demonstrate to our culture that true freedom is being yoked to what is true."[22] Freedom is not equivalent to radical autonomy; instead, freedom finds its real context in Truth.[23] We are to be Christ's "slaves of righteousness," to voluntarily "serve" (enslave) ourselves to God and to others.[24]

Geoffrey Brennan expresses it well:

Christ's commandment that we love our neighbors as ourselves clearly involves an obligation to care for the destitute and assist the needy...Yet it also implies that we crave for others what we most crave for ourselves. Christians, as a minority, crave for themselves liberty to dream their own dreams and strive to make them come true, liberty to embrace their own ideals and attempt to live by them, liberty to cherish their own vision of the 'good life'—a vision which for them centers in the Christ—and to struggle to transform that vision into a reality...It is precisely that liberty we must crave for our neighbors, in full knowledge that their visions of the 'good life' may be quite other than ours.[25]

Freedom is a crucial Biblical concept and usually runs counter to the extension of government power.[26] As such, I have argued that our political pursuits are often at odds with promoting personal, corporate, intellectual, emotional, and spiritual freedom. Although I believe that I have stated my case well, I anticipate that my Biblical and logical arguments will not be well received—at least in some circles.

But this comes as no surprise. As we have seen in Biblical examples and contemporary politics, the status quo often screams loudly at any attempt to reform. As Machiavelli observed: "There is nothing more difficult to carry out, nor more doubtful of success, nor more dangerous to handle, than to initiate a new order of things. For the reformer has enemies in all those who profit by the old order, and only lukewarm defenders in all those who would profit by the new order...on every opportunity for attacking the reformer, his opponents do so with the zeal of partisans, the others only defend him half-heartedly, so that between them he runs a great danger."[27] When truth and tradition differ, for which one are we more zealous? Are we lukewarm about ideas that deserve our energies? Do we have passion for godly goals and methods?

Machiavelli concluded that "all armed prophets have conquered and unarmed ones failed." My prayer is that I am armed with the truth. And God willing, my efforts will be armed by the sovereignty of God and the power of His Word.

Endnotes

Chapter 1: Introduction

1.   For a brief discussion of the causes of 20th century failures in this regard, see: R. Hittinger, "How Now Shall We Bear Witness?", *Touchstone*, March 2000.

John Yoder's *The Politics of Jesus* (Grand Rapids: Eerdmans, 1972) is a notable exception. Interestingly, Yoder's book was written in the early-1970's when a dominant mindset in evangelical Christian circles was that politics should be mostly avoided. Thus, he argues "that the ministry and claims of Jesus are best understood as presenting to men not the avoidance of political options, but one particular social-political-ethical option" (p. 22-23). Following Yoder, this book is an attempt to define that "option."

Jim Wallis' *The Soul of Politics* (New York: The New Press, 1994) is another exception. He criticizes the extremes of the political (left-right) spectrum. And his prescriptions are atypical for one with his beliefs about the inefficacy of markets: he relies heavily on exhorting Christians to service in lieu of grand calls to political activism. In criticizing political discourse, he calls for "something more truthful, more insightful, more compassionate, more wise, more humble, and more human" (p. 20; see also: p. 29-30). Hopefully the style and substance of my book will answer his call.

In *Cease Fire: Searching for Sanity in America's Culture Wars* (Grand Rapids: Eerdmans, 1995), Tom Sine surveys the range of Christian political beliefs and critiques what he considers to be the radical fringes of both sides of the left-right spectrum. Although he does not provide much of a positive case for any alternative, his critique is designed to make his prescriptions relatively attractive in comparison. As such, he seeks a "third way" (see: p. 4, 5, 220; chapters 9 and 10). That said, perhaps my approach should be labeled a "fourth way." For a "moderate" approach with more positive prescriptions, see: R. Frame and A. Tharpe, *How Right Is the Right?*, Grand Rapids: Zondervan, 1996.

2. Lynn Buzzard, *The Door*, interview, March/April 1991, p. 10.

3. Lawrence Adams finds considerable contradiction and confusion in the political views of Americans in general and in the church in particular (*Going Public: Christian Responsibility in a Divided America*, Grand Rapids: Brazos Press, 2002; see: especially, chapter 4). For a distillation of the book, see: "Christians and Public Culture in an Age of Ambivalence", *Christian Scholar's Review*, Fall 2000, p. 11-36.

4. Gregory Gronbacher: "[The Christian Right's] internal inconsistencies arise from its own lack of a coherent political theory capable of incorporating its moral, religious, and social views...On the one hand, the Christian Right abhors government meddling in cultural, moral, and economic affairs. Whether the complaint is excessive taxation or governmental promotion of a leftist, radical moral agenda, the Christian Right gives the appearance of being in favor of limited government. However, when it comes to legally enshrining their favored moral agenda, the Christian Right appears to be in favor of the activist state." ("The Christian Right in America: A Movement at a Crossroads", Grand Rapids: Acton Institute, 2000.)

5.   A number of other authors have called for a consistent Christian philosophy of government. In addition to Buzzard, see: M. Noll, *The Scandal of the Evangelical Mind*, Grand Rapids: Eerdmans, 1994; O. Guinness, *Fit Bodies, Fat Minds: Why Evangelicals Don't Think and What to Do About It*, Grand Rapids: Baker Books, 1994; J. Whitehead, *Christians Involved in the Political Process*, Chicago: Moody Press, 1994, p. 36; L. Smedes, "The Evangelicals and the Social Question", in *Salt and Light: Evangelical Political Thought in Modern America*, ed. A. Cerillo, Jr., and M. Dempster, Grand Rapids: Baker Books, 1989, p. 48; Frame and Tharpe, p. 100; R. Sider, *Books and Culture*, "Can We Agree to Agree?", January/February 1997, p. 27; R. Sider, "Toward an Evangelical Political Philosophy", in *Christians and Politics Beyond the Culture Wars: An Agenda for Engagement*, ed. D. Gushee, Grand Rapids: Baker Books, 2000, p. 79-96; J. Skillen, "Civic-Minded *and* Heavenly Good", *Christianity Today*, November 18, 2002, p. 50-53.

One should note that forming a consistent political philosophy— even one based on the Bible—is a formidable task. Adams notes that "the articulation of a coherent and viable political philosophy has been the goal of contending thinkers since the earliest human history"; "the existence of and need for a comprehensive public philosophy has been a matter of extensive and vigorous discussion in the years surrounding the dawn of the 21st century"; and "the volume of work attempting to sketch out a Christian approach to public life is enormous" (p. 29,30,32; see also: p. 104-105's list of authors). Interestingly, some Christian thinkers have argued that we don't need a political philosophy. But one should worry whether this view is—or will be taken as—an excuse for continuing to think in a sloppy manner about such things.

6. Acts 17:2,17, 18:4,19. (All Scripture quotations will be from the New International Version unless otherwise specified.)

7. Galatians 5:25. This is true for both sins of omission and commission. With respect to sins of omission, we underestimate the benefits or overestimate the costs of obedience.

8. G. Stigler, *Memoirs of an Unregulated Economist*, New York: Basic Books, 1988, p. 4.

9. Arguably, sin suffers from the same information problems to the extent that the natural and supernatural worlds distort the true costs and benefits of a decision.

10. I Timothy 1:8.

11. This has not always been the case. For example, almost all of the first 100 universities in America were established by churches. Guinness cites Puritan support for the belief that all towns should have a school: "Satan, the enemy of mankind, finds his strongest weapons in the ignorance of men." Moreover, "the Puritans [and] the evangelicals around Wilberforce were described as a group whose brains and brilliancy would not be denied even by those who sneered at their religion." (p. 151, quoting E. Howse, *Saints in Politics*, London: George Allen & Unwin, 1952, p. 24-25.)

12. There was less need for a political philosophy in the past—when government intervention was less complex and intrusive, and when Christian involvement in politics was limited to relatively few topics.

13. Quoted in Guinness, p. 12.

14. Ibid., p. 10-11. Or to borrow a phrase from a Norm Geisler talk: "Our heads are not just hood ornaments."

15. C.S. Lewis, *Mere Christianity*, New York: Macmillan, 1960, p. 75.

16. Quoted in Guinness, p. 137; D. Sayers, *Her Life and Soul*, New York: St. Martin's Press, 1993, p. 368.

17. Guinness, p. 139-140.

18. II Corinthians 10:5.

19. J. Belz, *World*, May 6, 1995.

20. S. Shaughnessy, *Walking on Alligators* (quoted in *Christianity Today*, April 24, 2000, p. 110): "Cultures are always dancing with denial. Writers tap us on the shoulder and say, 'May I cut in?'"

21. Mark 3:21, Acts 26:24.

22. G. K. Chesterton argues, reasonably, for giving tradition the benefit of the doubt. "It [tradition] is trusting to a consensus of common human

voices...It is quite easy to see why a legend is treated, and ought to be treated, more respectfully than a book of history. The majority of people in the village, who are sane, generally makes the legend. The book is written by the one man in the village who is mad...Tradition means giving votes to the most obscure of all classes, our ancestors. It is the democracy of the dead." (*Heretics/Orthodoxy*, Nashville: Thomas Nelson, 2000, p. 217.)

23. For a much shorter (but far less comprehensive) version of the ideas in this book, see: "Common Ground Between the Philosophies of Christianity and Libertarianism", *Markets and Morality*, Fall 2002, p. 439-457.

24. Among other things, "correctly handling the word of truth" involves exegesis (reading meaning from out of the text) rather than eisegesis (reading meaning into the text). Another phrase comes to mind as well: a verse out of context is merely a pretext.

Chapter 2: The Bible on the Role of Government

1. Augustine: "It is recorded of Cain that he built a city, which Abel, as though he were merely a pilgrim on earth, built none. For the true City of the saints is in heaven, though here on earth it produces citizens in whom it wanders as on a pilgrimage through time looking for the Kingdom of eternity." (*City of God*, New York: Doubleday, 1958, p. 325) For a comprehensive and balanced discussion of cities, see: D. Hay, *Economics Today*, Grand Rapids: Eerdmans, 1989, p. 42-43.

2. The earlier episodes: Abraham with Pharaoh (Genesis 12), in the battle of the kings (Genesis 14), and with Abimelech (Genesis 20-21); Lot's apparent position in Sodom's government (Genesis 19:1); Isaac with Abimelech (Genesis 26); and Joseph with Potiphar and Pharaoh (Genesis 39-50).

3. I Samuel 8:5,19-20. As G. Campbell Morgan notes: "They asked for a king like the nations. Their glory and their power had consisted in their unlikeness to the nations in this very fact." (*Life Applications from Every Chapter of the Bible*, Grand Rapids: Revell, 1994, p. 3.)

4. I Samuel 8:9.

5. There is a story about an American joking with an Englishman about winning the Revolutionary War. The Englishman asked why the war was fought. The American replied: "taxation without representation." The Brit quipped, "OK, so how do you like it *with* representation?" Just as Americans today bear a much larger burden of government than the Colonialists, the Israelites would learn God's lesson the hard way.

6. The Northern Kingdom failed to produce a single godly ruler; the Southern Kingdom's record was decidedly mixed.

7. II Kings 22-23.

8. See: Ezekiel 16:8, Hosea 2:16,19-20; for Christ and the Church, see: Ephesians 5:21-33, Revelation 20:7-9.

9. See: Ezekiel 16 and Revelation 18.

10. Isaiah 2:22. See also: Psalms 118:9, 146:3.

11. See especially: Ezekiel 23:20. See also: II Kings 15:19-20, 17:3 for examples and Jeremiah 46:25, Hosea 5:13, 7:8-11, and Lamentations 5:6 for other references. In addition to idolatry, relying on those who have at best divided interests and loyalties is impractical. As Machiavelli noted, in such cases, "ruin is only deferred as long as the assault is postponed...The cause of this is that they have no love or other motive to keep them in the field beyond a trifling wage, which is not enough to make them ready to die for you." (*The Prince*, New York: Penguin, 1980, p. 73.)

12. Morgan, p. 80.

13. Lawrence Adams: "The growing disappointment of the American people with national government follows their high expectations for it and their dependence upon it. As noted, Americans still expect the national government to be primarily responsible for the solution of national problems—meaning that Americans may lack a robust sense of the importance of other institutions." (*Going Public: Christian Responsibility in a Divided America*, Grand Rapids: Brazos Press, 2002, p. 122.)

14. Luis Lugo notes that "give" is more properly translated "render," implying that to which Caesar was rightfully entitled. ("Caesar's Coin and the Politics of the Kingdom: A Pluralist Perspective", in *Caesar's Coin Revisited: Christians and the Limits of Government*, ed. M. Cromartie, Grand Rapids: Eerdmans, 1996, p. 8.) John MacArthur notes that Christ changed the word that Pharisees had used for their question to emphasize the point. (*Why Government Can't Save You: An Alternative to Political Activism*, Nashville: Word Publishing, 2000, p. 61.)

15. Luke 20:20,25.

16. See also: Luke 4.

17.   In his definition of Satan, Ambrose Bierce relates a fictional dialogue between God and Satan. "Satan made himself multifariously objectionable and was finally expelled from Heaven. Halfway in his descent he paused, bent his head in thought a moment and at last went back.
    Satan: 'There is one favor that I should like to ask.'

God: 'Name it.'

Satan: 'Man, I understand, is about to be created. He will need laws.'

God: 'What, wretch! You his appointed adversary, charged from the dawn of eternity with hatred of his soul—you ask for the right to make his laws?'

Satan: 'Pardon; what I have to ask is that he be permitted to make them himself.'

It was so ordered."

18. J. Yoder, *The Politics of Jesus*, Grand Rapids: Eerdmans, 1972, p. 98. See also: Hebrews 4:15.

19. See: John 6:15. "Jesus didn't seize political power, whether it was offered to him by Satan or his followers. He didn't run for Congress or try to pass laws...the way God changes his world [is] through servanthood, meekness, and humility." Frederica Mathewes-Green, *The Door* interview, March/April 1995, p. 10-11.

20. John 18:36. Bob Briner says that "we are to be ambassadors of the One to whom we belong. It is important to remember that ambassadors do not meddle in the internal affairs of the country to which they are sent. They merely represent the interests and carry the messages of their homeland." (*Deadly Detours: Seven Noble Causes that Keep Christians from Changing the World*, Grand Rapids: Zondervan, 1996, p. 35.)

21. Christ's words in Matthew 6:1-4 make the pursuit of government less attractive as well. To some extent, calls for government activism often amount to a show of self-righteousness as opposed to working "quietly" behind the scenes, one-on-one. In Matthew 17:24-27, Christ claims an exemption from the temple tax—since the king and his sons are usually exempted—but decides to pay anyway "so that we may not offend."

22. See also: Ezra 6:10b, Jeremiah 29:7, I Thessalonians 4:11-12.

23. See also: Titus 3:1-2. For my attempt to find legitimate exceptions to this command, see: "The Ethics of Tax Evasion Within Biblical Christianity", in *The Ethics of Tax Evasion*, ed. R. McGee, South Orange, NJ: The Dumont Institute for Public Policy Research, 1998, p. 144-157.

24. "When Christ said, 'Render unto Caesar the things that are Caesar's, and unto God the things that God's', those words...gave to the civil power, under the protection of conscience, a sacredness it had never enjoyed, and bounds it had never acknowledged; and they were the repudiation of absolutism and the inauguration of freedom." (Lord Acton, "The history of freedom in antiquity", p. 29; quoted in K. DeYoung, Acton graduate student essay contest winner, 2001.) Similarly, C. S. Lewis remarked that: "If individuals live only seventy years, then a state, or a nation, or a civilization, which may last for a thousand years, is more important than an

individual. But if Christianity is true, then the individual is not only more important but incomparably more important, for his life is everlasting and the life of a state or a civilization, compared with his, is only a moment." (*Mere Christianity*, New York: Macmillan, 1960, p. 73.) Finally, note that people were "amazed" at Christ's specific teachings only three times: his teachings about the resurrection and no marriage in eternity (Matthew 22:33), the difficulty for the rich to get into heaven (Mark 10:24,26), and his Caesar/God comment (Luke 20:26). The first will always be amazing; interestingly, the second and third were amazing in their contemporary context but are taken as axiomatic today.

25. Acts 4:16-21, 5:28-29,33. Three vignettes in the book of Daniel (chapters 1, 3, and 6) also serve as excellent examples of appropriate responses to government. See also: Exodus 1, Joshua 2. Augustine (p. 113): "When it is considered how short is the span of human life, does it really matter to a man whose days are numbered what government he must obey, so long as he is not compelled to act against God or his conscience?"

26. There are two potential errors here: one can submit too little or too much to the State. This is analogous to the conditions under which one should submit (or not) to parents, employers, or a spouse.

27. See also: Isaiah 30:33. A sobering, contemporary application of this combination is the marriage of Islam and the use of force through the State and terrorism. Note also that martyrdom in Islam is connected to battles and war—whereas martyrdom in Christianity is connected to persecution for the faith.

28. Using some simplifying assumptions, John Cobin calculates that non-theocratic government policies were evil more than 90% of the time and more than 60% of theocratic government policies were evil (*Bible and Government: Public Policy from a Christian Perspective*, Greenville, SC: Alertness Books, 2003, p. 97-98, 106-111).

29. John MacArthur reproduces the classic prayers of this sort by Clement of Rome and Justin Martyr (p. 82-84). See also: Matthew 5:41's call to go the extra mile.

Chapter 3: The Theory vs. the Practice of Government

1. This is one of the prominent topics in Ramsey MacMullen, *Christianity and Paganism in the 4th to 8th Centuries*, New Haven, CT: Yale University Press, 1997 (especially chapters 1-2).

2. Contemporary understanding of the "establishment clause" of the First Amendment—that "Congress shall make no law respecting an establishment of religion, or prohibiting the free exercise thereof"—is highly flawed. People often assume that the State should be completely free of religion. Geisler and Turek cite a number of instances where the early American government directly funded religious activities. (*Legislating Morality: Is it Wise? Is it Legal? Is it Possible?*, Minneapolis: Bethany House, 1998, p. 81-82.)

3. For an interesting discussion of this and the role of Christianity in American history, see: Steven Keillor, *This Rebellious House: American History and the Truth of Christianity*, Downers Grove, IL: InterVarsity Press, 1996 (especially chapter 4). See also: K. Wald, *Religion and Politics in the United States*, 2nd cd., Washington, DC: CQ Press, 1992, p. 4.

4.   Note also that it is difficult to motivate the righteousness of the Revolutionary War in light of its context and Biblical injunctions to submit to government authority. During this time, "the Bible was used as a reservoir of images, moral principles and types...Serious exegesis, however, of what would seem to us like the relevant passages (such as Romans 13) was very rare...Patriots and Loyalists were both much more likely to add scriptural authority to political reasoning rooted in some other ideology than they were to attempt reasoning from the ground up on the basis of Scripture." (M. Noll, "Was the Revolutionary War Justified?" *Christianity Today*, February 8, 1999, p. 70. See also: M. Noll, "Ordinary People, Extraordinary Times", *Books and Culture*, July/August 2001, p. 27-29— especially his review of a book favorable to George III [of the same title] by Christopher Hibbert [New York: Basic Books, 1998].)

     John MacArthur argues that the American Revolution was a violation of Romans 13:1-7 and concludes that "the United States was actually born out of a violation of New Testament principles, and any blessings that God has bestowed upon America have come in spite of that disobedience by the Founding Fathers." (*Why Government Can't Save You: An Alternative to Political Activism*, Nashville: Word Publishing, 2000, p. 6.) Francis Schaeffer defends the American Revolution as protest and then self-defense, but only on the basis of the Declaration of Independence and Samuel Rutherford's "model" of *Lex Rex*—"Law is King." (*A Christian Manifesto*, 2nd ed., Wheaton, IL: Crossway Books, 1982, p. 127.) Finally, Ambrose Bierce defines "revolution": "In politics, an abrupt change in the form of misgovernment. Specifically, in American history, the substitution of the rule of an Administration for that of a Ministry, whereby the welfare and happiness of the people were advanced by a full half-inch. Revolutions are usually accompanied by a considerable effusion of blood, but are accounted worth it—this appraisement being made by beneficiaries whose blood had not the mischance to be shed."

5. From the supposed connection between legality and morality often voiced by politically-conservative evangelicals, the Founding Fathers apparently condoned drug use since they passed no laws against it.

6. D. Bandow, *Beyond Good Intentions: A Biblical View of Politics*, Wheaton, IL: Crossway Books, 1988, p. 146; J. Hunter, *Culture Wars: The Struggle to Define America—Making Sense of the Battles over the Family, Art, Education, Law, and Politics*, New York: Basic Books, 1991, p. 36, 201; R. Murphy, "The Origins of the Public School", *The Freeman*, July 1998, p. 403-406. Edward Larson quotes U.S. Census figures and reports that public high school enrollments increased from 200,000 in 1890 to two million in 1920. (*Summer for the Gods: The Scopes Trial and America's Continuing Debate over Science and Religion*, New York: Basic Books, 1997, p. 24.)

7. Ibid. A similar battle goes on today although the arguments are now based as much on science and logic as religious conviction—noting the differences between the facts of so-called "micro-evolution" and "macro-evolution" as a comprehensive theory for explaining the development of life.

8. Wald, p. 59. R. Reed, *Active Faith: How Christians Are Changing the Soul of American Politics*, New York: Free Press, 1996, p. 55. A. Crippen II, "The Public Square: Naked or Sacred?" in *Reclaiming the Culture: How You Can Protect Your Family's Future*, ed. A. Crippen II, Colorado Springs: Focus on the Family Publishing, 1996, p. 15-16, 38. The phrase was also written into the second verse of the Star Spangled Banner. In 1864, the Mint Act placed "In God We Trust" on the two-cent piece.

9. I Samuel 14:35. It is fashionable in evangelical circles to point to the 1960's as the genesis of America's supposed decline. In fact, an overall decline is debatable (a topic we will revisit in chapter 6)—and even assuming a decline, the catalysts would clearly extend further back into our history. For example, Lawrence Adams finds the root of our current problems in the Colonial period (*Going Public: Christian Responsibility in a Divided America*, Grand Rapids: Brazos Press, 2002, p. 58-65.)

10. Stewardship of the environment is another important issue, but beyond the scope of this book. Dallas Willard provides an excellent discussion of the distorted gospels presented by the Religious Left and Religious Right. (*The Divine Conspiracy: Rediscovering our Hidden Life in God*, San Francisco: Harper Collins, 1998, p. 42-59.) Most pertinent here is his critique of the Religious Left and its "Social Gospel" (p. 50-55).

11. Their agenda also prominently includes school prayer and other public education issues, as well as abortion. See: T. Sine, *Cease Fire: Searching for Sanity in America's Culture Wars*, Grand Rapids: Eerdmans, 1995, p. 150-151, for a connection between "legislating morality" and "legislating justice." Abortion is a separate and special case and will be dealt with in two later chapters.

12. Cal Thomas in C. Thomas and E. Dobson, *Blinded by Might: Can the Religious Right Save America?*, Grand Rapids: Zondervan, 1999, p. 94.

13. J. Haltemann, "The Market System, the Poor, and Economic Theory" in *Toward a Just and Caring Society: Christian Responses to Poverty in America*, ed. D. Gushee, Grand Rapids: Baker Books, 1999, p. 101.

14. P. Heyne, *The Catholic Bishops and the Pursuit of Justice*, Washington, DC: Cato Institute, 1986, p. 23.

15. As Ralph Reed notes (p. 8), "A dictatorship is efficient, quiet, and inhumane. In the chilling phrase about fascist Italy, Mussolini made the trains run on time. In a democracy, the trains sometimes run late, the conversation is loud, and disputes can turn contentious and occasionally downright nasty. But that dissent is a small price to pay for freedom. Indeed, this noise is not a sign of weakness; it is a sign of strength."

16. Heyne, p. 21.

17. Thomas Jefferson: "Sometimes it is said that man cannot be trusted with the government of himself. Can he, then, be trusted with the government of others?"

18. In *Death by Government* (New Brunswick, NJ: Transaction Press, 1997), R.J. Rummel estimates that governments have killed more than 170 million people.

19. II Kings 25:7.

20. As William Miller notes, "Here the fault often is idealism. The idealist begins with an abstract list of good things, drawn out of the mind— equality, peace, justice—instead of with the world as it is. He misses the fact that politics is not just about pure ideals, but about policy—that is, about relating particular objectives to other objectives and to what's possible; especially, he ignores the facts about power and interest and responsibility." (*The Protestant and Politics*, Philadelphia: Westminster Press, 1958, p. 36-37.)

21. G. K. Chesterton speaks to this as well—in distinguishing between ideals and reality: "Now, I have not lost my ideals in the least; my faith in fundamentals is exactly what it always was. What I have lost is my old

childlike faith in practical politics...As much as I ever did, more than I ever did, I believe in [Classical] Liberalism. But there was a rosy time of innocence when I believed in Liberals." (*Heretics/Orthodoxy*, Nashville: Thomas Nelson, 2000, p. 205.)

22. F. Hayek, *The Road to Serfdom*, chapter 10—"How the Worst Get on Top", Chicago: U. of Chicago Press, 1944. Or as P.J. O'Rourke puts it: "Giving money and power to government is like whiskey and car keys to teenage boys." G. K. Chesterton shares this concern (p. 272): "The man should rule who does *not* think that he can rule...we must take the crown in our hands, and go hunting in dry places and dark corners of the earth until we find the one man who feels himself unfit to wear it...We have not got to crown the exceptional man who knows he can rule. Rather, we must crown the much more exceptional man who knows he can't."

23. Quoted in Bandow, p. 107. See also: p. 107-115 and L. von Mises, *Liberalism: The Classical Tradition*, Irvington-on-Hudson, NY: Foundation for Economic Education, 1996, p. 55,56. Jonathan Rauch makes a similar point: "Idealistic activists can be much more expensive that cynical opportunists. A man who wants to take your car just for the money can often be warded off by an alarm, which may make the effort not worth the trouble. But the man who believes he is entitled to your car can be much more persistent." (*Demosclerosis: The Silent Killer of American Government*, New York: Random House, 1994, p. 77-78.)

24. R. Neuhaus, *The Naked Public Square: Religion and Democracy in America*, 2nd ed., Grand Rapids: Eerdmans, 1997, p. 8.

25. In Noll's words, when Christians have exercised power, the cross is typically set aside for the crown. In contrast, when believers have been a distinct minority, "they have not needed to be instructed about the cross." (*Adding Cross to Crown: The Political Significance of Christ's Passion*, Grand Rapids: Baker Books, 1996, p. 25.)

26. Quoted by Richard John Neuhaus, *First Things*, March 2000, p. 113.

27. The example of Billy Graham during the Nixon administration is instructive. See: Cal Thomas, "Silence of the Shepherd", *World*, March 16, 2002, p. 25.

28. Richard John Neuhaus very nicely defends "the morality of compromise" in chapter 7 of *The Naked Public Square* (see especially: p. 114-115, 123-124).

29. Ambrose Bierce defines a "mugwump" as "In politics, one afflicted with self-respect and addicted to the vice of independence. A term of contempt." In his essay, "Liberalism's Religion Problem," Stephen Carter

relates the story about Fannie Lou Hamer's unwillingness to compromise with Vice-President Hubert Humphrey—from Charles Marsh's book, *God's Long Summer*. He concludes that Mrs. Hamer "has much to teach us about what can happen when strong religious commitment runs up against the world of secular politics." (*First Things*, March 2002, p. 21.)

30. I Peter 4:11.

31. See also: Isaiah 52:5, Ezekiel 36:22.

32. P. Yancey, *Christianity Today*, February 6, 1995. See also: Miller, p. 25.

33. Thomas and Dobson, p. 194.

34. MacArthur, p. ix.

35. C.S. Lewis, *The Screwtape Letters*, New York: Macmillan: 1982, letter #7, p. 35. Ambrose Bierce is a bit more cynical, defining a patriot as "The dupe of statesmen and the tool of conquerors."

36. D. Gushee, "From Despair to Mission", in *Christians and Politics Beyond the Culture Wars: An Agenda for Engagement*, ed. D. Gushee, Grand Rapids: Baker Books, 2000, p. 39. Leith Anderson quotes Bill Bennett: "Our first task is to recognize that it is foolish, and futile, to rely primarily on politics to solve moral, cultural and spiritual afflictions."—and concludes that "rather than argue politics and philosophies and strategies, is not our highest calling to 'live Christianly'." (*Winning the Values War in a Changing Culture: Thirteen Distinct Values that Mark a Follower of Christ*, Minneapolis: Bethany House, 1994, p. 39, 24.) John MacArthur (p. 34) concurs: "The contemporary church seems to have largely forgotten that the priorities for effecting change in society are faithful prayer, godly living, and diligent evangelism rather than persistent lobbying, self-righteous confrontation, and political organizing." Lawrence Adams (p. 131) makes the same argument from the angle that contemporary political philosophy is so convoluted that "any Christian strategy for the reconstruction of public culture [through politics] currently has little chance of wide acceptance," before concluding that "the practice of faithfulness may indeed be the best goal."

37. Interestingly, Jerry Falwell had an interesting reversal on this matter. In March 1965, he preached that pastors should eschew political activism in civil rights and in fighting communism to focus on evangelism. "Preachers are not called to be politicians but to be soul winners...Nowhere are we commissioned to reform the externals. The gospel does not clean up the outside but rather regenerates the inside." (Quoted in Neuhaus, p 10.) As Neuhaus then notes, "By 1980, 1965 seemed like a very long time ago."

38. See: I Corinthians 7-11, I Corinthians 6:12, Galatians 5:1,13, etc. The biggest possible exception to this principle is Paul's "self-defense" in Acts—at Philippi and especially in dealing with the Roman government. But in all of the cases, one could argue that he had other agendas at the forefront of his motivations—protecting the new Philippian church and trying to get an audience for the gospel to Roman leaders. In any case, his defense goes no further than self-preservation.

39. Noll, p. 73.

40. Neuhaus, p. 59. Or as Joel Belz puts it: "local churches need to be more careful not to become precinct offices for the Republican party." (*World*, June 8, 2002, p. 3.)

41. See: Sine, p. 133-135, 160, 225.

42. II Corinthians 10:1-5. Ironically, Tom Minnery approves of pastor Neal Laybourne's use of this text, causing him to be "fully confident that a political protest movement was an act of righteousness." (*Why You Can't Stay Silent: A Biblical Mandate to Shape our Culture*, Wheaton, IL: Tyndale House, 2001, p. 13.)

43. Von Mises, p. 64.

44. A. W. Tozer, "Organization: Necessary and Dangerous".

45. Neuhaus, p. 30.

46. Neuhaus (p. 181): "...every governmental decision produces unhappiness as well as satisfactions...Vindication tends to be a brief satisfaction, while the sense of being violated goes on and on. Since they tend to manufacture resentments, there is wisdom in the bias that favors limiting the number of government decisions. Nonetheless, the form of governance is tolerable so long as it is assumed that there will always be another inning, another election...there are no final winners or final losers, and everybody understands that she will get her way only part of the time."

47. C.S. Lewis, "Membership" in *The Weight of Glory and Other Addresses*, Grand Rapids: Eerdmans, 1965, p. 36.

48. Chesterton, p. 206.

49. P. Cleveland, "Economic Liberty", paper delivered at the conference on Economics and Christianity, Baylor University: Waco, TX, November 7-9, 2002. Cleveland primary focus here is in discussing the work of Frederic Bastiat.

50. D. Bandow, *The Politics of Envy: Statism as Theology*, New Brunswick, NJ: Transaction Publishers, 1994, p. xviii.

51. Ibid., p. 5.

52. M. Skousen, *Religion and Liberty*, "Civilization Held Together by Persuasion, not Force", May/June 1996, p. 1. See also: Von Mises, p. 51.

53. Jeremiah 17:10; Bandow, *Politics of Envy*, p. 6.

54. Ibid., p. 4.

55. J. Elshtain, *Augustine and the Limits of Politics*, Notre Dame, IN: University of Notre Dame Press, 1998, p. 101. For the record, Elshtain wisely notes the complexity of Augustine's work and cautions against using "slices" or isolated quotes (p. 23-24). Curtis Chang: "For Aquinas especially recognized that Christ's strategy differed profoundly from the fallen human pattern of coercion and violence...In Christ, God rejects any coercion to correct humanity. Instead God offers himself in Christ as a free gift of grace. This grace is the antithesis of violence..." (*Engaging Unbelief*, Downers Grove, IL: InterVarsity Press, 2000, p. 149-150.)

56. "The problem with making unlimited government our savior, according to Lewis, is that it undermines human dignity and ignores human depravity. It undermines human dignity because it does not take seriously the connection between freedom and human excellence...Lewis granted that the freedom required for virtue to flourish also makes evil possible but this is the price that must be paid..." (J. West, "Public Life in the Shadowlands: What C.S. Lewis Can Teach Us About Politics", Grand Rapids: Acton Institute, 1998, p. 8.)

57. Quoted in Bandow, *Beyond Good Intentions*, p. 20. William Martin reports that Tim LaHaye's American Coalition for Traditional Values held a conference in December 1985 on how to win elections. Unfortunately, a magazine revealed that one of the organization's biggest supporters was the Reverend Sun Myung Moon's Unification Church. (*With God on our Side: The Rise of the Religious Right in America*, New York: Broadway Books, 1996, p. 270.)

58. C. Thomas, "More Than Politics", *(Louisville) Courier-Journal*, March 22, 1995.

59. C. Colson, *Power Religion: The Selling Out of the Evangelical Church*, ed. M. Horton, Chicago: Moody Press, 1992, p. 36, quoted in J. Whitehead, *Christians Involved in the Political Process*, Chicago: Moody Press, 1994, p. 32. Colson also notes that "One of the reasons I have written books and given speeches warning Christian leaders not to be seduced by the wiles and the attractiveness of power in the White House, and to keep our distance and never mix the gospel with politics, is that I saw how well I

exploited religious leaders when I was in that job." (Quoted in Martin, *With God on our Side*, p. 99.)

60. W. Bennett, "Revolt Against God: America's Spiritual Despair", in *Reclaiming the Culture*, p. 15-16.

61. M. Olasky, *The Tragedy of American Compassion*, Washington, DC: Regnery Gateway, 1992, p. 122. Reed (p. 50) notes an example of a similar idolatry toward unions: "The union label is a religious emblem. It is a religious act to buy goods to which this label [is] attached, an act blessed on earth and honored in heaven."

62. Pope Paul VI, "Octogesima Adveniens", #46, Vatican City, 1971.

63. Pope Paul VI, "Populorum Progressio", #33, Vatican City, 1967. He continues with a warning: "But let take care to associate private initiative and intermediary bodies with this work. They will thus avoid the danger of complete collectivization..." But after his initial remark, the follow-up seems like chasing after the wind. See also: #60-61.

64. Sirico's preface in Bandow, *Politics of Envy*, p. ix. See: Schlossberg's *Idols for Destruction: The Conflict of Christian Faith and American Culture* (Wheaton, IL: Crossway Books, 1990) for an excellent discussion of the State as one of many idols. He also argues that redistribution results from an "idolatry to mammon" with its "insistence that it is more blessed to receive than to give." (p. 137)

65. D. Chilton, *Productive Christians in an Age of Guilt Manipulators: A Biblical Response to Ronald J. Sider*, 3rd ed., Tyler, TX: Institute for Christian Economics, 1985, p. 64.

66. The memorial service for Senator Paul Wellstone was a poignant example of idolatry in action. Richard John Neuhaus: "One columnist referred to the Wellstone memorial/rally as a sacrilege. I expect that many, perhaps most, of the people there would simply be puzzled by that assertion. Sacrilege assumes an understanding of the sacred, and they were celebrating what was sacred for them. The occasion was an unabashed, full-throated, vulgar declaration that politics is the first thing. They were there not to honor but to use the memory of Paul Wellstone in the service of their highest good, political power." (*First Things*, December 2002, p. 84.)

67. Deuteronomy 13:6-10.

68. Deuteronomy 13:15.

69. Schlossberg (p. 8) writes that idolatry "explains the vehemence with which attacks on someone's assumptions are met; they are often attacks on that person's unacknowledged religion." To the extent that this is a matter

of idolatry, persuasion may be difficult. Jeremiah died without seeing the people change, but at least they remembered his words when they were in exile!

70. P. Wehner, *World*, "Principled Withdrawal?", March 11, 1995, p. 26.

71. Thomas, "More Than Politics".

Chapter 4: Pursuing Godly Goals with Godly Methods

1. Romans 6:13, I Thessalonians 1:3.

2. Galatians 2:20.

3. Galatians 5:22-23, I Thessalonians 5:19.

4. Galatians 4:19, 5:1,13.

5. Romans 14:23.

6. Revelation 3:15-16. See also: Isaiah 27:4-5.

7. *Christianity Today*, October 6, 1997, p. 53.

8. As Richard John Neuhaus notes, "There is tolerance, and then there is tolerance. There is the tolerance of indifference to truth, and then there is the tolerance (from *tolerare*—to endure) that is the fortitude to bear with people...who do their worst to make themselves unbearable. The latter is indeed a virtue." (*First Things*, January 1998, p. 71.)

9. Luke 8:7,14.

10. Luke 18:18-30; John 18:28-40; James 1:6-8; Numbers 13-14; Judges 4-5.

11. J. Wallis, *The Soul of Politics*, New York: The New Press, 1994, p. 195.

12. See also: Zephaniah 1:12, Matthew 22:5.

13. Galatians 4:18.

14. See also: Genesis 11's tower of Babel, Genesis 19 for Lot's wife and her passion for Sodom, Genesis 37 for the avid jealousy of Joseph's brothers in selling him into slavery, and the Israelites' persistent grumbling against God and Moses in the wilderness.

15. Jeremiah 10:5. In Isaiah 44, the prophet notes the stupidity of using half a block of wood for fire and half as something to worship. See also: Daniel 2 for the usually practical Nebuchadnezzar's expenditures on a 90-foot tall golden image of himself.

16. Jeremiah 2:20-25.

17. Galatians 5:13, Ephesians 4:30.

18. Galatians 5:1.

19. C.S. Lewis, *The Great Divorce*, New York: Touchstone, 1996, p. 95.

20. See: Hebrews 4:12, Romans 14:23, I Corinthians 4:5, John 5:30, 15:5.

21. Proverbs 19:2, I Corinthians 8:1, 13:3.

22. See also: John 16:7, Galatians 5:16-26, Romans 6-8. This is a complex, but crucial topic. For those who do not understand it or its importance, I recommend *The Saving Life of Christ* by Ian Thomas (Grand Rapids: Zondervan, 1961) and *The Normal Christian Life* by Watchman Nee (Wheaton, IL: Tyndale House, 1985).

23. Thomas, p. 82.

24. Although he didn't deceive anyone in the latter case, it would have been more gracious to simply offer the famished Esau some food.

25. See also: Abraham's failures to trust God with respect to protecting his wife in foreign lands (Genesis 12, 20).

26. His failure to get into the Promised Land was caused by a similar mistake. Contrast Exodus 17 with Numbers 20.

27. Matthew 26:51-54, Luke 9:51-56.

28. See Matthew 23, especially verse 15.

29. Philippians 3:6 and Galatians 1:14.

30. Romans 10:2. See also: Proverbs 19:2.

31. In the words of Donald Hay, "However laudable the ends, the means could be quite intolerable." (*Economics Today*, Grand Rapids: Eerdmans, 1989, p. 88.) Unfortunately, Hay advocates many policies with "intolerable" means.

32. In *God Tells the Man who Cares*, A. W. Tozer makes a similar point within the church: "What foreign relation board actually seeks to follow the guidance of the Lord?...They all think they do, but what they do in fact is to assume the scripturalness of their ends and then ask for help to find ways to achieve them...Christ is desired as their helper, not as their Lord. Human means are devised to achieve ends assumed to be divine. These harden into policy, and thereafter the Lord doesn't even have a vote."

33. Dallas Willard: "We must beware of believing that it is okay for us to condemn as long as we are condemning the right things. It is not as simple as all that. I can trust Jesus to go into the temple and drive out those who were profiting from religion, beating them with a rope. I cannot trust myself to do it." The same question must also be asked of the State; good intentions are not sufficient. (*The Divine Conspiracy: Rediscovering our Hidden Life in God*, San Francisco: Harper Collins, 1998, p. 221.)

A Note on Defining Legislating Morality and Justice

1. John Paul II, "Reconciliatio et Paenitentia", #16, 1984; quoted in *The Social Agenda: A Collection of Magisterial Texts*, ed. R. Sirico and M. Zieba, Vatican City: Pontifical Council for Justice and Peace, 2000, p. 88.

2. L. Spooner, *Vices Are not Crimes: A Vindication of Moral Liberty*, 1875, chapter I. Spooner then argues that "unless this clear distinction between vices and crimes be made and recognized by the laws, there can be on earth no such thing as individual rights, liberty, or property..."

3. R. Reed, *Active Faith*, New York: Free Press, 1996, p. 278.

4. In "Libertarianism in One Lesson," Tibor Machan notes another overlap. In distinguishing between "the Right's idealism"—seeking to regulate "spiritual or mental actions" ("the crafting of people's souls")—and "the Left's materialism"—seeking to regulate "economic or material actions," he notes that the two intersect "since body and soul aren't ever sharply divided." He then cites examples of this overlap—the Right seeking "blue laws" and affecting commerce and the Left restricting free speech and thought at the expense of social freedoms.

5. E. Scheske, "Is There no Privacy?", *Touchstone*, July/August 2001, p. 13.

6. A related argument is that the indirect costs are not particularly indirect—for example, a supposedly strong causation between pornography and child abuse. But, in addition to questions about whether this connection is merely correlation, we still run into the same difficulty—should Christians advocate prohibitions against cars, alcohol, guns, legalistic homes, and so on? If one argues that pornography is different because it is "worthless," they should at least be wary of giving powers to a government which may someday view Christianity as a worthless folly. If one argues that pornography is different because the costs are substantial, to be consistent, we also need to vocally pursue LM on issues like extramarital sex, false religions, and smoking cigarettes.

7. "Such a thing as government, formed by voluntary association, would never have been thought of, if the object proposed had been the punishment of all vices, impartially; because nobody wants such an institution, or would voluntarily submit to it. But a government, formed by voluntary association, for the punishment of all *crimes* is a reasonable matter; because everybody wants protection for himself against all crimes by others, and also acknowledges the justice of his own punishment, if he commits a crime." (Spooner, Chapter XI.)

8. Lynn Scarlett lists other minor "externalities": "Leaves from one person's tree fall onto another's yard; a car door sounds across the road, jolting someone from his midday reverie; a plane flies 30,000 feet overhead, leaving an unnatural scratch upon the sky; and neon pink trim around the windows of a house offends a neighbor's sense of aesthetics and propriety." (*Reason*, March 1999, p. 64.)

9. The same is true in economics. If markets do not function particularly well, as in the cases of externalities (e.g., pollution), "public goods" (e.g., national defense), significant degrees of monopoly power, etc., government can improve the workings of the market—at least in theory.

10. J. Wallis, *The Soul of Politics*, New York: The New Press, 1994, p. xxiv.

11. Quoted in *From Irenaeus to Grotius: a Sourcebook in Christian Political Thought, 100-1625*, ed. O. O'Donovan and J. O'Donovan, Grand Rapids: Eerdmans, 1999, p. 360.

12. For example, see: M. Bauman, "The Falsity, Futility and Folly of Separating Morality from Law", *Christian Research Journal*, p. 21ff. Likewise, Geisler and Turek's *Legislating Morality: Is it Wise? Is it Legal? Is it Possible?* (Minneapolis: Bethany House, 1998) suffers from the same failure, arguing simply that consensual sins impact others too (see: p. 33-34, 44-45). As such, sadly, their efforts add much less to the debate than they should. Tom Minnery's *Why You Can't Stay Silent: A Biblical Mandate to Shape our Culture* (Wheaton, IL: Tyndale House, 2001) argues for Christian political involvement in broad terms (LM and LJ), but then almost exclusively provides examples of LJ or leaves the matter undefined. (See: p, 20-25, 29, 47, 49, 53-54, 65, 67, 68. The other examples are using zoning laws in trying to reduce abortion and laws restricting gambling—topics we will discuss later.)

13. "We see that as soon as we surrender the principle that the state should not interfere in any questions touching on the individual's mode of life, we end by regulating and restricting the latter down to the smallest detail...[The individual] becomes a slave of the community, bound to obey the dictates

of the majority." (L. Von Mises, *Liberalism: The Classical Tradition*, Irvington-on-Hudson, NY: Foundation for Economic Education, 1996, p. 54.)

14. G. Jesson, "The Train Wreck of Truth and Knowledge", in *Reclaiming the Culture: How You Can Protect Your Family's Future*, ed. A. Crippen II, Colorado Springs: Focus on the Family Publishing, 1996, p. 50.

Chapter 5: What Does the Bible Say? What Would Jesus Do?

1. MacArthur qualifies his similar conclusions in a similar manner: "By making such criticisms...I want to affirm clearly that I am still unalterably opposed to the sins of abortion and homosexuality." (*Why Government Can't Save You: An Alternative to Political Activism*, Nashville: Word Publishing, 2000, p. 26.) Clifford Thies reasonably critiques the Libertarian party on similar grounds: "The Libertarian Party comes close to, but misses the mark set out by Romans 13 because it declares itself neutral on moral issues...Instead of saying that [it] does not take positions on moral issues, it should affirm that virtue is only possible in a free society, that a free society best induces virtuous behavior, and that the candidates of the Libertarian Party will, if elected, promote virtue through non-coercive means." ("Must a Christian Be a Libertarian?", www.self-gov.org/christian/thics.htm, January 28, 2003, p. 2.)

2. The law defines "consent" as pertaining to adults only. Other questions about "mental competence," legal and moral distinctions between adults and children, the degree to which other parties are affected, and so on, are relevant and interesting but tangential to the principles developed here. For the proper response to Christians who have committed sin, see: Matthew 18, I Corinthians 5:1-6:8, Galatians 6:1.

3. Geisler and Turek's book (*Legislating Morality: Is it Wise? Is it Legal? Is it Possible?*, Minneapolis: Bethany House, 1998) fails to ask or answer this question. It's ironic and sad that Geisler is such an excellent apologist for Christianity and the Bible, but fails to address the question for which their subtitle absolutely begs: "Is it Biblical?"! They close by asking for "a well-reasoned rebuttal" with the request that it include "the standard by which you judge." Again, it would seem that Scripture should have a prominent place in deciding whether or not one should legislate morality.

4. See also: Nehemiah 13's "blue laws."

5. Moreover, the Canaanites had options. Instead of actively fighting against God and Israel, they could flee, repent (as Rahab), or "negotiate" (as the Gibeonites). See: my book, *Inheriting our Promised Land: Lessons in*

Victorious Christian Living from the Book of Joshua (Greenville, SC: Alertness Books, 2003) for an in-depth study of Joshua. See also: Genesis 15:16's prophecy of this.

6. See: C.S. Lewis, *Mere Christianity*, New York: Macmillan, 1960, Book 2, Chapter 3.

7. Matthew 13:24-30. This is also very much evident in God's relationship with Elijah and the nature of his ministry to Israel.

8. Galatians 5:1,13. See also: I Corinthians 6:12's "Everything is permissible but not everything is beneficial."

9. Romans 1:24,26,28. In Luke 15, the father gives the "Prodigal Son" the freedom to hang himself. See also: Acts 14:16.

10. Ironically, the tree may have been even more enticing with a fence around it. And arguably, Adam &/or Eve constructed a fence by adding "do not touch" to God's command not to eat of the fruit (Genesis 2:17, 3:3).

11. R. Bass, "Liberty and the Judeo-Christian Heritage", unpublished paper, Bowling Green State University, Department of Philosophy. Of course, this quote does not solve all of the relevant questions, but does serve as a cautionary tale.

12. D. Willard, *The Spirit of the Disciplines: Understanding How God Changes Lives*, San Francisco: HarperSanFrancisco, 1988, p. 52-53. See also: Joshua 24:15, Judges 5:2.

13. It becomes more difficult to condemn some seemingly sinful behaviors while other seemingly appropriate behaviors are deemed out-of-bounds (with "seemingly" determined by a spirit of the Law interpretation). As an example of the latter, one would not be able to justify having Bible classes for children at church since Scripture only mentions teaching children at home.

14. Dave Burchett asks "Would Jesus Spend His Time on This?" (*When Bad Christians Happen to Good People*, Colorado Springs: Waterbrook Press, 2002.)

15. Mark 10:17-22.

16. See: T. Sine, *Cease Fire: Searching for Sanity in America's Culture Wars*, Grand Rapids: Eerdmans, 1995, p. 132. Willard provides an excellent critique of this misconception in *The Spirit of the Disciplines*, Chapter 10: "Is Poverty Spiritual?" Or as Bandow remarks, "while Jesus demanded financial sacrifice on the part of His followers, he did not do so as part of an income redistribution program but to heal them spiritually." (*Beyond Good*

Intentions: A Biblical View of Politics, Wheaton, IL: Crossway Books, 1988, p. 104.)

17. For other interesting episodes, see: John 5:3-15, Luke 19:1-10. See also: Joshua's different battle strategies from God and I Chronicles 14 for David depending on God for direction. What role docs the Holy Spirit play in legislating morality?

18. In addition to using it as an example of upholding the Law in the story of the "rich young ruler" (Mark 10:19), Christ used adultery to 1.) talk about the heart (Matthew 15:19); 2.) stretch adultery to include lust (Matthew 5:28); 3.) make divorce seem worse (Matthew 5:32, 19:9); 4.) take a poke at the Pharisees (Luke 18:11); and 5.) refer to the idolatry of this "wicked and adulterous generation." (Matthew 12:39, 16:4; Mark 8:38)

19. N. Van Andel, letter to the editor, *Christianity Today*, August 14, 1996, p. 8.

20. Matthew 8:26, 16:8; Matthew 15:16; Luke 9:51-56; Luke 22:34.

21. John 20:24-31, Luke 10:38-42. Interestingly, it may be that Thomas had the most faith of any disciple since Christ appeared to him last. Perhaps the others needed to see Christ as soon as possible to maintain their (weaker) faith.

22. Mark 10:35-40.

23. Matthew 14:31.

24. Mark 16:7, John 21:15-18.

25. Ephesians 4:29, I Thessalonians 2:11-12, Colossians 3:16, 4:6; Proverbs 10:21.

26. See also: Christ as an extremely impolite dinner guest in Luke 11:37-52.

27. John 7:50-51, 19:39-40.

28. The life of John the Baptist provides a possible exception. In Luke 3:19, John may have publicly reproved Herod. In any case, the word for "reproved" is the same one John the gospel-writer used to describe how the Holy Spirit would convict the world of its sin (John 16:8)—hardly a loud or brute force method. Matthew 14:4 and Mark 6:18 report John telling Herod that he was wrong, but apparently in private. This supports further the idea of working "one-on-one" rather than going public. And even with the most favorable interpretation of this one verse, there is still not any meaningful case for publicly admonishing government officials. There is simply too much evidence to the contrary. Analogously, if I were to only cite a few verses, I could develop a "reasonable" case for salvation by works.

Presumably one's response would be that I should look at the totality of Scripture to gain an accurate picture. The same principle holds here.

29. Romans 2:24, Isaiah 52:5, Ezekiel 36:22.

30. The former chaplain at Harvard, George Buttrick, tells a story about students who would come into his office and say "I don't believe in God." Buttrick would reply: "Sit down and tell me what kind of God you don't believe in. I probably don't believe in him either." (*Christianity Today*, June 17, 1996, p. 32.)

31. Romans 16:17-18, II Thessalonians 3:6.

32. Matthew 18:15-20.

33. I Corinthians 5:9-13. See also: I Peter 4:17.

34. See also: Jonah 1 when God looks past the "great sins" of the sailors to work on "his man," Jonah.

35. Romans 12:19. As Doug Bandow (p. 99) notes, God "transferred authority to enforce [LM issues] from the civil authorities to the church...As a result, the sanctions are different—excommunication instead of execution, for instance—but the ultimate objective is the same, to maintain the purity of the Body of Christ...If this were not the case, the task for civil government would have become impossible in practice once Christ emphasized compliance with the law in thought as well as in deed...While the civil authorities may be able to detect and punish adultery, no official, without divine wisdom, can judge lustful looks..."

36. See also: John 17:14-15. David Gushee: "We are fixated on the one moral issue most remote from the daily experience of our membership, while we ignore a wide range of offenses far closer to home—divorce and materialism, to name two examples. This reverses the way Jesus taught his followers to deal with sin." ("The Speck in Mickey's Eye", *Christianity Today*, August 11, 1997, p. 13.)

37. Deuteronomy 22:22. The Law leaves the means of execution open-ended unless she happened to have been a "virgin pledged to be married" (Deuteronomy 22:23-24).

38. *Charlotte Observer* columnist Lew Powell asks wryly: "Do I prefer conservatism to conservatives, but liberals to liberalism?" In response, Joel Belz notes, "Neither conservatives nor liberals can take comfort while they wrestle with the implicit accusations" in the quote. He then asks readers which reputation they would rather have: "someone whose ideas are right but is always crotchety, or someone who is loved by all but whose ideas

can't stand the test of time." ("Trading Places", *World*, December 24, 1994.)

39. A proponent of LM should be able to answer why Christ did not allow her to die or even to be punished for her sin.

40. From beginning to end, Rick Scarborough's *Enough Is Enough: A Call to Christian Involvement* (Springdale, PA: Whitaker House, 1996) represents perhaps the antithesis of Christ's approach. The cover art depicts the upper arm of an angry white guy in a business suit, slamming his closed fist on a table, in a red-white-and-blue (patriotic?) arc. The book covers the usual litany of problems and prescriptions offered by the Religious Right. The final chapter's title ("Pray and Grab a Hoe") and one of its opening lines ("I believe the only hope for restoration of this nation is the church.", p. 241) seem to hold some promise, but then his five prescriptions include four that are exclusively political and one that recommends establishing a church committee to advertise "moral concerns"!

41. Of course, not having many opportunities to interact with unbelievers is a separate problem (I Peter 2:11-12).

42. For a noteworthy example, see Paul's response to slavery in Ephesians 6:5, Colossians 4:1, and the letter to Christian slave-owner Philemon. The one pseudo-exception to this is Paul's brief critique of slave-*trading* in I Timothy 1:10.

Chapter 6: Practically Speaking—What Are the Costs?

1. Luke 14:28-33.

2. J. Ortberg, "Do They Know Us by Our Love?", *Christianity Today*, May 19, 1997, p. 25.

3. Luke 19:10.

4. Romans 3:9-10,22-23.

5. Ephesians 2:3.

6. I Corinthians 6:9-11.

7. Matthew 23:25-28, II Timothy 3:5.

8. J. MacArthur, *Why Government Can't Save You: An Alternative to Political Activism*, Nashville: Word Publishing, 2000, p. ix.

9. Galatians 1:8-9. It is also noteworthy that God gave the Law to the Israelites after he delivered them from their bondage in Egypt.

10. At the extreme, the position can reduce itself to caricature. For example, John Freeman argues that "Alcohol was designed by the Creator to meet certain needs in the chemical world...It was never intended to be used as a beverage." And he claims that "The story of the Good Samaritan should impel every Christian to be both a total abstainer from alcoholic beverages and a vigorous opponent of the entire liquor industry...To give consent to the traffic in alcoholic beverages because one is an abstainer and is not hurt by the traffic is like asserting lack of responsibility for letting a blind man run into a pit which careless man has left uncovered." (*Shadow Over America*, Nashville: Convention Press, 1957, p. 3, 123-124.) All this is reminiscent of Ambrose Bierce's definitions of teetotaler ("One who abstains from strong drink, sometimes totally, sometimes tolerably totally") and rum ("generically, fiery liquors that produce madness in total abstainers").

11. Galatians 5:10.

12. Luke 11:52.

13. Revisiting John Freeman (p. 82), he reasonably argues that "There is lack of wisdom when a nation places strict prohibitions against the misuse of opiates and refuses to safeguard the public against the misuse of narcotics." Of course, whether a Christian should seek to prohibit either is debatable! Francis Schaeffer notes the enforcement of blasphemy laws in the 19th century (*A Christian Manifesto*, 2nd ed., Wheaton, IL: Crossway Books, 1982, p. 37). Justinian argued that inheritances should not be allowed to pass to heretics. In the absence of orthodox family members, the proceeds of the estate would go to the State or the Church. (Codex I.5.18, in *From Irenaeus to Grotius: a Sourcebook in Christian Political Thought, 100-1625*, ed. O. O'Donovan and J. O'Donovan, Grand Rapids: Eerdmans, 1999, p. 191-192.)

14. Matthew 7:3-5.

15. See: Acts 16:21's "unlawful to accept or practice."

16. C.S. Lewis, *The Great Divorce*, New York: Touchstone, 1996, p. 95. This memorable line is in the middle of a fascinating discussion on a debatable topic—whether increased morality is a stumbling block or stepping stone to establishing or deepening a relationship with God. "There's something in natural affection which will lead it on to eternal love more easily...But there's also something in it which makes it easier to stop at the natural level and mistake it for the heavenly...And if it finally refuses conversion its corruption will be worse than the corruption of what you call the lower passions. It is a stronger angel, and therefore, when it falls, a fiercer devil...The false religion of lust is baser than the false religion of

mother-love or patriotism or art; but lust is less likely to be made into a religion." (p. 95-96)

17. It might seem as if this argument conflicts with Romans 3:5-8. However, that passage addresses the prospective abuse of grace by believers, not the behavior of unbelievers. This is not meant to imply that we should encourage immorality among unbelievers, but merely that to the extent that it occurs, Christian behaviors would stand in starker contrast.

18. Or as C.S. Lewis asks, how far should Christians "try to force their views on marriage on the rest of the community by embodying them in the divorce laws? A great many people seem to think that if you are a Christian yourself you should try to make divorce difficult for everyone. I do not think that. At least I know I should be very angry if the Moslems tried to prevent the rest of us from drinking wine." (*Mere Christianity*, New York: Macmillan, 1960, p. 101.) Touche!

19. B. Briner, *Deadly Detours: Seven Noble Causes that Keep Christians from Changing the World*, Grand Rapids: Zondervan, 1996, p. 10, 14-15. This is a prominent theme in Thomas and Dobson's book, *Blinded by Might: Can the Religious Right Save America?* (Grand Rapids: Zondervan, 1999). For example, Ed Dobson argues that "the Religious Right has abandoned the greater priority of communicating the gospel for the lesser priority of sanctifying the state. The net result is that they accomplished neither very well." (p. 109) Tom Minnery, in his response to Dobson and Cal Thomas, acknowledges this issue in noting Focus on the Family's limited political agenda. (*Why You Can't Stay Silent: A Biblical Mandate to Shape our Culture*, Wheaton, IL: Tyndale House, 2001, p. 129-130.)

20. See: T. Sine, *Cease Fire: Searching for Sanity in America's Culture Wars*, Grand Rapids: Eerdmans, 1995, p. 133. See also: Matthew 6:33 and Luke 8:7,14's seed among the thorns.

21. L. Spooner, *Vices Are not Crimes: A Vindication of Moral Liberty*, 1875, Chapter VIII.

22. An amusing but telling example of this: Winnipeg's efforts to separate children under 18 from second-hand smoke in public places. The result was that many businesses catered to smokers, declining to hire children for work and refusing service to adults accompanied by children. (C. Freund, "Child-Free Dining", *Reason*, April 2002, p. 12.)

23. Spooner, Chapter XIII.

24. Clifford Thies ("Must a Christian Be a Libertarian?", www.self-gov.org/christian/thies.htm, January 28, 2003, p. 3.): "God's will is revealed to us through the laws of nature and history. It is wrong for the government

to try to protect us from, and thus undermine the laws of nature and history." Frederic Bastiat (quoted in P. Cleveland, "Economic Liberty", presented at "Economics and Christianity", Baylor University: Waco, November 7-9, 2002): "All error breeds suffering. And this suffering either falls upon the one who erred, in which case it sets in operation the law of responsibility; or else it strikes innocent parties, in which case it sets in motion the marvelous reagent that is the law of solidarity. The action of these laws, combined with the ability...of seeing the connection between cause and effect, must bring us back, by the very fact of suffering, to the path of righteousness and truth...But if evil is to fulfill this purpose...the freedom of the individual must be respected."

25. Interview with Walter Wangerin, *The Door Interviews*, p. 289-290.

26. Spooner, Chapter XVI.

27. Ibid.

28. A related issue is building laws to deal with the problems of a small portion of the population. Curiously, Freeman (p. 52) concludes that "the state was ordained of God for the protection and welfare of all citizens (Romans 13:7) not to provide legal sanction under which a very small minority may carry on the manufacture and sale of beverages which enslave so many."

29. In Norway, Kirsti Larsen spent two days in jail because she wouldn't pay a $200 fine for violating a law by giving her son a name that was deemed unacceptable by the government. The name *Gesher* which is Hebrew for "bridge," was not on the approved list. (*World*, January 9, 1999, p. 10.) In Texas, some seminaries are not allowed to call themselves seminaries unless they purchase a "certificate of authority" from the State and make "expensive adjustments to meet 25 state standards." (*World*, April 7, 2001, p. 35.) Some European countries already regulate Jehovah's Witnesses and Scientologists. Finally, would Isaiah have had his ministry restricted by the State—or even religious conservatives—in Isaiah 20:2-4?!

30. As Florence King quips in her "cautionary tale [for] the Nanny State": "When they came for the smokers I kept silent because I don't smoke. When they came for the meat eaters I kept silent because I'm a vegetarian. When they came for the gun owners I kept silent because I'm a pacifist. When they came for the drivers I kept silent because I'm a bicyclist. They never did come for me. I'm still here because there's nobody left in the secret police except sissies with rickets." (*The Florence King Reader*, p. 330.) Tom Minnery (p. 59): "A pastor who believes that his congregation can simply sit out the culture war and then somehow resist at the end is foolish." Paraphrasing his valid point, one should wonder about the wisdom

of using government force against others and our ability to resist the same in the future.

31. Matthew 12:39, 17:17; Luke 11:29.

32. Ezekiel 16:47-48. See also: Amos 1-2.

33. Although John MacArthur would presumably be highly sympathetic to my argument, he provides a long list of ways in which the country has diminished (p. 3-5). Schaeffer (p. 17-18) points to "a shift in world view...*away from* a world view that was at least vaguely Christian...*toward* something completely different—toward a world view based upon the idea that the final reality is impersonal mater or energy shaped into its present form by impersonal chance."

34. See: S. Coontz, *The Way We Never Were: American Families and the Nostalgia Trap*, New York: Basic Books, 1992.

35. M. Olasky, *Abortion Rites: A Social History of Abortion in America*, Wheaton, IL: Crossway Books, 1992, p. 291-292.

36. Sine, p. 136. See: p. 135-141 for his critique of this mindset, including the pursuit of materialism and a lack of idealism and passion for the things of God. Further, he notes that "the American middle class suburban version that the Religious Right is so keen on protecting has been around for less than 60 years" (p. 141). See also: A. W. Tozer's chapter, "The Waning Authority of Christ in the Churches" in *God Tells the Man who Cares* and Herbert Yeuell's turn-of-the-century sermon, "Our Modern Evangelistic Problem", delivered in Carnegie Hall (October 19, 1909). Yeuell critiques the need for church members to be entertained, the "money-crazed age," materialism and mysticism, science's encroachment on religion, a secular media bias, and "the relegation of the Bible to a mere book of history and tradition...no longer taught in the schools...in the popular mind, no longer a book of authority."

37. F. Mathewes-Green, "Abortion in the Tides of Culture", *First Things*, December 2002, p. 16-17.

38. D. Neff, "Doctrine Still Matters", *Christianity Today*, September 9, 2002, p. 7.

39. L. Buzzard, interview in *The Door*, March/April 1991, p. 10.

40. R. Frame and A. Tharpe, *How Right Is the Right?*, Grand Rapids: Zondervan, 1996, p. 136-137. Peter McWilliams argues that our glorified view of the 1950's comes from a TV world that, in fact, did not exist. (*Ain't Nobody's Business if You Do*, Los Angeles: Prelude Press, 1993, p. 554.)

41. M. Hamilton and J. Yngvason, "Patrons of the Evangelical Mind", *Christianity Today*, July 8, 2002, p. 42.

42. A similar issue today is the low-cost availability of pornography on the Internet.

43. Of course, Christians are called to a higher standard (see: Matthew 5:47, 20:25-26).

44. An interesting statistic in this regard is Gallup Poll numbers which reveal that the percentage of people who report that "someone says grace or gives thanks aloud to God at family meals" rose from 43% in 1947 to 69% in 1996. (*The American Enterprise*, September/October 1999, p. 92.) More broadly, two recent books reflect a growing consensus of optimism toward the growth of Orthodoxy Christianity. (See: C. Carroll, *The New Faithful: Why Young Adults Are Embracing Christian Orthodoxy*, Chicago: Loyola Press, 2002; and R. Webber, *The Younger Evangelicals: Facing the Challenges of the New World*, Grand Rapids: Baker Books, 2002.)

45.   "Family values" are important but can be overemphasized. On the one hand, family environs are important in raising children. The 5th Commandment—reinforced in Ephesians 6:1-3—is to honor one's parents. In I Timothy 5:4,8, Paul says that one is "worse than an unbeliever" if they don't take care of the financial needs of their family. And in the last act of his life, Christ asked John to take care of his mother (John 19:25-27). See also: Matthew 15:3-6, I Samuel 19:1-2.

    On the other hand, Christ repeatedly put family well below following his call. (See also: Deuteronomy 13:6-10!) Christ didn't marry—defying cultural and familial norms as well as religious tradition. The Gospels reveal little about Christ's family and when they're mentioned, the portraits are less than flattering. (See: Matthew 10:34-37, 12:46-50; Mark 3:21, 3:31-35, 13:12-13; Luke 9:59-62, 14:26, 21:16, John 7:15.) Christ also redefined family to mean the "family of God". In a word, it is far more important to join God's family (Ephesians 1:5, 3:15; John 1:12, I John 3:1).

    Moreover, Gregory Gronbacher points out that "The rhetoric of family values, upon close examination, is found to be empty. What is a family value? Honesty? Are not...single folk also interested in honesty? It would appear that there is a small, limited set of values that pertain to family life per se. Yet the rhetoric of family values is employed in the absence of a political theory to justify and promote legislation and public policy that is friendly to families." ("The Christian Right in America: A Movement at the Crossroads", Grand Rapids: Acton Institute, 2000.)

46. With respect to patriotism, see Jerry Falwell's "Ninety-five Theses for the 1980's" (in *Salt and Light: Evangelical Political Thought in Modern America*, ed. A. Cerillo, Jr., and M. Dempster, Grand Rapids: Baker Books,

1989, p. 160-165). In the section entitled "Concerning America," he lists "love and honor the flag" just before "just and equal treatment under the law" and rights to religious freedom and peaceful assembly. (And he argues that each of the 11 sexual sins listed is wrong "because it is anti-family.")

47. R. Reed, *Politically Incorrect*, Dallas: Word, 1994.

48. For an interesting discussion of this and the role of Christianity in American history, see: S. Keillor, *This Rebellious House: American History and the Truth of Christianity*, Downers Grove, IL: InterVarsity Press, 1996 (especially chapter 4) and K. Wald, *Religion and Politics in the United States*, 2nd ed., Washington, DC: CQ Press: 1992, p. 4. "A careful study of the facts of history shows that early America does not deserve to be considered uniquely, distinctively or even predominantly Christian, if we mean by the word 'Christian' a state of society reflecting the ideals presented in Scripture. There is no golden age to which Christians may return." (M. Noll, N. Hatch, and G. Marsden, *The Search for Christian America* (Westchester, IL: Crossway Books, 1983, p. 17, cited in Sine, p. 118.) Lynn Buzzard again: "The notion that we are really God's favorite people and we just need to clean up our act is a terrible illusion. The problem is not the Supreme Court; the problem is not the law; the problem is not sex education in the schools; the problem is that we live in a thoroughly pagan society." William Martin argues that Christianity in America peaked by the mid-19th century—citing splits over slavery and the Civil War, industrialization, urbanization, immigration, secularism, the Social Gospel, evolution, and historical criticism of the Bible as causes for the decline. (*With God on our Side: The Rise of the Religious Right in America*, New York: Broadway Books, 1996, p. 5-6.)

49. See: Philippians 1:12-14, 2:14-15, 4:11-13; I Corinthians 7:17-24.

50. Matthew 24:12.

51. Quoted in O'Donovan, p. 664. Augustine offered an intriguing use of law as an indirect teacher—law as a waiting period of sorts to allow truth to come to the fore. "The thing to be considered when anyone is coerced is not the mere fact of coercion but the nature of that to which he is coerced, whether it be good or bad; not that any one can be good in spite of his own will, but that, through fear of suffering what he does not desire, he...is compelled to examine the truth of which he had been contentedly ignorant...and now willingly holds what he formerly rejected." (Quoted in O'Donovan, p. 132.) While Augustine's point is provocative, it raises as many questions as it seems to answer—for example: Is it acceptable to use coercion to move people toward *anything* that is good? Does the threat of coercion move people to Christ more often than allowing them to hit rock bottom through pursuing that which is bad for them?

52. Martin Luther King Jr.: "There are always those who say legislation can't solve the problem. There is a half-truth involved here. It is true that legislation cannot solve the whole problem. It can solve some of the problem. It may be true that morality can't be legislated, but behavior can be regulated. It may be true that legislation cannot change the heart, but it can restrain the heartless. It may be true that the law cannot make a man love me, but it can keep him from lynching me, and I think that's pretty important." (*First Things*, March/April 2003, p. 88; quoting from Nigel Rees' newsletter "Quote...Unquote".)

53. Thomas is an evangelical syndicated columnist and a former writer for the Moral Majority. Dobson is currently a pastor in Minneapolis and was formerly a lieutenant in the Moral Majority. John MacArthur's *Why Government Can't Save You* makes many of the same points, but was less accusatory and inflammatory, and perhaps not surprisingly, received far less attention.

54. See: J. Hitchcock, "Blinded by Ambition?" *Touchstone*, November/December 1999, p. 46-48; and J. Bolt, "'We Were Wrong!' Yes: Hook Then, Slice Now", *Religion and Liberty*, November/December 1999, p. 11-13.

55. *World*, May 15, 1999; and *Christianity Today*, September 9, 1999.

56. Minnery, *Why You Can't Stay Silent*. The primary (negative) point of the book is to take Thomas & Dobson (p. 98-104) and John MacArthur (p. 104-106) to task for their calls for Christians to reconsider their attraction to political means. Interestingly, Minnery opens the book by asserting the effectiveness of the 1985 Attorney General's Commission on Pornography ("able to blow a crater in the crusted world of hard-core pornography...a glimmer of hope") which was then reversed solely "*because* libertines in the Clinton Justice Department did absolutely nothing...hope was dashed" (italics mine)—implicitly communicating his faith in government. Ironically, many of his best examples in how to respond to social problems are non-political. (See: p. 14-15, 136-137's boycotts, p. 118's description of Henry Hyde's winsome character within the political arena, and p. 200's thorough call to "local school involvement.")

57. In a fundraising letter, Randall Terry called the book more dangerous than child pornography at Barnes & Noble. (*The [Southeast] Outlook*, Louisville, KY: Southeast Christian Church, September 2, 1999, p. A10.)

58. Bolt, p. 11.

59. Dobson's analysis and activism suffers from the earlier-discussed failure to distinguish between issues of LJ and LM. For example, he compares Thomas and Dobson to one who would "accommodate Hitler's

henchmen." Moreover, his rationale for involvement seems to be pragmatism (e.g., "steadily winning the battle...no chance of winning") and tradition ("the greatest weakness of the authors' thesis is with its departure from the historic posture of the church")—rather than Scripture. (*Christianity Today*, "The New Cost of Discipleship", September 6, 1999, p. 56-58.)

60. Hitchcock (p. 47) notes that "the book alludes to but then ignores—how to distinguish genuine religious issues from mere conservative politics." In commenting on his review, Richard John Neuhaus describes "the excesses" of the Religious Right as a "target-rich environment." (*First Things*, October 2000, p. 96.)

61. Bolt, p. 12.

62. Eberly, "We're fighting the wrong battle", *Christianity Today*, September 6, 1999, p. 52-53.

63. II Timothy 4:2-3.

64. O. Guinness, *Fit Bodies, Fat Minds: Why Evangelicals Don't Think and What to Do About It*, Grand Rapids: Baker Books, 1994, p. 16. Eberly (p. 53) says that "religious conservatives have put their stock in a model for moral renewal that awakens a deep, native resistance."

65. H. Nouwen, quoted in Thomas and Dobson, p. 53.

66. Too often, the Christian's motivation, in this and related areas, is the pursuit of "safety" over God's will. Like many things, safety is desirable, but it can get out-of-balance. It often reduces to not wanting to see or confront these behaviors on an individual level.

Chapter 7: What Should We Do Instead (of Legislating Morality)?

1. Matthew 16:15-18,21-23.

2. As is famously observed, Matthew 28:18-20 talks about making disciples not converts. Ironically, chapter 12 of Leith Anderson's *Winning the Values War in a Changing Culture: Thirteen Distinct Values that Mark a Follower of Christ* (Minneapolis: Bethany House, 1994) is entitled "Making More Disciples" but is entirely about evangelism.

3. At least in terms of discipling men, Kurt Sauder (the Men's Minister at Southeast Christian Church in Louisville, KY) and I have co-authored a 21-month discipleship program of Bible study, Bible reading and Bible memorization for self-study and small group interaction—broken up into

seven sections of 9-11 weeks each. If you're interested in learning more about our material, please contact Kurt (ksauder@secc.org) or me (dschansb@ius.edu).

4. T. Evans, *Are Christians Destroying America: How to Restore a Decaying Culture*, Chicago: Moody Press, 1996, p. 14. Or as the old Chinese proverb puts it: "Better to light one small candle than to curse the darkness."

5. L. Crabb, *The Silence of Adam: Becoming Men of Courage in a World of Chaos*, Grand Rapids: Zondervan, 1995, p. 167-168.

6. Actually, few non-Christians handle it well too. Note the recent Catholic priest scandals and an overwhelming aversion to connect the bulk of the sexual abuse to homosexuality. Note also the inconsistency between criticizing the Catholics and not allowing the Boy Scouts to avoid homosexual Scout masters.

7. The most obvious references are Leviticus 18:22, 20:13, Romans 1:27. (See also: the repeated condemnation of all forms of sexual immorality throughout the New Testament.) The Romans passage is made more interesting by the possibility that Paul was writing in the style of Amos— luring his audience in with the sins of the pagans (as in Amos 1-2), before pointing to their own unrighteousness with Romans 1:29-32's list of more common sins and Romans 2:1-4's condemnation of their judgment. The discussion of marriage in Genesis 1-2—and references to that passage by Christ and Paul—provide additional indirect evidence. Genesis 1 emphasizes the equality of men and women while Genesis 2 focuses on their complementarity. Genesis 1-2 indicates that marriage is designed for procreation (1:28) as well as mutual joy, comfort and pleasure (2:24-25; see also: Song of Solomon).

8. Life expectancies are dramatically lower for men who engage in homosexual conduct, approaching those of men in the mid-19th century. (See: "Modeling the Impact of HIV Disease on Mortality in Gay and Bisexual Men", *International Journal of Epidemiology*, Vol. 26, #3, 1997, p. 657-661.)

9. Frederica Mathewes-Green argues that the fuel for the "gay rights" movement is hatred—at least its perception. As such, she advises Christians to be especially careful to avoid its perception or reality. (*Touchstone*, "Facing the Homosexual Void", July/August 1998, p. 30.)

10. Interview with Joe Dallas, *The Door*, May/June 1997, p. 15. The dialogue between Jerry Falwell and Mel White is a counterexample. (Lynn Rosellini, "An Unlikely Friendship, a Historic Meeting", *U.S. News & World Report*, November 1, 1999, p. 68.)

11. D. Gushee, *Christianity Today*, "The Speck in Mickey's Eye", August 11, 1997.

12. Of these, adultery is arguably the worst in God's eyes. After all, the 7th Commandment speaks to it instead of all other types of fornication. And it is a perversion of a vital, God-ordained institution, marriage. Moreover, conservatives implicitly ignore Christ's words equating lust with adultery, believing that an unbeliever's commission of carnal sexual sins is somehow far more heinous than a believer's commission of spiritual sexual sins. Of course, Christians have less of an excuse to engage in any type of sin.

13. Interestingly, sodomy is defined as "abnormal" sexual activity. Depending on cultural norms and legal definitions, this can and sometimes does include oral and anal sex within marriage.

14. At present, 13 states have anti-sodomy laws (down from 24 in 1998), including four who legally apply the law to homosexuals only. The Supreme Court recently overturned a 1998 conviction which will have broader implications for other anti-sodomy laws.

15. One could argue that "the ground" cried out; Genesis 4:10 records that after Cain kills Abel, his blood cried out to God from the ground. Regardless, the Hebrew word for "cry out" implies a response to some act of violence. (For example, see: Exodus 3:7-8a.) In addition, contemporary Western understanding typically understates the importance of hospitality in that culture and thus, the sin of such tremendous inhospitality. Even a casual reading of Genesis reveals the high value placed on treating visitors well.

16. Ezekiel 16:47-48.

17. See: Deuteronomy 29:23, 32:32; Isaiah 1:9-10, 3:9; Jeremiah 23:14; Amos 4:11. In Judges 19:22-30, Sodom is not expressly mentioned, but this story about the Israelites is an almost perfect parallel to Genesis 19.

18. See: Lamentations 4:6, Ezekiel 16:46-50, Matthew 10:15, 11:23-24. See: Isaiah 13:19, Jeremiah 50:40; Jeremiah 49:18; and Zephaniah 2:9 for descriptions of how Babylon, Edom, and Moab would be overthrown like Sodom. Luke 17:29 uses Sodom to describe the sudden judgment which would accompany the establishment of God's kingdom. See also: Revelation 11:8.

19. Evans, p. 38. Or as Doug Bandow notes, "it was the lack of ten righteous men, not the absence of a municipal vice squad, that caused God to destroy Sodom." (*Beyond Good Intentions: A Biblical View of Politics*, Wheaton, IL: Crossway Books, 1988, p. 97.)

20. Genesis 19:15, II Peter 2:8; Genesis 19:14.

21. In a letter to the editor of *Christianity Today*, John Freeman points to the problem of self-labeling as both Christian (assuming chastity in this matter) and homosexual (speaking of orientation or temptations): "There is danger in labeling oneself by besetting temptations, however deeply felt. Temptation does not equal orientation. Biblically speaking, we become oriented to that which we repeatedly give our hearts..." See also: I Corinthians 6:9-11.

22. F. Mathewes-Green, *World*, October, 29, 1994, p. 30. Scientific research indicates that "highly motivated homosexuals" can become heterosexuals. ("Some gays can become straight, study suggests", *(Louisville) Courier-Journal*, May 9, 2001—citing research by Robert Spitzer at Columbia University, presented at the annual APA meeting the same day. See also: W. Throckmorton, "Efforts to modify sexual orientation: A review of outcome literature and ethical issues", *Journal of Mental Health Counseling*, 1998, p. 283-304.) Biblically, I Corinthians 6:9-11 and II Corinthians 5:17 imply that a "change in orientation" is a distinct possibility—although not a certainty—for new believers. And perhaps if the church preached and practiced more seriously what the Bible says about divorce and pre-marital sex, we'd be far more credible on this issue.

23. Andrew Small (letter to the editor of *Touchstone*): "To be a Christian celibate homosexual is to be a minority within a minority within a minority, and that is neither fashionable, socially acceptable, nor (let's face it) much fun."

24.   "Gay rights" is a related issue. It's beyond the scope of this work, but the entire debate about "employment at will" and an employer's right to hire as they please is relevant to this question. In any case, a practical concern with allowing employers to fire or not hire homosexuals because of their lifestyles is that they may someday reject or fire Christians because they "choose that lifestyle" or because they read their Bibles—even though it's "in the privacy of their own homes."

So-called "same-sex marriage" is another related issue. But concerns in this realm are often overblown or at least unexplained. For instance, "same-sex marriage" further legitimizes homosexual behavior but is seemingly unrelated to the efficacy of traditional marriages. In any case, isn't divorce—especially that within the church—a far larger issue?

The optimal arrangement would be to remove the State from any connection to (religious) marriage—and then to allow employers to compensate employees however they wish. In Puritan Massachusetts, it was illegal for clergy to officiate at a wedding—because marriage was understood as a state (not a religious) function. (S. Carter, "Remedial History", *Christianity Today*, July 8, 2002, p. 60.) And as David Sant argues, the state should only provide marriage certificates rather than marriage licenses: "A license asserts the claim of the state over the family to regulate marriage; whereas a marriage certificate is merely a legal document bearing witness to the marriage." ("Resisting State Licensure of the Family")

Note also that employer provision of health insurance is connected to its subsidy as a non-taxed fringe benefit. Taxing fringe benefits would move health insurance back to an individual's decision outside of work—in addition to many other benefits to the market for health care. (See: chapter 11 of *Poor Policy: How Government Harms the Poor* [D. Schansberg, Boulder, CO: Westview Press, 1996] for more detail.)

25. Richard John Neuhaus (*First Things*, June/July 2002) quotes Benedict Groeschel at length from his essay "The Pastoral Care of Those Who Are Not Yet Disposed to Follow the Commandments" (in *With Mind and Heart Renewed*, University Press of America)—on the difficulty of ministering to many in similar situations: "The thorny problem of the pastoral care of those who desire to participate in the life of the Church, and who are yet either unwilling or unable to observe its moral teachings, is one that many pastors and pastoral workers encounter every day. In every good-sized parish, there are people beginning to experience a real call to conversion, but who are involved in moral difficulties ranging from invalid marriages and homosexual relationships to addiction to alcohol and drugs...What can be done for them without becoming an enabler..."

26. T. Schmidt, "A Pastoral Manifesto", *Christianity Today*, November 11, 1996, p. 38-39. Schmidt also suggests replacing the slogan "Hate the sin; love the sinner." He describes it as "known and despised by homosexuals...tired and needs to be replaced." But C.S. Lewis notes that "For a long time I used to think this a silly straw-splitting distinction: how could you hate what a man did and not hate the man? But years later it occurred to me that there was one man to whom I had been doing this all my life—namely myself." (*Mere Christianity*, New York: Macmillan, 1960, p. 105.)

27. The analogy is not relevant in that homosexuality involves behavior while the Samaritan's key characteristic is his (innate) nationality. However, the key element of Christ's story is that the Samaritans were despised by the Jews, as homosexuals are by many in contemporary society and even in religious audiences. In "Facing the Homosexual Void", Frederica Mathewes-Green puts it this way: "There's a saying that we all stand on level grounds at the foot of the Cross. If we feel disgust at the thought of standing there next to a homosexual but feel complacent about rubbing shoulders with an adulterer, we are not seeing things with God's eyes."

28. Bob Briner asks why we are so willing to minister in prisons to mass murderers, but less than eager to work with homosexuals. (*Deadly Detours: Seven Noble Causes that Keep Christians from Changing the World*, Grand Rapids: Zondervan, 1996, p. 46-47.) C. Everett Koop notes that leprosy provided much of the impetus for Christian mission work in the 19th century. (W. Martin, *With God on our Side: The Rise of the Religious Right in America*, New York: Broadway Books, 1996, p. 253.)

29. One problem with the definition emerges immediately since Christians do not believe in "chance" per se, but rather, in God's sovereignty. What the world calls coincidence, we call God's providence. Perhaps we can amend the definition to include games which use little or no skill.

30. J. Stapleford, *Bulls, Bears and Golden Calves: Applying Christian Ethics in Economics*, Downers Grove, IL: InterVarsity Press, 2002, p. 158-160. (See also: all of his chapter 12.)

31. Ibid. Stapleford reports that lotteries were outlawed in most states by 1840 and were not resuscitated until the Civil War and the rebuilding that followed. Troubles returned over time and legal gambling was vastly diminished by the end of the 20th century's first decade. Gambling returned again in the Great Depression as Nevada embraced it to build its tourism industry. State lotteries reappeared, beginning in 1964 and have grown steadily ever since.

32. In one church newspaper, an editorial writer advocated majority rule (through a referendum) on a gay rights ordinance and then advocated leaving it up to the state's elected leaders on whether gambling should be legal. Why the difference? Pragmatism over principle: The outcome of majority rule favored her side in one case and not the other!

33. Moral virtue promoter Bill Bennett's avid interest in gambling—either an expensive hobby or an "addiction"—is a bit odd and not at all helpful to politically conservative gambling opponents.

34. C. Clotfelter (Professor of Economics, Duke University), "Do Lotteries Hurt the Poor? Well, Yes and No", testimony before the U.S. House of Representatives, April 19, 2000.

35. There are also two interesting ironies here for the Religious Right given their usual admiration for the Founding Fathers. Lotteries were used to fund the Revolutionary War and a variety of public works projects in post-colonial times. And a hero of the faith, George Washington, kept records of his gambling pursuits. (T. Stafford, "None Dare Call It Sin", *Christianity Today*, May 18, 1998, p. 37; P. McWilliams, *Ain't Nobody's Business if You Do*, Los Angeles: Prelude Press, 1993, p. 267; R. Rogers, *Seducing*

America: Is Gambling a Good Bet?, Grand Rapids: Baker Books, 1997, p. 66.)

36. According to Rogers (p. 99,101), estimated bingo revenues exceed $4 billion per year. With respect to sweepstakes, spending your valuable time and $.34 for a stamp makes it "a gamble".

37. See: Isaiah 65:11.

38. Rogers (p. 63-64) tries to hand-wave this point by arguing that any gambling is a "waste of time" and "unwholesome" and that it "debilitates...debases" and prevents one from being a "proper steward of one's God-given resources." In contrast, John Cobin notes that "a family that spends $5 per month on lottery tickets is not going to harm itself financially any more than a family that spends $5 per month at Blockbuster video. Like any form of entertainment, the value...is always determined by subjective individual preferences...Just because I am not very entertained by renting and viewing *Mary Poppins* or by playing skee-ball in an arcade does not mean that they do not entertain others. Is there a point at which expenditures for entertainment for a Christian turn into excess? Of course there is, but that point is *not* usually a bright line that can be objectively determined by others." ("Bare, Beer, Baby Ruth and Blessings"; www.policyofliberty.net, February 2003.)

39. A related argument is concern about gambling as a stumbling block for others. But if applied consistently, this principle would be paralyzing. Moreover, this view typically ignores the impact of legalism as a stumbling block (Luke 11:52).

40. Moving the standard definition beyond gaming to similar activities introduces some difficulties. Defining it as introducing risk rather than dealing with risk seems helpful, but falls short when one recognizes that dealing with risk can also be done poorly and that making any type of investment is risky. On futures markets, see: D. Lee, "Speculation and Risk", *The Freeman*, September 1998, p. 50-51. Another possibility would be to describe the activity in terms of its expected payoff: an expected loss or no gain but with the opportunity for a big payoff. (The middleman has a positive payoff; without the middleman, it would be zero-sum.) But again, this gets uncomfortably close to a number of standard investment decisions—e.g., starting a business.

41. The hedging aspect is similar to locking in an interest rate on a mortgage or a buyer and seller pinning down a price before a contract is fully executed.

42. A relevant public policy: the double taxation of dividends has made capital gains more attractive to firms and investors. Unfortunately, this

promotes speculation, greed, and stock-market bubbles since the rhetoric of a firm's asserted profitability is not as often backed up by the cash paid out in dividends.

43. Clotfelter, "Do Lotteries Hurt the Poor?". Average expenditures do not vary with income; thus, the percentage decreases as income rises.

44. Clotfelter (ibid.) notes that this spending pattern does not necessarily indicate "exploitation" or inappropriate targeting of the poor—any more than if a company was trying to sell its product to a certain niche in the market. And aside from fraud, one can use force to exploit others. Here, the issue would be whether the government establishes a state-run or state-endorsed gambling entity with significant monopoly power. As with all such government endeavors, this would be inequitable and inefficient. But there are far greater reasons for concern on this point which we will develop in chapters 8-10.

45. Thomas Sowell: "One of the problems with the market from the standpoint of those who think they are the brightest, the best, and ought to be telling the rest of us groundlings what to do, is that the market allows ordinary people to go out there and make their own decisions. And people who think they have the Truth and the Light don't want that; they want no part of that. It's really what they hate most, I think, about a market system." (*Reason*, December 1980.) Lysander Spooner: "If government has the right, and is bound, to prohibit any one act—that is not criminal—merely because it is supposed to tend to poverty, then, by the same rule, it has the right, and is bound, to prohibit any and every other act—though not criminal—which, in the opinion of the government, tends to poverty. And, on this principle, the government would not only have the right, but would be bound, to look unto every man's private affairs ad every person's personal expenditures, and determine as to which of them did, and which of them did not, tend to poverty..." (*Vices Are not Crimes: A Vindication of Moral Liberty*, 1875, Chapter XXI.)

46. This may explain the frustration in some circles that relatively educated pastors are willing to battle gambling but their relatively uneducated congregations feel no such passion. See also: prohibiting nudity in night clubs, but enjoying or condoning it in art, movies, and theater.

47. Rogers, p. 165. John Piper somehow falls into this by calling the advertising slogan "this could be your ticket out [of the inner city]"—"shameless." Likewise, Piper calls gambling "exploitation of the poor" and "plunder." ("Wages from Sin", *World*, January 11, 2003, p. 31.)

48. Tom Minnery: "Repeatedly the Bible admonishes Christians to ensure that the poor are not oppressed, and there is no clearer example of such

exploitation than legalized gambling." (*Why You Can't Stay Silent: A Biblical Mandate to Shape our Culture*, Wheaton, IL: Tyndale House, 2001, p.100) This is an amazing statement—both for the ignorance it ascribes to the poor who gamble and its ignorance of vastly more important economic/political issues for the poor.

49. See, for example: R. Rogers, "America's New Love Affair with Gambling", *Christian Research Journal*, January-March 1998, p. 23; Rogers, *Seducing America*, p. 72-74; R. Goodman, *The Luck Business*, p. xi, 163-166.

50. An entire issue of *Managerial and Decision Economics*, edited by Earl Grinols and David Mustard, has been devoted to the topic of gambling (Volume 22, Issue 1-3, 2001).

51. James Dobson has voiced his pleasure at class-action suits against casinos. Without evidence of fraud, this is an odd stance for a "conservative", given its reliance on trial lawyers and its emphasis on blame-shifting (to business!) over individual responsibility and self-restraint. Jim Babka wryly re-labels Dobson's organization "Focus on the State" before warning that "When you give politicians the power to prohibit peaceful behaviors you don't like, you have also given them the power to prohibit peaceful activities you do like...It is possible that future politicians and trial lawyers will attempt to regulate Christian evangelism using words very similar to Dr. Dobson's."

52. This topic is developed more fully in chapter 9 of *Poor Policy*.

53. Who promised Christians that our decisions to follow God would be without significant costs? The pros and cons of the decision to educate students in public, private, or home schools could easily be the subject of a book of its own.

54. Perhaps ironically, Louis Tarsitano argues the same point in critiquing homosexual activists for trying to conquer the Boy Scouts rather than starting their own organization. (*Touchstone*, April 2001, p. 8.)

55. Briner, p. 23. "For so many Christians to spend so much time, energy, effort, and resources on the non-issue of legalizing school prayer is appalling and heartbreaking." (p. 20) Instead, Briner recommends following in the footsteps of *Moms In Touch*, an international group of mothers who pray about the schools (p. 25-28): "Do you think that those in Moms In Touch worry very much about what Congress or the Supreme Court says about prayer in schools? Of course not. They're too busy praying!"

56. If we don't believe that public schools are effective in teaching "the 3 R's" (reading, writing, and arithmetic), why would we ask them to teach the

4th R of religion?! Stephen Carter notes that "the decisions to ban school prayer were correct, resting on an important if rarely articulated truth: the religious education of children is both the right and the responsibility of the family. This role is older than the Constitution, and the state has no power to interfere with it." ("A Quiet Compromise", *Christianity Today*, February 4, 2002, p. 82; see also: S. Carter, "Uncle Sam Is not your Dad", *Christianity Today*, May 21, 2002, p. 68.)

57. Ralph Reed: "To compel individuals to participate in a prayer with which they don't agree is a form of tyranny; therefore I would oppose any statute or constitutional amendment that mandates prayers composed or led by teachers, principals or other school officials." (*Active Faith*, Free Press: New York, 1996, p. 278.)

58. M. Hunter, "Evangelist Calls for Restoration of Prayer in U.S. Public Schools", *New York Times*, July 31, 1980, p. A14 (cited in J. Hunter, *Culture Wars: The Struggle to Define America—Making Sense of the Battles over the Family, Art, Education, Law, and Politics*, New York: Basic Books, 1991, p. 368).

59. Taken from a direct mail solicitation advertising the book, *America: To Pray or Not to Pray?* (Washington, DC: Concerned Women for America, 1988), cited in J. Hunter, p. 368.

60. This is driven by the assumption that illegality led directly to conformity with the law. In fact, compliance was very slow in following the Supreme Court decisions. (K. Wald, *Religion and Politics in the United States*, 2nd ed., Washington, DC: CQ Press: 1992, p. 159.) "The 1962 and 1963 decisions that ended officially sponsored prayer and devotional reading in the public schools had been met by howls of outrage and predictions of every sort of evil consequence...Though the causal connection may have been tenuous, the undeniable appearance of all the predicted phenomena not only convinced critics of the Court that they had been right, but made the restoration of school prayer an evergreen item on the conservative agenda." (W. Martin, *With God on our Side*, p. 192.)

61. Briner, p. 23.

62. As Bandow argues (p. 147), "believers should not waste time attempting to insert formalistic, ceremonial religion into public institutions. Non-denominational prayer led by an unbelieving teacher is not only meaningless, but is also unfair to non-Christians who must attend public institutions."

63. "And the Word Turned Secular", *Christianity Today*, May 21, 2001, p. 84. Carter's primary topic is the 2000 case *ACLU vs. Capitol Square Review and Advisory Board* where an upper court allowed Ohio to keep

"With God, all things are possible" (Matthew 19:26) as their state motto. The judges decided that there is "nothing uniquely Christian about the thought" and that people "are unlikely to have even the vaguest notion of the source from which [the] motto was drawn." Carter concludes: "In other words, the phrase, lifted from its biblical context, is utterly mundane."

64. A school in Ecru, MS speaks to the power and glory of voluntary prayer. After a 1996 court ruling that prayer and Scripture-reading over the intercom were unconstitutional, more than 90% of the student body have gathered voluntarily for the same activity. (S. Morris, "An Answer to Prayer", *World*, February 15, 1997.)

65.   Another popular reform effort is the attempt to "put the Ten Commandments back in the classroom." While this presents the same Biblical concerns as mandating school prayer, it has fewer practical problems—probably because we would be letting God do the talking! On the other hand, maybe such reforms reduce God's word to mere tokenism and emphasize the morality of the Old Covenant over Christianity. Anthony Tomasino: "The remedy, some seem to believe, could be as simple as giving our children two tablets of stone and checking the moral temperature again in the morning...We need to bear in mind that the Ten Commandments possess no magical powers...Knowing the Ten Commandments by heart is nothing. The Devil, I'm sure, knows them by heart." (*Written upon the Heart: The Ten Commandments for Today's Christian*, Grand Rapids: Kregel Publications, 2001, p. 8.) Dallas Willard asks "where do we find churches, right or left, that put them on their walls?" (*The Divine Conspiracy*, San Francisco: HarpersSanFrancisco, 1998, p. 56) Tom Lehrer: "I think one of the hilarious things is that they're trying to put the Ten Commandments in the schools—which I think is wonderful because all these little kids are going to be enjoined not to commit adultery. I love that idea. There's been too much adultery going on in the third grade: we've got to put a stop to that. And then coveting their neighbors' wives too. I notice there's a lot of that going on. So we've got to stop that." (*The Door*, March/April 2002, p. 12.)

Worrying about "under God" in the Pledge of Allegiance is a similar issue. Ironically, the Pledge was written by an avowed Socialist, Francis Bellamy (brother of Edward Bellamy) in 1892 to promote allegiance to the Flag and the State. The phrase "under God" was added in 1954 by Congress in response to a campaign led by the Knights of Columbus. Douglas Wilson rips the phrase, noting that the god of the pledge is the generic god of American civil religion, not the God of the Bible. He concludes by saying "If this all seems a little extreme, try to imagine what would happen if we altered the Pledge by dropping 'indivisible' and labeling its god as 'the Triune God'." ("One Little Word

Shall Fell Him", *Credenda Agenda*, Volume 13, Issue 6; www.credenda.org.) Richard John Neuhaus suggests that we should "understand 'under God' to mean under the judgment of God...[not] that God is angry with America, although I should suppose he is indeed angry with much that is done by Americans and in the name of America. Rather, under judgment means more importantly that there is a transcendent point of reference to which we as a people are accountable." (*The Naked Public Square: Religion and Democracy in America*, 2nd ed., Grand Rapids: Eerdmans, 1997, p. 76.)

66. J. Gwartney, "A Positive Approach to Improve our Schools", *Cato Journal*, Spring/Summer 1990, p. 166.

67. Thomas Hazlett: "The state is not about subtle trade-offs...but about the brutish task of deriving and enforcing one-size-fits-all rules...Take the public schools: Can there be a more contentious slice of social life to place in the hands of the state? Can we create any more political dyspepsia than to mandate that everyone's (or no one's) kids be rustled away and taught moral values, condom technique, Creationism, 'lifestyles'—not to mention literature, history, and civics. Is *Heather Has Two Mommies* the appropriate text—or would the Jimmy Swaggart Redemption Sermon Video be preferred?...Not only *could* reasonable people disagree—we can predict with absolute certainty that reasonable people *will* disagree...Why not simply choose freedom...Free to choose, people could themselves weigh costs and benefits of rival theories of education, rather than thrusting them upon the rest of us." (*Reason*, June 1998, p. 74.)

68. For those who at least implicitly believe that monopoly power in economic markets is rampant and troubling, the idea of a government entity with tremendous monopoly power over the poor should be especially bothersome. Another irony here is that government has so vigorously fought the supposed monopoly power of Microsoft while itself possessing control over 90% of the market for education.

69. To his credit, Tom Minnery argues for active involvement in local school district (p. 200).

70. S. Alder, "Education in America", *The Freeman*, February 1993, p. 63-67. See also: J. Hunter, p. 36, 201. Marvin Olasky notes this and warns about so-called Blaine Amendments in 37 states. ("Breaking through Blaine's roadblock", *World*, August 24, 2002, p. 14-17.)

71. Unfortunately, voucher programs are often called "educational choice" programs which leads to some confusion. Note also that higher voucher amounts could be arranged for secondary vs. elementary education and for

students with special needs. Today, voucher programs are operating in Milwaukee, Cleveland, Florida—and have been newly enacted in Colorado.

72. This approach allows private producers to have a level playing field with the government schools. Currently, government schools receive a subsidy of nearly $8,000 per student enrolled. Of course, private schools receive little such assistance (except tax subsidies as non-profit organizations)—a tremendous disadvantage to operating in this market.

73. In Arizona, businesses and individuals can donate up to $500 per year to finance private scholarships and receive a dollar-for-dollar tax credit. From 1997 to 2001, scholarship groups raised $32 million and funded 19,000 scholarships. In 2001, Pennsylvania and Florida passed similar legislation. (L. Vincent, "Unstoppable Choice?", *World*, September 8, 2001, p. 22) Pennsylvania's law allows businesses to have tax credits of 75-90% of donations up to $100,000. (L. Vincent, "Inventive Incentive", *World*, August 11, 2001, p. 40.)

74. With respect to teaching evolutionary theories as a comprehensive scientific explanation for the development of life: if people want their kids to be taught a combination of bad religion and quasi-science, that should be their prerogative. As an introduction to the topic, see: Phillip Johnson's *Darwin on Trial* (Downers Grove, IL: InterVarsity Press, 1993).

75. Other opposition comes from Christians who understandably worry about government subsidies in private schools and the regulation that might follow. (See: Douglas Dewey, "An Echo, not a Choice", *Policy Review*, November/December 1996, p. 28-32.) But regulation can be avoided (as with food stamps and grocery stores). The "cleanest" alternatives in this respect are the various types of tax credits.

76. This is not a comprehensive case for increasing competition in the market for education. (See also: chapter 10 later in this book and chapter 9 in *Poor Policy*.) The most popular argument against vouchers is that they would cause the public schools to be a dumping ground for unruly and hard-to-educate students. Of course, inner-city public schools are already a "dumping ground" of a sort. Moreover, entrepreneurs would eagerly vie for the opportunity to educate children well—and pocket the vouchers. Finally, the private sector already takes care of many of our most challenging children, using the equivalent of vouchers.

77. Moreover, causation here is probably overrated. For example, the Japanese have far more violent programming on TV, but much less trouble with violent crimes. Briner (p. 82) prescribes that Christians should enter the entertainment industry as an occupation. "We need to see the television industry as a mission field and television technology as a powerful means

of telling who Jesus is and why he came." Elsewhere, Briner notes that "It is infinitely easier to boycott objectionable television programs than it is to create, produce, sell, and distribute a quality television program... Participating in a boycott of the products of companies sponsoring trashy television programs might make us feel good and righteous, but it has very little to do with being salt in the world." (*Roaring Lambs: A Gentle Plan to Radically Change the World*, Grand Rapids: Zondervan, 1993, p. 40-41.)

78. W. Smith, "Learning to be Quiet", *World*, August 23/30, 1997, p. 26.

Chapter 8: The Biblical Case for Legislating Justice

1. There are many types of justice: commutative (defining fair economic processes), distributive (outcomes and allocation), procedural (legal processes), retributive (punishment for misdeeds), and so on. But I will leave such distinctions to interested readers. See also: chapter 13 of E. Opitz, *Religion and Capitalism: Allies, not Enemies* (2nd ed., Irvington-on-Hudson, NY: Foundation for Economic Education, 1992).

2. Job 37:23, Psalms 9:16, 11:11, 33:5; Isaiah 9:7, 28:17, 30:18, 61:8; Jeremiah 9:24, I John 1:9, Revelation 15:3.

3. Proverbs 22:2, Romans 2:11, Ephesians 6:9, Colossians 3:25.

4. Deuteronomy 27:19, Isaiah 10:1-3, Jeremiah 5:26-29, 7:5-7; Ezekiel 18:12, 45:9-10; Amos 2:7, 4:1, 5:11, 8:4-7; James 5:1-6. Hay observes that "the failure to observe the Law in its social and economic aspects is an important theme in the proclamation of the prophets from the eighth century onwards." (D. Hay, *Economics Today*, Grand Rapids: Eerdmans, 1989, p. 39.)

5. Exodus 3:7-8a, 6:5-7, Deuteronomy 10:18, 26:6-8; Job 5:15-16, Psalms 10:15-18, 12:5, 68:5, 72:4, 107:41, 140:12, 146:7; Isaiah 25:4, Malachi 3:5, Luke 1:53. On the other hand, as Chilton notes, "God is against certain poor people"—sluggards (Proverbs 6:6-11), law-breakers (Proverbs 28:6), those who covet and then curse God (Proverbs 30:7-9), and so on. Chilton concludes that "whose side is God on?" is the wrong question. Rather, as Moses said in Exodus 32:26, we should ask "who is on the Lord's side?" (D. Chilton, *Productive Christians in an Age of Guilt Manipulators: A Biblical Response to Ronald J. Sider*, 3rd ed., Tyler, TX: Institute for Christian Economics, 1985, p. 80-85.)

6. Exodus 23:3,6; Leviticus 19:15, Deuteronomy 1:17, 16:18-20.

7. Proverbs 8:15, Isaiah 3:14-15, Jeremiah 21:12, Daniel 4:27, Amos 5:15. See also: Psalms 72 and Ezekiel 34.

8. Romans 13:4. See also: Romans 13:2, Proverbs 21:15, 28:5.

9. II Samuel 8:15, I Chronicles 18:14. See also: Psalms 71:1, Luke 3:10-14.

10. I Kings 10:9. However, Solomon failed to live up to this standard; even the wisest man in the world was responsible for some very poor policy and bad personal decisions. See the forced labor and high taxation of I Kings 5:13-18 and the polygamy and idolatry of I Kings 11. Richard Friedman notes that Solomon imposed a disproportionate tax burden on the Northern tribes (land and money) while disproportionately building up military defenses in the South. (*Who Wrote the Bible?*, Englewood Cliffs, NJ: Prentice Hall, 1987, p. 44-45.) Ironically, these events follow God's "measureless" provision of wisdom to Solomon in I Kings 4:29-34. An extension of Solomon's unjust "heavy yoke" by his son Rehoboam (I Kings 12:4) eventually led to the division of his kingdom.

11. Ecclesiastes 5:8.

12. I Timothy 5:21, James 2:1,9.

13. Psalms 82:2-4, Proverbs 17:5, 31:8-9, Isaiah 1:17, 58:3,6-11; Jeremiah 22:3-5,13-17.

14. Psalms 52:7, Proverbs 22:22, Isaiah 3:14, Ezekiel 22:29, 45:9; Amos 2:7, 5:11-12, 8:4-7; Micah 2:1-2, 6:10-12; Zechariah 7:9-10, James 2:6.

15. Psalms 112:5, Proverbs 19:17, I Timothy 6:18-19, I John 3:17.

16. Proverbs 21:3, Amos 5:21-24, Micah 6:7; Deuteronomy 16:20. Ambrose Bierce defines "injustice" as "a burden which of all those that we load upon others and carry ourselves is lightest in the hands and heaviest upon the back."

17. See also: I Corinthians 5:11, 6:9-11.

18. Proverbs 29:7, 21:15, Psalms 37:21. See also: Job 29:12-17, Proverbs 22:9.

19. Proverbs 14:31, 19:17.

20. In fact, Matthew 25:40,46 tells us that as we do these things for others, we do them for Christ.

21. Jeremiah 23:5.

22. There are a number of potential reasons for this: Perhaps the poor and powerless were more receptive to his message. Perhaps the organization of the church made appealing to the poor more practical. Perhaps it was a matter of justice. At the least, his teaching countered a contemporary religious bias in favor of the rich—a natural conclusion from the "blessings

equal obedience" formula of the Old Covenant. See: Luke 16:19-31's parable of the rich man and Lazarus, Matthew 19:23's pithy analogy, Luke 6:24's "woe", Luke 12:21's parable of the rich fool, and Luke 21:1's account of the widow's offering. See also: Luke 4:18, 7:22b; James 2:1-5, 5:1-6.

23. Matthew 23:23.

24. II Corinthians 5:21.

25. Luke 23:34.

26. But see also: Luke 4:25-29.

27. Matthew 21:12-13, Mark 11:15-17, Luke 19:45-46, John 2:14-16.

28. Matthew, Mark, and Luke record this while John's account has Christ critical of turning his "Father's house into a market."

29. Deuteronomy 14:24-26.

30. The Religious Left often criticizes "monopoly power" in economic markets. As such, the high prices may have been the result of a "cartel"—a voluntary arrangement among sellers to charge high prices and earn higher profits. But a cartel is difficult to maintain since the members of the cartel have a tremendous incentive to undercut their competitors. Thus, the existence and extension of monopoly power is usually the result of government intervention at the behest of interest groups—in political markets. Another source of monopoly power is highly imperfect information—in particular, when sellers can exploit an information advantage over buyers. This market was probably characterized by some natural monopoly power (customers needing to purchase at that location, little information about prices, and so on), but probably not enough to raise Christ's ire.

31. If pushed far enough, a passion for justice can become an idol; legislating justice can then degenerate into works-based religion and legalism. For example, Sider seems to cross the line numerous times on salvation by faith vs. works. He says that "salvation is by grace alone, not works-righteousness," but he also says that "there comes a point when neglect of the poor is not forgiven. It is punished. Eternally." (_Rich Christians in an Age of Hunger_, Dallas: Word Publishing, 1990, p. 59, 60.) When the gospel is perverted by a "Social Gospel", Christians need to be adamant in defending the infinite value of our Savior's atoning death on the cross (Galatians 1:8-9). At least in later writings, Sider does explicitly reject idolatry of government elsewhere: "When a social problem emerges, the first question should _not_ be, What can government do?" (_Just Generosity: A_

New Vision for Overcoming Poverty in America, Grand Rapids: Baker Books, 1999. p. 91.)

32. C. Henry, "Evangelicals in the Social Struggle", in *Salt and Light: Evangelical Political Thought in Modern America*, ed. A. Cerillo, Jr., and M. Dempster, Grand Rapids: Baker Books, 1989, p. 33.

33. An exception to this would be when a majority of people benefit from an injustice. Even in these cases, Christians should value justice over people-pleasing.

34. Certainly there are exceptions to this latter point. For instance, many people recognize their bondage to carnal sin and seek help. On a one-to-one basis, we should seek to address their "felt needs" as well.

35. In 1997, the 20th-anniversary 4th edition appeared with a note on the cover proclaiming its 350,000 copies in print. In the latest edition, Sider admits to changing many of his views, but as the numbers attest, most people will be familiar with the earlier editions of the book. Even so, Sider still (at least occasionally) confuses the causes of "oppression". In *Just Generosity* (p. 72), his misinterpretation of Ecclesiastes 4:1 ("power was on the side of their oppressors") requires government to be a solution to market problems, when at least in a modern context, such problems are much more likely to be caused by government in the first place. At other times, he's begun to look like a Libertarian! "What should be legislated and what not?...1.) individuals should normally be free to harm themselves but not be free to harm others; 2.) laws must be enforceable in a way that does not undermine other important values...." ("Toward an Evangelical Public Philosophy", in *Christians and Politics Beyond the Culture Wars: An Agenda for Engagement*, ed. D. Gushee, Grand Rapids: Baker Books, 2000, p. 92.) Although never seemingly as enamored with government solutions as Sider, it would seem that Jim Wallis, another prominent leader within the so-called Religious Left, has also become more "moderate" over time—with respect to the efficacy of markets and the practical uses of public policy to address the problems of the poor. (M. Tooley, "Sojourn to the Center", *Touchstone*, April 2002, p. 54-55.)

36. Many of Sider's views on population and the environment are suspect. For instance, he remarks that foreign aid is "probably the *only* way to check the population explosion in time to *avoid global disaster.*" (*Rich Christians*, p. 205; italics added) Further, Sider calls for "legislation that *justly compels* all businesses to *end* pollution." (p. 196; italics added) Moreover, within these beliefs, he expresses a number of contradictions. First, with respect to population growth, he is bothered by low life expectancies and high infant mortality rates, but he is also concerned by increasing population which is a function of longer life spans (p. 8-14). Second, he argues that there are

limits to economic growth (p. 15-17); although there are plenty of predictions from doomsayers, there is no historic support for such a belief. Third, he laments the impact of continuously declining prices of natural resources and agricultural products on the income of less-developed countries. In fact, the decline of resource prices for thousands of years provides strong evidence that we are not running out of resources! If we were, those prices would be rising over time as the resources became more scarce (p. 112-116, 189). Finally, he complains that rich countries import more than they export, but he is also critical of import restrictions by rich countries—i.e., rich countries did not import enough (p. 133-138, 112-116). See: chapter 19 of my book, *Poor Policy: How Government Harms the Poor* (Boulder: Westview, 1996) for a discussion of "the cause and effect of population, resources and food."

37. On Isaiah 10:2, Alec Motyer notes that "Both *dal* (poor) and *ani* (oppressed) have the same general ambience...The latter, however, also includes the sense of "humiliated, downtrodden"—not only uninfluential but because uninfluential, manipulated by the authorities as existing only for others' advantage." (*The Prophecy of Isaiah*, InterVarsity Press: Downers Grove, IL, 1993, p. 111.) Matthew Henry observes that "if the poverty and helplessness of their state was not an argument with them to keep them from sin, they could not expect it should be an argument with God to protect them from judgments."

38. Sider, *Rich Christians*, p. 61. Chapter 6 also has a number of examples where Sider draws causation between poverty and oppression.

39. James 5:4. Ironically, the government forces employers to "withhold" wages by mandating that they collect income and payroll taxes from workers, even the working poor (see: chapter 10). Economists condemn "withholding" to the extent that it makes the cost of taxation unnecessarily subtle to workers. Some have even argued that this would be the quickest way to reduce the size of government. Imagine, instead, a world where you would send a check to the government for your tax bill once per month or per quarter!

40. Proponents of government activism often assert that monopoly power or "economic power" in economic markets is rampant. The requisite article of faith is that our markets feature limited competition; if competition is limited, the concern has merit, but not otherwise. However, in today's economy, with 20th century advances in communication and transportation technologies, this is a difficult position to hold. (Even in less-developed countries, where competition is more limited, it requires tremendous faith in government to believe that political markets will be an improvement over economic markets.) To note, even if I know that I can "take advantage of

you", it would be very difficult to pay you lower wages than your productivity. In competition, I cannot pay you $5 if you produce revenues of $10 because it will be in someone's best interests to offer you $8, and so on. Finally, the existence of "economic power" would still be irrelevant to the godliness of certain choices. Should Esau be excused because Jacob had "economic power" over him in Genesis 25?

41. "The phrase 'economic power' is a tricky one. If it means no more than ownership, it is misleading and clumsy. If it is used, as is customary, to convey the implication that ownership gives the designated person some sort of power over others, it is dishonest. Strictly speaking, there is only one power structure in a society, and that is government; all other usages of the word power in a sociological context are metaphorical." (Opitz, p. 49.)

42. This section borrows from Sider, *Rich Christians*, p. 97-99; D. Willard, *The Spirit of the Disciplines: Understanding How God Changes Lives*, San Francisco: HarperSanFrancisco, 1988, Ch. 10; and Nee, *Love Not the World*, Wheaton, IL: Tyndale House, 1978, Chapter 11.

43. David Chilton (p. 10-12), in citing the number of times that Sider says that possessions and riches are "dangerous", wryly notes that "what seems most strange is that Sider goes on to request us to share these dangerous things with others." But as Chilton notes, "the problem is sin, not possessions." Unfortunately, advocates of greater income equality argue for voluntary or coercive redistribution of wealth while simultaneously criticizing materialism among the wealthy. Is a focus on money and material possessions appropriate or not? (See: for example, J. Wallis, *The Soul of Politics*, New York: The New Press, 1994, p. 166.) Finally, H. Schlossberg (*Idols for Destruction: The Conflict of Christian Faith and American Culture*, Wheaton, IL: Crossway Books, 1990, p. 61) argues that "it is fitting that the war on poverty should come at the same time as the apogee of materialism. Modern materialism is not only an ethical philosophy that places a high value on money and possessions but a social philosophy that says that human relations are determined by material factors."

44. As John Stott notes in looking at I Timothy 6:6-10, Paul "is not for poverty against wealth, but contentment against covetousness." (*Guard the Truth*, Downers Grove, IL: InterVarsity Press, 1996, p. 154.) See also: I Timothy 3:2-3, Hebrews 13:5; Proverbs 11:28, 15:16, 21:6.

45. I Timothy 6:18. See also: Proverbs 3:9-10, 29:4,7,26. Commenting on I Timothy 6:17-18, John Stott (p. 161) observes that "We are not to exchange materialism for asceticism."

46. R. Sirico, "Acton Notes", Grand Rapids: Acton Institute, June 2001.

47. II Corinthians 8:9, Philippians 2:5-7.

48. Matthew 11:19.

49. John 12:4.

50. Proverbs 10:22, 22:9, Psalms 112.

51. To explain this, Willard argues that Christ was dealing with a contemporary religious bias in favor of the wealthy—given the Old Testament's tight correlation between obedience and blessings. That said, Willard believes that the religious bias today is in favor of the poor. Stephen Mott and Ron Sider note that God's attention to the poor does not imply bias and compare it to firefighters who are "partial" to people with fires and parents who devote more tutorial resources to a child who struggles in school. ("Economic Justice: A Biblical Paradigm", in *Toward a Just and Caring Society: Christian Responses to Poverty in America*, ed. D. Gushee, Grand Rapids: Baker Books, 1999, p. 27, 30.)

52. J. Schneider, "The Good of Affluence", *Religion and Liberty*, March/April 2002, p. 6-8. (The essay is a distillation of his book, *The Good of Affluence: Seeking God in a Culture of Wealth* [Grand Rapids: Eerdmans, 2002]. See also: K. Elzinga, A. Hartropp, R. Klay, C. Blomberg, E. Noell, J. Schneider, "Weighing the Good of Affluence: A Symposium", *Faith and Economics*, Fall 2002, p. 1-25.) "This generally negative [Christian] attitude toward affluence under capitalism grows from powerful influences that are now as antiquated as they influential...the moral analysis of Marx...the grand thesis of Max Weber...[and] in Christian history, almost all spiritual and moral teaching on affluence has been quite negative...[C]ontemporary Christian thinkers have almost no models in their tradition that might encourage a more favorable disposition toward the condition of affluence...On the contrary, our heroes are almost one-sidedly people who have delivered prophetic judgments against the rich."

53. Willard, p. 193.

54. Nee, p. 123-124.

55. Willard, p. 194-195. Luke 16:13 tells us we cannot serve both God and Mammon, but Luke 16:9,11 provides instructions on how to properly use Mammon. See also: Deuteronomy 21:20, Proverbs 23:20-21, 28:7, Matthew 6:19-21.

56. Luke 18:18-30, 19:1-10, 19:11-27. (See also: Matthew 25:14-30, 13:44-46.) This is followed by the "Parable of the Ten Minas"—on how to handle one's resources well. See also: E. Noell (Professor of Economics, Westmont College), "Wealth and Market Exchange in the Gospels: Re-

examining the Evidence", presented at Christianity and Economics, Baylor University: Waco, TX, November 7-9, 2002.

57. Willard, p. 198. If one gives away everything, "the virtue or discipline here is in the giving, not in the resultant state of poverty." (p. 199) For a notable exception, see Paul's description of Christ in Philippians 2:7-8, II Corinthians 8:8-9. Ronald Nash notes that Christ taught that we have obligations to care for parents (Matthew 15:3-9) and to support worthy causes (Matthew 6:2-4)—and "it is rather difficult to fulfill such obligations unless one has certain financial resources." (*Poverty and Wealth: Why Socialism Doesn't Work*, Richardson, TX: Probe Books, 1986, p. 164.)

58. Willard, p. 202. Clement of Alexandria on wealth and worldly goods: "They lie at our disposal like materials or like instruments that can be well used by those who know how."

59. See: Chapter 1 of my book *Poor Policy* for more details.

60. In the mid-1960's, economists estimated the cost of a nutritionally adequate diet, and knowing that the poor spent about 1/3 of their incomes on food, multipled that cost by three to get the original poverty lines.

61. The statistic is biased in the other direction when people have moderate income but huge unavoidable expenses—for example, with large medical bills.

62. This and other related topics are the subjects of the excellent book by Michael Cox and Richard Alm, *Myths of Rich and Poor: Why We're Better Off Than We Think*, New York: Basic Books, 1999. For an example of a failure to understand this point, see: Sider, *Just Generosity*, p. 27, 42.

63. I Corinthians 15:41. On differential rewards in heaven, see: e.g., I Corinthians 3:11-15, II Corinthians 5:10; I Corinthians 9:25-27, I Thessalonians 2:19-20, II Timothy 4:8, Hebrews 11:6, James 1:12, I Peter 5:2-4, Revelation 2:10; Matthew 25:21, Daniel 12:3, Luke 18:30, II Timothy 2:12a. A great book on the topic is Joe Wall's *Going for the Gold: Reward and Loss at the Judgment of Believers* (Chicago: Moody, 1991). Note also that in the parable of the talents (Matthew 25:14-30) and the parable of the workers in the vineyard (Matthew 20:1-16), Christ does not even try to justify the inequalities of the situations.

64. Moreover, people are confused in thinking that income inequality *causes* poverty. For example, George Monsma Jr. writes that "The highly unequal distribution of income in the United States *leaves* many people living in poverty." (italics mine; "Income Distribution in the United States", in *Toward a Just and Caring Society*, p. 167.)

65. J. Boersema, *Political-Economic Activity to the Honour of God*, Winnipeg: Premier Publishing, 1999, p. 81.

66. Would you oppose a policy which made all people better off but made the wealthy moreso? For an example, see: capital gains tax reductions.

67. The same is true for labor markets; does a given worker have few or many options in the labor market? If there are many options, then employers will have to satisfy their employees; if not...

68. Boersema, p. 222-224.

69. C. Pinnock, "The Pursuit of Utopia", in *Freedom, Justice and Hope: Toward a Strategy for the Poor and the Oppressed*, ed. M. Olasky, H. Schlossberg, P. Berthoud, C. Pinnock, Westchester, IL: Crossway Books, 1988, p. 67. Why is this? In a word, "The market approach works well because it is realistic about human nature. Socialism works poorly because it presupposes saints." (p. 80)

70. Winston Churchill: "The inherent vice of capitalism is the unequal sharing of the blessings. The inherent blessing of socialism is the equal sharing of misery." (Of course, the latter holds except for those in power!). In any case, as Pinnock (p. 66) notes: "It is neither wise nor prudent to side with an ideology which...has such a bad record in regard to reducing the misery of poor people."

71. W. McGurn, *First Things*, August/September 2002, p. 16.

72. Sider, *Rich Christians*, p. 90. In contrast, Michael Novak has written much about the spiritual basis of capitalism. See: *The Spirit of Democratic Capitalism*, New York: Simon and Schuster, 1982, and *The Catholic Ethic and the Spirit of Capitalism*, New York: Free Press, 1993.

73. J. Haltemann, "The Market System, the Poor, and Economic Theory", in *Toward a Just and Caring Society*, p. 72.

74. Michael Budde and Robert Brimelow's *Christianity Incorporated: How Big Business Is Buying the Church* (Grand Rapids: Brazos Press, 2002) is replete with examples of these problems. The book does provide a useful critique of some aspects of Christian business behavior and the extent to which the Church has been allured to the American culture of consumerism. In addition to their confusion about capitalism, the other irritating feature of the book is how they fail to define key terms and answer the (often valid) questions they ask about others' political and economic beliefs (especially in chapter 6).

75. W. Marty, "A Christian Political Economy: Some Dilemmas", *Journal of Interdisciplinary Studies*, Vol. 3, #1/2, 1991, p. 107-120.

76. Llewellyn Rockwell Jr. sings the praises of the inn-keeper responsible for housing the Christ child at his birth. "The inns were full to overflowing in the entire Holy Land because of the Roman emperor's decree that everyone be counted and taxed...Luke doesn't say that [Mary and Joseph] were continually rejected at place after place. It tells of the charity of a single inn owner, perhaps the first person they encountered...There is no mention that the innkeeper charged the couple even one copper coin, though given his rights as a property owner, he certainly could have...And yet we don't even know the innkeeper's name. In 2000 years of celebrating Christmas, tributes today to the owner of the inn are absent. Such is the fate of the merchant throughout all history: doing well, doing good, and forgotten for his service to humanity." Likewise, he observes that the location of the Last Supper was also in a *kataluma* (the same Greek word) "before Jesus was crucified by the government. Thus, private enterprise was there from [his] birth, through life, and to death." ("Bethlehem's Economic Lessons"; www.mises.org, posted on December 19, 2001.)

77. In contrast, it would be sinful if economic gains came through fraud, coercion, or sinful activity. (With the last category, conservatives are actually anti-capitalism.) And of course, what one does with his income is another important issue. Ironically, Sider is as much of a capitalist as the misleading stereotype he criticizes. He puts time, effort, and money into writing books, his social activism, and teaching at a seminary. Through his self-interested pursuits, he presumably makes others better off. Finally, note that most of our "selfless acts" are in our self-interests. We typically choose to do X because it gives us the most warm fuzzies, imperishable rewards in heaven, and so on. For another example of confusion about capitalism, see: *Rich Christians*, p. 156's 3rd paragraph on mutually beneficial trade; and S. Keillor, *This Rebellious House: American History and the Truth of Christianity*, Downers Grove, IL: InterVarsity Press, 1996, p. 162's 1st paragraph on motives.

78. R. Sirico, *Acton Notes*, Grand Rapids: Acton Institute, July 1996.

79. See: Nehemiah 3:28.

80. Ironically, markets also require a number of virtues to be most effective. For example, if most people were dishonest, it would be extremely costly to regulate behavior and prevent cheating on contractual agreements. Thus, the success of economic markets is a function of a country's cultural norms, moral beliefs, legal framework, work ethics, and so on.

81. Schneider, *Religion and Liberty*.

82. Schlossberg (p. 241) pointedly asks, "Do church leaders who inveigh against 'obscene profits' have any idea what would constitute adequate

profit? Do they know the function of profit? Have they considered the ways in which profit is similar to and different from a salary?"

83. Ronald Reagan: "Government's view of the economy could be summed up in a few short phrases. If it moves, tax it. If it keeps moving, regulate it. And if it stops moving, subsidize it." Winston Churchill: "Some see private enterprise as a predatory target to be shot, others as a cow to be milked, but few are those who see it as a sturdy horse pulling the wagon."

84. Sider, *Rich Christians*, p. 147. Nash (p. 70) notes that "Many times, critics of capitalism demonstrate that they have no idea what capitalism is. The capitalism they attack is a caricature, a straw man...many of the objections to a market system result from a simple but clearly fallacious two-step operation. First, some undesirable feature is noted in a society that is allegedly capitalist. Then it is simply asserted that capitalism is the cause of this feature."

85. Sine criticizes those who believe in "the magic of the marketplace" (*Cease Fire: Searching for Sanity in America's Culture Wars*, Grand Rapids: Eerdmans, 1995, p. 115, 131-133). My effort is not meant to place the outcomes of economic markets on a pedestal per se, but rather to acknowledge that it is a system whose lack of coercion is most consistent with what the Bible advocates. Likewise, aside from the inappropriateness and inequities of using government as a tool, Sine and others on the "Religious Left" could easily be criticized for believing in "the magic of government."

86. See: Boersema, p. 176-179. Sidney Hook: "I was guilty of judging capitalism by its operations and socialism by its hopes and aspirations."

87. John Mueller opens his book by arguing that "Democracy and free-market capitalism seem to suffer from image problems—opposite ones, as it happens. Capitalism is much better than its image, while democracy has turned out to be much worse that its image." He continues by pointing to the merits and virtues within a market economy and the inevitable success of special interest groups within democracies at the expense of the general welfare of the public—a key theme in the next two chapters of this book. (*Capitalism, Democracy, and Ralph's Pretty Good Grocery*, Princeton, NJ: Princeton University Press, 1999.)

88. See: D. Schansberg, "Does the Free Market Undermine Culture?", *Markets and Morality*, 1999, p. 125-131.

89. O. Guinness, *Fit Bodies, Fat Minds: Why Evangelicals Don't Think and What to Do About It*, Grand Rapids: Baker Books, 1994, p. 30.

90. John Stapleford's *Bulls, Bears and Golden Calves: Applying Christian Ethics in Economics* (Downers Grove, IL: InterVarsity Press, 2002) is meant to be a supplemental text for Principles of Economics courses, but it is also a nice supplement to this book as well.

Chapter 9: Explaining Redistribution to the Non-Poor

1. The themes in this chapter are developed more fully in chapter 4 of my book, *Poor Policy: How Government Harms the Poor*, "Reversing Robin Hood: How to Transfer Income to the Non-poor" (Boulder, CO: Westview, 1996). The following analysis is a subset of "Public Choice" economics—a combination of political science and economics. The seminal idea is that people behave in self-interested ways in political markets as well as economic markets. Instead of merely viewing government officials as benevolent "public servants," we understand that they may also be interested in enhancing their careers and increasing their incomes. To some, this may seem like old news, but this follows years of growing cynicism toward government. When James Buchanan and Gordon Tullock developed Public Choice theory in the early 1960's, it was a novel approach. Subsequently, Buchanan was awarded the Nobel Prize for Economics in 1986.

2. Note that attempts to legislate morality are closely aligned with what is described here as political market activity. There is at least one difference—the freedoms taken away from A by C are not given to B, although B often lobbies for such laws and presumably benefits in some way.

3. One could argue that using such terminology in the context of a democracy is too strong. Given the subtle costs and the methods invoked for such redistribution (described below), persistent fraud might be a better term. Nonetheless, political markets are certainly more coercive than economic markets.

4. Poorly formed expectations and degrees of fraud can prevent transactions from being mutually beneficial. But few would argue that the former is any cause for political activity. In cases where fraud is significant, this amounts to coercion of a type and the law can be invoked to punish offenders. And again, political market activity suffers from a higher degree of the same concerns.

5. Ignoring its inefficiencies, political market transactions are a "zero-sum game"—A loses $5, B gains $5; the sum is $0. In contrast, economic activity is "positive-sum." For instance, when I buy a shirt for $20, nothing physical changes—there is still one shirt and one $20 bill. But wealth is still created since I value the shirt more than the $20, and the storeowner values

the $20 more than the shirt. The difference in our subjective valuations allows there to be an increase in well-being.

6. There is often a middleman in economic markets as well. Although he is paid for his services, his efforts reduce transaction costs for the buyer and seller. Again, this is voluntary, mutually beneficial trade.

7. David Myers blames "libertarian values" for many of our contemporary problems. To be more precise, it is selfish personal values in combination with anti-libertarian political values which cause so much trouble in this regard. (*The American Paradox: Spiritual Hunger in an Age of Plenty*, New Haven, CT: Yale University Press, 2000, p. 7.)

8. For a brilliant description of why the costs of organizing have decreased and the benefits of organizing have increased over time, see: J. Rauch, *Demosclerosis: The Silent Killer of American Government*, New York: Random House, 1994, p. 50-58.

9. In other words, people have a greater interest in the relatively few things they sell (their income) as opposed to the innumerable things they buy.

10. "Poor Returns", *Wall Street Journal*, April 13, 1998.

11. Rauch, p. 153-154.

12. J. Schlesinger, "Systems Analysis and the Political Process," *Journal of Law and Economics*, October 1968, p. 281.

13. The 10th Commandment, injunctions against moving boundary stones (Deuteronomy 19:14, Proverbs 23:10, Hosea 5:10), and the concepts of tithing and sacrifice (out of what one owns and controls) also support strong property rights. See also: Micah 4:4, Matthew 25:14-30, and Genesis 3's original sin which centered around theft.

14. H. Schlossberg, *Idols for Destruction: The Conflict of Christian Faith and American Culture*, Wheaton, IL: Crossway Books, 1990, p. 118. See also: Ecclesiastes 4:1, 5:8-9. Augustine said that the only difference between the state and a band of highwaymen is its justice and supposed legitimacy: "Justice being taken away, then, what are kingdoms but great robberies? But what are robberies themselves, but little kingdoms? The band itself is made up of men; it is ruled by the authority of a prince; it is knit together by the pact of the confederacy; the booty is divided by the law agreed upon." (Quoted in D. Bandow, "The Necessity of Limited Government", in *Caesar's Coin Revisited: Christians and the Limits of Government*, ed. M. Cromartie, Grand Rapids: Eerdmans, 1996, p. 147.)

15. There is one category that is different—when the money is used to support the common good, rather than simply to redistribute from A to B.

To promote coercive ends, Joseph McKinney cites Joseph's advice to Pharaoh to tax the Egyptian harvests by 20% during the years of plenty to prepare for the years of famine (Genesis 41). But even if an appropriate prescription, the ends were to promote the general welfare and not at all to promote any private interests. Note also that for the prescription to be practical required omniscience and a benevolent dictator—an unlikely combination. ("The Public Sector and the Poor", in *Political Principles and Economics: The Foundations*, volume 2, ed. R. Chewning, Colorado Springs: Navpress, 1989, p. 235.) Isaiah 22:10 may provide another example. For confusion in labeling health care as what economists call a "public good", see: C. Cochran, "Health Policy and the Poverty Trap: Finding a Way Out", in *Toward a Just and Caring Society: Christian Responses to Poverty in America*, ed. D. Gushee, Grand Rapids: Baker Books, 1999, p. 236-239, 244.

16. R. Heinlein, *The Moon Is a Harsh Mistress*, New York: Ace Books, 1965, p. 63.

17. Quoted in L. Burkett, *The Coming Economic Earthquake*, Chicago: Moody Press, 1991, p. 33. Dwight Lee draws an analogy to shortening the life of every American by five seconds in order to lengthen a friend's life by 41 years. ("The Perversity of Doing Good at Others' Expense", *The Freeman*, September 1997, p. 525-528.) Grover Cleveland: "When we consider that the theory of our institutions guarantees to every citizen the full enjoyment of all the fruits of his industry and enterprise, with only such deduction as may be his share toward the careful and economical maintenance of the Government which protects him, it is plain that the extraction of more than this is indefensible extortion and a culpable betrayal of American fairness and justice." (Quoted in R. Higgs, *Crisis and Leviathan*.)

18. Schlossberg, p. 281. Wilhelm Roepke: "The morally edifying character of a policy which robs Peter in order to pay Paul cannot be said to be immediately obvious. But it degenerates into an absurd two-way pumping of money when the state robs nearly everybody and pays nearly everybody, so that no one knows in the end whether he has gained or lost in the game." *A Humane Economy: The Social Framework of the Free Market*, 3rd ed., Wilmington, DE: ISI Books, 1998, p. 165.)

19. Psalms 109:11. "If one does not acknowledge transcendent truth, then the force of power takes over, and each person tends to make full use of the means at his disposal in order to impose his own interests or his own opinion, with no regard for the rights of others. People are then respected only to the extent that they can be exploited for selfish ends." (John Paul II, Centesimus Annus, #44-45, 1991; in *The Social Agenda: A Collection of*

Magisterial Texts, ed. R. Sirico and M. Zieba, Vatican City: Pontifical Council for Justice and Peace, 2000, p. 99.)

20. Likewise, it is impossible for Christians to reconcile advocacy of coercive versions of "affirmative action". Again, the goal is reasonable, but aside from the many practical difficulties, the method involves taking a job from A to give to B who has discriminated against by C. If this were appropriate, we would have to condone people who burglarize others because they have been burglarized by someone else.

21. D. Bandow, *Beyond Good Intentions: A Biblical View of Politics*, Wheaton, IL: Crossway Books, 1988, p. 51.

22. Even avid libertarians recognize that economic markets aren't particularly adept at dealing with: 1.) "externalities" such as pollution, because of the existence of substantial costs (or benefits) external to, and usually ignored by, the agent making the decisions. In such cases, the market produces more (or less) than the socially optimal level; and 2.) "public goods" such as infrastructure or national defense. Here, the market can produce the optimal amount, but because providers cannot exclude those who do not pay, we may observe "free riding". (Why should I pay if I can sponge off my neighbor's purchase?) Thus, the supplier may not be able to collect revenues adequately enough for economic markets to provide this effectively. In such cases, government (political markets) *can be* "efficiency-enhancing" or "socially optimal"; they may be capable of doing a better job than economic markets. However, efficiency-enhancing is not at all assured. For example, in the provision of national defense, Congress might approve money for a weapon system that is ineffective for defending the country but accomplishes political purposes.

23. An interesting potential counter-example is in the Israelites accepting money from the Persian king in rebuilding the temple (Ezra 6:4,8-9, 7:15). Note that the money was volunteered not requested and God might have considered it a form of "back-pay" (as in Exodus 12:35-36).

24. L. Spooner, *Vices Are not Crimes: A Vindication of Moral Liberty*, 1875, Chapter XX.

25. Exodus 23:8. See: Deuteronomy 16:19, Ecclesiastes 7:7. See also: Deuteronomy 10:17, 28:25; Job 15:34-35, 36:18; Psalms 15:5, 26:9-10; Proverbs 15:28; Isaiah 5:23; Micah 3:9-12.

26. Exodus 18:21.

27. I Samuel 12:3-4.

28. Amos 5:11-12. One can draw a moral distinction between taking and paying bribes. See: my essay, "The Ethics of Tax Evasion Within Biblical

Christianity: Are There Limits to 'Rendering unto Caesar?'", in *The Ethics of Tax Evasion*, ed. R. McGee, South Orange, NJ: The Dumont Institute for Public Policy Research, 1998, p. 156.

29. Presumably I don't have any conflicts of interest, but of course, readers should also weigh my remarks carefully—like the Bereans (Acts 17:11).

30. Bierce defines "vote" as "the instrument and symbol of a freeman's power to make a fool of himself and a wreck of his country." Again, given the machinations of political markets, don't expect too much from democracy, especially when people feel little compunction in using government to make themselves better off at the expense of others!

31. Further, any new requirements are usually "grandfathered"— incumbents are immune to the new restrictions. If the well-being of consumers was the primary motivation, presumably all suppliers would have to measure up to the new standards.

32. Schlossberg, p. 118.

33. Often, proponents of government programs will argue that those with the created jobs will spend their money, creating more jobs, etc. Of course, the same reasoning holds for the jobs destroyed by taxing the public to pay for the programs. This returns us to the "shell game" idea.

34. Expenditures on infrastructure may be an exception, assuming that the investment is productive (not digging holes in the ground) and that the private sector would be hampered by the "public goods" aspect of the investment. The difference is the positive by-products for people completely independent of those receiving the income transfer. In other words, taxpayer A benefits in addition to recipient B. For instance, with a new or improved road, the cost of transport for everybody would diminish with less traffic congestion or fewer potholes. Of course, government can do many other things to encourage economic growth and job creation—by creating an environment where productive behavior is encouraged. These include the provision of secure property rights, law and order, a stable monetary system, and so on. The minimal level of government needed to accomplish this legal infrastructure also benefits the common good.

35. Schlossberg (p. 90) draws an analogy to alchemy—the fictitious practice of turning lead into gold. Both give "the illusion of creating wealth where none existed before. But all [they do] is redistribute the wealth that is already present."

36. Again, this holds unless economic markets are highly inefficient—as, for example, with "public goods" and externalities.

37. Politicians give cash to sympathetic groups (e.g., the elderly, the poor, those dealing with disasters), but use more subtle mechanisms to redistribute wealth to other groups.

38. In recent times, only OPEC's control over oil and DeBeer's monopoly power over diamonds have been notably successful. DeBeer's has been especially effective because it controls elements of both the supply and demand sides of the diamond market. This also explains why stories about "predatory pricing" are so unlikely. Even if a firm can handle losing all the money it would take to drive all of its rivals out of a market, subsequent attempts to raise prices too much will likely cause those rivals to reenter or new competitors to emerge.

39. W. Williams, *All It Takes Is Guts*, Washington, DC: Regnery Gateway, 1987, p. 68. Will Rogers: "The business of government is to keep out of business—that is, unless business needs government aid." See also: I Kings 20:34a.

40. G. Bauer (*Our Hopes, Our Dreams: A Vision for America*, Colorado Springs: Focus on the Family Publishing, 1996, p. 70-71) finds himself "asking whether the free-trade mantra is being used to play American families for suckers." He then notes that "a 10% tariff on imports from Japan would raise $12 billion a year", without recognizing (or at least mentioning) that American consumers would be among the losers in this version of the shell game. Besides, where is the Biblical justification for this populist policy?

41. "A Sweet Deal for Big Sugar Daddies", *U. S. News and World Report*, August 6, 2001, p. 36. In 1991, the sugar program cost consumers $3.2 billion—$50 from the average family of four. ("Hidden Monopolies: Driving Up Prices for Consumers," *U.S. News and World Report*, February 3, 1992, pp. 42-48.)

42. Ibid. It is a $560 million subsidy, about $65 million of which goes to one family, the Fanjul's.

43. James Bovard's comment that "democracy must be something more than two wolves and a sheep voting on what to have for dinner" is apt except that in most cases the sheep doesn't know what's for dinner!

44. Jonathan Rauch (p. 242) compares our current climate (of using government to redistribute income to interest groups) to monkeys and dogs reflexively gnawing at parasites. Depending on the context, individuals are either the victim of parasites or parasites themselves. "Who will repudiate the politics of blame and tell the people the truth...we are the special interests...John Kennedy told Americans to ask what they could do for their

country, not what their country could do for them. They adored him and ignored his counsel. Now they must listen or pay the price."

45. G. North, "The Politics of the 'Fair Share'," *The Freeman*, November 1993.

46. *U.S. News and World Report*, November 14, 1994, p. 39.

47. For an interesting version of this point in the context of sin and self-interest, see: W. Miller, *The Protestant and Politics*, Philadelphia: Westminster Press, 1958, p. 62-65.

48. John Claypool observes that Southern Baptists used to be "poor tenant farmers" who were not used to having much power in the community at large. As a result, in the past, they focused on issues of private morality rather than corporate justice. Likewise, he notes that Episcopalians (and other mainline Protestants) have been more influential, and thus, had a stronger sense of social responsibility. Unfortunately, as we'll see later, that sense of responsibility has not always been well-directed. (*The Door Interviews*, p. 130.)

49. Isaiah 59:14-16.

50. Proverbs 21:15.

51. See: Acts 16. Interestingly, the only two recorded instances where Paul is harassed by Gentiles, the subject is money and the force of government is used to persecute him.

52. Luke 22:4-6.

Chapter 10: Ending Redistribution to the Non-Poor

1. This section borrows heavily from chapter 5 of my book, *Poor Policy: How Government Harms the Poor* (Boulder, CO: Westview, 1996). See also: K. Schmiesing, "Free Economy Farming", Grand Rapids: Acton Institute, 2001.

2. In 1998, median net family wealth was $71,600 and mean equity for farmers (with sales of more than $10,000) was $406,664 (*Statistical Abstract of the United States*, 2000, Tables #764, 1104, 1111).

3. The Bureau of Land Management subsidizes grazing fees to ranchers on public lands; in 1992, the annual fee was $1.92 per animal compared to $9.26 for private landowners. From 1988-1992, the Farmers Home Administration wrote off $11.5 billion in bad loans—a staggering amount, especially considering that principal on current loans amounts to $13.8 billion. (S. LaFranierc, "Though They Owe, Still They Rcap," *Washington*

368   *Turn Neither to the Right nor to the Left*

Post National Weekly Edition, February 28-March 6, 1994.) California subsidizes the purchase of water by farmers; they use 80% of the state's water at prices discounted up to 94% of cost. (S. Hayward, "Muddy Waters," *Reason*, July 1991.)

4. *Statistical Abstract of the United States*, 1993, Table #1109.

5. J. Donahue, "The Corporate Welfare Kings," *Washington Post National Weekly Edition*, March 21-27, 1994. See: www.ewg.org/farm for great data!

6. B. Copple, "Insuring Failure", *Forbes*, March 20, 2000, p. 100; and "Higher subsidy boosts crop-insurance sales", *(Louisville) Courier-Journal*, May 13, 2001. The latter also notes that the insurance subsidy was 58% in 2000. For what it's been worth, the "Freedom to Farm Act of 1996" was supposed to reduce such programs, but political talk has greatly exceeded political walk.

7. J. Bovard, *Fair Trade Fraud*, New York: St. Martin's Press, 1991, p. 96. The U.S. International Trade Commission has estimated that the quotas nearly double the effective price of peanuts and peanut butter. In the most recent farm bill, legislators have proposed a $1.3 billion buy-out of the quotas along with new subsidy system. (E. Becker, "Peanut Proposals Put a new Wrinkle on Farm Subsidies", *New York Times*, March 4, 2002.)

8. "End of the Citrus Cartel," *Wall Street Journal*, December 15, 1992.

9. *Agricultural Outlook*, various years.

10. Bovard, p. 10, 65-70.

11. 60% of American farmers receive no subsidies at all (N. Kristof, "Farm Subsidies that Kill", *(Louisville) Courier-Journal*, July 7, 2002).

12. Ibid.

13. Bovard, p. 36.

14. Ibid.; *Economic Report of the President*, 1989, p. 172; C. Oliver, "The Ghost of Christmas Presents," *Reason*, January 1990.

15. Ibid.

16. R. Sider, *Rich Christians in an Age of Hunger*, Dallas: Word Publishing, 1990, p. 113. Edward Opitz reports that the U.S. Congress' first law was a tariff. (E. Opitz, *Religion and Capitalism: Allies, not Enemies*, 2nd ed., Irvington-on-Hudson, NY: Foundation for Economic Education, 1992, p. 250.)

17. Dana Frank provides an excellent overview of the (American) history of protectionism in *Buy American* (Boston: Beacon Press, 1999).

18. Dave Barry on farm subsidies: "Perhaps you're asking yourself: 'Wait a minute! Isn't this kind of like, I don't know...WELFARE?' No it is not. Welfare is when government gives money to people who produce nothing. Whereas the farm-money recipients produce something that is critical to our nation: votes...So as we see, it's not welfare at all! It's bribery."

19. This section is a distillation of chapters 6 and 7 of my book *Poor Policy*.

20. See also: D. Schansberg, "Does the Free Market Undermine Culture?", *Markets and Morality*, 1999, p. 125-126.

21. This explains why engineers are not paid $7.00 per hour and why firms in competitive product markets cannot charge "outrageous prices." (For an inability to recognize differences in worker skills, and more important, worker productivity—and their impact on wages and confusion about minimum wages, see: M. Budde and R. Brimelow, *Christianity Incorporated: How Big Business Is Buying the Church*, Grand Rapids: Brazos Press, 2002, p. 151.) Note however that when firms have substantial degrees of monopoly power, the outcome can be different. Recent examples include government as the sole employer in a fully socialistic economy, the NCAA cartel concerning college athletes, professional sports in the absence of "free agency," and slavery. Note also that, in the past, when labor markets were not (as) competitive, one could more easily make a justice argument for government intervention to regulate business' monopoly power in labor markets—for example, with a 19th century coal mining town.

22. This assumes an "effective" wage floor—one that exceeds the market rate for that skill level. If not effective, then the law will have no binding effect (positive or negative)—just as if Congress passed a law mandating that McDonald's sell Big Macs for at least $.25. In our now-booming economy, one could easily argue that the current minimum is largely irrelevant to the workings of labor markets. In any case, many people advocate substantially higher minimum wages—at levels that would clearly constrain the market in the manner described.

23. See: S. Malanga, "How the 'Living Wage' Sneaks Socialism into Cities", *City Journal*, Winter 2003.

24. For a critique of the National Conference of Catholic Bishop proposal, see: S. Borland, *First Things*, February 2001, p. 14-17.

25. *Statistical Abstract of the United States*, 2000, Table #674. These numbers began to worsen in the 1950's when the real minimum wage and the proportion of jobs covered both increased. In the early 1950's, black and white teen males had almost identical labor force participation and unemployment rates. Note also that the minimum wage, by causing a

surplus of unskilled workers, makes discrimination costless, and therefore, more likely.

26. Unlike the stereotype around which the policy is built, very few minimum wage workers are full-time employed and heads of households. Many are food servers who supplement their incomes with tips, middle-class teenagers, or other part-time workers. As such, the following policy prescriptions would reward work *and* more effectively target assistance to the poor.

27. David Bernstein's entire book makes this point about the impact of Progressive Era and New Deal labor market restrictions on minorities. (*Only One Place of Redress*, Durham, NC: Duke University Press, 2001; see: especially, p. 103-110.)

28. *The Freeman*, February 1994, p. 67, citing "Rates of Wages for Laborers and Mechanics on Public Buildings of the United States," *Congressional Record* (1931), #6504, #6513.

29. C. Wenman, "Beastly Burden", *Reason*, October 1996, p. 16.

30. Similarly, "big business" often lobbies for an employer mandate when it already meets the standard. By requiring that small businesses provide the same, they can increase their costs and limit their ability to compete.

31. Low-quality service or products may be reduced, but arguably, people should not have their choices restricted to accomplish this. (A range of quality is particularly important to the poor.) And while average quality in licensed markets may increase, the improvement is costly: prices will rise, possibly limiting the ability of the poor to obtain any service at all. Moreover, quality might diminish. If barriers to entry are large enough, incumbents would be relatively unconcerned with providing high-quality service. Many government enterprises serve as excellent testimony to this effect of limited competition.

32. Imagine that a state passed a law requiring people to have a "qualified" tax consultant prepare their returns (as in Oregon). The legislature might say that it wants to prevent the public from receiving low quality tax returns. Clearly, accountants in the state would benefit from the restricted competition. Consumers would be worse off by being forced to obtain "Cadillac service" or none at all. And the relatively less skilled people who often prepare returns would be eliminated from this labor market.

33. See: p. 67-68 of *Poor Policy* for examples.

34. Midwives and chiropractors are also heavily restricted in many states. In the market for dental and legal services, dental assistants and paralegals face similar barriers—at the behest of the ADA and ABA.

35. Many argue that unions were (or even are) necessary for workers to avoid exploitation. But wages were increasing even before unions were ascendant. And again, competition in labor markets will avoid significant and systematic exploitation. Remember also that all sellers (here, of labor) have an incentive to collude in order to achieve higher prices (here, wages) for the things (labor) they sell.

36. Among unions, those in the public sector are especially effective. With the deep pockets of taxpayers as well as the incentives of budget-maximizing bureaucracies, public sector unions could continue to grow well into the future, increasing the transfer of income from taxpayers to upper and middle-class union workers.

37. Unfortunately, Ron Sider repeatedly supports labor unions and higher minimum wages. This policy conclusion is especially ironic since he recognizes the role of interest groups in manipulating government for its own ends at the expense of others (*Rich Christians*, p. 112-113; *Just Generosity: A New Vision for Overcoming Poverty in America*, Grand Rapids: Baker Books, 1999, p. 89, 118.) But see also: Sider's support of the EITC over a minimum wage (ibid., p. 104).

38. R. Armey, "Review Merits of Flat Tax", *Wall Street Journal*, June 16, 1994.

39. In 1999, 26% of tax filers had no tax liability at all, while the top .5% of taxpayers paid 28% of total income tax revenues; 553,380 people were responsible for $877 billion, averaging more than $1.5 million each. In 2000, the top 5% of income earners (with adjusted gross incomes greater than $128,336) were responsible for 56%; the top 50% were responsible for 96%. ("The Non-Taxpaying Class", *Wall Street Journal*, November 20, 2002, p. A20.)

40. With lower marginal tax rates, one would expect people to report more income, seek fewer tax shelters, cheat less often on income tax returns, and to work harder. (The latter is arguable since individuals may respond to greater take-home pay by consuming more leisure. Either way, people are better off.) See also: Proverbs 12:24 and Joshua 17:13's additional taxation on "undesirables". John Anderson notes, somewhat with tongue in cheek, that David seems to have responded to tax incentives in winning the hand of his wife (I Samuel 17:25). But just "as the Christian understands that David was motivated by factors other than tax breaks and the offer of the king's daughter, so the contemporary Christian policy observer understands that modern behavior is not driven entirely by tax incentives. Yet the tax system is a powerful tool for implementing incentives for individuals and firms to alter their behavior." ("Taxation and Economic Justice", in *Toward a Just*

and Caring Society: Christian Responses to Poverty in America, ed. D. Gushee, Grand Rapids: Baker Books, 1999, p. 261-262.)

41. Our earlier discussion of income dynamics in chapter 7 is relevant here as well. Since people usually face a life-cycle of earnings, the marginal tax rates they will face over their careers may well vary. See: R. Hubbard, "Measure Tax-Cut 'Fairness' Over a Lifetime", *Wall Street Journal*, January 8, 2003.)

42. The "14-day rule" is an interesting loophole. It allows people to exempt *all* rental income as long as they rent out their homes for 14 days or fewer each year. For example, the loophole is popular in Augusta, Georgia— where the Masters golf tournament generates considerable income for some residents.

43. Grover Norquist suggests pursuing a series of smaller reforms instead of the one large reform of embracing a flat tax: eliminate the estate tax, stop taxing capital gains, end the Alternative Minimum Tax, make all savings tax free, let businesses write off investments in a single year, and then charge everyone the same marginal tax rate. "This...program has the advantage that each of its elements has its own built-in constituency, while support for an official flat tax is far more diffuse." ("Five Easy Steps to Tax Reform", *The American Enterprise*, December 2002, p. 18.)

44. One-half of the $66 billion subsidy goes to those with incomes greater than $100,000 per year. (*Just Generosity*, p. 126.) Sider also notes that the tax exemption per child in the 1940's was more than twice as much as today's exemption after accounting for inflation. Likewise, the tax subsidy for excluding employer contributions for health care expenditures is nearly $70 billion, and again, pocketed disproportionately by those with above average incomes. (*The Atlantic Monthly*, January/February 2003, p. 81.)

45. Actually, workers bear most of the "employer's share" of the Social Security tax as well—through lower wages and other compensation. The imposition of a tax is irrelevant to determining who bears the long-run burden of that tax. Since workers have few reasonable options in trying to avoid the tax (work illegally, work in one of the few areas of the economy not exposed to the tax, or don't work at all), and firms have some flexibility with their inputs, workers end up bearing the brunt of even the employer's share of the tax. An example might be instructive: although the gas tax is imposed on and collected from gas stations, who do you think bears the burden of the tax? (For more detail, see: M. Wilson, "A Look at Who Pays the Payroll tax", Washington, DC: Heritage Foundation, August 2001.)

46. The cap applies to the 12.4% Social Security tax, not the 2.9% Medicare tax.

47. As a result of these two provisions and the other deductions available to avoid income taxation, 75% pay more in direct Social Security taxes than in federal income taxes.

48. One rationale for the Earned Income Tax Credit (EITC) was to alleviate the burden of Social Security (payroll) taxes on the working poor. But given that Social Security is purely income redistribution from current workers to current retirees (rather than forced savings by each individual), there is no necessary reason for the working poor to bear any of its burden. As such, an EITC along with the elimination of payroll taxes on the working poor—or a tax credit to compensate for its burden on the working poor—would seem to be the an equitable and efficient solution. For recent scholarship, contemporary detail, and an historical account of the EITC, see: *Making Work Pay: The Earned Income Tax Credit and its Impact on America's Families*, ed. B. Meyer and D. Holtz-Eakin, New York: Russell Sage Foundation, 2001.

49. The numbers in this paragraph come from annual reports released by the Center on Budget & Policy Priorities in Washington, DC (www.cbpp.org).

50. Alabama's state income tax became more infamous on a state and national level after Susan Pace Hamill's master's thesis on the topic became published and gained national attention. See: "An Argument for Tax Reform Based on Judeo-Christian ethics", *Alabama Law Review*, Fall 2002, p. 1-112; and "Seminary Article Sparks Alabama Tax-Code Revolt", *Wall Street Journal*, February 2003, p. A1.

51. When one includes the fact that employers shift most of their Social Security tax burden to workers in the form of lower wages, the monthly bill is about $280 per month.

52. See: B. McIntyre, "State and Local Taxes Hit Poor and Middle Class Far Harder than the Wealthy", Washington, DC: Institute on Taxation and Economic Policy, January 2003.

53. J. Belz, *World*, February 3, 1996, p. 5. Of course, the tithe didn't have "personal deductions"; all income was subject to the tithe. Note also that some sacrifices were income-dependent. All that said, it is arguable whether this is relevant since the New Testament does not use the tithe as its concept of giving; instead, giving is described as voluntary and flexible but self-sacrificing. For details on "the tithe", see: J. MacArthur, *Why Government Can't Save You: An Alternative to Political Activism*, Nashville: Word Publishing, 2000, p. 57. For an interesting academic article on tithing within the Mormon church, see: G. Dahl and M. Ransom, "The 10% Flat Tax: Tithing and the Definition of Income", *Economic Inquiry*, January 2002, p. 120-137.

54. This section distills chapter 9 of *Poor Policy*. See also: the May/June 1996 issue of *Prism*.

55. *Statistical Abstract of the United States*, 1999, Tables #313, 315.

56. D. Lee and R. McKenzie note that at the inception of the loan programs in 1957, assistance was limited to low-income families. But over time, interest groups for higher education asserted themselves and the programs were expanded. For example, from 1977 to 1981, guaranteed student loans rose from $1.5 to $7.8 billion. (*Failure and Progress*, Washington, DC: Cato Institute, 1993, p. 127-128.)

57. The National Center for Education Statistics reports that 52% of parents were "very satisfied" with their children's public schools. For those with choice among public schools, the percentage rose to 62%. For those in private schools, the rate was 82%.

58. 22% vs. 10%. *Imprimis*, March 1992; and "Education Reform Breakout," *Wall Street Journal*, December 17, 1993. In 1990, more than 40% of public school teachers sent their children to private schools in the following cities: Baltimore, Boston, Cleveland, Dayton, Grand Rapids, Honolulu, Milwaukee, New Orleans, and Pittsburgh (1990 Census Data compiled by Denis Doyle, *The American Enterprise*, September/October 1996, p. 18).

59. *Statistical Abstract of the United States*, 2002, Tables #198, 199. Tuition at private schools is somewhat lower than the cost since the education is often subsidized by churches. The primary factor in the higher cost of government education is the bureaucracy characteristic of any socialistic endeavor. For example, in New York City, public schools have 10 times more employees per student and 60 times more administrators per student than the city's Catholic schools. (M. Perry, "The Educational Octopus", *The Freeman*, February 1995, p. 127.) In Washington, D.C., Catholic schools have a central administration of only 17 people for 50,000 students; the public schools have 1,500 administrative employees for 81,000 students, 50 times more per student. ("The Exodus", *U.S. News and World Report*, December 9, 1991, p. 71, cited in G. Bauer, *Our Hopes, Our Dreams: A Vision for America*, Colorado Springs: Focus on the Family Publishing, 1996, p. 88.) Moreover, teacher salaries are much higher in the taxpayer-financed sector of the market for education—in 2001-2002, $44,500 per school year. (www.nea.org/edstats/reupdate02.html, cited in *School Reform News*, Heartland Institute: Chicago, February 2003.)

60. Http://Nces.ed.gov/pubs/2002/2002367.pdf, cited in *School Reform News*, December 2002, p. 18.

61. Ibid.

62. In 1999, there were 46.8 million students in public schools and 6.02 million in private schools. If educational vouchers would save taxpayers $3,109 each for all public school students and would cost an additional $4,983 for existing private school students, the total savings would be $115.5 billion. (*Statistical Abstract of the United States*, 2002, Tables #198, 199.)

63. It is often asserted that poorer students receive less funding for public education. Although true to the extent that spending is connected with property taxes (see: J. Pinkerton, "A Grand Compromise", *The Atlantic Monthly*, January/February 2003, p. 115), there are many counter-examples where spending is comparable or even far greater than average. For example, in Washington D.C., where schools are routinely described as an unmitigated disaster, spending is more than $11,000 per student. (Http://Nces.ed.gov/pubs/2002/2002367.pdf, cited in *School Reform News*.)

64. R. Reed, *Active Faith*, New York: Free Press, 1996, p. 74.

65.   Sider advocates experimenting with vouchers (*Just Generosity*, p. 163). Frame and Tharpe advocate educational vouchers—but only for the poor (*How Right Is the Right?*, Grand Rapids: Zondervan, 1996, p. 105). This approach is more politically expedient, if not more equitable. Charter schools provide another avenue for enhancing competition and choice. Tax credits are the "cleanest" reform (avoiding direct contact with government funding), but would benefit so few people—and the rich, disproportionately—that this is politically infeasible and doesn't begin to address the current injustices. For details on contemporary reform, see: *The School Reform News*, published by the Heartland Institute out of Chicago.

Meanwhile, there is a growing academic attention to and debate about the impact of vouchers. See: *Charter Schools in Action: Renewing Public Education*, ed. C. Finn Jr., B. Manno, and G. Vanourek, Princeton, NJ: Princeton University Press, 2000; J. Witte, *The Market Approach to Education: An Analysis of America's First Voucher Program*, Princeton, NJ: Princeton University Press, 2000; F. Bergstrom and M. Sandstrom, "School Choice Works: The Case of Sweden", working paper for the Research Institute of Industrial Economics, Stockholm, 2002. For a debate within an academic journal, see: H. Ladd, "School Vouchers: A Critical View", *Journal of Economic Perspectives*, Fall 2002, p. 3-24; and D. Neal, "How Vouchers Could Change the Market for Education", *Journal of Economic Perspectives*, Fall 2002, p. 25-44.

66. The current system also violates the principles of "subsidiarity" and "sphere sovereignty"—that social groups nearest the challenge should have the most discretion in dealing with that problem. "Parents who have the primary and inalienable right and duty to educate their children must enjoy

true liberty in their choice of schools. Consequently, the public power, which has the obligation to protect and defend the rights of citizens, must see to it, in its concern for distributive justice, that public subsidies are paid in such a way that parents are truly free to choose according to their conscience the schools they want for their children." (Vatican Council II, *Gravissimum Educationis*, #20, October 28, 1965; quoted in J. Klesney, "School Choice and Parental Duty: Returning Subsidiarity to Education", Grand Rapids: Acton Institute, 2000.)

67.   Some people rightly worry that educational vouchers could be accompanied by government regulation. But as should be obvious from the grocery store analogy, overly burdensome regulation is not necessarily an issue. Fending off potential regulation is a separate, but important battle within the vouchers debate. But even if regulation followed, Christian schools would be no worse off since they could still choose to turn down the money. Finally, in defending their position, many of these vouchers opponents *sound* selfish and unconcerned with the plight of the inner-city poor.

    There is some debate in libertarians circles whether to accept any role—whether long-term or even short-term—for government funding of education. Joseph Bast notes that this greater reluctance is a relatively new thing—from some combination of philosophical change or the more practical point that educational subsidies for even the poor are now unimportant, given greater incomes and nearly universal literacy. That said, most Libertarians would support some degree of privatization in the short-term, in working toward complete privatization at some point. See: J. Bast, "Why Conservatives and Libertarians Should Support School Vouchers", *The Independent Review*, Fall 2002, p. 265-276.

68. Opponents often argue that vouchers violate the church-state provision of the Constitution. Besides having a questionable interpretation of the Constitution, the argument is a straw man in practice. In fact, the G.I. Bill empowered war veterans to purchase educational services at the university of their choice—public or private. Moreover, an untold number of Medicare and Medicaid recipients purchase health care services at hospitals run by churches. If one is consistent, this is not an issue.

69. See: C. Glenn, "Just Schools: Doing Right by Poor Kids", in *Toward a Just and Caring Society: Christian Responses to Poverty in America*, ed. D. Gushee, Grand Rapids: Baker Books, 1999.

70. Bill Clinton, Ted Kennedy, and Jesse Jackson are just a few of the famous opponents of educational vouchers who have chosen private schools for their children. In the U.S. House of Representatives, 70% of the Hispanic Caucus and 30% of the Black Caucus send their children to

private schools while mostly opposing educational vouchers. Nationally, 6% of Hispanics and 4% of Blacks send their children to private schools while a majority supports vouchers (*World*, May 20, 1995, p. 14, citing a study by the Heritage Foundation). In the recent vote to allow a small educational voucher experiment in Washington, D.C., "with one exception, no Senator who voted against the choice measure had ever chosen to send his or her children to the D.C. Public Schools" (*The American Enterprise*, September/October 1996, p. 15). See also: J. Rauch, "Reversing White Flight", *The Atlantic Monthly*, October 2002, p. 32.

Chapter 11: Redistribution to the Poor—Ethical and Practical Concerns

1. With respect to Catholic leaders, this has been most evident among the U.S. bishops. Over the last 100 years, the popes have often written on these topics, but their conclusions are general enough that one can read their own biases into the papal critiques of both socialism and capitalism. That said, among the works in the "Catholic Social Justice Canon", Leo XXIII's *Rerum Novarum* (1891) and John Paul II's writings (most notably, *Centesimus Annus*, 1991) provide an especially strong defense of property rights and a serious critique of the ethics and practice of government activism. (For an overview, see: Thomas Woods, Suffolk Community College, "Catholic Social Teaching and Economic Law: An Unresolved Tension", presented at Economics and Christianity, Baylor University: Waco, TX, November 7-9, 2002.) For an analysis of John Paul II's writings, see: W. Mott, Jr., *The Third Way: Economic Justice According to John Paul II*, Lanham, MD: University Press of America, 1999, p. 136-141. (Mott also tries to defend the policy prescriptions of the U.S. Bishops—p. 143-148.)

2. "Every alternative to the market economy and the system of liberty—when carried to its logical conclusion—relates a man's economic status to his political power; the higher he is on the political ladder, the greater his opportunities for acquiring wealth. Those without political power...are condemned to poverty—unless they acquire a patron, or resort to predation." (E. Opitz, *Religion and Capitalism: Allies, not Enemies*, 2nd ed., Irvington-on-Hudson, NY Foundation for Economic Education, 1992, p. 241.)

3. Because the economy of a church is "socialistic," its success in spite of the "free rider problem" (people can "consume" without paying anything) may mislead church leaders into believing the same about the economy. Moreover, they are prone to view money simply in terms of collection and

redistribution. Others believe that material pursuits should be discouraged, but of course, this should be left to individual choice.

4. See also: Leviticus 25:35-38.

5. See also: Deuteronomy 24:19-22. Every seventh year, the poor were to be able to eat produce from fallow land (Exodus 23:10-11).

6. See: Nehemiah 8:10, Numbers 18:24-29, Deuteronomy 14:28-29. Ron Sider claims that the Jubilee principle "underlines the importance of institutionalized mechanisms and...prescribes justice rather than haphazard handouts by wealthy philanthropists." (*Rich Christians in an Age of Hunger*, Dallas: Word Publishing, 1990, p. 67.) Although true for the Israelites, there were no mandates placed on those outside the community of believers. Further, Sider at least implicitly assumes that the Jubilee was only for promoting justice and equal economic outcomes (p. 66-69). However, it's not even clear that greater "economic equality" was even a goal of this facet of the Law; it may have been simply a by-product. One could easily argue that its purpose was to directly illustrate that everything we have belongs to God or merely to provide another analogy to God's grace. Finally, Chilton notes a number of instances when "the Jubilee actually furthered (income) inequality." (D. Chilton, *Productive Christians in an Age of Guilt Manipulators: A Biblical Response to Ronald J. Sider*, 3rd ed., Tyler, TX: Institute for Christian Economics, 1985, p. 157-159.)

7. Luke uses parallel passages within two chapters of each other to emphasize these principles and for other literary effects—in Acts 2, for Peter to invite new believers into an attractive community after calling them out of "this corrupt generation" (2:40); and at the end of Acts 4 to introduce Barnabas and contrast him with Ananias and Sapphira at the beginning of Acts 5.

8. See also: Luke 8:3, Acts 11:29-30, James 1:27.

9. Luke 10:25-37.

10. I love Frederick Buechner's definition of "neighbor" (*Wishful Thinking: A Theological ABC*, San Francisco: Harper & Row, 1973, p. 65-66): "When Jesus said to love your neighbor, a lawyer who was present asked him to clarify what he meant by *neighbor*. He wanted a legal definition he could refer to in case the question of loving one ever happened to come up. He presumably wanted something on the order of: 'A neighbor (hereinafter referred to as the party of the first part) is to be construed as meaning a person of Jewish descent whose legal residence is within a radius of no more than three statute miles from one's own legal residence unless there is another person of Jewish descent (hereinafter to be referred to as the party of the second part) living closer to the party of the first part than one is

oneself, in which case the party of the second part is to be construed as neighbor to the party of the first part and one is oneself relieved of all responsibility of any kind or sort whatsoever.' Instead Jesus told the story of the Good Samaritan, the point of which seems to be that your neighbor is to be construed as meaning anybody who needs you. The lawyer's response is left unrecorded."

11. For an example, see: Sider, p. 58 and his theses about the role of government in chapters 6 and 9. Elsewhere, Sider argues that charitable efforts by individuals are *inferior* to government redistribution because the former can lead to pride! (Cited in H. Schlossberg, *Idols for Destruction: The Conflict of Christian Faith and American Culture*, Wheaton, IL: Crossway Books, 1990, p. 244, and Chilton, *Productive Christians*, p. 172-173.)

12. P. J. O'Rourke: "There is no virtue in compulsory government charity, and there is no virtue in advocating it. A politician who portrays himself as 'caring' and 'sensitive' because he wants to expand the government's charitable programs is merely saying that he's willing to try to do good with other people's money. Well, who isn't? And a voter who takes pride in supporting such programs is telling us he'll do good with his own money—if a gun is held to his head."

13. Opitz (p. 91) describes welfare programs as "the apparatus of compulsion first deprives everyone of a portion of his resources, then impersonally redistributes this booty according to political expediency." G. Gordon Liddy has described a liberal as "someone who feels a great debt to his fellow man, which he proposes to pay off with your money." Isaiah 58:7 says you should give your food, not your neighbor's!

14. See: G. Brennan, "The Christian and the State", *CIS Occasional Papers* #7, St. Leonards, Australia: The Centre for Independent Studies, 1983, p. 5. He also notes that this is the very essence of grace. "God's love for man is a prime attribute of God; [yet] it is not borne of man's right to be loved." Lysander Spooner wrote that "Whatever moral claims a poor man...may have upon the charity of his fellow-men, he has no legal claims upon them. He must depend wholly upon their charity, if they so please. He cannot demand, as a legal right, that they either feed or clothe him, and he has no more legal or moral claims upon a government—which is but an association of individuals..." (*Vices Are not Crimes: A Vindication of Moral Liberty*, 1875, Chapter XXI.)

15. Quoted in *World*, April 23, 1994, p. 14.

16. II Thessalonians 3:10-12. See also: Proverbs 19:19, Ephesians 4:28, I Thessalonians 4:11-12.

17. Economists separate the work disincentive into two parts. First, with more income from the welfare benefits, recipients can "afford" to "consume" more leisure. Second, because the benefit reduction rate necessarily reduces the rewards for working, work becomes relatively less attractive and one is likely to substitute from work to leisure. (Note that "leisure" encompasses all "non-market activity", including labor supplied in underground markets.)

18. I encourage you to construct your own numerical example. Simply choose a maximum benefit level and a benefit reduction rate that you think will preserve work incentives. Unless you are heartless to the truly needy or believe that people will work despite financial disincentives, you will probably put most of the middle class on welfare. Murray illustrates this principle by using a thought experiment: the hypothetical implementation of a government anti-smoking policy. The problem is the impossibility of inducing smokers to quit without enticing non-smokers to start. (C. Murray, *Losing Ground: American Social Policy, 1950-1980*, New York: Basic Books, 1984, p. 205-211.)

19. Exodus 25:2. One could argue that tithes and offerings are less than completely voluntary given church membership. But this is rarely enforced, and in any case, is clearly less coercive than taxation. And taken further, mandating church offerings could be done through the tax code. Would that be desirable?

20. See also: Acts 12:12 for Mary's home ownership and the verb tenses in Acts 2:44-45 and 4:32-35 which imply a continuing redistribution of the early church's assets. See also: Acts 11:29-30.

21. See also: Elisha and the widow in II Kings 4:1-7.

22. M. Hengel, *Property and Riches in the Early Church*, Philadelphia: Fortress Press, 1974, p. 45.

23. Governor Thomas R. Marshall, "The Individual and the State", an address delivered at Logansport, IN, October 13, 1912.

24. "Authorities must beware of hindering family, social, or cultural groups, as well as intermediate bodies and institutions. They must not deprive them of their own lawful and effective activity, but should rather strive to promote them willingly and in an orderly fashion. For their part, citizens both as individuals and in association should be on guard against granting government too much authority and inappropriately seeking from it excessive conveniences and advantages, with a consequent weakening of the sense of responsibility on the part of individuals, families, and social groups." (Vatican Council II, *Gaudium et Spes*, #75, 1965.)

25. This error in "Christian" circles is called "Horizontalism". Jean Danielou defines it as reducing Christianity to the dimension of love of neighbor and "transforming it in to a vague philanthropy". It stems from seeing Christianity exclusively as a form of social service and minimizes its "vertical dimension". Ironically, "horizontalism is in error on the very nature of the love of neighbor. For dedication to another, a spirit of service, and kindness toward those in suffering are not at all an exclusively Christian prerogative...what characterizes Christian charity is not a greater or lesser spirit of dedication but a new depth." (J. Danielou, "Horizontalism", 1968, at www.ewtn.com/library/theology/horzntl.htm.)

26. Schlossberg, p. 315. He holds up the Macedonians as an example to follow: "Although suffering greatly, they refused to become dependent and instead became the servants of others."

27. Spending on social services for the poor (excluding education) was $416.6 billion in 2000. (*Statistical Abstract of the United States*, 2002, Table #516.)

28. Luke 18:22. Some have incorrectly interpreted these passages as universal injunctions for Christians to pursue poverty. See: T. Sine, *Cease Fire: Searching for Sanity in America's Culture Wars*, Grand Rapids: Eerdmans, 1995, p. 132. Willard provides an excellent critique of this misconception in Chapter 10: "Is Poverty Spiritual?" of *The Spirit of the Disciplines: Understanding How God Changes Lives*, San Francisco: HarperSanFrancisco, 1988.

29. "When we speak of the reform of institutions, the State comes chiefly to mind, not as if universal well-being were to be expected from its activity, but because things have come to such a pass through the evil of what we have termed 'individualism' that, following upon the overthrow and near extinction of that rich social life which was once highly developed through associations of various kinds, there remain virtually only individuals and the State. This is to the great harm of the State itself, for, with a structure of social governance lost, and with the taking over of all the burdens which the wrecked associations once bore, the State has been overwhelmed and crushed by almost infinite tasks and duties." (Pius XI, *Quadragesimo Anno*, #78, in *The Social Agenda: A Collection of Magisterial Texts*, ed. R. Sirico and M. Zieba, Vatican City: Pontifical Council for Justice and Peace, 2000, p. 101.)

30. Paul Jargowsky's book, *Poverty and Place: Ghettos, Barrios, and the American City* (New York: Russell Sage Foundation, 1997), is a wonderful study of the details of neighborhood poverty. For my review of his book, see: *Faith and Economics*, Spring 2000, p. 28-30.

31. Pope Pius XI: "Just as it is gravely wrong to take from individuals what they can accomplish by their own initiative and industry and give it to the community, so also it is an injustice and at the same time a grave evil and disturbance of right order to assign to a greater and higher association what lesser and subordinate organizations can do...The supreme authority of the State ought, therefore, to let subordinate groups handle matters and concerns of lesser importance, which would otherwise dissipate its efforts greatly...Therefore those in power should be sure that the more perfectly a graduated order is kept among the various associations, in observance of the principle of "subsidiarity function", the stronger social authority and effectiveness will be the happier and more prosperous the condition of the State." (*Quadragesimo Anno*, 1931, #79-80.)

32. See: "Sphere Sovereignty", *Abraham Kuyper: A Centennial Reader*, ed. J. Bratt, Grand Rapids: Eerdmans, 1998, p. 462-490. The Spring 2002 issue of *Markets and Morality* was dedicated to the writings of Kuyper, and to a lesser extent, John Paul II.

33. I Timothy 5:8. See also: I Timothy 5:16 and Leviticus 25:25,35 vs. 25:38.

34. John Paul II, *Centesimus Annus*, #48, in *Social Agenda*, p. 164-165. His caveat: "In exceptional circumstances, the State can also exercise a substitute function, when sectors or business systems are too weak or are just getting under way, and are not equal to the task at hand. Such supplementary interventions, which are justified by urgent reasons touching the common good, must be as brief as possible, so as to avoid removing permanently from society and business systems the functions which are properly theirs, and so as to avoid enlarging excessively the sphere of State intervention to the detriment of both economic and civil freedom."

35. Cited in M. Olasky, *The Tragedy of American Compassion*, Washington, DC: Regnery Gateway, 1992, p. 180.

36. In studying fraternal societies, David Beito notes that assistance within the fraternals ("reciprocal relief") was fundamentally different than standard government or charitable assistance ("hierarchical relief"). "Hierarchical relief was characterized by large, bureaucratic, and formalized institutions. The donors usually came from geographical, ethnic, and income backgrounds significantly different from those of the recipients. Reciprocal relief tended to be decentralized, spontaneous, and informal. The donors and recipients were likely to be from the same or nearly the same walks of life. Today's recipient could be tomorrow's donor." (*From Mutual Aid to the Welfare State: Fraternal Societies and Social Services, 1890-1967*, Chapel Hill: University of North Carolina Press, 2000, p. 18, 57, 58.) Going further back in history, for the early Church's efforts to help

the poor (which resemble the efforts of the fraternals), see: P. Brown, *Poverty and Leadership in the Later Roman Empire*, Hanover, NH: University Press of New England, 2002.

37. Olasky, p. 150.

38. J. Wallis, *The Soul of Politics*, New York: New Press, 1994, p. 22.

39. Poverty warrior Michael Bernick quickly returned from Washington, D.C. after learning that policymakers had "no understanding of how welfare operates at a local level: the dependency, the child care difficulties, the lack of skills and motivation..." (*Urban Illusions: New Approaches to Inner-City Unemployment*, New York: Praeger, 1987, p. 150.)

40. Olasky, p. 105.

41. From the Didache, chapter 12: "If he who comes is a traveler, help him as much as you can, but he shall not remain with you more than two days, or, if need be, three. And if he wishes to settle among you and has a craft, let him work for his bread. But if he has no craft, provide for him according to your understanding, so that no man shall live among you in idleness because he is a Christian. But if he will not do so, he is making traffic of Christ; beware of such." (*The Apostolic Fathers*, trans. K. Lake, Cambridge, MA: Harvard University Press, 1912, p. 359.)

42. Proposals requiring work from government welfare recipients are currently popular. Although "workfare" might be an improvement, it has a number of practical problems. For example, it is difficult to determine whether someone is adequately "seeking work". And if they cannot find work, government must provide opportunities for training or jobs. But the former are typically costly and ineffective; the latter often amount to "make-work" jobs. Thus, government spends money to create jobs for welfare recipients and bureaucrats while it simultaneously destroys private-sector jobs by lowering disposable incomes through higher taxation. Finally, with single heads-of-household, the desirability of having a parent working in the labor market—as opposed to staying home with his/her children—is not at all clear. (That said, recent research indicates that this is not a substantive concern—at least in a growing economy. See: P. Chase-Lansdale et. al., "Mothers' Transitions from Welfare to Work and the Well-Being of Preschoolers and Adolescents," *Science*, March 7, 2003, p. 1548-1552.) Again, local and voluntary efforts with categorization and discernment and individual solutions are more likely to be effective.

43. Sider, p. 163.

44. Ambrose argued that "If one were too trustful, one would quickly exhaust the funds meant for the relief of the poor. We need to be

methodical, so that beggars may not depart empty-handed, but neither will the paupers' fund be signed away as rich pickings for extortioners. We must act with a sense of proportion, not suppressing humane sympathy, not leaving true need without a recourse." (Quoted *From Irenaeus to Grotius: a Sourcebook in Christian Political Thought, 100-1625*, ed. O. O'Donovan and J. O'Donovan, Grand Rapids: Eerdmans, 1999, p. 88.)

45. M. Olasky, *Religion and Liberty*, September/October 1995, p. 5.

46. Olasky, *Tragedy of American Compassion*, p. 90 (paraphrasing Deuteronomy 15:7-8). In *Loving Your Neighbor: A Principled Guide to Charity* (Washington, DC: Capital Research Center, 1994, p. 1), Olasky notes that people usually assume that there are only two welfare options: "Social Universalism (redistribution upon request, no questions asked) and Social Darwinism (if she freezes during the winter, so be it)." The book is a compilation of essays on effective "tough love" charity.

47. Robert Sirico observes that it is no accident that we celebrate the Lord's incarnation with bread and wine—products of our work in combination with God's creation—rather than wheat and grapes.

48. See: Proverbs 6:6,10,11, 10:4, 12:24, 13:4, 14:23, 18:9, 19:15, 20:13, 24:33,34, 28:19; Colossians 3:23, I Thessalonians 5:14.

49. Matthew 25:14-30.

50. John 14:6-7. Christ seemed to be almost in a hurry to leave when he said "It is for your own good that I am going away. Unless I go away, the Counselor (Holy Spirit) will not come to you; but if I go, I will send him to you" (John 16:7).

51. Galatians 4:6, Galatians 2:20, Philippians 2:13.

52. Ezekiel 36:26-27 prophesied that God would give believers a new heart and a new spirit. See also: Jeremiah 31:31-34.

53. W. Nee, *The Normal Christian Life*, Wheaton, IL: Tyndale House, 1957, p. 97.

54. Sider (p. 65) notes that God requires a radical transformation in His people, including economic relationships. Unfortunately, Sider omits that it is the Christian's "new heart" and the Holy Spirit that allow this. He then endorses government solutions instead of relying on Christians with changed hearts and behaviors. Frame and Tharpe (p. 102-103) argue cryptically that "when the free market loses sight of fundamental principles of human dignity and fairness, it must be restrained" and "we the people have the right to authorize government to step in to protect citizens from the

moral abuses of the free market." Besides not specifying the ends, they are apparently prepared to embrace dubious means.

55. D. Bandow, *The Politics of Envy: Statism as Theology*, New Brunswick, NJ: Transaction Press, 1994, p. 17.

56. Chilton (p. 61) reports the following anecdote about the three-point lecture of a "well-known college professor" who "took a position similar to [Ron] Sider's": "First, he said, the individual has a duty to the poor. With an open Bible before him, he admirably defended this from Scripture. Second, he observed, the church has a duty to the poor; again he quoted copiously from Holy Writ. Third, he declared, the state has a duty to the poor. He then picked up the Bible, closed it, and put it aside."

Chapter 12: Past Government Activism & the Poor—Money vs. Compassion

1. D. Moloney, "'Saving' the Poor", *First Things*, May 1999, p. 39.

2. C. Murray, *Losing Ground: American Social Policy, 1950-1980*, New York: Basic Books, 1984, p. 151-152. Moreover, there are two reasons why these numbers would understate the true effects: the experimental group knew the benefits were only temporary, and the control group was not "pure"—they received a minimal level of benefits as well.

3. Ibid., p. 77.

4. Ibid., p. 124.

5. W. Raspberry, "Hollowed Communities", *Washington Post*, November 19, 1993.

6. Murray, chapter 9. While the percentage was diminishing before the Great Society, the rate of decrease greatly accelerated afterwards. The proportion of white children born into two-parent households also declined, but not as significantly as for blacks.

7. C. Murray, "Bad News About Illegitimacy", *The Weekly Standard*, August 5, 1996, p. 24-26; "The Coming White Underclass," *Wall Street Journal*, October 29, 1993. Demographic changes are also influential: higher divorce rates and married people bearing fewer children have also contributed to higher illegitimacy (percentage) rates. Although presumably not a catalyst, changing social norms have also been an influence over time.

8. R. Rector, "Welfare: Broadening the Reform", Washington, DC: Heritage Foundation, 2000, p. 2. David Blankenhorn reports some of the latest numbers and notes the difficulty (and subsequent confusion) in trying

to define these proxies ("The Reappearing Nuclear Family", *First Things*, January 2002).

9. "In the mid-1960's, America experimented with the idea, a reasonable guess on its face, that simply giving handouts to poor blacks would enable them to bypass the conventional route to self-realization. But today the data are in: a three-generations-deep welfare culture where work was an option rather than a given, where a passive and victimhood-based relationship to mainstream accomplishment was endemic. There is nothing 'black' about this, given that similar policies have left an equally bleak situation in Native American communities, as well as white ones in Appalachia." (J. McWhorter, "Blood Money: Why I don't want reparations for slavery", *The American Enterprise*, p. 20-21.)

10. Often, such children are said to be "born without a father"; as someone once quipped, "...and I don't mean the virgin birth!".

11. Murray, "The Coming White Underclass". Rector et. al. conclude that "the major underlying factors producing child poverty in the U.S. are welfare dependence and single parenthood...Black American children are more likely to live in poverty than are white children, primarily because black children are far more likely to live in single-parent families and to be on welfare...Race per se is not a factor in producing child poverty." (R. Rector, K. Johnson, and P. Fagan, "Understanding Differences in Black and White Poverty Rates", Washington, DC: Heritage Foundation, 2001.)

12. G. Duncan and S. Hoffman, "Teenage Behavior and Subsequent Poverty," in *The Urban Underclass*, ed. C. Jencks and P. Peterson, Washington, DC: Brookings Institution, 1991, p. 172.

13. On the importance of the government "getting serious" about poverty, see T. Sine, *Cease Fire: Searching for Sanity in America's Culture Wars*, Grand Rapids: Eerdmans, 1995, p. 139. Jim Wallis (*The Soul of Politics*, New York: The New Press, 1994, p. 90) argues that "the cold economic savagery of racism" is largely responsible for "family breakdown." This is a curious hypothesis given supposed improvements in civil rights since the 1960's. Has diminished racism caused more illegitimacy?

14. Murray, *Losing Ground*, p. 219. D. Bandow, *Beyond Good Intentions: A Biblical View of Politics*, Wheaton, IL: Crossway Books, 1988, p. 30. Joel Schwartz's *Fighting Poverty with Virtue: Moral Reform and America's Poor, 1825-2000* (Bloomington: Indiana University Press, 2000) presents themes developed in Marvin Olasky's *The Tragedy of American Compassion* (Washington, DC: Regnery Gateway, 1992) and Charles Murray's *Losing Ground*, but adds more detail on the move from late-19th

century approaches to poverty and considers the work and philosophies of Booker T. Washington and W. E. B. DuBois.

15. See also: Genesis 3:14-15, II Chronicles 21:11, Malachi 2:8, Matthew 18:7, Luke 17:1, I Corinthians 8:13, 10:32.

16. See: Romans 14:20-21, Matthew 13:41, 18:5-7.

17. In this way, welfare is similar to the sorts of redistributive efforts we modeled in chapter 9.

18. T. Funiciello, *The Tyranny of Compassion: Dismantling the Welfare System to End Poverty in America*, New York: Atlantic Monthly Press, 1993, p. 213, xvii. She also cites the salaries of heads of various foundations and charities which range as high as $500,000. (S. Greene, "How Much Should Charities Pay?" *Chronicle of Philanthropy*, March 24, 1992, p. 32, quoted by Funiciello on p. 248.) In *Urban Illusions: New Approaches to Inner-City Unemployment* (New York: Praeger, 1987), Michael Bernick ridicules (former U.S. Housing and Urban Development director) Jim Califano's description of himself as a "humanitarian who sacrifices" by noting the salary and perquisites which accompanied his job.

19. Joel Schwartz (*Fighting Poverty with Virtue*) contrasts the national/governmental emphasis of the Economic Opportunity Act of 1964 versus the emphasis on personal responsibility in the title of the 1996 welfare reform.

20. For a review of the distinctions between AFDC and TANF, see: G. Burtless and K. Weaver, "Reinventing Welfare...Again: The Latest Version of Welfare Needs a Tune-Up", *The Brookings Review*, Winter 1997, p. 26-29.

21. J. Leo, "Meet the parents", *U.S. News and World Report*, June 25, 2001, p. 12—citing a Center for Budget and Policy Priorities study by Wendell Primus. For example, the number of families receiving AFDC/TANF fell from 4.4 million in August 1996 when the bill was signed to 2.2 million in June 2000. Even with the sluggish economy since then, the rolls have continued to diminish—to 2.0 million in June 2002.

22. Jim Payne notes that this was almost inevitable given the length and complexity of the legislation (*Overcoming Welfare: Expecting More from the Poor—and from Ourselves*, New York: Basic Books, 1998). Reiterating themes heard most prominently from Marvin Olasky, Payne recommends "expectant giving"—requiring that recipients play an active role in receiving, rather than a something-for-nothing model.

23. D. Lee, "The Tradeoff Between Equity and Efficiency: Short-Run Politics and Long-Run Realities", *Public Choice*, Vol. 53, #2, 1987, p. 149-165.

24. Murray, p. 236.

25. Murray (ibid.) comments that "the barrier to radical reform of social policy is not the pain it would cause the intended beneficiaries of the present system, but the pain it would cause the donors."

26. M. Olasky, *The Tragedy of American Compassion*, Washington, DC: Regnery Gateway, 1992, p. 233. See also: J. Payne, *The Befriending Leader: Social Assistance Without Dependency*, Sandpoint, ID: Lytton Publishing, 1997.

27. W. Bennett, *Book of Virtues*, New York: Simon and Schuster, 1994, p. 665.

28. K. Kraakevik, "The Two Faces of Moral Poverty", Grand Rapids: Acton Institute, www.acton.org/publicat/books/remedy/hmention2.html, 2001. See also: D. Myers, *The American Paradox: Spiritual Hunger in an Age of Plenty*, New Haven, CT: Yale University Press, 2000.

29. I Timothy 6:18.

30. In fact, the dignity of the human person is a recurring theme in Scripture, but especially in God's special treatment of humanity in the Creation accounts. We were made in God's image (Genesis 1:26-27); we were endowed with God's breath of life (2:7); when man was created, God declared that His creation was *very* good (1:31); God expressed concern for Adam's subjective feelings of loneliness without Eve (2:18,20); God gave us freedom and self-determination as well as accountability and responsibility (2:16-17); and God equipped us with an intellect—to exert dominion over the creation, to work in the faithful stewardship of Eden, to discover order in the created universe (1:26-30, 2:15-18,20). Of course, ultimately, our inherent dignity can be inferred from God's plan of salvation—while we were still sinners, God's Son, who had no sin, became sin for us, to bear the sins of the world and to die on a cross (Romans 5:8; II Corinthians 5:21).

31. In *From Mutual Aid to the Welfare State* (Chapel Hill: University of North Carolina Press, 2000), David Beito underlines the importance of preserving dignity in his book on fraternal organization. He notes that people of the late 19th century avoided both private charity and public welfare because of a stigma and their desire to avoid dependence and one-sided giving. Within fraternals, members helped each other, but recipients always faced the likelihood that they would one day return the favor to

another member. The capacity for reciprocal giving added dignity to an otherwise undignified position. Likewise, we must work to preserve and enhance the dignity of the needy.

32. In Acts 3:1-10, the beggar asks for money, but Peter heals and empowers him instead.

33. Deuteronomy 24:6.

34. Genesis 47:19-24.

35. II Corinthians 8:2.

36. See: Charles Murray, *In Pursuit of Happiness and Good Government*, New York: Simon and Schuster, 1988; "Does Money Buy Happiness?", *The Atlantic Monthly*, January/February 2003, p. 42-43. Ron Sider (*Rich Christians in an Age of Hunger*, Dallas: Word Publishing, 1990) also correctly points to giving time as well as money (p. 165). He also notes the importance of building self-esteem and promoting freedom to make decisions (p. 187).

37. Murray, *In Pursuit of Happiness and Good Government*.

38. For example, see: John 5:1-9, Acts 3:1-10.

39. T. Stafford, "Why Volunteers Won't Save America", *Christianity Today*, April 29, 1996, p. 24.

40. R. Sider, *Just Generosity: A New Vision for Overcoming Poverty in America*, Grand Rapids: Baker Books, 1999, p. 121.

41. David Gushee has been very active in writing on these topics—and more positive angles on marriage. For example, see: "The Divorce Epidemic: Evaluating Policy Options that Can Reduce Divorce", in *Christians and Politics Beyond the Culture Wars: An Agenda for Engagement*, ed. D. Gushee, Grand Rapids: Baker Books, 2000, p. 143-164; "Rebuilding Marriage and the Family" in *Toward a Just and Caring Society: Christian Responses to Poverty in America*, ed. D. Gushee, Grand Rapids: Baker Books, 1999, p. 499-530; and "Marriage, Divorce, and The Kingdom of God: Revisiting the Biblical Witness", *Moral Leadership*, Vol. 2, #3, Fall/Winter 2000.

42. D. Gushee, "Marriage, Divorce, and The Kingdom of God".

43. See also: D. Schansberg and P. Donohue-White on "Does the Free Market Undermine Culture?", *Markets and Morality*, 1999, p. 125-139.

44. S. Alder, "Education in America", *The Freeman*, February 1993, p. 63-67. See also: J. Hunter, *Culture Wars: The Struggle to Define America—*

Making Sense of the Battles over the Family, Art, Education, Law, and Politics, New York: Basic Books, 1991, p. 36, 201.

45. For example, in 1986, the National (U.S.) Conference of Catholic Bishops (*Economic Justice for All: Pastoral Letter on Catholic Social Teaching and the U.S. Economy*, Washington, DC: U.S. Catholic Conference, 1986) advocated the public education monopoly (paragraph #205), a higher minimum wage (#197), and redistribution to the non-poor (farmers in #202-205, labor unions in #104,108). While no longer openly affirming socialism, they reaffirmed the major themes of their 1986 letter at their 1995 annual conference. (P. Steinfels, "Catholic Bishops Urge Rejection of Accords on Curbing Welfare and Cutting Tax Credit", *New York Times*, November 15, 1995.)

46. G. Brennan, "The Christian and the State", *CIS Occasional Papers*, St. Leonards, Australia: The Center for Independent Studies, 1983, p. 12.

47. Ironically, as William McGurn notes, theologians and those in the pulpit need to embrace the greater *hope* preached by market economists. ("Pulpit Economics", *First Things*, April 2002, p. 21-25.)

48. Brennan (p. 20) notes that "Goods which have not been produced cannot be distributed. An ethics of production must accompany an ethics of distribution." It is a rare event to have a member of the Religious Left enunciate either ethic.

49. See: Proverbs 19:2, Romans 10:2, Galatians 4:18. Schlossberg is critical of a prominent member of the Religious Left: "Sider has not bothered to learn anything about the economic processes on which he expresses such strong positions." (*Idols for Destruction: The Conflict of Christian Faith and American Culture*, Wheaton, IL: Crossway Books, 1990, p. 245.) In a recent interview, Sider said, "I admit that I didn't know a great deal of economics when I wrote the first edition of *Rich Christians*. In the meantime, I've learned considerably more, and I've changed some things as a result of that." (K. Miller, "The Rich Christian", *Christianity Today*, April 28, 1997, p. 69.) See also: D. D'Souza, "The Bishops as Pawns", *Policy Review*, Washington, DC: Heritage Foundation, p. 50-56.

50. W. Roepke, *A Humane Economy: The Social Framework of the Free Market*, 3rd ed., Wilmington, DE: ISI Books, 1998, p. 104. Samuel Gregg of the Acton Institute (a group devoted to education on these topics) wrote a book especially for this audience: *Economic Thinking for the Theologically Minded*. And in "The State of Economic Education in U.S. Seminaries," John Green and Kevin Schmiesing report the results of a survey of seminary professors (Grand Rapids: Acton Institute, 2001). They find that the respondents have a "mixed opinion" about many specific policy

prescriptions. Hopefully, this reflects humility in the face of their scarce training in economics and politics. Given the influential authors the respondents mention, one suspects that many of their views are driven by historical reality trumping liberal political ideology—in particular, the failure of socialism and the flaws of domestic social and economic policies—resulting in moderation and uncertainty.

51. As Clark Pinnock notes, "the market approach works well because it is realistic about human nature. Socialism works poorly because it presupposes saints." ("The Pursuit of Utopia", in *Freedom, Justice and Hope: Toward a Strategy for the Poor and the Oppressed*, ed. M. Olasky, H. Schlossberg, P. Berthoud, C. Pinnock, Westchester, IL: Crossway Books, 1988, p. 80.)

52. Donald Hay seems to understand this at times, but other times, not. Contrast p. 195 to p. 175 in *Economics Today*, Grand Rapids: Eerdmans, 1989.

53. P.T. Bauer, *Reality and Rhetoric*, Harvard University Press: Cambridge, MA, 1984, p. 84. C.S. Lewis argues that "the demand for equality has two sources; one of them is among the noblest, the other is the basest, of human emotions. The noble desire is the desire for fair play. But the other source is the hatred of superiority." (*Present Concerns*, ed. W. Hooper, New York: Harcourt, Brace and Jovanovich, 1996, p. 33.)

54. Ronald Nash continues: "only capitalism operates on the basis of respect for free, independent, responsible persons. All other systems in varying degrees treat men as less than this." (*Poverty and Wealth: Why Socialism Doesn't Work*, Richardson, TX: Probe Books, 1986, p. 80.)

55. Or as William Miller wryly notes, "Sincerity is not the only question, even about the individual. Remember Johnny, the boy next door? He was a very sincere trumpet player." (*The Protestant and Politics*, Philadelphia: Westminster Press, 1958, p. 35.)

Chapter 13: How We Can Help the Poor—Prescriptions

1. In this sense, one plays the role of a prophet—in exhorting both individuals and social institutions to repent. See: W. Mott, Jr., *The Third Way: Economic Justice According to John Paul II*, Lanham, MD: University Press of America, 1999, chapter 4 (especially p. 95-96).

2. W. Miller, *The Protestant and Politics*, Philadelphia: Westminster Press, 1958, p. 24.

3. And all things equal, Christians should advocate policies which enhance the efficiency of the economy. Promoting economic growth allows for greater charity, and more important, enhances opportunity for the poor.

4. Rauch (*The Atlantic Monthly*, October 2002, p. 32) is working from the research of Thomas Nechyba (an economist at Duke University). The premise is that many parents would choose to live in neighborhoods with lower-quality homes than otherwise—if they can still find attractive schooling options.

5. *World*, January 30, 1999, p. 16. The *(Louisville) Courier-Journal* (May 19, 1996) reported an Alan Guttmacher Institute study finding that 20% of children born to the 15-17 age group were fathered by men at least six years older.

6. Ironically, this is a type of discrimination perpetuated largely on minorities by other minorities. Again, while the intentions might be noble, the results are often ugly.

7. Galatians 6:10, I Timothy 5:8. Recent research by Ram Cnaan (a secular Jew at the University of Pennsylvania) indicates considerable activity and an immense desire to help—independent of theological beliefs. Cnaan was pleasantly surprised and expresses his admiration for these efforts. ("Counting [Helping] Hands: A Conversation with Ram Cnaan", *Books & Culture*, January/February 2003, p. 24-25.) Nonetheless, more can be done! On the efforts of John Wesley in this arena, see: F. Schaeffer, *A Christian Manifesto*, 2nd ed., Wheaton, IL: Crossway Books, 1982, p. 64-65.

8. T. Evans, *Are Christians Destroying America? How to Restore a Decaying Culture*, Chicago: Moody Press, 1996, p. 22. Evans also notes that the temple grain storehouses served three purposes: to provide food for the priests, the widows and orphans, and the poor Gentiles in their society (p. 169; Numbers 18:24-29, Deuteronomy 14:28-29).

9. In giving up control of welfare and education to the State a century ago, Grant Kuhn notes that it's as if Christians were praying anti-Jabez.

10. T. Campolo, *Is Jesus a Republican or a Democrat?*, Dallas: Word, 1995, p. 163-164. T. Sine, *Cease Fire: Searching for Sanity in America's Culture Wars*, Grand Rapids: Eerdmans, 1995, p. 275.

11. D. McGraw, "A New Kind of Book of Job", *U.S. News and World Report*, January 13, 1997, p. 47-48; J. Johnson, "The Ministry of Good Success", *Christianity Today*, October 1, 2001, p. 60-65. Caldwell's church is now working on a full-blown planned residential community with 452 single-family homes on 24 acres.

12. On the efforts of Bob Cote in this arena, see: S. Walter, "Rocky Mountain Sheriff", *The American Enterprise*, October/November 2002.

13. There is an interesting dilemma here over the role of one-on-one paternalism in helping people who systematically make poor decisions, as opposed to allowing recipients to have greater short-term levels of freedom, respect, and self-dignity.

14. Ecclesiastes 5:12a. Note also that God feeds the birds but He doesn't throw food in their nests. See also: M. Olasky, "The Beginning of Hope", in *Freedom, Justice and Hope: Toward a Strategy for the Poor and the Oppressed*, ed. M. Olasky, H. Schlossberg, P. Berthoud, C. Pinnock, Westchester, IL: Crossway Books, 1988, p. 134-135.

15. M. Olasky, "Breaking the Cycle", *World*, August 14, 1999, p. 34.

16. *American Enterprise*, November/December 1995, p. 15.

17. T. Stafford, "Why Volunteers Won't Save America", *Christianity Today*, April 29, 1996, p. 24.

18. See: C. Boyd, "The Ministry of Safe Play", *Christianity Today*, July 12, 1999, p. 18B on Urban Concern in Columbus, Ohio; and T. Stafford, "Taking Back Fresno", *Christianity Today*, March 6, 2000, p. 48ff.

19. Ruth 2:15-16. Christ's parable in Matthew 20 is meant to describe God's grace, but it applies to this principle as well. In contrast, consider James 5:1-6.

20. J. Veenker, "Chicago Bank Has New Faith in Credit-Poor Churches", *Christianity Today*, August 9, 1999, p. 23. This approach has also been very productive in less-developed countries—a practice called "micro-lending," referring to the small size of the loans required.

21. K. Kantzer in the Foreword to R. Sider, *Rich Christians in an Age of Hunger*, Dallas: Word Publishing, 1990, p. xi.

22. B. Lupton, *Discipleship Journal*, #86, 1995, p. 43.

23. "A Call for Church Welfare Reform", *Christianity Today*, October 6, 1997, p. 50.

24. For example, the church I attend encourages members to participate in at least one hour per week or worship, formal Bible study, and service each week.

25. Jim Wallis' *The Soul of Politics* (New York: The New Press, 1994) is useful in promoting a vision and passion for the poor. His lyrical writing weaves stories and exhortation together to communicate the great need and

opportunity in this realm. Although the book suffers somewhat from occasional rhetorical excess and politically-based ideological distractions, it is a great book for motivating believers to serve.

26. Regnerus et. al. conclude that "theological and political conservatives are currently *more* generous" in giving to the poor. ("Who Gives to the Poor? The Influence of Religious Tradition and Political Location on the Personal Generosity of Americans Toward the Poor", *Journal for the Scientific Study of Religion*, Vol 37, #3, 1997, p. 481-493. Moreover, people who give to religious causes also give substantially more to non-religious causes. Those who gave to congregations gave nearly four times more overall, gave 20% more to secular organizations, out-gave in all categories including the arts, education, and the environment, and volunteered more of their time. (See: "Faith and Philanthropy" at www.independentsector.org, cited in *The American Enterprise*, December 2002, p. 13.)

27. Spending on social services for the poor (excluding education) was $416.6 billion in 2000. (*Statistical Abstract of the United States*, 2002, Table #516.)

28. With respect to fraternal societies, David Beito says "There is reason to believe that a relationship existed between the emerging welfare state [of the New Deal] and the decline of fraternal services....Officials of the homes for the elderly and orphans of the SBA cited Social Security and other welfare programs as justification not only for rejecting applicants but for closing down entirely...The establishment of Social Security and other programs provided excuses to shed costly services." (*From Mutual Aid to the Welfare State: Fraternal Societies and Social Services, 1890-1967*, Chapel Hill: University of North Carolina Press, 2000. p. 228-229.)

29. The ideas I cite from Olasky's fine book are not especially controversial. That said, some of his conclusions are more debatable. See: K. Schaefer, "The Privatizing of Compassion: A Critical Engagement with Marvin Olasky", in *Toward a Just and Caring Society: Christian Responses to Poverty in America*, ed. D. Gushee, Grand Rapids: Baker Books, 1999, p. 144-161, especially p. 148-149, 153-154.

30. R. McKenzie, "Was It a Decade of Greed?" *Public Interest*, Winter 1992, p. 91-96. McKenzie also found that in the 1980's, donations increased more quickly (58%) than spending on jewelry (41%) and eating out (22%). During the 1990-1992 recession, average household contributions fell by 7.1%. (D. Cross, "No Brother, I Can't Spare a Dime," *Washington Post National Weekly Edition*, April 25-May 1, 1994.)

31. See: McKenzie, "Was It a Decade of Greed?"; and C. Murray, *In Pursuit of Happiness and Good Government* (New York: Simon and Schuster, 1988, p. 276). D. Lee and R. McKenzie note that after the New Deal, charity began to shift away from helping the poor to supporting religious organization and the arts. (*Failure and Progress*, Washington, DC: Cato Institute, 1993, p. 116.)

32. www.aafrc.org/news.htm, May 24, 2000. The level of giving has been stagnant since 2000, but presumably this is a short-term phenomenon connected to the recession and plummeting stock market.

33. For more on this issue, see: M. Olasky, "The Right Way to Replace Welfare", *Policy Review*, March/April 1996, p. 46-50—an excerpt from *Renewing American Compassion* (New York: Free Press, 1996). Another option is for taxpayers to have control to allocate their tax dollars to charities of their choice. J. Goodman, "Welfare Privatization", *Wall Street Journal*, May 28, 1996.

34. For a more skeptical viewpoint, see J. Mason, "Marvin Olasky and Effective Assistance to the Poor", *Regeneration Quarterly*, Spring 1996, p. 14-15.

35. Richard John Neuhaus quotes Terry Golway in a *New York Observer* article about a common double standard in weighing the merits artists and religiously-based organizations receiving funding: "A generation of artists has come to believe that publicly funded grants are an entitlement, and those who oppose them outright or seek some sort of review process are nothing more than neo-Fascist shredders of the right to free expression...[S]ome of the very same people who believe cultural organizations owe no obligation to public sensibilities when they take taxpayer funds are prepared to argue that religious organizations must abide by the government's political dictates if they take the government's money." (August/September 2001, *First Things*, p. 96.)

36. Research indicates that church attendance (rather than stated beliefs) is highly correlated with physical, mental, and spiritual health, as well as academic performance and participation, perhaps because it develops discipline and provides a substantive hope.

37. The Center for Public Justice (in Washington, DC) publishes "Charitable Choice Compliance: A National Report Card" which grades the states on the extent to which they have gotten rid of old policies which discriminated against FBOs. The CPJ has also published a study by Amy Sherman on her survey of nine states and 84 new partnerships between FBOs and government. (For a summary of her study, see: "A Survey of Church-Government Anti-poverty Partnerships", *The American Enterprise*,

June 2000, p. 32-33.) She found less than .1% of clients complaining about even subtle pressure to attend church. And the survey revealed that "the vast majority" of FBOs "felt free to be religious."

38. Ron Sider wants to challenge secular providers to a competition along the lines of Elijah vs. the prophets of Baal in I Kings 18. He also argues cleverly that secular providers should be more "tolerant" and allow FBOs to help the poor without being discriminated against. ("Revisiting Mt. Carmel Through Charitable Choice", *Christianity Today*, June 11, 2001, p. 84-89.)

39. Joel Belz questions the relevance of the distinction, noting that "every organization in life is faith-based" and that all organizations try to persuade you of the merits of their cause. ("Everything's faith-based", *World*, April 21, 2001, p. 5.)

40. See: The Hudson Institute study, "Faithful Collaborators", and the Manhattan Institute study, "Working Faith: How Religious Organizations Provide Welfare to Work." Richard John Neuhaus (*First Things*, May 2000, p. 72-73) cites an article by Brian Anderson in *City Journal* which depicts the compromise of Catholic Charities and its receipt of government money (65% of its $2.3 billion annual budget). But, at least in this case, the compromise occurred prior to their receiving the money. As Anderson writes, "Catholic Charities officials already sincerely believed that government entitlements are the best way to help the needy..."

41. The *New York Times* slandered Samaritan's Purse (Franklin Graham's international relief agency) in its supposed use of government funds. After being corrected, the newspaper provided a tepid apology. ("Bad Ideas Have Consequences", *Christianity Today*, April 23, 2001, p. 29.)

42. That said, Joel Belz argues that charges of discrimination against employees or clients should not be relevant. He points to universities which have routinely "discriminated against" prospective faculty and students—by rejecting them for a variety of reasons—but have still received government money through students. ("The proof is in", *World*, March 9, 2001, p. 5.)

43. One can divide the important goals of an FBO Code of Ethics into three categories: Financial Independence, Freedom from Intrusive Regulation, and Financial Integrity. (A complete, sample Code of Ethics is available by request from the Acton Institute in Grand Rapids, MI.) Here, let me list some of the key considerations. With respect to Financial Independence: 1.) Avoid being dependent on any one funding source, especially the government; 2.) Do not take government funding for overhead costs or basic expenses; and 3.) Pursue funding from the lowest level of government possible. With respect to Freedom from Intrusive Regulation: 1.) Avoid regulation of program content by government; 2.) Refuse regulation of

hiring practices by government; and 3.) Be cautious about mission creep. With respect to Financial Integrity: 1.) Have frank discussions about the contexts in which it is appropriate to ask for money and to engage in public policy advocacy; and 2.) Keep government money strictly separate from other accounts and have separate employees handle it if possible.

44. Charles Freund makes a provocative argument in noting that state support for the arts has not only promoted mediocrity, but at the same time, attracted attention to the most controversial examples of public funding. Freund anticipates the same problem with Charitable Choice, concluding that "The state is no better prepared to act as religious benefactor than it has been to act as cultural patron." ("In God We Trust", *Reason*, April 2001, p. 27.)

Appendix: What About Foreign Aid?

1. See: Chapter 19 of my book, *Poor Policy: How Government Harms the Poor* (Boulder, CO: Westview, 1996) and D. Hay, *Economics Today*, Grand Rapids: Eerdmans, 1989, p. 248-264.

2. *Rich Christians in an Age of Hunger*, Word Publishing: Dallas, 1990, p. 192. See also: T. Sine, *Cease Fire: Searching for Sanity in America's Culture Wars*, Grand Rapids: Eerdmans, 1995, p. 206-208.

3. Proponents cite aid programs they perceive to have been successful, particularly the Marshall Plan which provided financial assistance to European governments after World War II. Sider (p. 209) reasons too hastily that "one has only to look at the material prosperity of Western Europe today to realize that it was the most successful aid program the world has ever seen." In fact, Europe's recovery may have been independent or even in spite of our assistance. Advocates of foreign aid can recite a few examples of seeming effectiveness, but in general, aid and growth do not appear to be related.

4. Stephen Saint discusses this problem in the context of the Huaorani ("Auca") Indians who became famous after making a martyr of Jim Elliot. After they were evangelized, Saint argues that the tribe has become dependent on assistance from outsiders, including the church. (*Christianity Today*, March 2, 1998, p. 42-45.)

5. T. Sowell, *The Economics and Politics of Race* (New York: William Morrow, 1985), p. 239. Bandow notes that "the IMF has been subsidizing the world's economic basket cases for years, without apparent effect." He then cites some long-term addictions to IMF assistance: as of 1989, six nations (Chile, Egypt, India, Sudan, Turkey and Yugoslavia) had been

relying on IMF aid for more than 30 years; 24 countries for 20-29 years; and 47 countries for 10-19 years. ("The IMF: A Record of Addiction and Failure," in *Perpetuating Poverty*, ed. D. Bandow and I. Vasquez, Cato Institute: Washington, DC, 1994, p. 19.)

6. Ron Sider (p. 120) notes that "too much of what was loaned was spent on the latest armaments or wasted because of official corruption. Faced with budget deficits, governments chose to cut education and health programs rather than their military budgets, and they printed money, which produced surging inflation." Thus, he belatedly concludes that "more foreign aid...would not necessarily improve the lot of the truly poor" and "might simply enable [them] to strengthen their repressive regimes." (p. 183)

7. As a general call to help the oppressed (properly defined), Sider's work is very powerful. However, it has much less to say about how to specifically reach those in poverty. Sider assumes too easily that we know how to help the poor, especially those in foreign countries, given our immense geographical and political ignorance, completely different cultures, and thousands of miles of distance.

8. G. Hancock, *Lords of Poverty: The Power, Prestige, and Corruption of the International Aid Business*, New York: Atlantic Monthly Press, 1989, p. 181.

9. *Statistical Abstract of the United States*, 2000, Tables #1320, 1321. Military aid was $3.86 billion; economic aid was $9.17 billion.

10. D. Bandow, "A Private Sector Solution to Poverty", *The Freeman*, November 1999; J. Wallis, *The Soul of Politics*, New York: New Press, 1994, p. 223.

11. As I develop in *Poor Policy*, foreign aid and overpopulation are largely irrelevant in contrast to the problems caused by the "poor policy" of poor countries. For a converse example in Africa, see Mauritius ("Mauritius, a Tiny Fish In a Big Ocean, Makes An Example Of Itself", *Wall Street Journal*, July 14, 1998.)

12. As Sider (p. 189) notes, "an ironic aspect of trade barriers is that economic theory suggests that both the developing and the industrialized nations would be better off after their removal."

13. J. Bovard, *The Fair Trade Fraud*, New York: St. Martin's Press, 1991, p. 48.

14. One should recognize that competition may be more limited and government mischief more likely in ldc's. A common bogeyman is the multi-national corporation, but in the absence of natural or government-provided monopoly power, they are merely a firm engaging in a series of

mutually beneficial trades. And even in a worst case scenario, multi-nationals represent another alternative for workers to choose; removing them hardly makes natives better off.

15. In recent years, Hernando deSoto has more than anyone to promote these ideas in the public arena. His books, *The Other Path: The Invisible Revolution in the Third World* (New York: Harper Collins, 1990) and *The Mystery of Capital: Why Capitalism Triumphs in the West and Fails Everywhere Else* (New York: Basic Books, 2003), are powerful in explaining why "assets" in countries are not productive as "capital"—unless the proper, efficiency-enhancing institutions are in place.

16. J. McClure and N. Van Cott provide a very useful example in comparing the relative freedom and prosperity of the Dominican Republic with the lack thereof in Haiti.

Chapter 14: Abortion—A Biblical and Historical Perspective

1. Or as Peter Kreeft asks ("Human Personhood", *Religious and Theological Studies Fellowship Bulletin*, March/April 1996, p. 3): "Am I reading this because I want to be the servant of truth or because I want truth to be my servant?...Am I willing, even eager, to admit I was wrong if reason proves me wrong?"

2. Some criticize the overwhelming focus of some pro-lifers on abortion. Of course, there are many "pro-life" issues—"world hunger", smoking, and so on. While this is a reasonable criticism to some degree, one should recognize that the analogy fails insofar as an abortion is more direct in its cause and effect. A corollary to this is the dilemma of voting with respect to a politician's position on abortion versus their positions on other issues, as well as their character, experience, ability, and so on. For example, would you vote for someone who was "pro-life" and an outspoken proponent of "family values," but had recently divorced his long-time wife to marry a staffer?

3. Divorce is a similarly complex issue. In the world's eyes, it is LM in that it is between two consenting adults—or at least the breaking of a voluntary contract by one of the two necessary parties. (To Christians, it is a covenant between a man, a woman, and God.) But when the married couple has children, justice issues emerge. In any case, this topic receives far too little attention in the church—probably because it is complex and hits too close to home.

4. Not all LM issues involve direct transactions of money. Nonetheless, the relevant parties engage in what they perceive to be "mutually beneficial trade".

5. The statistics: 1.31 million surgical abortions in 2000, down from a peak of 1.56 million in 1987 (*Touchstone*, January/February 2003, p. 62), for a total of about 40 million since 1973 (*Christianity Today*, June 10, 2002). About 44% of abortions are for those who have already had at least one; of total abortions, 79% were to unwed mothers, 46% to childless mothers, 54% to those under 25 years old, 89% to those less than 12 weeks pregnant; 62% to whites and 34% to non-whites (*U.S. News and World Report*, August 18, 1996 and January 19, 1998). African-Americans are 2.6 times more likely to get an abortion than whites (*First Things*, October 2001, p. 90). Chris Rice and Spencer Perkins discuss this and the differences in white and black perceptions of abortion in the context of understanding and reconciliation between whites and blacks (*More than Equals*, Downers Grove, IL: InterVarsity Press, 2000, p. 32-33). About 6% of all teenagers had an abortion in 1997 and the abortion rate for unmarried women is four times greater than for married women (J. Crouse, "Unsafe, Deadly, and Legal", *Touchstone*, January/February 2003, p. 15). Paul Fowler quotes Joseph Stalin—"One death is a tragedy; a million deaths is a statistic"—and asks if abortion has become "a mere statistic for us." (*Abortion: Toward an Evangelical Consensus*, Portland, OR: Multnomah Press, 1987, p. 209.)

6. See: F. Mathewes-Green, "The Dilemmas of a Pro-Life Pastor", *Christianity Today*, April 7, 1997, p. 27-31.

7. Beckwith, Bercot, and Fowler quote several early church fathers whose belief was that abortion was murder. (F. Beckwith, *Politically Correct Death: Answering Arguments for Abortion Rights*, Grand Rapids: Baker Books, 1993, p. 140-141; D. Bercot, *Will the Real Heretics Stand Up: A New Look at Today's Evangelical Church in Light of Early Christianity*, Tyler, TX: Scroll Publishing, 1989, p. 27; Fowler, p. 18.)

8. R. Ward, "The Use of the Bible in the Abortion Debate", *St. Louis Public Law Review*, vol 13:1, 1993; and an interview with Roy Ward, *The Door*, March/April 1995, p. 17. "There were several methods used for abortions in the ancient world: surgical procedures, manipulative procedures, abortifaciants applied as suppositories, and oral abortifaciants." The latter two were mostly herbal recipes which stemmed from folk experimentation and were popular in Greek medicine.

9. Likewise, debates over "just" wars and capital punishment are seemingly intractable.

10. This view implicitly assumes an "age of accountability" (Deuteronomy 1:39, Nehemiah 10:28, Isaiah 7:15-16) before which children are innocent in God's eyes. Other theological views hold that our "original sin" condemns even those who have not sinned (Romans 9:10-14). Assuming the former, this is not to say that one should kill their own (young or unborn) children to ensure their salvation, since that would be an inappropriate and ungodly means to an albeit desirable end. The fact that God can turn sin into blessings is no rationale for justifying or promoting sin.

11. Isaiah 59:1.

12. The Israelites' conquest of Canaan has been used to argue for restricted access to abortion. For instance, Katherine Ragsdale notes that "...we take life all the time...'Just war' theories try to take into account the multiple responsibilities, complexities, and constraints rulers operate under...make the best possible decisions about when to kill..." (*The Door*, interview, March/April 1995.) They then argue that abortion might be appropriate in certain circumstances—in particular, the cases of rape, incest, and health of the mother.

13. John Paul II has written about "a lack of [spiritual] freedom" that "leads people to consider children as one of many 'things' that an individual can have or not have, according to taste, and which compete with other possibilities. It is necessary to go back to seeing the family as the sanctuary of life." (*Centesimus Annus*, #39, 1991; in *The Social Agenda: A Collection of Magisterial Texts*, ed. R. Sirico and M. Zieba, Vatican City: Pontifical Council for Justice and Peace, 2000, p. 42-43.)

14. See: Jeremiah 7:6, 22:3,17; and Exodus 23:7. Deuteronomy 27:25 promises a curse for one who "accepts a bribe to kill an innocent person." Exceptions to this would include ectopic pregnancies and perhaps expectant mothers with uterine cancer.

15. Genesis 4:8-12.

16. Job 10:8-12, 31:15. See also: Genesis 25:23, Ecclesiastes 11:5, Isaiah 44:2,24. Job 10:18-19 also implies that life begins before birth. Interestingly, the Greek term "*brephos*" is used to denote a six-month old baby in the womb (Luke 1:26,39-41,44) *and* out of the womb (Luke 2:12,16, 18:15, Acts 7:19, II Timothy 3:15, I Peter 2:2). Some also refer to Amos 1:13's condemnation of Ammon "because he ripped open the pregnant women of Gilead." (See also: II Kings 8:12, Hosea 9:14,16; 13:16.) However, this verse is not particularly useful since it refers to an involuntary abortion as well as violence, and killing the mother or at least inducing permanent barrenness.

17. "Attacking the Tabernacle", *First Things*, November 1999, p. 15-16. The thesis of Leithart's essay stems from the Hebrew word for "woven" (*raqam*) in Psalms 139:15. Leithart notes that the term is rarely used in the Old Testament (eight times) and is [always] used in the context of producing the Tabernacle furnishings. He then connects the Tabernacle with the baby in the womb. "Abortion attacks not only a creature of God but a house of God."

18. Hosea 9:11, Ruth 4:13, and I Samuel 1:20 distinguish between birth and conception. If one reads the verses literally, they can be interpreted as distinguishing between conception and implantation of the fertilized egg.

19. Jeremiah 1:5. See also: Galatians 1:15.

20. Arguably, Christ's birth is a "special case"! But note the prediction of Samson's conception in Judges 13:5. See also: Psalms 119:73.

21. Frame and Tharpe argue that "Quoting the psalmist who said that God knew him when he was still in the womb is an oft-used but irresponsible Biblical argument against abortion. The literary genre of the Psalms is poetry, which is characterized by hyperbole and figures of speech intended to convey general impressions, and in this case, God's omniscience. To use such passages as arguments against abortion sets a precedent that would allow virtually anything to be proved from Scripture." (*How Right Is the Right?*, Grand Rapids: Zondervan, 1996, p. 120.) See also: the interpretation of Psalms 51:5.

22. Predestination is a prominent theme throughout the Bible. For example, writing to believers in Ephesians 1:4, Paul says that God "chose us in him before the creation of the world." But given our free will (another important Biblical theme), why would God allow these seemingly contradictory concepts to be in Scripture? Since free will is intuitively obvious to us, God must believe that predestination conveys something important about His character. Three things come to mind. First, incomprehensible doctrines show us that God is bigger than us. At some level this is merely a cop-out, but if God is a God worth worshipping, He must be "beyond" us. Second, predestination is a riveting way to describe God's sovereignty over all. If God foreknew Jeremiah's ministry, then He truly must have "the whole world in his hands." Third and most important, predestination provides a picture of "God chasing us" in addition to free will's "us chasing God". As C.S. Lewis once said, "It forearms one against subsequent fears that the whole thing was only wish fulfillment." In fact, God wants a passionate and intimate relationship with everyone; He is not a distant, disinterested God.

23. Interview with Roy Ward, *The Door*, p. 18. See also: Romans 9:11.

24. There are at least two other potentially troubling passages. First, Numbers 5:11-28 describes the "lab test" for whether a woman has been unfaithful to her husband. Unfortunately, the cost of her God-confirmed infidelity is the God-induced death of the unborn child and permanent barrenness. Second, Exodus 21:22 probably describes a non-elective abortion. (Some translations render it "give birth prematurely" as opposed to "miscarry." See also: Ward, "The Use of the Bible in the Abortion Debate", p. 396-397.) If translated "miscarry," this is troubling since the offense is only punishable by a fine. (Note also that verses 23-25 imply that the woman is injured since "tooth for tooth," "burn for burn," and the Hebrew words for "life for life" are not relevant to a baby in the womb.) But since the death of the child was accidental, one cannot draw any firm conclusions about the status of the child. Given how the Law treats accidental vs. pre-meditated acts, it is shaky at best to infer that accidentally hitting a woman who may not even appear to be pregnant and causing a miscarriage would be worthy of death.

25. See also: I Corinthians 14:7's use of *"apsuchos"*—meaning without life or breath. One criticism of this conclusion is that the breath is empowering an already-formed body (or bones).

26. Matthew 27:50, Mark 15:37, Luke 23:46, John 19:30.

27. Paul Fowler (p. 51-52) argues against this point by moving the description from the process to the sperm and egg separately. He quotes Robert Joyce who argues for a distinction between potential life (i.e., an embryo) and potential causes of life (i.e., the sperm and egg separately).

28. Beckwith, p. 157. Beckwith also notes that this pluralism is limited to the pro-choice view since pro-lifers are not legally allowed to act in concert with their beliefs (p. 158).

29. Ankenberg and Weldon, *When Does Life Begin?*, Brentwood, TN: Wolgemuth and Hyatt, 1989, p. 191-193. See: Ecclesiastes 11:5, especially the NIV's alternative translation "As you do not know...how life (or the spirit) enters the body being formed..."

30. J. Belz, "If There Is Mystery", *World*, August 18, 2001, p. 5.

31. J. Crosby, "The Imperatives of Ignorance", *Touchstone*, January/February 2003, p. 17-19.

32. Given the scientific evidences, how does a materialist/atheist argue for anything other than conception? Robert George argues that physical life begins at conception and notes the irony that pro-choice advocates are the ones who "typically want to transform the question into a metaphysical or religious one...the pro-choice position collapses if the issue is to be settled

purely on the basis of scientific inquiry..." ("God's Reasons: Science, Religion, and the Right to Life", *Touchstone*, May 2000, p. 23.)

33.   A few potentially troubling analogies/questions for pro-lifers: Would you be more, less, or equally likely to expend financial resources to save an innocent man from capital punishment or to save an unborn child from an abortion? Given a very high rate of natural "spontaneous" abortion, a significant rate of artificial (medical or surgical) abortions, and the proportion of adults who accept God's grace and choose (eternal) life with God—can you imagine a Heaven where the *vast* proportion of its human occupants would be former fetuses (and young children). Why don't we always mourn an early miscarriage as much as the death of a child? Why don't we always have funerals or memorial services for miscarriages? Should the punishment be as great for an abortion as for infanticide? Should an abortionist and an informed mother receive punishment in line with any other type of pre-meditated murder?

James Spiegel establishes a framework for describing the prospective starting assumptions and conclusions within abortion. He concludes that "a Christian *can* be coherently morally pro-life and politically pro-choice, but only if her (morally) pro-life conviction is weak." ("Can a Christian Be Coherently Morally Pro-Life and Politically Pro-Choice?", *Christian Scholar's Review*, p. 107-115.) In other words, given "a presumption in favor of liberty," a Christian might "argue that a significant theological case can be made for abortion as murder," but that "the evidence is not strong enough to justify one's believing that civil liberty on the matter should be proscribed." One would probably not find abortion restrictions troubling, but would not actively advocate those restrictions publicly.

34. That said, Robert Bowman, Jr. notes the interesting correlation between Christians who (do not) take Scripture as relatively authoritative and those who (do not) oppose abortion. (*Facts for Faith*, Q2, 2001, p. 49.) Likewise, the question of when death occurs is equally troublesome both Biblically and medically. In an interesting symposium on commerce and altruism with respect to vital organs, H. Tristam Engelhardt poses some very provocative hypotheticals to help argue that death occurs at brain death. (*Touchstone*, June 2001, p. 34.) Maureen Condic argues that death, and thus life, are connected with the ability "of the body's parts to function together as an integrated whole." ("Life: Defining the Beginning by the End", *First Things*, May 2003, p. 50-54.) Her essay is also useful in dividing views about when life begins into three types: "form, ability, and preference." A related issue is the Christian's stance on "euthanasia." Unfortunately, definitions vary widely. In the framework developed here, if a person wants to voluntarily end his own life, it would be a LM issue; if involuntarily, it

would be a LJ issue. In any case, it should not be subsidized by taxpayers. This still leaves difficult questions—in particular, when does refusing or withholding help become sinful (omission vs. commission)?

35. Joel Belz ("If There is Mystery") applies Ronald Reagan's maxim here: "If there's mystery involved, let's live on the safe side." Ironically, advocates of abortion are often opponents of the death penalty, reasoning that if there is some element of doubt, it would be better to play it safe. This is pure hypocrisy since the same standard here would imply no abortion either.

36. Crosby, "The Imperatives of Ignorance". He concludes: "It seems highly probable that my being as person should coincide with the start of my physical being...there is no point after conception that seems a more likely point for the onset of personhood than the completion of reproduction itself...No point after conception is as radical and complete a beginning as the point at which the embryo comes into being...[I] do not claim to prove incontrovertibly that the embryo is a person, only that its personhood has to be assumed, because no later point for the beginning of personhood can with certainty be demonstrated...The argument throws the burden onto our opponents, saying to them in effect: Try to find a later and morally safe beginning of the human person. You will see that it cannot be done conclusively."

37. "Although there are no direct and explicit calls to protect human life at its very beginning, specifically life not yet born, and life nearing its end, this can be easily explained by the fact that the mere possibility of harming, attacking, or actually denying life in these circumstances is completely foreign to the religious and cultural way of thinking of the People of God." (John Paul II, *Evangelium Vitae*, #44; in *The Social Agenda*, p. 5.)

38. Ibid. Peter Kreeft argues that a fetus is a "person"—more through logic than Biblical principles. ("Human Personhood", p. 3-8.) Given Genesis 9:6 and the Biblical connection between life and blood, another possibility is that life begins with the flow of blood. Or as the old joke goes, "life begins when your last child leaves home."

39. M. Olasky, *Abortion Rites: A Social History of Abortion in America*, Wheaton, IL: Crossway Books, 1992.

40. Ibid., p. xiv, xv.

41. For instance, in 1680, 3% of colonial brides had children within six months of marriage (8% within nine months). In the period 1760-1800, it was 17% and 33% respectively (ibid., p. 29).

42. There is little historical documentation of slaves' behavior in this regard.

43. The two statistics differ since women have fewer children today. The second number is based on the rate of 1.3-1.5 million abortions per year and the population of 260 million people from a few years back.

44. Ibid., p. 83.

45. Ibid., p. 90. More states passed laws in the decades that followed. Olasky (p. 94) argues that "what forced reluctant legislative hands in some states was the opening in the 1830's of the 'penny press'." Cheap advertising undermined the containment policy of abortion foes.

46. Ibid., p. 95.

47. Ibid., p. 103.

48. Ibid., p. 147.

49. By the late-1930's, newspaper accounts show that the concern had shifted to "unscrupulous" abortionists, not abortionists per se—a trend which continued to gain pace into the 1960's (ibid., p. 273-278).

50. Ibid., p. 251, 253. But ironically, polarization and even strongly held opinions within most Christian denominations did not occur until the late 1970's. (See: Fowler, p. 22-23 and chapter 3.)

51. W. Martin, *With God on our Side: The Rise of the Religious Right in America*, New York: Broadway Books, 1996, p. 240-241. Koop concluded, "they had an all-or-nothing mentality. They wanted it all, and they got nothing."

52. Olasky, *Abortion Rites*, p. 280-281. Candace Crandall points to "fortuitous timing" in the 1960's, with the emergence of civil rights and its effect on the courts, feminism and its demand for rights, and environmentalism and its concerns about over-population. ("Thirty Years of Empty Promises", *First Things*, January 2003, p. 14-17.)

53. Olasky, *Abortion Rites*, p. 283.

54. Ibid., p. 298.

55. Ibid., p. 298.

56. Ibid., p. 299.

Chapter 15: Abortion—What Should We Say? What Can We Do?

1. G. McKenna, "On Abortion: A Lincolnian Position", *The Atlantic Monthly*, September 1995, p. 51-68. For a counterexample, see: Cynthia Gurney's *Articles of Faith: A Frontline History of the Abortion Wars*, New York: Simon and Schuster, 1998. (For an admiring review of Gurney's book, see: Dave Andrusko's review, *First Things*, November 1998, p. 32-36.) Some of the reasons for our inability to talk about this and other "hot topics" are covered in chapter 5 of J. Hunter, *Culture Wars: The Struggle to Define America—Making Sense of the Battles over the Family, Art, Education, Law, and Politics*, New York: Basic Books, 1991.

2. Frederica Mathewes-Green suggests the use of surveys and focus groups with mediators to find surprising common ground and develop an understanding of the other sides true (vs. perceived) beliefs. (*Sojourners*, January/February 1999, p. 34.)

3. Actually, one could argue that women bear primary responsibility. For instance, in the misuse of guns and alcohol, many believe that sellers are only marginally responsible compared to buyers. Beckwith introduces but does not provide a compelling answer to the question of whether pregnant women should be prosecuted for smoking or drinking during pregnancy (*Politically Correct Death: Answering Arguments for Abortion Rights*, Grand Rapids: Baker Books, 1993, p. 120).

4. J. Mercer, letter to the editor, *Louisville Eccentric Observer*, July 12, 1995.

5. S. Waldman, E. Ackerman, and R. Rubin, "Abortions in America: So Many Women Have Them, So Few Talk About Them", *U.S. News and World Report*, January 19, 1998, p. 20.

6. C. Forsythe, "Abortion is not a Necessary Evil", *Christianity Today*, May 24, 1999, p. 63-64. About 200 women have died from legal abortion since 1973 (*Christianity Today*, June 10, 2002).

7. Paul Vitz: "Recall that the young Mary was pregnant under circumstances that today routinely terminate in abortion. In the important theological context of Christmas, the killing of the unborn child is a symbolic killing of the Christchild." (Quoted in Beckwith, p. 137.)

8. F. Mathewes-Green, "What Women Need: Three Bad Ideas for Women and What to Do About Them", *Touchstone*, July-August 2001, p. 20-25.

9. Mathewes-Green (ibid.) notes the ironies that both goals "are stubbornly contrary to the average woman's deepest inclinations" and "were adopted

unchanged from the worldview of the folks feminists claimed to hate—male chauvinists...We couldn't imagine any success except success in men's terms." And to be clear, she defines "careerism" as "a half-conscious ideology that holds that the most important thing in life is the prestige conferred by one's employment, and it's as bad for men as it is for women."

10. P. Swope, "Abortion: A Failure to Communicate", *First Things*, April 1998, p. 31-35. Swope is the Northeast Project Director of the Caring Foundation and President of LifeNet Services Inc.

11. F. Mathewes-Green, "Wanted: A New-Life Strategy", *Christianity Today*, January 12, 1998, p. 29.

12. E. Cole and A. Press, *Speaking of Abortion: TV and Authority in the Lives of Women* (Chicago: University of Chicago, 1999), reviewed in *First Things*, October 1999, p. 67-70. Swope notes "the clear bias of the authors," but says the book still offers "substantive insights into the abortion debate," especially in understanding women of different socio-economic backgrounds.

13. N. Wolf, "Our Bodies, Our Souls", *The New Republic*, October 16, 1995, p. 26-35.

14. F. Mathewes-Green, "A Labor of Love: Pregnancy Care Centers", in *Freedom, Justice and Hope: Toward a Strategy for the Poor and the Oppressed*, ed. M. Olasky, H. Schlossberg, P. Berthoud, C. Pinnock, Westchester, IL: Crossway Books, 1988, p. 81.

15. Similarly, Randall Terry refers to the Republican Party's platform plank as "the perennial pacifier." (W. Martin, *With God on our Side: The Rise of the Religious Right in America*, Broadway Books: New York, 1996, p. 359.)

16. One is reminded of Jonathan Swift's "A Modest Proposal" where he satirically suggests that Irish babies should be sold for food and to produce a soft leather that would be useful for the economy.

17. Stapleford points to the merits of natural family planning in this context (*Bulls, Bears and Golden Calves: Applying Christian Ethics in Economics*, Downers Grove, IL: InterVarsity Press, 2002, p. 224). On this combination, Patrick Henry Reardon writes that: "Another manifestation of the current severance from family is recourse to artificial contraception. The pill, the patch, and the condom have become...our culture's "first defense against childbirth", abortion serving only as a socially distasteful back-up...It is no small indication of our cultural decline that we now speak, not of procreation, but of reproduction." ("The Roots of *Roe v. Wade*", *Touchstone*, January/February 2003, p. 4.)

18. Interested readers may find the *Human Life Review* helpful in exploring these issues.

19. The failure rate was 8% in American clinic trials and 5% in the French trials. (*Christianity Today*, June 11, 2001, p. 60.)

20. S. Guthrie, "RU-486 Deaths Prompt Outcry", *Christianity Today*, June 10, 2002, p. 15.

21. *U.S. News and World Report*, October 9, 2000, p. 22.

22. *World*, August 3/10, 1996, p. 7; *National Review*, August 12, 1996, p. 22-24; *U.S. News & World Report*, February 28, 2000, p. 79.

23. And in many cases, so-called pro-choicers are not particularly pro-choice on other topics. An excerpt from Sheldon Richman's list of the frequent inconsistencies—Why wouldn't the woman also have the right to choose: 1.) not to pay for someone else's "right to choose" to have an abortion if it violates her convictions or if she simply doesn't want to; 2.) to send her kids to private schools without also having to pay taxes for the government schools; 3.) to decide how to plan and save for her own retirement and to opt out of Social Security; 4.) to buy imports from anywhere in the world...free of tariffs and quotas designed to protect domestic products she finds inferior or too expensive; 5.) to abstain from paying dues to a labor union she wishes not to join; 6.) to patronize doctors, lawyers, and other professionals whose credentials are vouched for by someone other than government licensing boards; and 7.) to keep a handgun in her purse and nightstand drawer without having to get permission from the government. (www.fff.org; August 8, 2000)

24. CNSNews.com, May 8, 2002.

25. *First Things*, January 2003, p. 86.

26. In contrast, John Paul II argues that "A mother welcomes and carries in herself another human being, enabling it to grow inside her, giving it room, respecting it in its otherness. Women first learn and then teach others that human relations are authentic if they are open to accepting the other person: a person who is recognized and loved because of the dignity which comes from being a person and not from other considerations, such as usefulness, strength, intelligence, beauty or health." (*Evangelium Vitae*, #99, 1995; in *The Social Agenda: A Collection of Magisterial Texts*, ed. R. Sirico and M. Zieba, Vatican City: Pontifical Council for Justice and Peace, 2000, p. 60.

27. C. Crandall, "Thirty Years of Empty Promises", *First Things*, January 2003, p. 14-17.

28. Wolf, "Our Bodies, Our Souls".

29. C. Hitchens, *The Nation*, April 24, 1989, p. 546.

30. McKenna, "On Abortion".

31. Eugenics is creating a superior race through murder and cloning is creating an inferior race for exploitation.

32. *First Things*, October 2001, p. 90.

33. In *The American* Feminist, quoted in *First Things*, May 2000, p. 74-75. Frederica Mathewes-Green ("What Women Need"): "We think of abortion as the defining, litmus-test issue of feminism, but it was not always a significant part of the package. When the feminist bible, *Sisterhood Is Powerful*, was published back in 1970, only one proportion of one essay focused on abortion. In 1967, when the National Organization of Women met for the first time...abortion appears only as the last word in the document." She concludes that "abortion rose to the top, mostly because it was concrete."

34. G. Veith, "Theory, not Practice", *World*, January 17, 1998, p. 22.

35. McKenna, "On Abortion". As Frederica Mathewes-Green ("Wanted", p. 29) notes, "No one saves up, hoping one day to have an abortion...Women don't want abortions. They are expensive, awkward, humiliating, painful, and potentially dangerous...[and] it breaks a mother's heart."

36. Further, Wolf ("Our Bodies, Our Souls") claims that her side's rhetoric errs by describing fetuses as "material" and by "emptying the act of [any] moral gravity." Wolf also criticizes Joycelyn Elders' remark that "We really need to get over this love affair with the fetus" by comparing it to the equally absurd notion that "we really need to get over our love affair with the terminally ill."

37. T. Lamer, "Linguistic Contortions", *World*, May 26, 2001, p. 43. Lamer notes that dermatologists are not called "skin doctors" or "skin care providers", before concluding that maybe proponents are not "just acting as propagandists...they may also be trying to fool themselves."

38. McKenna, "On Abortion".

39. *Washington Post*, February 5, 1989, cited in *Physician*, January/February 1993. See also: T. Burke and D. Reardon, *Forbidden Grief: The Unspoken Pain of Abortion*, Springfield, IL: Acorn Books, 2002.

40. J. Crouse, "Unsafe, Deadly, and Legal", *Touchstone,* January/February 2003, p. 15-16.

41. Crouse, ibid; and I. Gentles, "Women's Health After Abortion: The Medical and Psychological Evidence", Toronto: de Veber Institute, 2002.

Late-term abortions are particularly dangerous—handled by abortionists as an outpatient procedure, when if done for medical reasons, is worthy of the care equivalent to labor-and-delivery.

42. Gentles et. al., "Women's Health". The link between breast cancer and abortion is especially well-documented. R. Rubin, "Debating Abortion and Breast Cancer", *U.S. News and World Report*, October 21, 1996. Richard John Neuhaus (*First Things*, October 1999, p. 95) reports a study which finds a 190% higher incidence with one abortion and a 260% higher incidence with two. Dr. Joel Brind et. al. find a positive link in 27 of 33 studies, estimating an increased risk of 30% (*Journal of Epidemiology and Community Health*, 1997).

43. "Building a Culture of Life: A Call to Respect Human Dignity in American Life" (reprinted in part in *Touchstone*, May 2002, p. 46-49) is a document formed by the Family Research Council and signed by representatives of Jewish, Catholic, Protestant, and Orthodox faiths.

44. L. Vincent, "Keeping Secrets", *World*, July 27, 2002, p. 14-17. Life Dynamics and Priests for Life have combined to write letters to school districts, warning them about their potential legal liability in they continue to refer children to Planned Parenthood in the midst of these allegations. (L. Vincent, "More Trouble than It's Worth", *World*, August 10, 2002, p. 29; the letter is available at www.priestsforlife.org/schools/certifiedletter.htm.)

45. In this sense, abortion is similar to other poor decisions where benefits and costs are not weighed properly out of ignorance.

46. Wolf, "Our Bodies, Our Souls".

47. For two very interesting articles trying to answer the potential difficulties with this stance, see: J. Fitzpatrick, "A Pro-Life Loss of Nerve", *First Things*, December 2000, p. 35-38; and C. Halloway, "Serpents, Doves, and Abortion", *First Things*, June/July 2001, p. 24-28.

48. See: F. Beckwith, "Civil Disobedience and Abortion: A Moderate Defense", *Christian Research Journal*, Spring 1995.

49. I Corinthians 6:12.

50. F. Mathewes-Green, interviewed in *The Door*, March/April 1995, p. 10-11.

51. Ibid. The need for creativity and fresh approaches is implied by this later remark by Mathewes-Green on the general public's boredom with the topic of abortion: "It seemed to them like everything possible to say about abortion had already been said...the pro-life message was condensed to 'It's a baby!' while pro-choicers insisted that 'It's a woman's choice!' These two

arguments do not engage each other, but are locked in a futile clinch, punching ineffectively. After a few dozen years, no wonder the public's attention drifted." ("Abortion in the Tides of Culture", *First Things*, December 2002, p. 16-18.)

52. A 1983 *New England Journal of Medicine* article by John Fletcher and Mark Evans predicted the usefulness of ultrasound in this regard. Ultrasound machines cost about $30,000 apiece but "medical professionals are the major cost." (L. Driggers, "When a Picture Is Worth 1000 Lives", *World*, p. 84-86.)

53. Frederica Mathewes-Green ("What Women Need") avidly recommends post-abortion grief counseling. "You might think that once a woman has had an abortion, it is too late for a pregnancy center to be of any help. The opposite is true. Nearly half of the abortions done each year are done on women who have already had an abortion."

54. Ibid. Her other primary recommendations are abstinence education for boys and girls, uplifting marriage, and "the most important long-term strategy"—"restoring young men to the role of husband and provider...If he is there, problems look much less dire."

55. Mathewes-Green (ibid.) notes the irony that "While pro-choice advocates present abortion as an act of autonomy, pregnant women experience it rather as a response to abandonment."

56. A version of this plays out in research which finds a negative correlation between legalized abortion (by state) and crime rates. (S. Levitt and J. Donahue, "The Impact of Legalized Abortion on Crime", *Quarterly Journal of Economics*, May 2001, p. 379-420.) Since then, John Lott and John Whitley have tried to refute the Levitt-Donahue paper (http://papers.ssrn.com/sol3/papers.cfm?abstract_id'270126). In any case, all of this is irrelevant to the ethics of abortion as a means to an end. (For example, one could reduce crime by executing all people who commit felonies.) "By illegitimately shifting the discussion from the morality of abortion to whether one has a 'solution' to certain social problems, the abortion-rights advocate avoids the point under question. Although a clever move, it has nothing to do with whether or not abortion results in the death of human beings who have a full right to life or whether or not abortion is immoral." (Beckwith, p. 16.)

57. This question is not relevant to whether Christian opposition to abortion is ethical but has implications for the extent to which such opposition it is socially practical—in the way that Christians are perceived, and most important, in terms of the lives of these children.

58. R. Shearer and C. Shearer, "Gotcha Day", *World*, November 15, 1997, p. 34.

59. Another option is to pursue restrictions on a local level. Abortion opponents in Davenport, Iowa have been somewhat successful in preventing or at least delaying the provision of abortion services in their city. They have applied pressure to landlords and realtors since abortion clinics have fairly strong preferences about property characteristics—they want to be located near bus routes and to have big parking lots as private land that is inaccessible to protestors. (*Harper's*, p. 42.)

60. This procedure is described in grim detail in Lynn Vincent's "Piece-by-piece Abortion" (*World*, February 1, 2003, p. 22-25). Vincent cites CDC statistics that the number of abortions after viability increased by 23% in the 1990's, to more than 10,000 per year.

61. These protect pregnant women from unwanted third-party aggression against the mother and the fetus. About half of the states already have these. And, of course, it is somewhat difficult to reconcile these laws with a right to abortion.

62. This parallels waiting periods for the purchase of handguns. Proponents recognize that it would only be relevant some of the time, but nonetheless lobby for it on the basis of avoiding those occasions. The same argument holds for a waiting period for abortions. Another popular option is moving the battle over abortion back to the states. This may be an effective short-term solution, but in the long run, such a strategy may be inferior and more costly.

63. Texas and Minnesota are considering laws that would include information on fetal pain. And Texas, the proposed law would mandate that a woman who opts for abortion would have to agree to anesthetize her child beforehand. (B. Jones, "Thirty Years' War", *World*, January 18, 2003, p. 16-20.)

64. Another advantage of the incremental strategy is that it often reverses the charge of extremism. For example, it is the advocates of "partial-birth abortion" who are viewed as extremists in the court of public opinion.

65. *World* produced a study providing evidence of the effectiveness of parental notice &/or consent laws. "During the 1990's, states that implemented parental consent laws saw, on average, a decline in abortions among young teens that was triple that in states with no laws, and significantly bigger drops than states with parental notice laws." (L. Vincent, "The Parent Gap", *World*, January 18, 2003, p. 22-23.)

66. Richard John Neuhaus notes that "Some political theorists talk about questions that are pre-political or meta-political. Abortion may be such a question. That is, it may be prior to, or it may transcend, what is ordinarily meant by the political. As a result, it will never be resolved to the satisfaction of all, and quite possibly, no resolution will ever be supported by a stable consensus." (*The Naked Public Square: Religion and Democracy in America*, 2nd ed., Grand Rapids: Eerdmans, 1997, p. 27.)

67. For example, on October 10, 1997, President Clinton designated October 12th as "National Children's Day" and within an hour, vetoed the "Partial Birth Abortion Act." (*First Things*, March 1998, p. 76.)

68. M. Olasky, *World*, November 11, 1995.

69. McKenna, "On Abortion". Similarly, Virginia Postrel argues that Bill Kristol, a prominent conservative is abandoning the traditional argument against abortion (that it takes a life) and framed it as a choice that rebels against nature and tradition in order to broaden their attacks to other issues of choices considered inappropriate—everything from LM issues to trade protectionism. (*Reason*, April 1997, p. 5.) Kate O'Beirne has remarked that the Republicans are the pro-life party because they spend so much time in the fetal position. (*The American Enterprise*, November/December 1997, p. 11.)

70. P. Howington, "Lawyer Targets Abortion Malpractice", *(Louisville) Courier-Journal*, April 15, 1995. At the time of the article, Swendsen, Amshoff, Donovan, and Smith had reached four settlements worth $800,000. Medical malpractice suits, related to the known health risks for abortion, may be an effective weapon here as well. (See: J. Kindley, "The Fit Between the Elements for an Informed Consent Cause of Action and the Scientific Evidence Linking Induced Abortion with Increased Breast Cancer Risk", *Wisconsin Law Review*, 1998, p. 1595-1644.)

71. C. Crandall, "Legal but not Safe", *Wall Street Journal*, July 31, 1996.

72. Reardon, "The Roots of *Roe v. Wade*".

73. R. Bork, *First Things*, January 2003, p. 34-36. (Bork's essay is a response to Nathan Schleuter's preceding essay [p. 28-33] which argues that the 5th and 14th Amendments hold out some hope.) Bork opens by saying that "The exercise in which Schlueter engages, while interesting and nobly inspired, is entirely irrelevant to the future course of the law. *Roe* had nothing whatever to do with constitutional interpretation...The decision and its later reaffirmations simply enforce the cultural prejudices of a particular class of American society."

74. A. Scalia, "God's Justice and Ours", *First Things*, May 2002.

75. P. Linton, "How Not to Overturn *Roe v. Wade*", *First Things*, November 2002, p. 15-16.

76. Reardon, "The Roots of *Roe v. Wade*"; Fowler, p. 22

77. Mathewes-Green, "Wanted".

78. Mathewes-Green ("Abortion in the Tides of Culture"). "What 30's drunkenness and contemporary free sex have in common is backlash, rebellion against a prior standard." Harry Poe notes that *In the Heat of the Night* (which "hit the country like a blockbuster with its treatment of race relations") strikes an odd chord with those who watch it today—not for its approach to race, but that "the white southern lynch mob decides not to bother Sidney Poitier...when they discover that Poitier's accuser is involved in an abortion operation." ("Politics After the Culture Wars", in *Christians and Politics Beyond the Culture Wars: An Agenda for Engagement*, ed. D. Gushee, Grand Rapids: Baker Books, 2000, p. 98.)

79. D. Smolin, "The Jurisprudence of Abortion" (a review of Hadley Arkes, *Natural Rights and the Right to Choose*, Cambridge: Cambridge University, 2002), *First Things*, February 2003, p. 56.

80. A reliance on visual effects is similar to two Biblical stories: the Levite dismembering his murdered concubine and sending the 12 pieces to the 12 tribes in Judges 19:29-30 and Saul cutting two oxen and sending the pieces across the country to rouse the Israelites in I Samuel 11:7.

81. Wolf, "Our Bodies, Our Souls". Wolf goes on to note the irony of a feminist holding this implicit opinion: "The judgment that women are too inherently weak to face a truth about which they have to make a grave decision. This view of women is unworthy of feminism."

82. Hitchens, p. 546.

83. A. Tsiaras and B. Werth, *From Conception to Birth* (New York: Doubleday, 2002) uses the latest technology to detail the unborn baby throughout a pregnancy.

84. G. Veith, "Pro-life Photography", *World*, September 28, 2002, p. 13.

85. See: Olasky, *Wall Street Journal*. Ralph Reed argues that "a vigorous political strategy tempered by a humble acknowledgment that children will never ultimately be safe in their mothers' wombs until we change people's hearts...But as a purely tactical matter, while I personally support all measures to protect human life—including legal and constitutional remedies—it has become apparent that amending the Constitution may be the least practical and most remote weapon at our disposal at this time." (*Active Faith*, New York: Free Press, 1996, p. 271)

86. Olasky, *Abortion Rites*, p. 305-306.

87. *World*, August 26, 1995, p. 16.

88. In addition, her position on abortion evolved further after her conversion—from moderately to strictly pro-life. Again, gradual change worked.

Chapter 16: The Conclusion of the Matter—Defining and Pursuing True Freedom

1. See also: Mordecai in the book of Esther.

2. Quoted in K. Wald, *Religion and Politics in the United States*, 2nd ed., Washington, DC: CQ Press, 1992, p. 123.

3. In contrast, in a more private matter, Gideon tore down his father's idol (Judges 6).

4. While there are some advantages for Christians in both capitalism (e.g., freedom) and socialism (e.g., greater faith in the midst of persecution, and stronger evidence with respect to motives in many contexts since the financial incentives for moral behavior are greatly diminished), Richard John Neuhaus warns "the romanticizing of persecution is only possible for those who have not taken the measure of history's horror." (*The Naked Public Square: Religion and Democracy in America*, 2nd ed., Grand Rapids: Eerdmans, 1997, p. 164.)

5. J. Belz, *World*, March 30, 1996, p. 5

6. Daniel 2:14, 6:4.

7. R. Reed, *Active Faith*, New York: Free Press, 1996, p. 280.

8. Reed, p. 267. This is very similar to Schlossberg's recurring theme that understanding the limits of X allows one to most fully exploit its (limited) usefulness. (H. Schlossberg, *Idols for Destruction: The Conflict of Christian Faith and American Culture*, Wheaton, IL: Crossway Books, 1990.)

9. B. Briner, *Deadly Detours: Seven Noble Causes that Keep Christians from Changing the World*, Grand Rapids: Zondervan, 1996, p. 38.

10. J. Belz, *World*, "Give Us a King", April 27/May 4, 1996, p. 5.

11. P.J. O'Rourke, *All the Trouble in the World: The Lighter Side of Overpopulation, Famine, Ecological Disaster, Ethnic Hatred, Plagues and Poverty*, New York: Atlantic Monthly Press, 1994, p. 15.

12. Cal Thomas in C. Thomas and E. Dobson, *Blinded by Might: Can the Religious Right Save America?*, Grand Rapids: Zondervan, 1999, p. 90.

13. Jotham's parable in Judges 9:7-15 illustrates the Israelites choosing the least qualified and most unproductive candidate for king, who not surprisingly, tyrannizes them. David Chilton calls this episode "a libertarian exhortation for free, responsible self-government." (*World*, June 17/24, 1996, p. 26.)

14. Exodus 18:17-27.

15. D. Willard, *The Spirit of the Disciplines: Understanding How God Changes Lives*, San Francisco: HarperSanFrancisco, 1988, p. 238. See for example: II Timothy 2:12a.

16. Willard, p. 238.

17. Judges 17:6, 21:25.

18. Willard, p. 242. See also: Psalms 37:4

19. With respect to legalism, see Galatians; with respect to carnality, see I Corinthians; with respect to government, see I Samuel 8, many previously-cited excerpts from the Old Testament, the experience of the early church, and the church's prophesied experience in the "end times".

20. Any remaining "honest disagreements" would be judged by a trustworthy leader whose decision would be followed.

21. K. DeYoung, "The Freedom of Religion", Grand Rapids: Acton Institute, 2001.

22. Interview of Stanley Hauerwas, *The Door*, May/June 1993, p. 10. Augustine said that "whatever injury wicked masters inflict upon good men is to be regarded, not as a penalty for wrong-doing, but as a test for their virtues. Thus, a good man, though a slave, is free; but a wicked man, though a king, is slave. For he serves, not one man alone, but what is worse, as many masters as he has vices." (*City of God*, New York: Doubleday, 1958, p. 88.)

23. John Paul II: "True freedom is not advanced in the permissive society, which confuses freedom with license to do anything whatever, and which, in the name of freedom, proclaims a kind of general amorality. It is a caricature of freedom to claim that people are free to organize their lives with no reference to moral values." (1981 World Day of Peace Message; in *The Social Agenda: A Collection of Magisterial Texts*, ed. R. Sirico and M. Zieba, Vatican City: Pontifical Council for Justice and Peace, 2000, p. 27.)

24. Romans 6:18.

25. G. Brennan, "The Christian and the State", *CIS Occasional Papers*, St. Leonards, Australia: The Center for Independent Studies, 1983, p. 22.

26. Of course, the world's pursuits within economic markets can be highly flawed as well. John Paul II: "The individual today is often suffocated between two poles represented by the State and the marketplace. At times it seems as though he exists only as a producer and consumer of goods, or an object of state administration. People lose sight of the fact that life in society has neither the market nor the State as its final purpose, since life itself has a unique value that the State and the market must serve." (*Centesimus Annus*, #49; in *The Social Agenda*, p. 31.)

27. Machiavelli, *The Prince*, New York: Penguin, 1980, p. 49-50.

Selected Bibliography

L. Adams, *Going Public: Christian Responsibility in a Divided America*, Grand Rapids: Brazos Press, 2002.

L. Anderson, *Winning the Values War in a Changing Culture: Thirteen Distinct Values that Mark a Follower of Christ*, Minneapolis: Bethany House, 1994.

Augustine, *City of God*, New York: Doubleday, 1958.

D. Bandow, *Beyond Good Intentions: A Biblical View of Politics*, Wheaton, IL: Crossway Books, 1988.

G. Bauer, *Our Hopes, Our Dreams: A Vision for America*, Colorado Springs: Focus on the Family Publishing, 1996.

F. Beckwith, *Politically Correct Death: Answering Arguments for Abortion Rights*, Grand Rapids: Baker Books, 1993.

D. Beito, *From Mutual Aid to the Welfare State: Fraternal Societies and Social Services, 1890-1967*, Chapel Hill: University of North Carolina Press, 2000.

D. Bernstein, *Only One Place of Redress*, Durham, NC: Duke University Press, 2001.

A. Bierce, *The Devil's Dictionary*, Oxford: Oxford University Press, 1999.

J. Boersema, *Political-Economic Activity to the Honour of God*, Winnipeg: Premier Publishing, 1999.

B. Briner, *Deadly Detours: Seven Noble Causes that Keep Christians from Changing the World*, Grand Rapids: Zondervan, 1996.

B. Briner, *Roaring Lambs: A Gentle Plan to Radically Change the World*, Grand Rapids: Zondervan, 1993.

P. Brown, *Poverty and Leadership in the Later Roman Empire*, Hanover, NH: University Press of New England, 2002.

M. Budde and R. Brimelow, *Christianity Incorporated: How Big Business Is Buying the Church*, Grand Rapids: Brazos Press, 2002.

G. K. Chesterton, *Heretics/Orthodoxy*, Nashville: Thomas Nelson, 2000.

D. Chilton, *Productive Christians in an Age of Guilt Manipulators: A Biblical Response to Ronald J. Sider*, 3rd ed., Tyler, TX: Institute for Christian Economics, 1985.

J. Cobin, *Bible and Government: Public Policy from a Christian Perspective*, Greenville, SC: Alertness Books, 2003.

J. Elshtain, *Augustine and the Limits of Politics*, Notre Dame, IN: University of Notre Dame Press, 1998.

T. Evans, *Are Christians Destroying America? How to Restore a Decaying Culture*, Chicago: Moody Press, 1996.

P. Fowler, *Abortion: Toward an Evangelical Consensus*, Portland, OR: Multnomah Press, 1987.

R. Frame and A. Tharpe, *How Right Is the Right?*, Grand Rapids: Zondervan, 1996.

N. Geisler and F. Turek, *Legislating Morality: Is it Wise? Is it Legal? Is it Possible?*, Minneapolis: Bethany House, 1998.

O. Guinness, *Fit Bodies, Fat Minds: Why Evangelicals Don't Think and What to Do About It*, Grand Rapids: Baker Books, 1994

D. Hay, *Economics Today*, Grand Rapids: Eerdmans, 1989

J. Hunter, *Culture Wars: The Struggle to Define America—Making Sense of the Battles over the Family, Art, Education, Law, and Politics*, New York: Basic Books, 1991.

P. Jargowsky, *Poverty and Place: Ghettos, Barrios, and the American City*, New York: Russell Sage Foundation, 1997.

S. Keillor, *This Rebellious House: American History and the Truth of Christianity*, Downers Grove, IL: InterVarsity Press, 1996.

C. S. Lewis, *Mere Christianity*, New York: Macmillan, 1960.

J. MacArthur, *Why Government Can't Save You: An Alternative to Political Activism*, Nashville: Word Publishing, 2000.

W. Martin, *With God on our Side: The Rise of the Religious Right in America*, New York: Broadway Books, 1996.

W. Miller, *The Protestant and Politics*, Philadelphia: Westminster Press, 1958.

T. Minnery, *Why You Can't Stay Silent: A Biblical Mandate to Shape our Culture*, Wheaton, IL: Tyndale House, 2001.

L. von Mises, *Liberalism: The Classical Tradition*, Irvington-on-Hudson, NY: Foundation for Economic Education, 1996.

W. Mott, Jr., *The Third Way: Economic Justice According to John Paul II*, Lanham, MD: University Press of America, 1999.

C. Murray, *In Pursuit of Happiness and Good Government*, New York: Simon and Schuster, 1988.

C. Murray, *Losing Ground: American Social Policy 1950-1980*, New York: Basic Books, 1984.

D. Myers, *The American Paradox: Spiritual Hunger in an Age of Plenty*, New Haven, CT: Yale University Press, 2000.

R. Nash, *Poverty and Wealth: Why Socialism Doesn't Work*, Richardson, TX: Probe Books, 1986.

R. Neuhaus, *The Naked Public Square: Religion and Democracy in America*, 2nd ed., Grand Rapids: Eerdmans, 1997.

M. Noll, *Adding Cross to Crown: The Political Significance of Christ's Passion*, Grand Rapids: Baker Books, 1996.

M. Noll, *The Scandal of the Evangelical Mind*, Grand Rapids: Eerdmans, 1994

M. Olasky, *Abortion Rites: A Social History of Abortion in America*, Wheaton, IL: Crossway Books, 1992.

M. Olasky, *The Tragedy of American Compassion*, Washington, DC: Regnery Gateway, 1992.

E. Opitz, *Religion and Capitalism: Allies, not Enemies*, 2nd ed., Irvington-on-Hudson, NY: Foundation for Economic Education, 1992.

J. Rauch, *Demosclerosis: The Silent Killer of American Government*, New York: Random House, 1994.

W. Roepke, *A Humane Economy: The Social Framework of the Free Market*, 3rd ed., Wilmington, DE: ISI Books, 1998.

R. Rogers, *Seducing America: Is Gambling a Good Bet?*, Grand Rapids: Baker Books, 1997.

R. Scarborough, *Enough Is Enough: A Call to Christian Involvement*, Springdale, PA: Whitaker House, 1996.

F. Schaeffer, *A Christian Manifesto*, 2nd ed., Wheaton, IL: Crossway Books, 1982.

D. Schansberg, *Poor Policy: How Government Harms the Poor*, Boulder, CO: Westview Press, 1996.

H. Schlossberg, *Idols for Destruction: The Conflict of Christian Faith and American Culture*, Wheaton, IL: Crossway Books, 1990.

J. Schneider, *The Good of Affluence: Seeking God in a Culture of Wealth*, Grand Rapids: Eerdmans, 2002.

R. Sider, *Just Generosity: A New Vision for Overcoming Poverty in America*, Grand Rapids: Baker Books, 1999.

R. Sider, *Rich Christians in an Age of Hunger*, Dallas: Word Publishing, 1990.

T. Sine, *Cease Fire: Searching for Sanity in America's Culture Wars*, Grand Rapids: Eerdmans, 1995.

L. Spooner, *Vices Are not Crimes: A Vindication of Moral Liberty*, 1875.

J. Stapleford, *Bulls, Bears and Golden Calves: Applying Christian Ethics in Economics*, Downers Grove, IL: InterVarsity Press, 2002.

C. Thomas and E. Dobson, *Blinded by Might: Can the Religious Right Save America?*, Grand Rapids: Zondervan, 1999.

K. Wald, *Religion and Politics in the United States*, 2nd ed., Washington DC: CQ Press, 1992.

J. Wallis, *The Soul of Politics*, New York: The New Press, 1994.

J. Whitehead, *Christians Involved in the Political Process*, Chicago: Moody Press, 1994.

D. Willard, *The Spirit of the Disciplines: Understanding How God Changes Lives*, San Francisco: HarperSanFrancisco, 1988.

J. Yoder, *The Politics of Jesus*, Grand Rapids: Eerdmans, 1972.

Caesar's Coin Revisited: Christians and the Limits of Government, ed. M. Cromartie, Grand Rapids: Eerdmans, 1996.

Christians and Politics Beyond the Culture Wars: An Agenda for Engagement, ed. D. Gushee, Grand Rapids: Baker Books, 2000.

Freedom, Justice and Hope: Toward a Strategy for the Poor and the Oppressed, ed. M. Olasky, H. Schlossberg, P. Berthoud, C. Pinnock, Westchester, IL: Crossway Books, 1988.

From Irenaeus to Grotius: a Sourcebook in Christian Political Thought, 100-1625, ed. O. O'Donovan and J. O'Donovan, Grand Rapids: Eerdmans, 1999.

Making Work Pay: The Earned Income Tax Credit and its Impact on America's Families, ed. B. Meyer and D. Holtz-Eakin, New York: Russell Sage Foundation, 2001.

Political Principles and Economics: The Foundations, volume 2, ed. R. Chewning, Colorado Springs: Navpress, 1989.

Reclaiming the Culture: How You Can Protect Your Family's Future, ed. A. Crippen II, Colorado Springs: Focus on the Family Publishing, 1996.

Salt and Light: Evangelical Political Thought in Modern America, ed. A. Cerillo, Jr., and M. Dempster, Grand Rapids: Baker Books, 1989

The Social Agenda: A Collection of Magisterial Texts, ed. R. Sirico and M. Zieba, Vatican City: Pontifical Council for Justice and Peace, 2000.

Toward a Just and Caring Society: Christian Responses to Poverty in America, ed. D. Gushee, Grand Rapids: Baker Books, 1999.

Index of Bible Verses Referenced

Index of Biblical Names and Places

Index of Persons

Index of Topics

About the Author

D. Eric Schansberg (Ph.D. Economics, Texas A&M University) is Professor of Economics at Indiana University (New Albany). Eric is the author of numerous academic articles and popular press essays—as well as two other books: *Poor Policy: How Government Harms the Poor* (Westview Press, 1996) and *Inheriting Our Promised Land: Lessons in Victorious Christian Living from the Book of Joshua* (Alertness Books, 2003). He is also the co-author (with Kurt Sauder) of a 21-month Discipleship Curriculum for Men. He is active in teaching at his church and has led expository Bible studies for more than ten years. Eric and his wife, Tonia, have three children (so far!) and live in Jeffersonville, Indiana.

About Alertness Books

Alertness Books is dedicated to publishing scholarly work that will be useful to academic, professional, and general audiences. Areas of interest include public policy, free market economics, regulation, social issues (e.g., abortion), legal studies, and applied biblical/Christian studies. The company serves as an outlet for Evangelical (conservative or classically liberal) scholars to publish their work in these fields. Of special interest are unique, counter-intuitive or revolutionary ideas that are often of little interest to mainstream publishers. Most works are published as PDF e-books, although books with superb market potential are published in paperback. If you have an interest in submitting a manuscript for consideration, please contact us by the email link above. Include your vita and a summary of your book or position paper.

Alertness Books
▽▲▽

Quick Order Form

Fax: 413-622-9441
Phone: 866-492-2137 (toll-free) or 864-444-3728
On-line: http://www.policyofliberty.net
Email: dschansb@ius.edu
Postal: Alertness Books, Box 25686, Greenville, SC 29616

Please send me:

Books by Dr. Eric Schansberg			Quantity
Turn Neither to the Right nor to the Left:			
A Thinking Christian's Guide to	Paperback	$15.00	___
Politics & Public Policy	PDF	$5.00	___
Poor Policy: How Government			
Harms the Poor (1996)	PDF	$3.00	___
Inheriting Our Promised Land:			
Lessons in Victorious Christian Living	Paperback	$10.00	___
from the Book of Joshua	PDF	$5.00	___

Books by Dr. John Cobin			Quantity
Bible and Government: Public Policy	Paperback	$10.95	___
From a Christian Perspective	PDF	$3.95	___
Pro-Life Policy	PDF	$2.95	___
A Primer on Modern Themes	PDF	$5.95	___

Name: _____
Address: _____
City/State/Zip: _____
Phone/Email: _____

Please add 5% for products shipped to South Carolina addresses.
Shipping by ground: $2 per book (with credit card); $2 for first book; $1 for each additional book (with check).
Quantity Discount: 20% on orders of 10 or more books.
Make checks payable to Alertness Ltd.

Credit Card: Visa / MasterCard / Optima / Amex / Discover (circle one)
Card Number: _____ Expiration Date: _____
Name on Card: _____